lonely planet

Best Road Trips

AUSTRALIA

SARAH REID, ANTHONY HAM, BLAZE LOPES, BRETT ATKINSON, ANDREW BAIN, CRISTIAN BONETTO, SAMANTHA FORGE, PAUL HARDING, TRENT HOLDEN, ANITA ISALSKA, ANNA KAMINSKI, TATYANA LEONOV, VIRGINIA MAXWELL, HUGH MCNAUGHTAN, KATE MORGAN, CHARLES RAWLINGS-WAY, ANDY SYMINGTON, STEVE WATERS

CONTENTS

INDONESIA
Savu Sea
Timor Sea
Bathurst Island
Melville Island
Arafura Sea
Torres Strait
Thursday Island
Cape York
PAPUA NEW GUINEA
Coral Sea
Darwin
Jabiru
Arnhem Land
Joseph Bonaparte Gulf
Katherine
Gulf of Carpentaria
Cape York Peninsula
Weipa
Daintree National Park
SOUTH PACIFIC OCEAN
Kununurra
Cape Leveque
The Kimberley
Daly Waters
Port Douglas
Cairns
NORTHERN TERRITORY p207
INDIAN OCEAN
Broome
Great Barrier Reef
Townsville
Port Hedland
The Pilbara
Tennant Creek
Mt Isa
Karratha
Airlie Beach
North West Cape
Mackay
Exmouth
Winton
WESTERN AUSTRALIA p233
Gibson Desert
Uluru-Kata Tjuta National Park
Alice Springs
QUEENSLAND p135
Rockhampton
Yulara
Simpson Desert
Birdsville
Bundaberg
Shark Bay
Little Sandy Desert
Charleville
Fraser Island
SOUTH AUSTRALIA p169
Noosa
Great Victoria Desert
Mt Magnet
Coober Pedy
Brisbane
Lake Eyre South
Geraldton
Byron Bay
Nullarbor Plain
NEW SOUTH WALES & THE AUSTRALIAN CAPITAL TERRITORY p65
Kalgoorlie-Boulder
Eucla
Coffs Harbour
Port Augusta
Perth
Great Australian Bight
Port Macquarie
Fremantle
Eyre Peninsula
Great Dividing Range
Newcastle
Bunbury
Esperance
Port Lincoln
Mildura
Hay
Sydney
Margaret River
Albany
Kangaroo Island
Adelaide
ACT
Canberra
VICTORIA p97
Mt Kosciuszko
Tasman Sea
Geelong
Melbourne
SOUTHERN OCEAN
King Island
Bass Strait
Flinders Island
Launceston
TASMANIA p257
Hobart
0
1,000 km
0
500 miles

WELCOME TO AUSTRALIA

Australia is custom-made for road trips. All across this vast and wildly beautiful country, roads – ribbons of tarmac – unfurl to the far horizon. They take you into the outback and along the continent's beautiful shores, across deserts and through rainforests, past bustling cities and into the heart of an ancient land rich in the storytelling traditions of its First Nations peoples.

The 39 road trips in this book are as diverse as the country they traverse, and each one is an adventure in itself. Some routes are long journeys through landscapes cinematic in beauty and scale. On others, you'll take a week to go 100km as they meander through intimate valleys and historic small-town Australia. Whether the starting point – to a trailhead, or a surf beach, or a foodie experience – or a destination in its own right, each drive offers a precious window onto a very special country.

Gibb River Road (p62), Kimberley

BEE.DUB/SHUTTERSTOCK

MY PERFECT ROAD TRIP

SARAH REID

CAIRNS & THE DAINTREE, p156

Rolling off the ferry across the croc-filled Daintree River and into the wilds of Cape Tribulation feels like entering another realm, but the final section of this road trip is just the icing on a journey that immerses you in wondrous nature, Aboriginal cultures and the tropical way of life up here in equal measure. I've driven this spectacular Queensland route multiple times, and it never gets old.

ANTHONY HAM

CLARE VALLEY & THE FLINDERS RANGES, p200

There's something elemental about the road from Clare Valley into the Flinders Ranges. It begins amid the deep greens of the lush valley, and by journey's end I'm surrounded by the intense reds and oranges of an ancient mountain range beneath the deep blues of an outback sky. It's a fascinating human journey, too, from the renowned South Australian vineyards, to the Indigenous stories of Ikara-Flinders Ranges.

AUSTRALIANCAMERA/GETTY IMAGES

Daintree National Park (p156)

BEST SCENIC DRIVES

1. **Uluṟu & the Red Centre** The drama of the outback peaks here.
2. **Western Wilds** Tasmania's historic towns and natural beauty collide.
3. **Kimberley Crossing** The ultimate outback wilderness adventure.
4. **Snowy Mountains** Immerse in the rugged beauty of the Australian Alps.
5. **Yorke & Eyre Peninsulas** Wild coastlines with oysters, birdlife and beaches.

BEST URBAN DRIVES

1. **Sydney to Melbourne** Explore relaxed coastal towns linking two capitals.
2. **Canberra & the South Coast** A mix of city cool and charming regional towns.
3. **Victoria's Goldfields** Cruise between storied gold-rush-era towns.
4. **Margaret River Wine Region** Gourmet indulgence awaits south of Perth.
5. **Heritage Trail** Visit historic towns between Hobart and Launceston.

BLAZE LOPES

CORAL COAST TO BROOME, p248

There's nowhere in Australia where contrast feels as vivid as the Coral Coast – red earth meeting turquoise water, remote stations giving way to reef just metres from shore. The stretch from Coral Bay to Exmouth changed the way I travel, not only for Ningaloo's outrageous beauty, but for the community it draws. Surfers chasing swell, divers drifting through coral gardens, birdwatchers and hikers following the light. Here, you move with the country, not through it – and if you let it, it changes you.

KAI EGAN/SHUTTERSTOCK

Scuba diving, Coral Coast (p248)

BEST FAMILY DRIVES

1. **Cairns & the Daintree** Spot crocs, cassowaries and other rainforest critters.
2. **Darwin to Daly River** Frolic in waterfalls and get a taste of outback life.
3. **Sydney to Byron Bay** Beach swims, 'Big Things' and coastal rainforests in spades.
4. **Great Ocean Road** An easy adventure from Melbourne with many 'wow' moments.
5. **Turrakana / Tasman Peninsula** Great learning opportunity for budding history buffs.

COASTAL JOURNEYS

With around 35,000km of coastline, Australia has an incredible network of roads that hug the shore. In fact, there's nothing more Australian than setting out by car and driving from one beach to the next. Whether you have a surfboard on the roof, hiking boots for the hinterland, or you're simply in love with beach life Aussie-style, these road trips will get you there.

① SYDNEY TO BYRON BAY

Follow the footsteps of generations of Aussie families and backpackers along NSW's north coast. p68

② GREAT OCEAN ROAD

Track the contours of Victoria's wild southwestern coast, passing the Twelve Apostles en route. p100

③ QUEENSLAND COASTAL CRUISE

Journey from Brisbane to the high tropics along a coastline fringing the Great Barrier Reef. p138

④ CORAL COAST TO BROOME

Rack up the kilometres out west, passing gorge-filled national parks, reefs and glorious deserted beaches. p248

⑤ EAST COAST TASMANIA

Explore the jewel in Tasmania's crown, with an unrelenting panorama of beautiful bays and islands. p260

Left: Great Barrier Reef (p138), Queensland
Right: Great Ocean Road (p100), Victoria

TRAVEL SEASONS

Across Australia's north, the year divides into two, rather than four, seasons; the May-to-October Dry is the best time to travel. Across northern WA, the NT and Queensland, the wet season runs from November to March or April; even paved roads can flood.

CYCLONES

In northern Australia, the cyclone season runs from November to April, but January to March is when there's the greatest risk.

STAY WITH YOUR VEHICLE

If you get stuck, or your car breaks down, stay with your vehicle. Your chances of survival drop dramatically if you don't.

PHONE COVERAGE

Mobile (cell) phone coverage is often non-existent between towns. Consider carrying a satellite phone.

INTO THE OUTBACK

If your idea of a road trip is a ribbon of tarmac unfurling to the very far horizon, then the outback has you covered. So many Aussie highlights – Uluṟu, Kata Tjuṯa, Karlu Karlu (Devil's Marbles), the Bungle Bungles and Coober Pedy, to name just a few – reside in remote yet accessible corners of the Australian interior. Building a road trip around reaching them will feel like planning a quintessentially Australian odyssey.

① ALICE SPRINGS TO ADELAIDE

Drive into the heart of the continent via the underground opal town of Coober Pedy. p52

② KIMBERLEY CROSSING

Explore one of the outback's most beautiful corners across northern WA and into the NT. p58

③ OUTBACK NEW SOUTH WALES

Leave behind the bright lights of Sydney for the starry skies of NSW's west. p90

④ OUTBACK QUEENSLAND

Australia's true big-sky country is a hallucinatory landscape of droughts and flooding rains. p164

⑤ ULUṞU & THE RED CENTRE

Drive from one glorious landform to the next, including Uluṟu, Kings Canyon and the West MacDonnell Ranges. p210

LEFT TO RIGHT: ELETEURTRE/SHUTTERSTOCK, KEN GRIFFITHS/SHUTTERSTOCK

Left: Stranded car in the Australian outback
Above: Outback Queensland (p164)

HISTORY'S STORY

FUEL TYPES

Unleaded and diesel fuel are widely available. In remote communities, only diesel may be available.

History is everywhere as you drive through Australia. You just need to know where to look. Rock art (in Kakadu in the NT, or Murujuga National Park in WA's Pilbara), First Nations art centres and tours run by Aboriginal guides provide an unbroken thread to 45,000-plus years of continuous settlement in the country. Elsewhere, convict-era architecture and sites tell a very different story from the early days of European settlement.

1 VICTORIA'S GOLDFIELDS

Explore some of Australia's best-preserved historic towns that date back to Victoria's mid-19th-century gold rush. p116

2 ALONG THE MURRAY

River travel may belong to the past, but former ports such as Echuca, Swan Hill and Mildura retain some of their historical charm. p128

3 DARWIN & KAKADU

Explore rock-art sites dating back tens of thousands of years; they tell the story of Aboriginal Australia. p222

4 HERITAGE TRAIL

Tasmania has done a better job than most states of preserving its historic towns; drive from one to the next. p266

5 TURRAKANA /TASMAN PENINSULA

Driving to haunting Port Arthur, a former convict penal colony, takes you through lonely, wildly beautiful landscapes. p272

Sovereign Hill, Ballarat (p120)

NOVIYANTO UTOMO/SHUTTERSTOCK

ROB WALLS/ALAMY

Sullivans Cove Distillery, Richmond (p273)

WINE & WILDLIFE TRAILS

All across Australia's southern half, wine regions offer the very best kind of road tripping, with a gourmet sensibility infusing every corner of the regions through which you'll pass. Often, as an added bonus, you'll find these regions close to areas where wildlife is a major attraction, from whales and penguins in coastal areas from WA to Tasmania, to the animal abundance of resilient Kangaroo Island.

WORLD'S BEST WHISKY

Sullivans Cove *(sullivanscove.com)* in Tasmania is the only Australian whisky distillery to win the world's best single malt (in 2014) for its French Oak Cask variety.

① ADELAIDE HILLS & THE BAROSSA VALLEY

Get to know one of Australia's oldest wine-producing regions, just a short drive from Adelaide. p172

② MCLAREN VALE & KANGAROO ISLAND

Aficionados rate McLaren Vale among Australia's best wine regions, while Kangaroo Island is fabulous for wildlife. p178

③ SOUTHWEST COAST OF WA

Cool-climate wine regions lie just inland from the south coast, while whales are the main attraction offshore. p236

④ MARGARET RIVER WINE REGION

Arguably Australia's premier wine region, Margaret River also does every possible gourmet experience. p240

⑤ TAMAR VALLEY GOURMET TRAIL

In northern Tasmania, sample wines and fresh produce, then go looking for penguins. p276

NATIONAL PARKS

Australia has more than 500 national parks and they protect some of the country's most remarkable landscapes, including rainforests, vast tracts of empty outback, strips of coastal dunes and rugged mountain ranges. Most have roads running through them and public access is encouraged. Book a parks pass online and plan on staying in park campgrounds – ideal if you value the silence that descends after the day-trippers leave.

1 SNOWY MOUNTAINS

Traverse the high country of southern NSW, including Kosciuszko National Park, home to Australia's highest mountain. p76

2 GIPPSLAND & WILSONS PROM

Go as far south as you can on mainland Australia through wildlife-rich Wilsons Promontory National Park. p110

3 CAIRNS & THE DAINTREE

Drive along some of Australia's northernmost paved roads through the rainforests of Daintree National Park. p156

4 CLARE VALLEY & THE FLINDERS RANGES

Begin in wine country and end where the South Australian outback begins. p200

5 DARWIN & KAKADU

Discover a tropical paradise of wildlife, millennia-old rock art and towering escarpments in Kakadu National Park. p222

Left: Kosciuszko National Park (p79), New South Wales
Right: Ikara-Flinders Ranges National Park (p204), South Australia

LEFT TO RIGHT: ARTEFOTOGRAF/SHUTTERSTOCK, ADWO/SHUTTERSTOCK

STATE PARKS & PETS

State parks and forests are owned by state governments and have fewer regulations. Many have camping grounds, walking trails and signposted forest drives. Pets are not allowed in most national parks, but some state parks permit horses and dogs.

JOINT PARK MANAGEMENT

Most national parks are administered by states, but Booderee, Kakadu and Uluṟu-Kata Tjuṯa are federally managed in conjunction with Aboriginal communities.

WHEN TO GO

It's always a good time to be somewhere in Australia. As a general rule, go north in winter, south in summer, and east and west anytime.

I LIVE HERE

I LOVE DRIVING HERE

Anthony Ham
Lonely Planet writer

I love the big outback horizons, the empty roads, the red sand by the roadside. On a recent visit to Uluṟu, which lies at the end of just such a road, clouds began to gather close to sunset. It was December and fiercely hot. It began to rain. Cursing my ill luck, I began to drive back to my hotel, before a glimpse of Uluṟu in my rear-view mirror made me stop. Hundreds of waterfalls were cascading down off the rock, a cooling breeze brought relief and the desert was suddenly transformed.

Summer is synonymous with beach weather, but it's not always the case in Australia. In the southern states, summer is short and sweet, with January and February bringing the most comfortable conditions for a dip. Snow falls in alpine regions of NSW, Victoria and Tasmania from May to September. Winter also promises superb whale watching along east and west coasts (roughly May to November) and cooler, less humid weather that's ideal for coastal bushwalking.

Winter temperatures become milder (and summers hotter) as you travel north. When southern Australia is cold and rainy, it's the best time to visit the Top End (Tropical North Queensland,

Port Douglas, Queensland (p158)

NEAL PRITCHARD PHOTOGRAPHY/GETTY IMAGES

WEATHER WATCH: SYDNEY

JANUARY	FEBRUARY	MARCH	APRIL	MAY	JUNE
Avg. daytime max: **27°C** Days of rainfall: **8**	Avg. daytime max: **27°C** Days of rainfall: **9**	Avg. daytime max: **26°C** Days of rainfall: **10**	Avg. daytime max: **24°C** Days of rainfall: **8**	Avg. daytime max: **21°C** Days of rainfall: **8**	Avg. daytime max: **18°C** Days of rainfall: **9**

XAVIER HOENNER/SHUTTERSTOCK

Dark Mofo

northern WA and northern NT). During peak summer months further south, the north is in the midst of its wet (and low) season (November to April).

SEASONAL ACCOMMODATION

Much of the accommodation in Australia is seasonal. Prices in beach areas soar in summer, historic towns close to capital cities are often booked out on weekends and many places across tropical northern Australia close during the Wet.

WET & DRY

Rather than dividing the year into summer, winter, autumn and spring, a better benchmark in Australia's tropical north is the Wet (November to March or April, when it's steamy and hot, and torrential rains are common) and the Dry (May to October, when temperatures are more bearable).

BIG TICKET FESTIVALS

Sydney Mardi Gras
Australia's biggest and most iconic pride festival paints a rainbow across Sydney, culminating in a joyously extravagant parade along Oxford St. **February and March**

Melbourne International Comedy Festival
Laugh until your sides hurt at Australia's largest comedy festival, which runs for nearly a month, with more than 500 shows to choose from. **March and April**

Adelaide Fringe
World's second-largest fringe festival (after Edinburgh) is an absolute hoot, with hundreds of shows over an entertaining month. **February and March**

Dark Mofo
Live music, quirky arts, bonfires, red wine and a nightly Winter Feast in Hobart in the half-light of June's winter solstice. **June**

JULY
Avg. daytime max: **18°C**
Days of rainfall: **7**

AUGUST
Avg. daytime max: **19°C**
Days of rainfall: **6**

SEPTEMBER
Avg. daytime max: **22°C**
Days of rainfall: **6**

OCTOBER
Avg. daytime max: **24°C**
Days of rainfall: **8**

NOVEMBER
Avg. daytime max: **24°C**
Days of rainfall: **9**

DECEMBER
Avg. daytime max: **26°C**
Days of rainfall: **8**

GET PREPARED FOR AUSTRALIA

Useful things to load in your bag, your ears and your brain

CLOTHING

Formal or casual? Australians are a casual lot. Unless they're on their way to work, a wedding or a fancy restaurant, many people dress as if they might head for the beach at short notice.

Shorts or long pants? It's pretty unusual to see long pants in Australia's Top End, where they take casual to a whole new level. T-shirts, shorts and thongs (flip-flops) are acceptable in most situations.

Light waterproof jacket It can, and does, rain anytime in most coastal regions. Even summer evenings can be chilly, especially in the southern states.

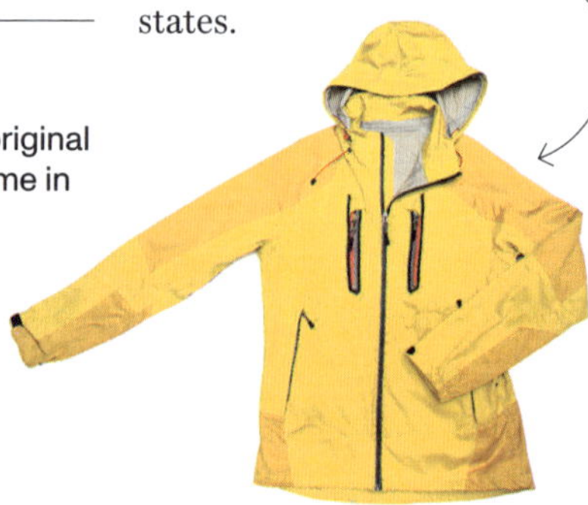

Walking shoes Bring a pair with enough support for pounding city footpaths. For more serious bushwalking, breathable walking shoes or boots with ankle coverage are best.

Casual and smart casual clothes Nicer restaurants and bars command a (usually unspoken) dress code. Shorts and nice sandals are fine, but thongs are not – south of the Tropic of Capricorn, at least.

Swimwear Have you even been to Australia if you didn't take a dip?

Layers Handy if you're visiting cooler zones or multiple regions.

Slip, slop and slap Apply SPF50+ or above before you head out during the day (even when it's overcast).

WATCH

- **Gallipoli**
  (Peter Weir; 1981)
  Devastatingly brilliant story of two mates who enlist in WWI.
- **The Castle**
  (Rob Sitch; 1997)
  Classic satirical comedy about an underdog Aussie family taking an unjust government to court.
- **Muriel's Wedding**
  (PJ Hogan; 1994)
  Rivals *The Castle* for best comedy-drama with a working-class family at its core, starring Toni Collette as Abba-obsessed Muriel.
- **Rabbit-Proof Fence**
  (Phillip Noyce; 2002)
  Three young stolen Aboriginal children try to reach home in the 1930s.

FROM LEFT TO RIGHT: ALLIANCE IMAGES/SHUTTERSTOCK, LANDSCAPEMANIA/SHUTTERSTOCK, VALZAN/SHUTTERSTOCK, MARTIN VALIGURSKY/SHUTTERSTOCK

South Bank (p152), Brisbane

WORDS

ambo ambulance
arvo afternoon
booze bus police van or bus used as a checkpoint to test and catch drunk drivers
brekkie breakfast
bush can refer to the outback, or anywhere beyond a city or town
chock-a-block/chockers full
Chuck a U-ie U-turn
clocked caught speeding
Fair dinkum? Really? Honestly? Are you serious? If not used as a question, it can mean 'authentic'.
g'day hello/hi
Good on ya Great work
hoon dangerous driver
How ya goin'? How are you?
K(s) Kilometre(s)
prang a (small) road accident
rego vehicle registration
servo petrol station
speedo speedometer
ute utility vehicle, pickup-style vehicle
woop woop middle of nowhere

LISTEN

Diesel & Dust
(Midnight Oil; 1987) Pick any Midnight Oil album as your driving soundtrack and you're halfway towards being an Aussie.

Longing
(Pete Murray; 2025) The Aussie folk rock singer-songwriter's latest album was made for coastal road trips.

Triple J
The national ad-free radio station features Australian artists of all genres.

Full Story
(Guardian Australia; 2019-ongoing) Guardian journalists go behind the headlines every weekday on this podcast.

READ

Talking to My Country
(Stan Grant; 2016) Powerful and personal meditation on race, culture and national identity by a Wiradjuri media figure.

Welcome to Country
(Marcia Langton; 2019) A travel guide to Aboriginal Australia, with sections on West Coast Australia.

Cloudstreet
(Tim Winton; 1991) Classic Aussie novel about two Perth families by a master storyteller.

ROAD TRIPS

Outback Australia
ELSALASS/SHUTTERSTOCK

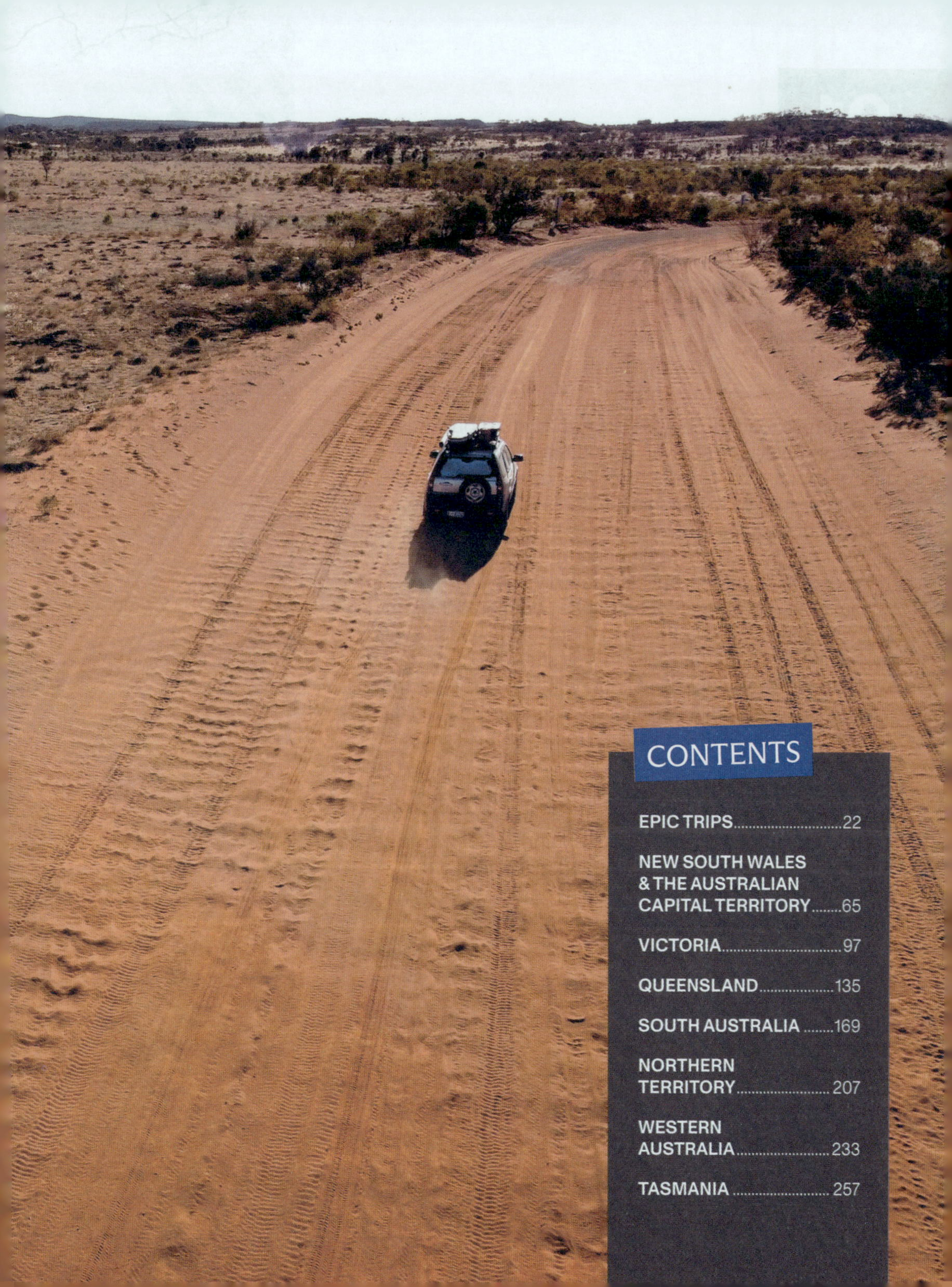

CONTENTS

01

EPIC TRIP: THE LAP

The ultimate road trip in Australia is the Lap. Thousands of people hook up a caravan or outfit their van to live on the road for 6, 12 or 48 months covering the 20,000-odd kilometres it takes to traverse the continent's coastline. It's a rite of passage for Australians – they return home (sometimes) with a renewed understanding of not only how vast the country is, but also how diverse it is.

Blaze Lopes / *@barefoot.blaze* has completed the Lap twice, the first time in 2020 when much of the country was in lockdown due to COVID-19 and, as she says, 'the one where I was 22 and didn't yet know what I was capable of'. While this isn't a traditional itinerary, we've provided links to trips in this book where you can retrace Blaze's steps and get a taste of what such an epic road trip entails.

Blaze wrote this coming-of-age story disguised as a road trip in her first van, Hurley, the same one that carried her around an entire country and, in her words, 'quietly reshaped the way I see it and myself. It gave me more than kilometres. It gave me perspective, confidence, community – and a home.'

BY BLAZE LOPES

Marking stops on the Lap
BLAZE LOPES/@BAREFOOT.BLAZE

SOUTH AUSTRALIA
VICTORIA
TASMANIA

EPIC TRIP

★ BEST FOR:

WILDLIFE LOVERS

Gorges and waters of the North West Cape.

Sunrise near Kununurra, Kimberley

DURATION: 6-12 MONTHS (IF POSSIBLE, NO TIME LIMIT!)

DISTANCE: APPROX 20,000KM / 12,400 MILES

GREAT FOR: NATURE LOVERS, SLOW TRAVEL

BEST TIME TO GO: FOLLOW THE SEASONS: SOUTH IN SUMMER, NORTH IN WINTER.

LINK YOUR TRIP

02 Sydney to Melbourne
Fresh green coastlines connecting two capitals like a deep breath

26 Yorke & Eyre Peninsulas
Wild coastlines, oysters and beaches that don't try to impress.

03 Across the Nullarbor
Vast horizons where nerves, curiosity and courage quietly collide.

34 Coral Coast to Broome
Red earth, turquoise reefs and Australia at its rawest beauty.

05 Kimberley Crossing
Ancient gorges and boabs in a landscape almost surreal.

29 Alice Springs to Darwin
Vast horizons where nerves, From desert heartlands to waterfalls, Australia beats loudest here.

17 Queensland Coastal Cruise
Sun-drenched islands, reef swims and easy tropical living.

06 Sydney to Byron Bay
Beloved beaches, big skies and a coastline that hums.

The only way I can describe taking off on a lap of Australia is: it's like skydiving. You don't realise how high you are until you jump – and Australia is the same. You don't truly grasp how vast this country is until you take the leap.

One minute you're staring at a map, tracing imaginary lines. The next, you're kissing loved ones goodbye and pulling out of The Drive:way. At first, leaving feels familiar. The streets out of town, the highways you've driven a hundred times before – it feels like any other road trip or weekend away. But then you hit the open road, and that's when it settles. Where the heck am I going?!

For me, the lap began in **Sydney**, New South Wales. I grew up in the heart of Bondi Beach, surrounded by some of the most beautiful coastline in the country and no shortage of opportunity. I'm very grateful for that upbringing – but by the time I hit the road, I felt ready for a different chapter.

My parents had already given us a taste of Australia's scale when we were kids. Every year, Mum (Vicki) and Dad (Mick) would pull my younger brother Brock and me out of school for a few weeks and load up the family Prado. We explored new corners of the country on each trip – from the red dunes of the Simpson Desert to endless sunsets at Eighty Mile Beach. Seeing Australia that young, when imagination runs wild, engrained something in me that I haven't been able to shake since. Even now, when 'Flame Trees' by Cold Chisel comes on, I'm instantly back in the rear seat, open plains stretching out along the Oodnadatta Track, Brock and I fighting over the last jelly snake.

Everyone has a different reason for lapping Australia. Some plan it for years; others stumble upon it. Mine sat somewhere in between. In August 2020, mid-pandemic, I bought my first van at 21. I'd done the Sydney thing – uni, full-

BLAZE LOPES/@BAREFOOT.BLAZE

time work – and I was ready for my glory days. Originally, that meant backpacking overseas…but COVID-19 had other plans. A time defined by lockdowns and closed borders opened me up to a life of freedom and adventure – ironic, hey? I think it forced a lot of us to explore our own backyard, and I'm bloody glad it did.

Buying that first van was equal parts excitement and fear. What do I need? What if it breaks down? What if I get it wrong? What I didn't know back then, and what I now tell anyone keen to hit the road, is that there's no such thing as the perfect setup. You figure it out as you go. All I really needed was a comfortable bed, a reliable engine and, after a bit of designing, bright-blue flower decals splashed across the body…perfect! It was an ex-rental Toyota Hiace with 480,000km on the clock. I'll never forget my dad finishing the test drive, glancing over and saying, 'I hate to admit it, but she drives like a dream.' Bloody oath she did.

The months leading up to departure blurred together – short trips, small tweaks, learning very basic mechanics. But one thing stuck with me. One day my mum said, 'Blaze, buying this van has been the best decision you've ever made.' She was right. Then suddenly, the day came. All I had was a map of Australia and a loose plan shaped by the seasons: south for summer, north for winter. There were driveway hugs, a few teary goodbyes, promises to call and then…I drove off.

My parents are travellers, so they were more excited than worried. Still, thinking back on that moment – the look in their eyes – it feels like they knew I'd fall in love with the life that lay ahead of me. The big, bad, beautiful world. And this was only the beginning. The open road. Holy sh*t! There's a moment – somewhere just beyond the city – where it hits you. Not excitement or fear, but something way deeper. A gut feeling that swells in your chest, almost to the point of squealing, and leaves your cheeks aching from smiling. Pure freedom.

JOHN CARNEMOLLA/SHUTTERSTOCK

Pambula, New South Wales

01 New South Wales South Coast

The South Coast of NSW felt like a deep breath. Not quite home – just ease. Sunrise swims, simple towns where life moves a little slower. It was the place I realised leaving didn't have to feel dramatic. This was where the road gently taught me how to leave.

Rolling over the **Sea Cliff Bridge** was when the adventure really sank in. The ocean opened up beside me, the road curved away from everything I knew, and town after town slid past – familiar, but just different enough to remind me I was moving forward.

Further south, the distances between towns stretch. Around places like **Merimbula** and **Pambula**, time feels slower. My Nonna and Nonno used to bring my dad here as a kid. I've seen the photos. Same beaches, same roads. It felt like stepping into a memory I didn't create, but somehow shared – one that lived in my grandparents' photos and stories, and now, in me.

There was a subtle confidence that settled in as I crossed into Victoria. We'd driven these roads my whole life (four times a year, every year), always heading somewhere specific. Family, obligations...a reason. This time, though, there was no one expecting me. No timetable, no reason except my own. For the first time, I wasn't following a path – I was writing one.

Among travellers, Victoria is often rushed – boosted straight through – but it deserves more than that. Slow down, and it rewards you. We'll come back to that.

02 Tasmania

Then came Tasmania. I couldn't tell if it was the swell or the realisation settling in, but crossing the Bass Strait – my home on wheels strapped down beside me – I felt nervous in a way I hadn't yet. Not scared, just aware. A quiet understanding that I was officially outside my safety net. I couldn't just turn around and drive home if things got tough.

But by the time we docked, that nervous energy had shifted. The air felt sharper. The anticipation had kicked in. Tasmania welcomed me like it knew I'd crossed more than just water.

Tassie doesn't let you rush. Cool mornings, quiet towns, conversations that lingered longer than expected. It was an early reminder

EPIC TRIP

Choosing a Touring Setup

Australia is vast. Distances are long, towns are sparse, so reliability matters more than anything. You want something that not only goes the distance, but is common enough that mechanics know it well and parts are easy to find.

I've done two laps in Toyotas (a Hiace and a Troopcarrier), both with high kilometres. Between them, my biggest issues were a starter motor and a fuel filter. Simple, fixable, no drama.

That said, your vehicle is personal. What works for one might not suit another. A van offers comfort – you can sit up inside when it rains, cook properly, and live out of it long-term with ease. A 4WD gives you access to more remote tracks and rougher terrain – places that simply aren't reachable in a 2WD.

But some of the best memories of my lap happened in carparks, campsites and bakeries, not on extreme tracks. Capability expands your options, but adventure isn't reserved for one type of setup.

Start simple. You can refine and update as you go. Whatever you choose, know you'll naturally gravitate towards people travelling similarly to you. Conversations often start with, 'Love your setup' – and before you know it, you're sharing camps, meals and k's. Almost all of my closest friendships on the road started with a chat about our vehicles.

There's a community waiting for you. Vans, caravans and 4WDs all come with their own tribes, rhythms and meeting points – and sometimes, that sense of belonging ends up being just as important as the vehicle itself.

Touring setup

BLAZE LOPES/@BAREFOOT.BLAZE

that the lap wasn't about ticking places off, but about learning how to be right where you are.

For such a small place, it's full of surprises. Some of the most grounding moments came from the simplest things – 'RV friendly' signs that genuinely meant it, hikes that knocked the wind out of me both physically and mentally, and bumping into Tony Abbott at the summit of **Cradle Mountain**. Only in Tasmania.

Tasmania invites you in. And before you realise it, you're moving slower – not because you should, but because it feels rude not to.

03 Great Ocean Road

When the ferry docked back on the mainland, I expected comfort. Familiar faces, familiar places. The Great Ocean Road waiting, like it always had. My family lives along that stretch. I'd driven those bends more times than I could count. It should've felt grounding but instead, it felt...strange.

There were long lunches with my beautiful Nanna (grandmother). Nonna and Nonno trailing their fingers across my map. Proper beds, full fridges, love everywhere. And yet, beneath it all, there was an itch I couldn't quite scratch.

Something in me had shifted. I'd tasted a kind of independence that's hard to explain – the only way I can describe it is that glow-up feeling after a breakup. When you stop asking for permission, you trust your gut and everything you do is unapologetically yours.

Coming back to the safety of knowing exactly where I was confused me. The Great Ocean Road was as beautiful as ever – limestone cliffs plunging into open ocean, the Apostles etched into the horizon – but it felt like a place I loved, not one I needed.

It wasn't until the air dried out beyond the Otways and the horizon stretched toward South Australia that I felt it again. That quiet pull toward the unknown. It was the first time in my life that familiarity didn't feel like comfort. I wasn't chasing home anymore – I was chasing space.

04 South Australia

South Australia met me with a steadiness I didn't expect. Towns where people look you in the eye and have a proper chat. No rush. Subtle. True blue. The kind of place that parks a Loch Ness monster in the desert and doesn't feel the need to explain itself.

But it was the **Eyre Peninsula** that got me. Australia stripped back to its best bits – barren, exposed and bloody beautiful.

In Port Lincoln, I hung in a shark cage, heart hammering...and saw absolutely nothing. Not a fin, not a shadow. Bugger.

Coffin Bay, though – the finer things at their simplest. Oysters for nine dollars a bag from the servo, shucked with a screwdriver on sun-bleached cliffs above electric-blue water. Wind in your hair. Nowhere to be. You beauty.

A few clicks west, I slowed for a family of emus crossing the bitumen – long legs, quiet confidence like they owned the joint.

Not far beyond **Streaky Bay**, a crew of surfers living out of rusty Cruisers, boards stacked on the roof, waxing up in the wind. Same long limbs (and longer hair), same unbothered energy, same look in their eyes like they'd cracked the code.

Windows down, dust trailing behind me, I realised something: South Australia doesn't try to impress anyone. It just does.

05 Nullarbor

And then, almost without warning, the **Nullarbor** begins. That single, straight line on my map I'd only ever imagined. We love to dramatise it. Total isolation, nothing for hundreds of kilometres.

These days? It's a highway of road trains, grey nomads towing half their house, backpackers rattling along in setups that shouldn't legally exist. It's not empty, but it's bloody long. And in between the quiet stretches, there's the wave – that subtle two-finger lift off the wheel as you pass another traveller. No words. Just: living the dream.

For all its scale, it feels strangely communal.

The trees thin, the bends disappear. No side roads, no 'we'll stay another night'. It was forward or nothing. Right on cue, my stereo carked it.

06 Western Australia

And just when I thought I had it handled, I rolled up to the WA border and had to surrender every fresh vegetable I'd bought the day before. Apparently Western Australia is harder to get into than a wet wetsuit.

That's the Nullarbor. Not remote the way people think – just exposing. It strips away distraction. And somewhere between the dead-straight bitumen and the edge of the **Bunda Cliffs** – staring into sheer nothingness – you realise there's nothing left to drown out the quiet. When the road offers no detours, no signal, no Cold Chisel, you finally hear yourself think.

Then, somewhere after that strange 15-minute time-zone shift and the turnoff at Norseman, the colour comes back. The first glimpse of **Esperance** felt like someone had turned the saturation up. Sand so

EPIC TRIP

The Quiet Confidence of the Road

I didn't grow up as a free spirit, that's for sure. I was a homebody in every sense of the word – the kid who avoided sleepovers and needed Mum to tickle her back every night. I don't know if I was scared of the world or just unsure of it, but comfort lived very close to home. That's why the road surprised me.

Travelling this way – especially solo – became a gentle gateway into independence. Van life gave me a constant. No matter where I parked, I had my bed, my familiar, my own four walls. Home came with me: 'my space, in every place'. That small certainty made the unknown feel manageable, even inviting.

I've travelled solo, in relationships and in convoys of mates. Each dynamic teaches you something different. Solo travel showed me just how capable I actually am.

There's a reason road trips are so universally loved: there's something undeniably magical about them. Road trips strip life back to its most basic rhythm. You rise with the sun and move from A to B. And when you're driving, there's nothing to do but watch the country unfold – talk, think, or sit in blissful silence. My favourite form of meditation.

There are stretches (often without reception) where you realise how freeing it is to be unreachable. In a world obsessed with urgency, that kind of disconnection feels almost rebellious. There's no scrolling, no emails, no instant distractions.

And yet, you're still moving forward – physically, visibly. You can feel the progress in the kilometres ticking by. You cover ground and make decisions. You never question stopping for a road-trip snack or a bakery feed in a town you've never heard of. On the road, everything feels justified. Everything feels like an adventure.

Living simply, outdoors, day after day, is indescribably empowering. Even the mundane becomes memorable – making lunch out the back of your setup, dust everywhere, flies buzzing, nowhere else you need to be. It sounds ridiculous but it feels extraordinary.

The lap changes you – not because of the destinations, but because of who you become between them. What you think matters at the start slowly shifts. You begin trusting yourself. You learn that discomfort doesn't mean danger, and uncertainty doesn't mean failure. The road didn't create confidence for me – it revealed it. That's when 'she'll be right' stopped being a saying and started being something I lived by.

I hope everyone gets the chance to experience that feeling at least once, because that quiet confidence – earned slowly, kilometre by kilometre – is what stays with you long after the engine switches off.

Sea Cliff Bridge, New South Wales

BLAZE LOPES/@BAREFOOT.BLAZE

white you needed sunnies, water so blue it looked edited. After the beige of the Nullarbor, it felt like clicking refresh.

We camped at **Lucky Bay** and swam at sunrise – the kind of swim that shocks you awake. Kangaroos bouncing along the shoreline like it was just another Friday. I remember floating there thinking, is this actually happening?

It was windier than I expected. One afternoon I genuinely had to shoulder my driver's door open just to get back inside. Sand in every nook and cranny, hair crustier than my bare feet. But boy, I felt alive.

At **Twilight Beach**, I started talking to a group of girls after we all spotted dolphins. No introduction, just a shared excitement. I've been lucky enough to keep bumping into these girls ever since.

When the weather turned – more unpredictable than my Spotify shuffle – we'd retreat inland. Into trees, into pubs with leather stools and sun-faded signs, into bakeries claiming Australia's best pie. Those warm, ordinary moments balanced the wildness of the coast.

Further west, the palette softened. Blues into greens. Granite boulders guarding calm bays. It's a beauty that stops conversation mid-sentence.

By the time I reached **Margaret River**, I wasn't chasing the next sticker anymore – I was just moving with the days. Caves Rd became the rhythm. Forest one minute, ocean the next. Surf checks that turned into full days, carpark chats that stretched late into the night.

There's a migration that happens in the southwest. Travellers follow the seasons. You start seeing the same rigs, the same faces swapping stories, surf reports and bakery recommendations. WA is geographically massive, but anyone who's travelled here understands just how small it can feel.

I didn't know it then – somewhere between forest camps, wineries and beach days – but this was the beginning of something bigger. The first time the road stopped feeling like an escape and started feeling like home.

Somewhere north of Perth, the light changes. I remember because I was on the phone to Dad. He'd lived in WA at 18, chasing his own freedom, and I'd called him half-deflated. It had been bucketing, and I'd started wondering if the magic had worn off. He just said, 'Keep driving until the sky opens up.' And then,

Twilight Beach, Western Australia

HANS WISMEIJER/SHUTTERSTOCK

just beyond the **Pinnacles**, it did. The clouds split and the sun punched through. The ocean shifted from steel to aqua in minutes. From that moment on, the north felt different. The kilometres stopped mattering and the Indian Ocean took over.

But it wasn't the places everyone talks about that shaped me – it was what sat just offshore: the **Abrolhos Islands**. Four weeks living with a local crayfisherman we'd met. No reception, no distractions. Just reefs so alive they barely looked real, odd jobs around camp, and whatever the ocean decided to feed us that day. Crayfish, fresh fish, supplies flown in from **Kalbarri**. Days weren't planned – they unfolded. And for the first time on the lap, I felt exactly how people imagined my life to be: free, raw, uncomplicated.

Travel comes with head noise. You carry yourself everywhere. Out there, it stopped. I wasn't trying to live the dream, I was just living. It remains one of the greatest privileges of my life.

Back on the mainland, the road north offered quick resets. **Geraldton** for creature comforts, **Billabong Roadhouse** for the obligatory photo. **Shark Bay** shimmered, Shell Beach crunched. **Francois Peron National Park** flashed red dirt against turquoise – a teaser of what was coming.

Then the coastline hardened. Stations, the kind only the northwest can pull off. On paper: nothing, no reception or signage. But somehow, it's everything.

The road in rattles your setup and your thoughts in equal measure. And at the end of it: Red Bluff. Dry wind, big swell. Surfers, Troopys and goats. No agenda beyond the tide, no distraction or overcomplicating. The Abrolhos magic – just on land.

We followed faint coastal tracks north, red earth on one side and the Indian Ocean on the other. It was the only time on the entire lap I truly felt like there was nobody else around. Not lonely – sacred.

And then, just as the rawness reached its peak, **Coral Bay** rolled in like a reward. Clear water, reef straight off the shore. A boat ramp that felt more like a community noticeboard than a destination.

07 Exmouth & Ningaloo

It was there I overheard someone talking about **Exmouth** – casually, like it was inevitable. I hadn't even heard of it. That was it. A throwaway conversation, a quiet redirect. I arrived in Exmouth on my 23rd birthday, and to this day, I think 23 was my favourite year. I had a glow that year – I just didn't know Exmouth was about to light the fuse.

Exmouth looks like the kind of place that should change you. The reef, the canyons, the swell. Warm, clear water. And it does, but not in the way you expect. Because the thing that reshaped me most wasn't offshore – it was a dusty carpark at Town Beach.

When I first rolled in (July 2021), WA was locked at the borders. Somehow, especially for those of us from the East Coast, we'd all ended up there. There was this unspoken understanding between us. We were lucky, stranded in the best possible way, and Town Beach became the village square. You didn't know people by surnames – you knew them by their rigs. The Transit, the bus, the bloke with the tinny. I was 'Hurley' because of the sticker on my van.

We'd spend entire days there, sunburnt from all-day tinny missions on the west side. Hair salted stiff, reapplying tinted zinc like it was makeup. Quick rinse in the public showers, op-shop outfit on. Then it was Froth, potshot, repeat. It sounds simple, but it was the life!

It felt like we were all living on the same frequency. Plans didn't get made – they unfolded. Someone would say, 'We're heading out to the west side tomorrow,' and suddenly you were too. Someone found a manta? Everyone was there by lunchtime. No overthinking or curating, just constant motion and constant presence.

Ningaloo is one of the most diverse stretches of coastline in the country. Reef off the shore, canyons inland, warm water year-round. For nature lovers, it's outrageous. But Exmouth isn't just stunning – it's shared. And that's what makes it different. You can visit beautiful places anywhere, but Exmouth taught me that beauty multiplies when you experience it together.

I arrived on my 23rd birthday, and left three months later glowing. Leaving Exmouth didn't feel like moving on – it felt like carrying something forward. The glow didn't fade, but the pull to keep moving grew louder.

Bullara was the gateway. A cattle station caught between coast and outback – one last shared dinner under fairy lights before the red dirt took over.

Then finally **Karijini** swallowed me whole. I remember driving in with the *Lion King* soundtrack blaring, tears welling as the landscape took my breath away. Lazy afternoons at Hamersley before a sunrise hike up Mt Bruce powered by stubbornness and an iPhone torch that had no business leading the way. I didn't feel overwhelmed – I felt capable.

And then, the universe checked me. I was camped at **Cape Keraudren**, still quietly rattled from leaving Exmouth, when a group of older women (all solo travellers, 65-plus) waved me over. Wine in hand, fire

EPIC TRIP

Exmouth: Learning to Slow Down

If there's one place that changes the way you move through Australia, it's Exmouth, WA. Among those who have visited, it's often described as a vortex – an oddly perfect word. Days stretch and soften. A schedule? Haven't had one since I took a photo at the iconic 'Welcome to Exmouth' sign. Life stops revolving around hours and starts responding to swell, wind and tides. I had never experienced anything quite like myself – faded away. Eventually, I hit the road again. Three days had turned into three months, and that's when I discovered the beauty of travelling without limits.

Exmouth didn't just show me beauty – it reshaped the way I travelled for the rest of the lap. It taught me to move with the country, not through it.

It was also the first place on my lap where I felt like I truly belonged, surrounded by people I'm lucky enough to now call lifelong friends. It gave me confidence. It gave me my glow. And of all the places the lap introduced me to, Exmouth is the one I'll always be grateful for – for the time, perspective and permission to slow down.

Ningaloo Reef, (p31), Western Australia

VIOLETA BROSIG/SHUTTERSTOCK

VIKTOR POSNOV/ALAMY

Lake Argyle, Western Australia

crackling. 'Bring a chair over, love.' Bloody oath! I sat with them for hours, laughed, cried a little, felt held in a way I hadn't realised I needed. Before bed, one of them called, 'Batten down the hatches, ladies – it'll be blowy tonight.'

At 3am my van started rocking. I assumed it was the wind. It wasn't. I was rolling. Instinctively, I jumped out as my entire home – my life – slid downhill toward the ocean, the full moon lighting it up like a stage. Between cries and attempts of slowing it down, I remember thinking, this cannot be happening. A single boulder stopped it. I sat there until sunrise, heart pounding, wheels airborne, waiting for the tide to confirm I was safe. When the women emerged, they wrapped me in hugs and made tea while I cried into their arms.

A local with a ute winched me back to solid ground soon after. Three years later, a mate working in the mines rang me laughing: she'd overheard a bloke telling that exact story around a table. It was him!

That night stripped something away – not confidence, but illusion. I'd left my comfort zone, and the road made sure I understood what that meant. It could've shaken me off the lap, but instead, it steadied me.

From there, the north unfolded like a reward. **Broome** shimmered – camels padding along Cable Beach at sunset, red dirt meeting electric blue. The Kimberley stretched wide – gorges glowing at golden hour, corrugations reminding you to pay attention. Waterfalls earned, not handed out.

And then **Lake Argyle**. I floated at sunset on a pool noodle, prosecco in hand, drifting as the sky softened to peach and gold. After everything the wild west had offered, it felt like WA was raising a glass. A subtle, final cheers. And I cheersed it right back.

08 Northern Territory

Crossing into the Northern Territory felt like the start of a new season. The air heavier, the sun less forgiving. **Litchfield** was immediate – waterfalls you dive straight into. **Kakadu** ancient and humbling.

Darwin? Listen to the lyrics of 'Darwin Nights' by Adam Harvey – Bundy, barramundi and NT time: not today, not tomorrow. Brilliant. And it was hot, the kind that makes you question living in a tin can on wheels.

Lying on the Darwin foreshore one afternoon, completely melted, a conversation turned into a last-minute house sit in **Humpty Doo**. Like it always seemed to on this lap, the universe intervened. We thought we'd scored air-con and stability, a break from van life. What we actually got was 150 free-range chickens, two cows and a bull. Overnight, we transformed from van girls to farmers. Chickens escaped daily (one regularly ended up in my bed). We'd race back from Litchfield to feed them before sunset. It was absolute chaos. But it was also one of the funniest, most grounding chapters of my entire lap — because the Territory makes you earn your stories, handing you heat, livestock and unpredictability, and watching what you do with it.

Somewhere between waterfalls and rogue chickens, I realised something: I didn't need perfect conditions anymore. I could handle the unexpected. By the time we pulled into **Daly Waters** – Mum first on the dance floor – I felt it in my gut. Not just adventure but capability. Whatever the road threw at me, I'd find my way through it.

09 Queensland

And suddenly, that road was pointing east. Not toward the unknown this time, but toward home – or at least, the version of it I'd left behind. Well...a very long home stretch. Because, according to some locals I met at a rest stop, if there's one thing you should do before heading east, it's watch your final sunset over the water at **Karumba**. Karumba is a small fishing town on the edge of the Gulf of Carpentaria. Understated, mostly missed. I had one last drink at a perfectly imperfect pub overlooking the water, overhearing local fisherfolk yarn about the croc that had tried to jump into their tinny earlier that day.

Somewhere inland, I caught up with a childhood friend I hadn't seen in decades. We sat at a country pub (after replacing my flat tyre) with ginger beers, laughing at how wildly different our lives had turned out. Same starting point, completely different roads – and yet, both exactly where we were meant to be.

Then the landscape flipped. Leaving the Gulf and winding through the **Atherton Tablelands** felt like driving into another country. After

Daly Waters, Northern Territory

PETAR B PHOTOGRAPHY/SHUTTERSTOCK

EPIC TRIP

Why the Lap Is Financially Possible

Here's what I wish someone had told me before I left: everyone laps Australia differently. But you don't need to be a millionaire to live the dream.

I've never travelled with a strict budget. Instead, I focus on removing my biggest expense. For most people, that's accommodation.

Travelling in a setup that allows free or low-cost camping changes everything. Free camps, donation sites and national parks quickly become the backbone of long-term travel. Apps like WikiCamps help you find them, and Petrol Spy helps you avoid overpaying for fuel.

National park passes are worth researching early. In Western Australia, for example, a 12-month pass is often cheaper than paying individual entry fees, and you can register two vehicles on one pass – meaning you can split the cost with a mate.

Caravan parks still have their place. I use them strategically for a reset: showers, laundry, water refills and charging everything in one hit. With laundromats costing around $7 per load (plus the cafe stop that somehow turns into lunch), a powered site can actually be better value.

Fuel is usually the biggest ongoing expense, especially in older vehicles. But Australia isn't going anywhere. Embracing the slow lane saves more than you'd expect over time. People often ask for exact numbers, but the truth is the lap flexes with how you travel. Cook most meals, free-camp regularly, move slower, and it becomes sustainable. Once accommodation stops dictating your decisions, the road feels far less expensive – and far more possible.

Family road trip, outback Australia

BLAZE LOPES/@BAREFOOT.BLAZE

months of red dust and dry heat, the green felt almost theatrical. Ferns crowded the road, waterfalls appeared without warning. The air felt softened.

That's when it clicked: I thought I knew the East Coast (I grew up on it!), but after two years away I realised I'd only ever seen it from one angle.

Cairns hit differently now – not just a gateway to the reef, but a town run by backpackers and adventure. The Daintree whispered bigger adventures. Queensland stretched wider than I remembered – louder, longer, more layered.

Agnes Water was where I saw the first swell since Broome. I ran into it without scanning for crocs or stingers. **Airlie Beach** wasn't just the Whitsundays anymore – it was chaos and youth and long dinners on boats with questionable engines. The **Sunshine Coast** wasn't flashy but lush and easy, and warmer than memory. The **Gold Coast** still pulsed at 4am with promenade walkers and surf clubs, and sausage sizzles that smelled like childhood.

Yes, the traffic between Brisbane and the Gold Coast still sucked. Some things hadn't changed. But I had.

The funny thing about coming home is that it moves faster. The unknown stretches out, the familiar starts to feel smaller. Before you know it, you're back where you started – except you're not.

10 Home Stretch

Byron rolled in with linen, longboards and incense. **Yamba** and **Crescent Head** stitched nostalgia to new friendships. The highway between towns felt less like commuting and more like reminiscing. And then, my toll beeped. The first time in almost two years. A tiny, unimpressive sound that somehow carried the weight of the entire lap.

I used to lie in the back of the van, staring at that laminated map on my ceiling, tracing the coastline with my finger, wondering how something so vast could ever feel familiar. Two years later, I realised: it never shrinks. You grow into it.

When the 'Welcome to Sydney' sign appeared, I lost it. Not sadness or relief, but something bigger. An overwhelming sense of gratitude. For the landscapes, for the strangers who became family, for the version of me who left – and the one who returned.

I pulled into Bondi Beach car park and there they were – my family. Two years later. The map that had hung above my bed finally complete. The same coastline I'd grown up on, the same ocean, the same city. Just a different pair of blue eyes looking at it.

You leave thinking the lap will show you Australia. But what it really shows you is how much bigger home becomes once you've left it.

I didn't do it alone. To the family who answered every call, to the mates who met me in the middle of nowhere, to the strangers I'm lucky enough to now call friends, to the online community who followed every chaotic kilometre, and to Hurley and Kewpie, the tin cans on wheels that carried me safely around an entire country (twice): thank you.

Because in the end, the simplest truth held up. Home isn't just where you're from, it's who you become along the way. And sometimes, home truly is where you park it.

Ningaloo Reef, (p31), Western Australia

BLAZE LOPES/@BAREFOOT.BLAZE

02

EPIC TRIPS

SYDNEY TO MELBOURNE

DURATION: 5–7 DAYS

DISTANCE: 1100KM / 683 MILES

GREAT FOR: NATURE, FAMILIES & HISTORY

BEST TIME TO GO: NOVEMBER TO MARCH FOR WARM WEATHER AND A GOOD CHANCE OF CLEAR SKIES.

★ BEST FOR:

FAMILIES

Wildlife around Merimbula includes kangaroos on the beach and passing whales in the spring.

Batemans Bay

Australia's most popular stretch of its famous Route 1 shadows a stunning coastline, passing pristine stands of tall-tree forest. Jervis Bay, Mallacoota and Cape Conran provide the most picturesque stretches of coastal wilderness, while Central Tilba charms with artistic finds, fine wine and cheese. For lovers of wildlife, there are koalas at Paynesville, seals and seabirds at Barunguba Montague Island and kangaroos aplenty near Merimbula.

LINK YOUR TRIP

06 Sydney to Byron Bay
If you've done Sydney–Melbourne in reverse, continue up the coast for 879km to Byron Bay.

13 Gippsland & Wilsons Prom
This route through Victoria's Gippsland region shares the Princes Hwy for part of The Drive: - detour to Phillip Island before arriving in Melbourne.

01 Sydney

Sydney (Warrane) may be one of the world's most beguiling cities, but for our purposes it's merely the starting point of this classic coastal route to Melbourne (Narrm).

THE DRIVE: Drive south of Sydney along Rte 1. At Loftus, and not long after leaving Sydney's urban sprawl, take the turnoff for Bundeena and Royal National Park.

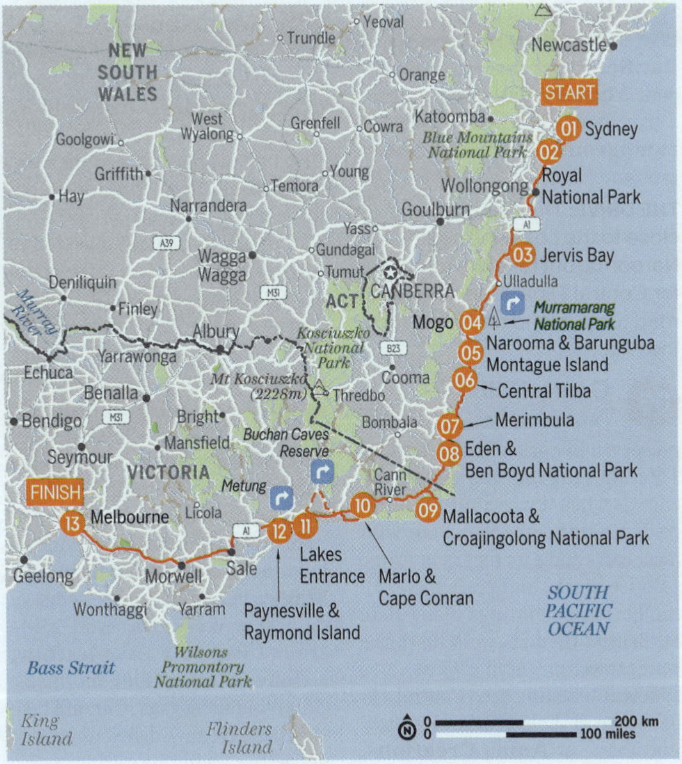

LEAH-ANNE THOMPSON/SHUTTERSTOCK

02 Royal National Park

The coastal **Royal National Park** *(nationalparks.nsw.gov.au)* protects almost 151 sq km of saltwater wetlands, subtropical rainforests and beaches lapped by azure waves. It's the world's second-oldest national park (1879) and its 32km coast alternates between forbidding cliffs and inviting beaches. **Garie and Wattamolla** are two of the easier beaches to reach. Access roads close at 8.30pm and there's a $12 fee for vehicles. Side roads to the smaller beaches close at 8.30pm. Even if you don't get out and walk, Rte 68 loops through the park and is an utterly lovely drive.

THE DRIVE: Make sure you take the coast road along the Sea Cliff Bridge that links Clifton with Stanford Park – you'll catch your breath as you cross the cantilevered bridge, hanging out over the water beneath high sea cliffs (there's a small car park allowing a pause for up-close views). There are more dramatic views on the approach to Wollongong. Later, after Kiama, take the Jervis Bay turnoff.

03 Jervis Bay

One of the New South Wales coast's unarguable highlights, this large, sheltered bay is immensely popular for its snow-white sand, crystalline waters, national parks and frolicking dolphins. Seasonal visitors include droves of Sydney holiday-makers (summer and most weekends) and migrating whales (May to November). **Jervis Bay National Park** *(nationalparks.nsw.gov.au)*, chock-full of paddle-worthy waters and family-friendly beaches, begins near Callala Bay.

Getting out on the water here is almost obligatory, from the wildlife-spotting trips of **Dolphin Watch Cruises** *(dolphinwatch.com.au)* to closer marine-life encounters, like diving and snorkelling.

Just as much fun is grabbing some oars with **Jervis Bay Kayaks & Paddlesports** *(jervisbaykayaks.com.au)*.

THE DRIVE: Return to the main highway, then turn south, passing through towns like Milton, Ulladulla and Batemans Bay on your way into Mogo.

DETOUR

Murramarang National Park

Start: 03 Jervis Bay

Surfing, kayaking, wildlife spotting...the wave-lashed shores of coastal Murramarang National Park offer a host of enticing beachside pastimes. The protected Murramarang Aboriginal Area is here, too, with its ancient middens and tool-making sites.

Walking trails snake off from the beaches, and a steep but enjoyable walk is up Durras Mountain (283m). To get here, take Rte 1 from Jervis Bay all the way past Ulladulla. At Termeil, turn left (southeast) towards Bawley Point and then follow the roads along the coast to Durras. Many of the roads in the park are pretty rough, but those to Durras, Durras Lake, Depot Beach and Durras North are all sealed, as is Mt Agony Rd to Pebbly Beach (but not Pebbly Beach Rd).

04 Mogo

While Batemans Bay is the more popular place to linger along this section of the coast, Mogo, a historic strip of wooden houses with cafes and souvenir shops, makes an interesting and much quieter alternative.

Moruya, 15km on, warrants a closer look for the beaches strung south of Moruya Heads, waterside restaurant **The River** *(therivermoruya.com.au)* and an outstanding historic B&B, the **Post & Telegraph** *(postandtelegraph.com.au)*.

THE DRIVE: The road from Mogo meanders along the contours of the coastline, passing over Moruya's main bridge. Dense woodlands line the roadside into Narooma.

05 Narooma & Barunguba Montague Island

Somnolent seaside town Narooma sits at an inlet, with surf beaches draped on either side. Uncommonly good wildlife encounters distinguish it from other beach towns, in particular on pristine **Barranguba Montague Island** *(montague island.com.au)*. Divers and snorkellers leap onto boats bound for this pest-free island, plunging themselves into waters alive with fur seals that move through the depths with remarkable grace; **Underwater Safaris** *(underwatersafaris.com.au)* is one eco-minded boat operator. Birdwatchers are also drawn to the island, gazing skyward to spot 90 avian species. Little penguins nest here, too, especially from September to February. Whales can be spotted offshore around the same time. Three-hour guided tours by national-park rangers explore the island's natural and human history; book ahead. Back in Narooma, take a swim at the southern end of **Bar Beach** or press on to resplendent **Mystery Bay**, where there's a bare-bones but prettily located **campground** *(mysterybaycamp ground.com.au)*.

THE DRIVE: The road stays close to the coastline south of Narooma, but take the turnoff for Central Tilba soon after the road turns inland and head for the hills.

06 Central Tilba

One of Australia's best-preserved historic villages, Central Tilba aims to exude the same ambience as when it was a 19th-century gold-mining boom town…only with nicer cafes and a lot more souvenirs.

Coffee places and craft shops fill the heritage buildings along Bate St. Behind the pub, walk up to the water tower for terrific views.

More interesting than Central Tilba's souvenir shops are the eye-catching wares at **Apma Creations**, among them desert art, handicrafts and marvellous jewellery, all made by Aboriginal artists. Off the main street, **ABC Cheese Factory** *(tilbadairy.com.au)* produces dairy delights spiked with olives and local herbs; nibble a few samples before deciding.

Rich cheese from the all-Jersey herds pairs nicely with a bottle of riesling from rustic **Tilba Valley Wines** *(tilbavalleywines.com)*, where there's a magnificent view of vines and plenty of grass where kids (and adults) can loll in the sunshine.

THE DRIVE: From Central Tilba, take the coast road instead of Rte 1 wherever possible – via Bermagui, Mimosa Rocks, Tathra and Tura Beach – and stop regularly to take in the view.

07 Merimbula

Merimbula is one of those South Coast beach resorts to which families have been returning for decades.

Part of its appeal lies in the long, golden beach and a lovely inlet, but there are also plenty of activities and an above-average selection of eateries. But best of all is the range of wildlife experiences. Go dolphin watching in the bay, or whale watching from mid-August to November. A conservation project has safeguarded wetlands at **Panboola** *(panboola.com)*, which is threaded by all-abilities cycling and walking trails; look out for birdlife and, towards dusk, kangaroos.

For an entirely different kind of wildlife, join **Captain Sponge's Magical Oyster Tours** *(magical oystertours.com.au)* and glide around Pambula Lake learning a thing or two about molluscs. Groan-inducing gags, tranquil lake views and creamy, delicious oysters make this a winning outing.

THE DRIVE: There's no mystery about the route to Eden – just take Rte 1 for 26km.

08 Eden & Ben Boyd National Park

Eden is a sleepy place where often the only bustle is down at the wharf when the fishing boats come in. Migrating humpback whales and southern right whales can be seen feeding or resting in Twofold Bay during their southern migration back to Antarctic waters from late September to late November. Teach the kids to bellow 'Thar she blows!' upon a sighting, just as they did in the old whaling days. The town's whaling past and whale-watching present are laid bare at the **Killer Whale Museum** *(killerwhalemu-*

JINA IHM/SHUTTERSTOCK

Jervis Bay National Park (p39)

seum.com.au), complete with the skeleton of the bay's celebrity cetacean. The wilderness barely pauses for breath in **Beowa National Park** *(nationalparks.nsw.gov.au)*, two expanses of protected land on either side of Eden comprising almost 105 sq km. The northern section of the park, with striking ironstone cliffs and Aboriginal middens, can be accessed from the Princes Hwy north of Eden. The southern section's isolated beaches and historic buildings are reached by mainly gravel roads leading off sealed Edrom Rd, which leaves the Princes Hwy 19km south of Eden. At its southern tip, the elegant 1883 **Green Cape Lightstation** *(nationalparks.nsw.gov.au)* offers awesome views.

THE DRIVE: South of Eden, the Pacific Hwy leaves the coast and cuts inland, crossing into Victoria deep in forest. The traffic thins and settlements are tiny to nonexistent for much of the way. Soon after crossing the state border, at Genoa, take the Mallacoota turnoff.

09 Mallacoota & Croajingolong National Park

The most easterly town in the state of Victoria, Mallacoota roosts by a vast inlet, flanked by **Croajingolong National Park**'s rolling dunes and hills. The rewards for coming this far are as diverse as ocean-surf beaches, quiet swimming spots and kangaroos galore. Croajingolong is one of Australia's finest coastal wilderness national parks and covers 875 sq km, stretching for about 100km from the village of Bemm River to the NSW border. Windswept Gabo Island, 14km offshore, is crowned with an operating lighthouse and has one of the world's largest colonies of little penguins. Get there by boat with **Wilderness Coast Charters** *(03-5158 0701)*.

THE DRIVE: Return the 22km northwest back up the road to the Princes Hwy, turn left, then drive all the way down through Cann River. Just past Orbost, take the 15km road south to Marlo.

> PHOTO OPPORTUNITY
>
> JERVIS BAY
>
> White-sand beaches near Jervis Bay.

10 Marlo & Cape Conran

The quiet seaside town of Marlo snoozes at the mouth of the Snowy River. Picturesque and popular with anglers, it's especially beloved as the gateway to the **Cape Conran** *(parks.vic.gov.au)* section of what is known as the Wilderness Coast. This blissfully undeveloped part of the coast is one of Gippsland's most beautiful corners, with long stretches of remote white-sand beach. The 19km coastal route from Marlo to Cape Conran is particularly pretty, bordered by banksia trees, grass plains, sand dunes and the ocean.

THE DRIVE: South of Eden, the Pacific Hwy leaves the coast and cuts inland, crossing into Victoria deep in forest. The traffic thins and settlements are tiny to nonexistent for much of the way. Soon after crossing the state border, at Genoa, take the Mallacoota turnoff.

♥ WHY I LOVE THIS TRIP

ANITA ISALSKA, WRITER

It's hard to imagine a more crowd-pleasing road trip than the coastal route between Melbourne and Sydney. There are surf beaches and pioneer towns, huffing whales, gliding seals and somersaulting dolphins, water sports and hiking trails that rove into Aboriginal history. My detours always increase on the home stretch – I'll take any excuse to prolong a journey this heartbreakingly beautiful.

DETOUR

Buchan Caves Reserve

Start: 10 Marlo

The sleepy town of Buchan, in the foothills of the Snowy Mountains, is famous for the intricate cave system at **Buchan Caves Reserve** *(parks.vic.gov.au)*, open to visitors for over a century. Underground rivers cutting through ancient limestone formed the caves and caverns, and they provided shelter for Aboriginal Australians as far back as 18,000 years ago. Parks Victoria runs guided tours daily, alternating between the equally impressive **Royal** and **Fairy**

Cape Conran (p42)

JAN KOZAK/SHUTTERSTOCK

Caves. Royal has more colour and a higher chamber; Fairy has dainty stalactites (fairy sightings not guaranteed). The rangers also offer hard-hat guided tours to the less-developed **Federal Cave** during high season. The reserve itself is a pretty spot, with shaded picnic areas, walking tracks and grazing kangaroos. Invigoration is guaranteed when taking a dip in the icy **rock pool**.

11 Lakes Entrance

Lakes Entrance has a certain scruffy charm, which is forgivable because the setting is just lovely. A number of lookouts watch over town from the neighbouring hilltops (ask at the Lakes Entrance **visitor centre** for directions), and a footbridge crosses the shallow Cunninghame Arm waterway separating the town from the ocean beaches. On the other side, climb over the dunes covered with coastal heath and down onto Ninety Mile Beach, with its crashing waves and endless sand. There are also boat cruises and some terrific places to eat, with the freshest local seafood a speciality.

THE DRIVE: Rte 1 loops up and out of town heading west – don't miss the Jemmy's Point Lookout on the way out of town. The turnoff to Paynesville is at Lucknow on the Princes Hwy.

DETOUR
Metung
Start: 11 Lakes Entrance

Dubbed the 'Gippsland Riviera' by locals, postcard-perfect Metung is wrapped around Bancroft Bay. One of the Lakes district's most attractive little towns, Metung has developed a niche appeal as the sophisticated alter ego to the clamour of Lakes Entrance.

BOSSA ART/SHUTTERSTOCK

Koala, Raymond Island

12 Paynesville & Raymond Island

Paynesville feels a million miles from the busy coast road. Down here, water dictates the pace of life: some residents have boats moored right outside their houses on purpose-built canals. Foodies will want to make a booking for the acclaimed **Sardine Dining** *(sardinedining.com.au)*, an unpretentious fine-dining restaurant run by the former chef at the acclaimed Vue de Monde. A good reason to detour here is to take the ferry on the five-minute hop across to **Raymond Island** for some koala spotting. There's a large colony of koalas here, mostly relocated from Phillip Island in the 1950s. If you happen to be here on the last weekend in February, the popular **Paynesville Music Festival** is outstanding.

THE DRIVE: Return to the main highway and set your sights on Melbourne, 298km away. The reason is simple: the best of the road is behind you, and the final crossing of Gippsland has very little to recommend it.

13 Melbourne

The cosmopolitan charms of Melbourne await you at journey's end. This artsy city could be the starting point of a new journey, but it's a fabulous destination in its own right, with ample attractions to satisfy architecture, food and sporting buffs.

03

★ BEST FOR:

OUTDOORS

Watch for whales amid the epic beauty of Head of Bight.

EPIC TRIPS

ACROSS THE NULLARBOR

DURATION: 5-7 DAYS

DISTANCE: 2493KM / 1549 MILES

GREAT FOR: NATURE & HISTORY

BEST TIME TO GO: APRIL TO OCTOBER IS BEST FOR MILD WEATHER, BUT THIS ROUTE IS POSSIBLE YEAR-ROUND.

Coastal Residences near Ceduna

Crossing the Nullarbor is about the journey as much as the destination, so relax and enjoy the big skies and endless horizons. The Nullarbor is a vast, treeless desert, dotted with a few tiny settlements and roadhouses, its roadsides speckled with spinifex grass. The full effect begins after Ceduna, while the Head of Bight and Kalgoorlie are first-rate attractions, and not only because it will take you so long to reach them.

LINK YOUR TRIP

04 Alice Springs to Adelaide
Port Augusta is Stop 7 on the Alice to Adelaide trip (1500km), and the start/end point of the Nullarbor crossing.

32 Western Australia's Southwest Coast
There are three ways to begin Trip 32 – Perth to Bunbury (173km), Wave Rock to Ravensthorpe (195km) or Norseman to Esperance (202km).

01 Port Augusta

Utilitarian, frontier-like Port Augusta (population 13,810) is where your journey begins – it's the last town of any size before you reach Perth (Boorlo). Port Augusta is known as the 'Crossroads of Australia': from here, highways and railways roll west across the Nullarbor into Western Australia, north to the Flinders Ranges or Darwin (Garramilla), south to Adelaide or Port Lincoln, and east to Sydney. Not a bad position! The old town centre has considerable appeal, with some elegant old buildings and a revitalised waterfront: locals cast lines into the Spencer Gulf as kids backflip off jetties. **Wadlata Outback Centre** *(wadlata.sa.gov.au)* is a good place to start your explorations – a combined museum/visitor centre. Inside, the 'Tunnel of Time' traces local Aboriginal and European histories using audiovisual displays, interactive exhibits

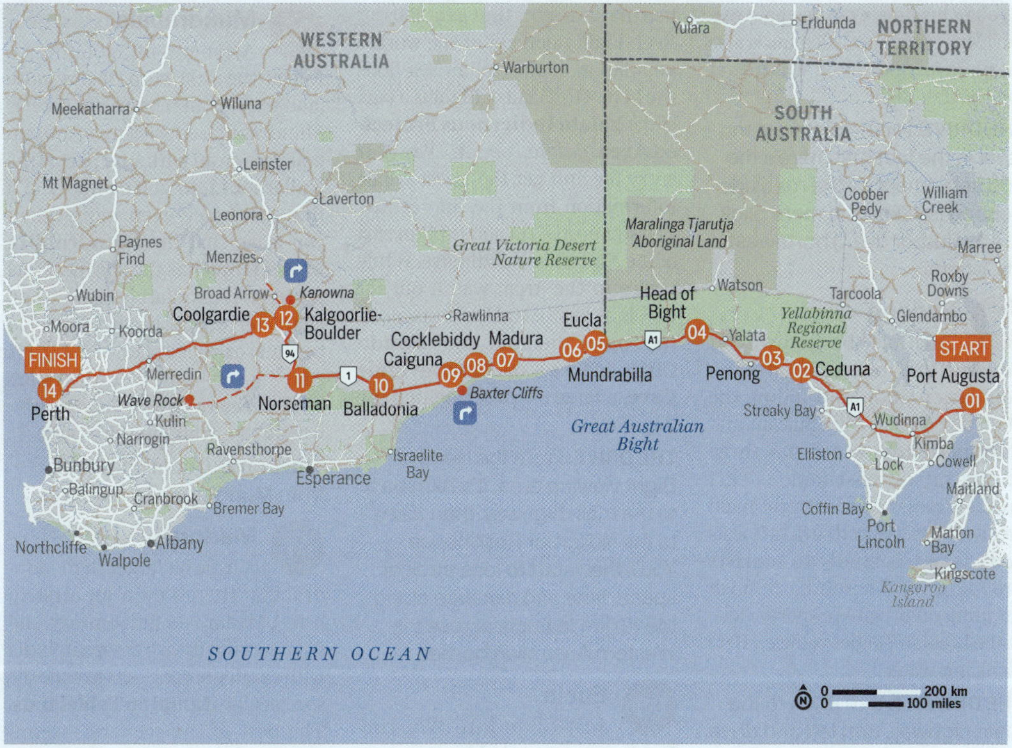

ICONSAUSTRALIA/ALAMY

and a distressingly big snake. Just north of town, the excellent (and free!) **Australian Arid Lands Botanic Garden** has 250 hectares of sandhills, clay flats and desert fauna and flora (ever seen a Sturt's Desert Pea?). Explore on your own – established walking trails run from 500m to 4.5km – or take a guided tour (10am Monday to Friday). To get a fix on the town's geography, climb to the top of the Water Tower Lookout in Port Augusta West. Not for the weak-kneed (see-through metal steps!), this 1882 turret affords a great view across the gulf and back to the town centre. Alternatively, 90-minute **Port Augusta Guided Walking Tours** depart the visitor centre.

THE DRIVE: From Port Augusta, the Eyre Hwy (A1) crosses the gargantuan Eyre Peninsula. Looping down to the southwest then veering northwest, the highway shadows the coastline of the Great Australian Bight, whose shores the road finally reaches at Ceduna, 497km after leaving Port Augusta. This is big-sky wheat-farming country: the towns along the highway are basic and functional.

02 Ceduna

Despite the residents' best intentions, Ceduna remains a raggedy fishing town that just can't shake its tag as a blow-through pit stop en route to WA (there are five caravan parks here). But the local oysters love it! **Oysterfest** *(cedunaoysterfest.com.au)* is the undisputed king of Australian oyster parties. The rest of the year, slurp a few salty bivalves at the Ceduna Oyster Bar. On a different tack, **Thevenard** is Ceduna's photogenic port suburb, on the peninsula south of town. The area delivers a gritty dose of hard-luck, weather-beaten imagery, with boarded-up shops, a pub with barred windows, dusty old iron-clad shacks...all loomed over by the massive silos next to the pier. If you're a painter or writer, this is fertile fuel for the imagination. Back in town, take a look at the sea-inspired works of local Aboriginal artists at the casual **Ceduna Arts & Culture Centre** *(facebook.com/ceduna aboriginalartsandculturecentre)*.

If you're heading west in whale season (May to October), Ceduna is also the place for updates on sightings at the Head of Bight.

THE DRIVE: Hit the highway and revel in the fact that there's the odd settlement by the roadside. Penong is 72km (the mere blink of a Nullarbor eye...) northwest of Ceduna.

03 Penong

Turn off the highway at **Penong** (the 'Town of Windmills'; population 200), and follow the 21km dirt road to Point Sinclair and **Cactus Beach**, which has three of Australia's most famous surf breaks. Caves is a wicked right-hand break for experienced surfers (locals don't take too kindly to tourists dropping in). There's basic bush camping on private property close to the breaks ($15 per vehicle); BYO drinking water.

THE DRIVE: Return 21km to the main highway, turn left and drive straight on through. Wheat and sheep paddocks line the road to Nundroo, after which you're in mallee scrub for another 100km. Around 20km later, the trees thin to low bluebush as you enter the true Nullarbor (Latin for 'no trees').

04 Head of Bight

The viewing platforms at the **Head of Bight** *(headofbight.com.au)* overlook a major southern right whale breeding ground. Whales migrate here from Antarctica, and you can see them cavorting from May to October. The breeding area is protected by the 45,822 sq km **Great Australian Bight Marine Park** *(australianmarineparks.gov.au/parks/south-west-marine-parks-network/great-australian-bight-marine-park)*, the world's second-largest marine park after the Great Barrier Reef. Eighty percent of the world's population of Australian sea lions live here. The Head of Bight is a part of the **Yalata Indigenous Protected Area** *(yalata.com.au)*. Pay your entry fee and get the latest whale information from the info centre. The signposted turnoff is 15km east of the Nullarbor Roadhouse. While you're in the area, watch out for the signs for coastal lookouts along the top of the 80m-high **Bunda Cliffs**, and check out **Murrawijinie Cave**, a large overhang behind the Roadhouse.

THE DRIVE: From the Head of Bight viewing area, it's 11km back to the main highway, then 15km to the Nullarbor Roadhouse. You'll then start to lose track of space, time and distance along the 197km to Eucla across the Western Australian border.

05 Eucla

Just 13km into WA, tiny **Eucla** is surrounded by stunning sand dunes and pristine beaches. It was once home to a booming population of 100 people and the busiest rural telegraph station in Australia. You can visit the atmospheric ruins of the 1877 telegraph station, 5km south of town and gradually being engulfed by the dunes; the remains of the old jetty are a 15-minute walk beyond.

THE DRIVE: It's 66km from Eucla to Mundrabilla through an endless red plain, with spinifex and the occasional roo.

> PHOTO OPPORTUNITY
>
> **90 MILE STRAIGHT**
>
> The sign '90 Mile Straight: Australia's Longest Straight Road (146.6km)'.

06 Mundrabilla

After waving goodbye to Eucla, the first stop of any note (and yes, it is all relative out here) is Mundrabilla, consisting of a roadhouse, caravan park, and part of the Nullarbor Links golf course. You'll like this place even more when you learn that the **Mundrabilla Motel Hotel** has the cheapest fuel prices on the Nullarbor, as well as a characterful pub, perfect for a cold beer and a heaped plate of pub grub. And did you know that Australia's biggest meteorite was found nearby, weighing a whopping 10 tonnes?

THE DRIVE: Count on 116km from Mundrabilla to Madura.

07 Madura

A little bit larger than Mundrabilla (there's even an airstrip here!), Madura – a 19th century stud farm serving British troops in India with cavalry horses – sits astride the spectacular **Hampton Tablelands**. The best of the scenery – semi-arid woodland sloping down off the escarpment, towards the Roe Plains and the Southern Ocean in the distance – is visible from along the road that rises up and over the Madura Pass. It's a stretch of road you'll remember, not least because so much of the rest of this road is flat, flat, flat... **The Madura Pass Oasis Motel** *(maduraoasis@bigpond.com)* has a very welcome pool.

THE DRIVE: From Madura, it's a mere 91km to that gloriously named Cocklebiddy.

08 Cocklebiddy

A welcome scattering of buildings amid scrubland, Cocklebiddy was originally established as an Aboriginal mission. Some 4km east, a short walking track just off the highway leads to the **Chapel Rock** formation, giving

ADWO/SHUTTERSTOCK

Start of the 90 Mile Straight

you a chance to stretch your legs. If you're in a 4WD, you might consider driving 32km south of Cocklebiddy to the Twilight Cove on the coast – a great spot for whale watching and a favourite of the local fishing community.

THE DRIVE: It's an uneventful 66km stretch from Cocklebiddy to Caiguna.

09 Caiguna

Consisting of a petrol station, roadhouse and airstrip, Caiguna itself is not a place you're likely to linger, especially as the roadhouse has the most expensive petrol on the Nullarbor and the welcome may be less than congenial.

It's well worth stopping at the **Caiguna Blowhole**, however (follow the signs 5km west of Caiguna). There you can hear the eerie howl of the sea as giant spouts of water are forced upwards through the rock.

THE DRIVE: The 181km drive from Caiguna to Balladonia includes the '90 Mile Straight' – Australia's longest stretch of straight road (146.6km). It's arguably the Nullarbor's most famous stretch of tarmac.

DETOUR

Baxter Cliffs

Start: 09 Caiguna

Experienced 4WD drivers shouldn't miss out on seeing the Baxter Cliffs – among the most spectacular in the world, reachable via a rough track 25km south of Caiguna. There, overlooking the Southern Ocean, is a memorial to John Baxter, John Eyre's overseer, who took part in the latter's historic east–west crossing of Australia. Baxter was murdered on 29 April 1841.

10 Balladonia

At Balladonia, loosely translated from an Aboriginal word meaning 'big red rock', the **Balladonia Hotel Motel** *(balladoniahotelmotel.com.au)* has a small museum.

The star exhibit here is the debris from Skylab's 1979 return to Earth that landed 40km east at the Woorlba Sheep Station. When Skylab's descent was imminent, there was much fear-mongering about the devastation it would cause.

With all due deference to the good folk of Balladonia, it is difficult to imagine that it caused anything more than a ripple in the heat haze out here...

GULLIVER'S TRAVELS IN CEDUNA?

According to map coordinates in Jonathan Swift's famous 1726 novel *Gulliver's Travels*, the islands of St Peter and St Francis, a few kilometres off the coast of Ceduna in the Nuyts Archipelago, are where the tiny folk of Lilliput reside. While we can neither confirm nor deny this possibility, it's likely Swift drew inspiration from the adventures of the 158 Dutch sailors aboard the *Gulden Zeepaert*, which sailed through these waters in 1627. You can gaze out at these inspirational islands from the lookout at Thevenard, Ceduna's raffish port suburb south of town.

THE DRIVE: It's 191km from Balladonia to Norseman. Close to the halfway mark is Fraser Range Station with heritage buildings, scenic bush walks and a camping ground. Near Norseman, the interminable red dirt and spinifex give way to the silver gums and eucalyptus-studded granite hills of the Fraser Range.

11 Norseman

You'll be almost dizzy with relief (or regret if the Nullarbor has you in its thrall) and with choice when you arrive in oasis-like, tree-studded Norseman.

From this crossroads township you could head south to Esperance, north to Kalgoorlie, westwards to Hyden and Wave Rock, or east across the Nullarbor. Stretch your legs at the **Beacon Hill Mararoa Lookout**, where there's a walking trail, stop at the **Historical Museum** and check out the stunning local photography at the **Gallery of Splendid Isolation**.

Pick up the Dundas Coach Road Heritage Trail brochure, for a 50km loop drive with interpretive panels. The **Ngadju Gateway Motel** *(ngadjugatewaymotel.com.au)* and **Gateway Caravan Park** *(acclaimparks.com.au)* are the pick of Norseman's lodgings, and you can treat yourself to authentic Thai food at the **Full Moon Cafe**.

THE DRIVE: After the distances you've crossed, the 187km trip into Kalgoorlie (via Kambalda) will seem very short indeed. Take the Coolgardie–Esperance Hwy north for 111km, then take the Kalgoorlie-Boulder turnoff.

DETOUR

Wave Rock

Start: 11 Norseman

Only on the Nullarbor would a 600km round trip be called a detour...

Large granite outcrops dot the central and southern wheat belts, and the most famous of these is the multicoloured cresting swell of **Wave Rock**, 350km from Perth and 300km from Norseman. Formed 60 million years ago by weathering and water erosion, Wave Rock is streaked with colours created by run-off from local mineral springs. To get the most out of Wave Rock, obtain the *Walk Trails* at Wave Rock and *The Humps* brochure from the **visitor centre** *(waverock.com.au)*. Park at Hippo's Yawn (no fee) and follow the shady track back along the rock base to Wave Rock (1km).

The road to Wave Rock from Norseman is unsealed, but suitable for 2WD vehicles in dry conditions. Check at Norseman before setting out.

The superb **Mulka's Cave** and the Humps are a further 16km from Wave Rock. Mulka's Cave, an easy stroll from the car park, is an important rock-art site with over 450 stencils and hand prints. The more adventurous can choose from two walking tracks. The **Kalari Trail** *(1.6km return)* climbs up onto a huge granite outcrop (one of the Humps) with excellent views, somehow wilder and more impressive than Wave Rock, while the **Gnamma Trail** *(1.2km return)* stays low and investigates natural waterholes with panels explaining Noongar culture.

12 Kalgoorlie-Boulder

With well-preserved buildings left over from the 1890s gold rush, Kalgoorlie-Boulder is still the centre for mining in this part of the state, flanked by a vast, open-pit gold mine that you can peer into from the **Super Pit Lookout** *(superpit.com.au/community/lookout)*. Historically, mine workers would come straight to town to spend up at Kalgoorlie's infamous brothels, or at pubs staffed by 'skimpies' (scantily clad female bar staff). Today 'Kal' is definitely more family-friendly – mine workers must reside in town and cannot be transient 'fly-in, fly-out' labour. It still feels a bit like the Wild West though, and the heritage pubs and 'skimpy' bar staff are reminders of a more turbulent past.

KYOHEI MIYAZAKI/SHUTTERSTOCK

Wave Rock

Mine tours by **Kalgoorlie Tours & Charters** *(kalgoorlietours.com.au)*, town and outback tours with **Goldrush Tours** *(goldrushtours.com.au)* and brothel tours by **Questa Casa** *(questacasa.com)* all take you behind the facade. Don't miss the outstanding **Western Australian Museum** *(visit.museum.wa.gov.au)* and if you're interested in Aboriginal culture, then a day or overnight tour with the **Bush Ghoodhu Wongutha Tours** is a must.

The **Bush Blossom Gallery** *(facebook.com/bushblossomgallery)* stocks a wealth of Aboriginal art from all over the outback.

Get a taste of local history by staying at the **Palace Hotel** *(palacehotelkalgoorlie.com)*. Kalgoorlie is also the place to treat your taste buds: stellar Thai at **Yada Thai**, craft beer at the hip **Beaten Track Brewery** *(beatentrackbrewery.com.au)* and superb coffee at **Just a Little Cafe**.

THE DRIVE: It's just 39km down the road to Coolgardie – so short you could almost walk.

DETOUR

Gold Ghost Towns & Lake Ballard

Start: 12 **Kalgoorlie-Boulder**

Easy day trips north from Kalgoorlie include the gold ghost towns of **Kanowna** *(18km northeast)*, **Broad Arrow** *(38km north)* and **Ora Banda** *(65km northwest)*. Little remains of Kanowna apart from the foundations of its 16 hotels (!), but its pioneer cemetery is interesting. Broad Arrow was featured in *The Nickel Queen* (1971), the first full-length feature film made in WA. At the beginning of the 20th century it had a population of 2400. Now there's just one pub, popular with Kal locals at weekends.

A longer and more worthwhile detour to the north involves driving to the remote salt flat of **Lake Ballard** *(182km)* via the former gold-rush town of **Menzies** *(131km)* on the Goldfields Highway. Lake Ballard is an ideal place to camp under the stars, in the middle of nowhere, but the main attraction here, besides glorious solitude, is the Antony Gormley masterpiece. **Inside Australia** *(antonygormley.com)* consists of 51 eerie metal sculptures, scattered across the vast expanse

♥ WHY I LOVE THIS TRIP

ANNA KAMINSKI, WRITER

There's an almost meditative quality to traversing the endless red plain. You get excited about the little things – a cold shower, a rough-and-ready roadhouse in the middle of nowhere. It's the whales frolicking offshore at the Head of Bight, it's driving the straightest road on the planet, it's Wave Rock. By the time you reach Kalgoorlie-Boulder, you've crossed the Nullarbor and feel a tremendous sense of accomplishment.

of dirty white saltbed, each one derived from a laser scan of a Menzies inhabitant.

Further north still, a mere 470km round trip from Kalgoorlie, the 1896 gold rush town of Gwalia was once home to the second-largest gold mine in Australia. Known as Little Italy, it employed newly arrived Italian immigrants, and its owner was Herbert Hoover, who later became a president of the United States. Today, the miners' tin shacks, the old hotel and other buildings of the **Gwalia Historic Site** *(gwalia.org.au)* are well worth a look, as is the giant open-pit mine. Stay at **Hoover House** *(gwalia.org.au)*, a gorgeous historic boutique hotel.

13 Coolgardie

In 1898, sleepy Coolgardie was the third-biggest town in WA, with a population of 15,000, six newspapers, two stock exchanges, more than 20 hotels and three breweries. It all took off just hours after Arthur Bayley rode into Southern Cross in 1892 and dumped 554oz of Coolgardie gold on the mining warden's counter. The only echoes that remain are stately historic buildings lining the uncharacteristically wide main road. The **Goldfields Museum & Visitor Centre** showcases goldfields memorabilia, including information about Herbert Hoover's days on the goldfields in Gwalia, as well as the fascinating story of Modesto Varischetti, the 'Entombed Miner'. There are also camel rides at the Camel Farm 4km west of town; book ahead.

THE DRIVE: There's an accumulating sense of approaching civilisation as you head west to Perth. It's still 555km into Perth, but the true Nullarbor is well and truly behind you by the time you leave Coolgardie.

14 Perth

Perth is, by some estimates, the most remote city on earth, and having crossed the Nullarbor, you'll need no convincing of this fact.

With its sunny optimism, sea breeze and fine places to stay, eat and drink, it's the perfect place to end this journey along one of the emptiest roads on the planet.

Abandoned house, Gwalia Historic Site
CHAMELEONSEYE/SHUTTERSTOCK

04

EPIC TRIPS

ALICE SPRINGS TO ADELAIDE

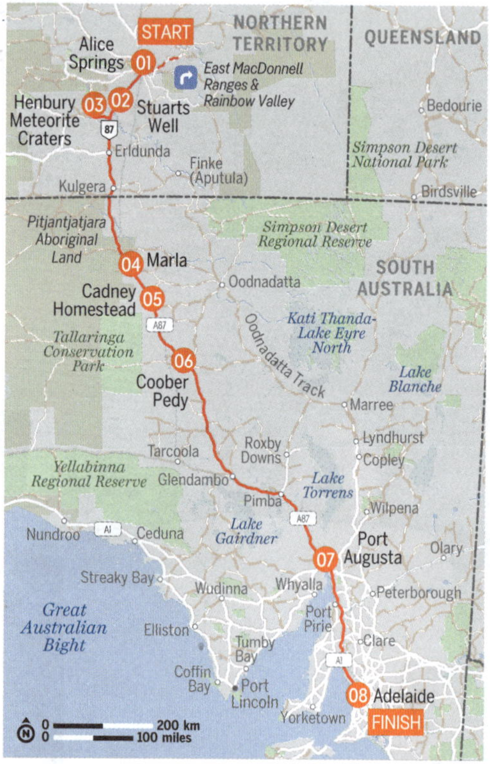

DURATION: 7 DAYS

DISTANCE: 1500KM / 932 MILES

GREAT FOR: NATURE & HISTORY

BEST TIME TO GO: YEAR-ROUND, ALTHOUGH SUMMER (DECEMBER TO FEBRUARY) CAN BE FIERCELY HOT.

Set the GPS and head south on 'The Track'. Soon enough there are a couple of fine local Northern Territory landmarks to enjoy before the long, long road down through the South Australian heartland takes you through Coober Pedy and on to the coast. 'The Track' is officially the Stuart Hwy, named after a 19th-century explorer who journeyed the whole way with camels; some sections were paved only in the 1970s.

LINK YOUR TRIP

29 Alice Springs to Darwin
If you've done this trip in reverse (ie from Adelaide to Alice), keep heading north to Darwin to cross the continent.

28 Uluṟu & the Red Centre
This trip to Uluṟu, Kata Tjuṯa, Kings Canyon and the West MacDonnell Ranges passes Alice Springs en route.

01 Alice Springs

There are many Alices to enjoy, from cultural capital of Aboriginal Australia to a base for all that's good about Australia's Red Centre. Begin by taking in the tremendous view, particularly at sunrise and sunset, from the top of Anzac Hill, known as Untyeyetwelye in Arrernte; it's possible to walk (use Lions Walk from Wills Tce) or drive up. From the war memorial there's a 365-degree view over the town down to Heavitree Gap and the Ranges. Outback creatures found nowhere else on the planet are another central Australian speciality – learn all about reptiles at **Alice Springs Reptile Centre** *(reptilecentre.com.au)*, then visit desert creatures at the **Alice Springs Desert Park** *(alicespringsdesertpark.com.au)*. And don't miss the galleries of Aboriginal art, such **Araluen Arts Centre** *(araluenartscentre.nt.gov.au)*, **Papunya Tula Artists** *(papunyatula.com.au)*, **Mbantua Gallery**

★ BEST FOR

CULTURE

The underground world of Coober Pedy is a classic outback subculture.

Left to right: Camel sculptures by Angelina Bradley, Daisybell Kulyuru & Imiyari Adamson. 2025.

(mbantua.com.au), **Tjanpi Desert Weavers** *(tjanpi.com.au)* and **Ngurratjuta Iltja Ntjarra** (Many Hands Art Centre; *manyhandsart.com.au*).

THE DRIVE: The Stuart Hwy, which cleaves the Northern Territory in two, continues south of Alice; 91km down the road (which you'll share with tour buses en route to Uluru) you'll come to Stuarts Well.

DETOUR

East MacDonnell Ranges & Rainbow Valley

Start: 01 Alice Springs

Although overshadowed by the more popular West Macs, the East MacDonnell Ranges are no less picturesque and, with fewer visitors, can be a more enjoyable outback experience. The sealed Ross Hwy runs 100km east of Alice Springs along the Ranges, which are intersected by a series of scenic gaps and gorges such as **Trephina Gorge** *(nt.gov.au/parks)* and **N'Dhala Gorge** *(nt.gov.au/parks)*, which are well worth exploring along hiking trails short and long. The gold-mining ghost town of Arltunga is 33km off the Ross Hwy along an unsealed road that is usually OK for 2WD vehicles.

Even better, south of Alice Springs, 24km off the Stuart Hwy along a 4WD track, the **Rainbow Valley Conservation Reserve** is a series of freestanding sandstone bluffs and cliffs, in shades ranging from cream to red. It's one of central Australia's more extraordinary sights. A marked walking trail takes you past claypans and in between the multihued outcrops to the aptly named Mushroom Rock. Rainbow Valley is most striking in the early morning or at sunset, but the area's silence will overwhelm you whatever time of day you are here.

02 Stuarts Well

Drivers are urged to 'have a spell' at Stuarts Well. It's worth stopping in for a burger and a beer at **Jim's House** *(stuartswellroad* *house.com.au)*, once run by well-known outback identity Jim Cotterill, who along with his father opened up Kings Canyon to tourism. Archival photos tell the story, but sadly Dinky the singing dingo is no longer with us.

THE DRIVE: Some 39km south-west of Stuarts Well, watch for the signs to the Henbury Meteorite Craters, 16km off the highway along an unsealed road.

03 Henbury Meteorite Craters

In the rush to the big-ticket attractions of the Red Centre, this cluster of 12 small craters, formed after a meteor fell to earth 4700 years ago, is often overlooked. These are no mere potholes – the largest of the craters is 180m wide and 15m deep – and the crater floors are, in most cases, sprinkled lightly with green trees, giving the deeper of them a palpable sense of lost, hidden oases. In some cases the craters are invisible from a distance and only reveal themselves when you reach the crater rim. The surrounding country is wildly beautiful in an outback kind of way – red-hued earth, sand dunes and rocky outcrops extend out as far as the eye can see.

THE DRIVE: Return 5km to the Ernest Giles Rd, a rough, 4WD-only back route to Kings Canyon, then 11km to the Stuart Hwy. Then it's 162km to the border, with a further 160km into Marla on the South Australian side. The last fuel before Marla is at Kulgera, 20km north of the border and 200km short of Marla.

04 Marla

Marla may be small (its transient population usually numbers fewer than 250) but it's an important service centre for long-haul drivers and the peoples of the Anangu Pitjantjatjara traditional lands that sweep away in endless plains of mulga scrub to the west. It's also a stop on *The Ghan*, the Adelaide-to-Darwin railway service, and it's here that the legendary, lonesome Oodnadatta Track, one of Australia's most famous 4WD traverses of the outback, begins or ends. The Oodnadatta Track is an unsealed, 615km road between Marla on the Stuart Hwy and Marree in

Henbury Meteorite Craters

LKPRO/SHUTTERSTOCK

the northern Flinders Ranges. The track traces the route of the old Overland Telegraph Line and the defunct Great Northern Railway. Kati Thanda–Lake Eyre, the world's sixth-largest lake (usually dry), is just off the road. As such, Marla is a crossroads town whose importance is far out of proportion to its size – treat it as such and you're unlikely to be disappointed.

THE DRIVE: Beyond Marla, the pancake-flat Stuart Hwy goes to Cadney Homestead (82km).

05 Cadney Homestead

Out here in the South Australian outback, small landmarks and lonely settlements take on singular importance, both in warding off the great emptiness and in orientating and servicing the needs of travellers. **Cadney Homestead**, 82km southeast of Marla, is one such place, with caravan and tent sites, serviceable motel rooms and basic cabins (BYO towel to use the shared caravan park facilities), plus petrol, puncture repairs, takeaways, cold beer, an ATM, a swimming pool…

Ask at the homestead about road conditions on the dirt track running west of the settlement – the track is usually passable in a 2WD vehicle, at least as far as the striking and rather aptly named **Painted Desert**. The track runs eventually to Oodnadatta.

THE DRIVE: It's 152km from Cadney to Coober Pedy.

06 Coober Pedy

As you pull into the world-famous opal-mining town of Coober Pedy, the dry, barren desert suddenly becomes riddled with holes, literally millions of them, and adjunct piles of dirt – quite suitably, the name derives from local Aboriginal words *kupa* (white man) and *piti* (hole). When you first get out of the car, you'll be greeted by a postapocalyptic wasteland – swarms of flies, no trees, 50°C summer days, cave-dwelling locals and rusty car wrecks in front yards. But it somehow all fits the outback's personality and the surrounding desert is jaw-droppingly desolate, a fact not overlooked by international filmmakers who've come here to shoot end-of-the-world epics like *Mad Max III*, *Red Planet*, *Ground Zero* and *Pitch Black*. You can't miss the **Big Winch** *(cooberpedy.com/big-winch)*, from which there are sweeping views over Coober Pedy. Take a tour with **Coober Pedy Tours** and a scenic flight with **Wrights Air** *(wrightsair.com.au)* to really take it all in.

THE DRIVE: It's 540km from Coober Pedy to Port Augusta, and it still feels like the outback all the way, with horizonless plains and shimmering salt pans shadowing the road as far as Woomera (366km). Thereafter, the road tracks southeast for 174km into Port Augusta.

STEPHEN KUCERA/SHUTTERSTOCK

Outback, Northern Territory

PHOTO OPPORTUNITY

South Australia–Northern Territory border, one of the remotest crossings on Earth.

♥ WHY I LOVE THIS TRIP

ANTHONY HAM, WRITER

This trip takes you halfway across the continent. Alice Springs is a fascinating place – I've always loved its Aboriginal art galleries and bush-tucker restaurants. Then it's a long road home, from the Aboriginal heartland around Uluṟu to the cultural riches of Adelaide. En route, you'll pass through remote outback homesteads, the partly underground opal-mining town of Coober Pedy, and lively Port Augusta, not to mention seemingly endless red-earthed desert miles.

07 Port Augusta

Port Augusta proclaims itself to be the 'Crossroads of Australia' and it's not difficult to see why – highways and railways roll west across the Nullarbor into WA, north to the Flinders Ranges or Darwin, south to Adelaide or Port Lincoln, and east to Sydney. Given that you've just come in from the never-never, there are two places that really speak to the spirit of the whole journey you're on. Just north of town, the excellent **Australian Arid Lands Botanic Garden** *(aalbg.sa.gov.au)* has 250 hectares of sandhills, clay flats and desert flora and fauna. Just as interesting is the **Wadlata Outback Centre** *(wadlata.sa.gov.au)*, a combined museum-visitor centre.

THE DRIVE: The final stretch from Port Augusta to Adelaide is the antithesis of where you've been so far – busy roadside towns at regular intervals, frequent glimpses of water, constant traffic and even a dual-carriage motorway for the last 95km into Adelaide.

08 Adelaide

Sophisticated, cultured, neat-casual – this is the self-image Adelaide projects and in this it bears little resemblance to the frontier charms of the outback. For decades this 'City of Churches' had a slightly staid reputation, but these days things are different. Multicultural flavours infuse Adelaide's restaurants; there's a pumping arts and live-music scene; and the city's festival calendar has vanquished dull Saturday nights. There are still plenty of church spires here, but they're outnumbered by pubs and a growing number of hip bars tucked away in lanes. You're also on the cusp of some of Australia's most celebrated wine regions, but that's a whole other story.

Australian Arid Lands Botanic Garden

STEPHANIE JACKSON - AUST WILDFLOWER COLLECTION/ALAMY

05

EPIC TRIPS

KIMBERLEY CROSSING

★ BEST FOR:

CULTURE

Aboriginal art centres, campgrounds and guided tours on Country at Mimbi Caves, Kununurra, Warmun and Mowanjum.

Jatbula Trail

DURATION: 14 DAYS

DISTANCE: 1920KM / 1193 MILES

GREAT FOR: NATURE & HISTORY

BEST TIME TO GO: APRIL TO OCTOBER TO AVOID CYCLONES, FLOODING AND ROAD CLOSURES.

This epic outback journey following the Savannah Way *(savannahway.com.au)* across the wild Kimberley from Katherine to Broome confronts nature at its most extreme, with excessive heat, vast distances and wandering wildlife – and 50m-long road trains (articulated trucks). Towns are few and far between in a land rich in Aboriginal culture and it's these vast spaces that you'll miss the most at journey's end.

LINK YOUR TRIP

29 Alice Springs to Darwin
Trip 5 starts from Katherine on the first section of this trip (when departing from Darwin).

34 Coral Coast to Broome
This trip from Perth to Broome connects with Trip 5 and could just as easily be done in reverse.

01 Katherine

Katherine is the largest town between Darwin and Alice Springs and the starting point for the sealed Victoria Hwy's 513km run to Kununurra in the Kimberley. The main attraction here is the exquisite **Nitmiluk National Park**, with its stunning gorges, waterfalls and walking tracks – the most renowned being the 66km **Jatbula Trail**, which normally takes four to five days to complete.

THE DRIVE: Heading southwest from Katherine there are termite mounds and low hills for 194km until Victoria River. Fuel up at tiny Timber Creek and watch for boabs – a sign the Kimberley is approaching. Dump food and turn back clocks 90 minutes at the WA border checkpoint (470km) and turn left shortly after for the final 34km into Lake Argyle Village.

ANDREW BAIN/ALAMY

02 Lake Argyle

Enormous **Lake Argyle**, where barren red ridges plunge spectacularly into the deep blue water of the dammed Ord River, is Australia's second-largest reservoir. Holding the equivalent of 18 Sydney Harbours, it provides Kununurra with year-round irrigation and important wildlife habitats for migratory waterbirds, freshwater crocodiles and isolated marsupial colonies. A cruise on the lake is not to be missed.

THE DRIVE: It's only a short 70km hop back to the highway and onto the delights of Kununurra, an oasis set among farmland growing superfoods, and tropical fruit and sandalwood plantations.

03 Kununurra

Kununurra, on Miriwoong Country, is every traveller's favourite slice of civilisation between Broome (Rubibi) and Darwin, with its relaxed vibe, excellent services, transport, communications and well-stocked supermarkets. Across the highway from the township, **Lily Creek Lagoon** is a mini-wetland with amazing birdlife, boating and freshwater crocs. Don't miss the excellent **Waringarri Aboriginal Arts Centre** *(waringarri arts.com.au)*, opposite the road to **Kelly's Knob**, a popular sunset viewpoint. On the eastern edge of town, the 'mini-bungles' of **Mirima National Park** are home to brittle red peaks, spinifex, boab trees and abundant wildlife. Try **Triple J Tours** *(triplejtours.com.au)* popular sunset 'BBQ Dinner' outings on **Lake Kununurra** or a cultural tour on Country from **Waringarri** *(waringarri arts.com.au/tours)*.

THE DRIVE: Cross the Diversion Dam heading west out of town and 46km later the Victoria Hwy disappears and you're on the Great Northern. Turn left 8km later onto the infamous Gibb River Rd and 25km of nice asphalt brings the Emma Gorge turnoff.

04 Emma Gorge

Pretty Emma Gorge features a sublime plunge pool and waterfall, one of the most scenic in the whole Kimberley. The attached **resort**

PHOTO OPPORTUNITY

The beehive-shaped Bungle Bungles glowing red in the late afternoon light.

(elquestro.com.au) has an open-air bistro. The gorge is a 40-minute walk from the resort car park.

THE DRIVE: Retrace your route back to the Great Northern, then turn left and follow the hills north 48km to Wyndham, where a giant 20m croc greets visitors entering town.

05 Wyndham

Wyndham is scenically nestled between rugged hills and the Cambridge Gulf, on **Balanggarra Country**, 100km northwest of Kununurra. Sunsets are superb from the spectacular **Five Rivers Lookout** on Mt Bastion (325m) overlooking the King, Pentecost, Durack, Forrest and Ord rivers entering the Cambridge Gulf. The historic port precinct is the northern terminus of the 3200km **Great Northern Hwy**. Birdwatchers should visit **Parry Lagoons Nature Reserve**, a beautiful Ramsar-listed wetland, 25km from Wyndham.

THE DRIVE: It's 56km to the Victoria Hwy junction; turn right and there's only boabs, eroded hills and lonely roadhouses for the next 200km to the Bungles turnoff. Grab a legendary burger and fuel at Doon Doon, and check out the incredible Warmun ochres. You'll need a 4WD for the Bungles, or join a tour from Warmun, Halls Creek or Mabel Downs.

06 Bungle Bungles

Looking like a packet of half-melted Jaffas, the World Heritage-listed **Purnululu National Park** is home to the incredible ochre-and-black-striped 'beehive' domes of the Bungle Bungle Range. The distinctive rounded rock towers are made of sandstone and conglomerates moulded by rainfall over millions of years. Rangers are based here from April to November and the park is closed outside this time. Although most Kimberley tour operators can get you to Purnululu and back – try **Bungle Bungle Expeditions** – you can also pick up tours at Warmun Roadhouse, Halls Creek and Mabel Downs.

THE DRIVE: Purnululu National Park lies 52km east of the Great Northern Hwy. Once back on the asphalt, head south, crossing several mostly dry rivers along the 108km section to Halls Creek.

♥ WHY I LOVE THIS TRIP

STEVE WATERS, WRITER

You're way beyond tripping on this epic journey across Australia's last frontier. I love the feeling of serious remoteness crossing the vast, boab-studded savannah of the ancient Kimberley where Indigenous culture shines brightly. It's the spaces between the sporadic towns – the incredible Bungle Bungles, hidden swimming holes, fern-fringed gorges, the brilliant Milky Way and the sparkling turquoise waters of the Indian Ocean – that define this once-in-a-lifetime trip.

07 Halls Creek

Halls Creek, on the edge of the Great Sandy Desert, is a small service town, home to Aboriginal communities of Kija, Jaru and Gooniyandi people, and offers free wi-fi and an excellent **art centre**. There's good swimming and camping at gorges along unsealed Duncan Rd. **Wolfe Creek Meteorite Crater** (880m across and 60m deep), 137km south of Halls Creek along the notorious Tanami Track, is best seen from a scenic flight with **Northwest Regional Airlines** *(northwestregionalair.com.au)*. According to the local Jaru people, Kandimalal, as the crater is traditionally known, marks the spot where a huge rainbow serpent emerged from the ground. Flights can also be extended to the Bungle Bungles.

THE DRIVE: Another 200km stretch of blistering sun, dry creeks and cattle stations finally brings relief at the Mt Pierre turnoff (right side) for Mimbi Caves, just past the Ngumban Cliffs. To break The Drive:, consider checking out the small Laarri Gallery at Yiyili at the 120km mark.

08 Mimbi Caves

One of the Kimberley's best-kept secrets, the vast subterranean labyrinth of **Mimbi Caves** *(mimbicaves.com.au)* lies 200km southwest of Halls Creek (90km southeast of Fitzroy Crossing) on Gooniyandi land at Mt Pierre Station. The caves house a significant collection of Aboriginal rock art and some of the most impressive fish fossils in the southern hemisphere. Aboriginal-owned **Girloorloo Tours** *(mimbicaves.com.au)* runs

Bungle Bungles Range

NAEEMPHOTOGRAPHER2/SHUTTERSTOCK

trips including an introduction to local Dreaming stories, bush tucker and traditional medicines.

THE DRIVE: Return to the Great Northern Hwy and there's only 90km of dry grasslands, salt pans and stunted bush as you head north to the crossing on the Kimberley's preeminent river, the Fitzroy.

09 Fitzroy Crossing

At the highway crossing of the mighty Fitzroy River lies a small, predominantly Aboriginal settlement. Local crafts include **Mangkaja Arts** *(mangkaja.com)*, where desert and river tribes interact producing unique acrylics, prints and baskets, and **Marnin Studio** *(mwrc.com.au)* whose women create jewellery, carve boab nuts and print textiles with traditional patterns. The main attraction, though, is the nearby magnificent **Geikie Gorge** where informative boat trips combine nature, Aboriginal culture and science.

THE DRIVE: Head north through the town to Geikie Gorge, 20km along a good sealed road. Afterwards, return to the highway and turn right for Derby. At 43km, a turnoff via Tunnel Creek and Windjana Gorge National Parks provides a spectacular alternative route to Derby for those with 4WD (244km, 130km unsealed). Otherwise, suck up another 213km of empty tarmac.

10 Derby

Surrounded by mudflats and marauding boabs on the tidal monster of **King Sound**, Derby has some excellent food, accommodation and vehicle-repair options. The mangrove-fringed circular **jetty** is a favourite late-afternoon strolling haunt for locals and tourists alike, while birdwatchers will appreciate the **wetlands** and history buffs the old **museum**. Art lovers should not miss nearby **Mowanjum** *(mowanjumarts.com)* with its powerful Wandjina figures, and in town **Norval Gallery** *(facebook.com/norvalgalleryderby)* always has something interesting.

But it's the **Horizontal Waterfalls** that people flock to see, an intriguing coastal phenomenon in the Buccaneer Archipelago north of Derby, where changing tides rush through narrow gorges. **Horizontal Falls Seaplane Adventures** *(horizontalfallsadventures.com.au)* and **North West Bush Pilots** offer scenic flights. Also consider a one-day cultural tour to **Windjana Gorge** and **Tunnel Creek**.

THE DRIVE: Mowanjum is 4km along the Gibb River Rd (sealed). Back on the Great Northern, it's 220km of nothingness to Broome, broken only by Willare Bridge Roadhouse. Beware of the late-afternoon sun as the highway heads west like a gunshot across the desolate Roebuck Plains. Keep straight when the Great Northern turns south to cross the Great Sandy Desert – Broome is 35km away.

11 Broome

The red pindan and turquoise waters of Yawuru Country provide a fitting finale to this most epic of drives. Before you lose yourself in the resorts, restaurants, camels and bars of Broome's iconic **Cable Beach** and historic Chinatown, keep the engine running out to **Gantheaume Point** and watch that setting sun drop into the Indian Ocean one last lonely time. Tomorrow, you can stretch your legs.

Broome, while having the best transport connections in the Kimberley, is also one of the remotest towns in Australia, a good 2000km from a capital city. Accommodation can be expensive, and if you have a 4WD there are better camping options out of town.

GIBB RIVER ROAD

Cutting a brown swathe through the scorched heart of the Kimberley, the legendary Gibb River Rd (GRR) provides one of Australia's most memorable outback 4WD experiences. Stretching 660km between Derby and Wyndham, the largely unpaved road is an endless sea of red dirt, big open skies and dramatic terrain. Rough, sometimes deeply corrugated side roads lead to remote gorges, shady pools, distant waterfalls and million-acre cattle stations. Rain can close the road at any time and it's permanently closed during the wet season. This is true wilderness with minimal services, so good planning and self-sufficiency are vital. Vehicles to tackle the Gibb can be rented in Broome and Darwin.

Gantheaume Point, Broome

DPA PICTURE ALLIANCE/ALAMY

QUEENSLAND
SOUTH AUSTRALIA
NEW SOUTH WALES
VICTORIA
ACT
CANBERRA
SOUTH PACIFIC OCEAN
TASMAN SEA
SOUTHERN OCEAN
06
07
08
09
10
Tweed Heads
Murwillumbah
Byron Bay
Ballina
Lismore
Tenterfield
Goondiwindi
Moree
Warialda
Inverell
Glen Innes
Grafton
Coffs Harbour
Nambucca Heads
Armidale
Narrabri
Tamworth
Nundle
Kempsey
Port Macquarie
Taree
Forster-Tuncurry
Muswellbrook
Singleton
Maitland
Newcastle
Gosford
Sydney
Royal National Park
Wollongong
Windsor
Lithgow
Bathurst
Orange
Mudgee
Merriwa
Wollemi National Park
Dubbo
Gilgandra
Coonabarabran
Coonamble
Walgett
Lightning Ridge
Brewarrina
Bourke
Mt Oxley (309m)
Macquarie River
Darling River
Cobar
Wilcannia
Tilpa
White Cliffs
Wanaaring
Tibooburra
Milparinka
Sturt National Park
Broken Hill
Menindee Lakes
Menindee
Mungo National Park
Wentworth
Mildura
Renmark
Robinvale
Balranald
Hay
Hillston
Lachlan River
Condobolin
Parkes
Forbes
Cowra
Young
Temora
Griffith
Narrandera
Wagga Wagga
Gundagai
Yass
Goulburn
Mittagong
Nowra
Ulladulla
Batemans Bay
Narooma
Cooma
Jindabyne
Thredbo
Mt Kosciuszko (2228m)
Bega
Eden
Cape Howe
Albury
Corowa
Wodonga
Tocumwal
Jerilderie
Deniliquin
Moama
Murray River
Bendigo
Horsham
Ballarat
Melbourne
Hamilton
Adelaide
Murray Bridge
Peterborough
0 200 km
0 100 miles

ANNALUCIA/SHUTTERSTOCK

Broken Hill (p94), New South Wales

NEW SOUTH WALES & THE AUSTRALIAN CAPITAL TERRITORY

EXPLORE

NEW SOUTH WALES & THE AUSTRALIAN CAPITAL TERRITORY

Driving from Sydney to Melbourne or Byron Bay (or vice versa) along the coast is something of a rite of passage for those looking to experience the best the Aussie road can offer. Stray inland from the coast, however, and you'll discover whole new worlds, from the rainforests of New England to one of the world's most unlikely capital cities, and the high-altitude surprises of the Australian Alps to vast outback plains. You could easily spend weeks getting to know the region. And in doing so, you'll get a pretty representative taste of Australia at its best.

Sydney

Most routes through New South Wales (NSW) at some point pass through the capital, Sydney. One of the most scenically situated cities on Earth, it has a sensational harbourside setting, fringed by Pacific Ocean beaches and national parks. Each neighbourhood has a different character, from the slick bars of the Central Business District (CBD) to more alternative Newtown in the Inner West. Fabulous food, good transport connections and a wide range of accommodation across all budgets make it an ideal start or end to any journey.

Canberra

There's more to Canberra than initially meets the eye. With no discernible centre, it can be a difficult city to get your head around, but it has some of Australia's best museums, a fascinating parliament house, a magnificent arboretum and a scenic outlook filled with lakes, forests and green hills. And when it comes to driving, the capital is a relaxed antidote to the traffic and sometimes-confusing road systems of Sydney.

Byron Bay

Come for a few days or a few months – Byron Bay is arguably Australia's most famous beach town. It draws backpackers, celebrities and just about everyone in between, and with good reason. Its coast is studded with magnificent beaches and

WHEN TO GO

Along the coast, November to March promises the best beach weather. This coincides with Tamworth's mid-January country music festival, while wider New England is glorious with autumnal colours from March to May. This is also a good time (along with spring) to be in the high country, while the outback is best April to October, thereby avoiding the searing summer heat.

the town itself has superb accommodation, terrific shopping and great food, while the hinterland is filled with charm and spectacle in equal measure. No wonder almost everyone tries to find an excuse to stay longer.

Bathurst

The oldest Australian colonial settlement beyond the coast, Bathurst is a quirky destination in its own right. Some visitors come for the museums and the architecture, while others visit for the car races on nearby Mt Panorama. But Bathurst also sits at the junction of many possible routes. With good places to stay and an emerging reputation for regional culinary excellence, it makes a fine alternative base if you're keen to avoid the clamour of Sydney. The oldest Australian colonial settlement beyond the coast, Bathurst is a quirky destination in its own right. Some visitors come for the museums and the architecture, while others visit for the car races on nearby Mt Panorama. But Bathurst also sits at the junction of many possible routes. With good places to stay and an emerging reputation for regional culinary excellence, it makes a fine alternative base if you're keen to avoid the clamour of Sydney.

TRANSPORT

So many incredible journeys begin in Sydney, which has good international and domestic flight connections. Canberra can also be a good place to fly into and begin. Regional airline **Rex** *(rex.com.au)* can also get you to some of NSW's smaller towns. Buses run up and down the coast, and trains cover the state surprisingly well.

Broken Hill

Way out west, Broken Hill is a fascinating outback town. It's a very long way from everywhere, and its pubs are central to its charm – one, the Palace, starred in the hit 1994 movie *The Adventures of Priscilla, Queen of the Desert.* Museums, art galleries and mining tours are part of the appeal, but it also has a growing culinary and cafe scene, quiet streets and a real sense of the vast outback lurking just beyond the city limits.

WHERE TO STAY

Sydney has an incredible (if generally expensive) array of accommodation spanning everything from five-star hotels to backpacker digs out in Bondi. The towns of Sydney's hinterland, as well as seaside towns such as Byron Bay, Port Macquarie, Jervis Bay and others, often have a good mix of atmospheric rural pubs, resorts, charming B&Bs and even the odd rainforest retreat. The further west you go, the more likely it is that you'll need to stay in a roadside motel at some point, though there are some fine national-park campgrounds. You might find the occasional station stay on a remote cattle station.

RESOURCES

- **NSW National Parks**
  Everything from campground reservations to wildlife and hiking trails.
  nationalparks.nsw.gov.au
- **Sydney Visitor Centre**
  Everything you need to know about visiting Sydney.
  sydney.com
- **Visit Canberra**
  Great source of info for the national capital and surrounding area.
  visitcanberra.com.au
- **Visit NSW**
  Australia's most populous state in all its glory. *visitnsw.com*

WHAT'S ON

- **Tamworth Country Music Festival**
  This rollicking 10-day mid-January festival draws 700 performers across 120 venues. *tcmf.com.au*
- **New Year's Eve**
  Australia's biggest, most spectacular New Year's Eve party, with fireworks around the harbour and on the bridge.
  sydneynewyearseve.com
- **Vivid Sydney**
  Sydney transforms in May and June with immersive light installations, 3D projections and more.
  vividsydney.com

06

NEW SOUTH WALES & THE AUSTRALIAN CAPITAL TERRITORY

SYDNEY TO BYRON BAY

DURATION: 7–10 DAYS

DISTANCE: 1100KM / 684 MILES

GREAT FOR: NATURE & FAMILIES

BEST TIME TO GO: NOVEMBER TO MARCH, WHEN THE WEATHER IS WARM AND THE LIVIN' IS GOOD.

Tearing yourself away from Sydney's singular charms is made easier by what lies ahead on this journey up the northern New South Wales coast. Classic beach resorts like Coffs Harbour share the road with more family-oriented places like Port Stephens and Port Macquarie, as well as national parks that protect some of the coast's more dramatic stretches. And don't miss the chance to explore hinterland villages and rainforests.

LINK YOUR TRIP

02 Sydney to Melbourne
This drive along the coast to connect Australia's two largest cities begins in Sydney, perfect for when you come back from Byron.

08 Canberra & the South Coast
This route starts in Wollongong, just 84km south of Sydney's Central Business District (CBD).

01 Sydney

Sydney's shimmering blue harbour is one of the most beautiful settings for a city you can imagine. Scratch the surface and it only gets better. Compared to its Australian siblings, Sydney is loud, uncompromising and in-your-face. Fireworks displays are more dazzling here, heels are higher, bodies more buff, contact sports more brutal, starlets shinier, drag queens glitzier and prices higher. Australia's best musicians, foodies, actors, models, writers and architects flock to the city to make their mark, and the effect is dazzling: a hyperenergetic, ambitious, and optimistic marketplace for the soul, where dreams are ripe for chasing.

THE DRIVE: The M1 freeway heads out of Sydney's suburbs through impressive bushland and across the Hawkesbury River. Ignore turnoffs to Gosford, Wyong and Newcastle,

★ BEST FOR:

FAMILIES

Port Stephens has wild dolphins, sand dunes and sheltered coves.

ANNE POWELL/SHUTTERSTOCK

Common dolphin, Port Stephens

but do no such thing when you see the Port Stephens sign not far beyond Newcastle. It's 206km from central Sydney to Port Stephens.

02 Port Stephens

Beloved by Sydneysiders looking for a slice of tranquil paradise without straying too far, Port Stephens inhabits a sheltered harbour along a submerged valley that stretches more than 20km inland. Framing its southern edge is the narrow Tomaree Peninsula, blessed with near-deserted beaches, national parks and an extraordinary sand-dune system. From the main centre, Nelson Bay, head out on a dolphin- and whale-watching cruise with **Moonshadow** *(moonshadow-tqc.com.au)* or **Imagine Cruises** *(imaginecruises.com.au)*.

Places in the vicinity to look out for include: One Mile Beach, a gorgeous semicircle of the softest sand and bluest water; the cult **Murray's Craft Brewing Co** *(murraysbrewingco.com.au)*; and the incredible **Worimi Conservation Lands** *(worimiconservationlands.com)*, the longest moving sand dunes in the southern hemisphere, and where it's possible to become so surrounded by shimmering sand that you'll lose sight of the ocean or any sign of life.

THE DRIVE: Return to the M1 and at Bulahdelah turn east and follow the signs to Myall Lakes National Park.

DETOUR

Hunter Valley Wine Region

Start: 02 Port Stephens

Just south of the turnoff to Port Stephens, A15 (New England Hwy) branches away to the northwest to Maitland, a non-descript regional centre that serves as a gateway to the Hunter Valley, one of Australia's favourite wine regions. Head for Pokolbin, the settlement at the heart of the area.

A filigree of narrow lanes criss-crosses this verdant valley, but a pleasant country drive isn't the main motivator for visitors – sheer decadence is. The Hunter is one big gorge-fest: fine wine, gourmet restaurants, boutique beer, chocolate, cheese, olives

– you name it. Bacchus would surely approve. The 150-plus Hunter wineries are refreshingly attitude-free and welcoming to novices. They nearly all have a cellar door with free or cheap tastings. The region is home to some of the oldest vines (1860s) and biggest names in Australian wine as well as some refreshingly edgy newcomers. It is known for its semillon, shiraz and, increasingly, chardonnay.

While some deride the Disneyland aspect of the Hunter Valley, the region also offers everything from hot-air balloons and horse riding to open-air concerts. Accordingly, it is a hugely popular weekender for Sydney couples, wedding parties and groups of friends wanting to drink hard while someone else drives. Every Friday they descend and prices leap accordingly. Visit midweek if you can.

The Hunter Valley is exceedingly hot during summer, so – like its shiraz – it's best enjoyed in the cooler months.

03 Myall Lakes National Park

On an extravagantly pretty section of the coast, the large Myall Lakes National Park incorporates a patchwork of lakes, islands, dense littoral rainforest and beaches. The lakes support an incredible quantity and variety of birdlife, and there are paths through coastal rainforest and past beach dunes at Mungo Brush in the south, perfect for spotting wildflowers and dingoes. The best beaches and surf are in the north around **Seal Rocks**, a bushy hamlet hugging Sugarloaf Bay. The beach has emerald-green rock pools and golden sand. Take the short walk to the **Sugarloaf Point Lighthouse** for epic ocean views. There's a detour to lonely **Lighthouse Beach**, a popular surfing spot. By the lighthouse is a lookout over the actual Seal Rocks – islets where Australian fur seals can sometimes be spotted. Humpback whales swim past during their annual migration.

THE DRIVE: Instead of returning to the M1, take the quieter coast road north through Forster-Tuncurry before rejoining M1 just south of Taree. From there it's 80km to the Port Macquarie turnoff, then 10km more into the town itself.

Sydney Harbour Bridge, Sydney (p68)

MAXIMILIANE WAGNER/SHUTTERSTOCK

04 Port Macquarie

Making the most of its position at the entrance to the subtropical coast, Port, as it's commonly known, has a string of beautiful beaches within short driving distance from the centre of town. Surfing is particularly good at Town, Flynn's and Lighthouse beaches; all of which are patrolled in summer. The rainforest runs down to the sand at Shelly and Miners beaches, the latter is an unofficial nudist beach. Whale season is May to November: there are numerous vantage points around town, or you can get a closer look on a whale-watching cruise with **Port Jet Cruise Adventures** *(portjet.com.au)*. While you're in town, don't miss the local seafood or the wonderful **Port Macquarie Coastal Walk**, a 9km, eight-beach stroll that can be broken into shorter segments.

THE DRIVE: The first stretch runs inland; for a scenic 17km detour, take Tourist Drive 14 through Stuarts Point and the eucalyptus forest to Grassy Head, then Yarriabini National Park and Scotts Head on your way back to the highway. After passing laid-back Nambucca Heads, it's a further 25km north, then 12km west to Bellingen.

05 Bellingen

Buried in deep foliage on a hillside above the Bellinger River, this gorgeous town dances to the beat of its own bongo drum. 'Bello' is flush with organic produce, and the switched-on community has an urban sensibility. Located between the spectacular rainforest of Dorrigo National Park and a spoiled-for-choice selection of beaches, it is a definite jewel on the East Coast route. Eating in Bellingen is a pleasure: it has a large and ever-growing number of cafes and casual restaurants, most of which use local organic produce. Check out our favourite, the Hearthfire Bakery.

A half-hour drive west of Bellingen, the 119-sq-km **Dorrigo National Park** *(nationalparks.nsw.gov.au/visit-a-park/parks/dorrigo-national-park)* is part of the Gondwana Rainforests World Heritage Area and home to a huge diversity of vegetation and more than 120 species of bird.

THE DRIVE: Head back to the highway and turn north once more for the short drive to Coffs Harbour.

DETOUR

Waterfall Way

Start: 05 Bellingen

Considered New South Wales' most scenic drive, the 190km Waterfall Way links a number of beautiful national parks between Coffs Harbour and Armidale, taking you through pristine subtropical rainforest, Edenic valleys and, unsurprisingly, spectacular waterfalls. As you emerge into the tablelands, there is green countryside and wide plains. Bellingen is the natural starting point for this route. Even a fairly short foray along it will result in some stunning views.

Guy Fawkes River National Park *(nationalparks.nsw.gov.au/guy-fawkes-river-national-park)* and the stunning Ebor Falls are 50km past Dorrigo, which is itself 30km northwest of Bellingen. Make your way into the **Cathedral Rock National Park** *(nationalparks.nsw.gov.au/cathedral-rock-national-park)* or take a detour down Point Lookout Rd to **New England National Park** *(nationalparks.nsw.gov.au/new-england-national-park)*, a section of the Gondwana Rainforests World Heritage Area. Further west, **Oxley Wild Rivers National Park** *(nationalparks.nsw.gov.au/oxley-wild-rivers-national-park)* is home to the towering beauty of Wollomombi Falls.

06 Coffs Harbour

Despite its inland city centre, Coffs has a string of fabulous beaches. Equally popular with families and backpackers, the town offers plenty of water-based activities, action sports and wildlife encounters, not to mention the kitsch yellow beacon that is the Big Banana. Getting out on the water is easy in Coffs, whether learning to catch the breaks with **Lee Winkler's Surf School** *(surfschoolcoffsharbour.com.au)* or taking a scenic paddle while learning about Aboriginal culture

WHY I LOVE THIS TRIP

ANDY SYMINGTON, WRITER

The trip to Byron is a rite of passage for Australians of all ages, a legendary road trip along a majestic coast of endless beaches, proud Aboriginal heritage, picturesque inlets, unspoiled national parks and leaping dolphins. For me and other Sydneysiders, heading north symbolises throwing off the stress and shackles of city life and embracing the summer, the sand and the great outdoors.

with **Wajaana Yaam Adventure Tours** *(wajaanayaam.com.au)*. And then there's **Muttonbird Island** *(nationalparks.nsw.gov.au/muttonbird-island-nature-reserve)*. The Gumbainggir people know it as Giidany Miirlarl, meaning Place of the Moon. It was joined to Coffs Harbour by the northern breakwater in 1935. The walk to the top (quite steep at the end) provides sweeping vistas. From late August to early April, this eco treasure is occupied by some 12,000 pairs of wedge-tailed shearwaters, with their cute offspring visible in December and January.

THE DRIVE: The road north of Coffs passes beneath tall, tall trees, within sight of the Big Banana, then almost as close to the coast as you can get. Before it sweeps inland, just after Sandy Beach, you'll hit Woolgoolga.

07 Woolgoolga

Woolgoolga is home to one of coastal Australia's more incongruous combinations – Woopi, as locals call it, is famous for its surf-and-Sikh community. If you're driving by on the highway, you're sure to notice the impressive Guru Nanak Temple, a Sikh gurdwara (place of worship). In September the town goes all out with the annual **Curryfest** *(curryfest.com.au)* celebration, with three days of food stalls, cooking demonstrations and cultural activities (Indian dance class, anyone?). It's a refreshing change from some of the somewhat monocultural beach towns elsewhere along the coast.

THE DRIVE: A mere 7km north of Woopi, where the M1 again arcs inland, take the Red Rock turnoff along a much quieter road that sticks to the coast.

08 Red Rock

The village of Red Rock (population 412) is set between a beautiful beach and a glorious fish-filled river inlet. It takes its name from the red-tinged rock stack at the headland. The local Gumbainggir people know it by a more sombre name: Blood Rock. In the 1880s a detachment of armed police slaughtered the inhabitants of an Aboriginal camp, chasing the survivors to the headland, where they were driven off. The area is considered sacred. The **Yarrawarra Aboriginal Cultural Centre** *(yarrawarra.com.au)* has an interesting art gallery and a bush-tucker cafe, where dishes are created using native ingredients such as lemon myrtle. It also holds bush-medicine tours and art classes; call ahead if you want to join one.

North of Red Rock, the **Yuraygir National Park** *(nationalparks.nsw.gov.au/yuraygir-national-park)* is the state's longest stretch of undeveloped coastline, covering a 65km swathe of pristine coastal ecosystems. The isolated beaches are outstanding and there are bushwalking paths where you can view endangered coastal emus.

THE DRIVE: Return back down the road to the M1, turn right (northwest) and follow it all the way north through flat agricultural country, passing Grafton and Maclean en route.

09 Yamba & Angourie

At the mouth of the Clarence River, the fishing town of Yamba is growing in popularity thanks to its gently bohemian lifestyle, splendid beaches and excellent cafes and restaurants. Often-heard descriptions such as 'Byron Bay 20 years ago' are not unfounded.

Neighbour Angourie, 5km to the south, is a tiny, chilled-out place that has long been a draw for experienced surfers and was proudly one of Australia's first surf reserves.

Serious surfers head for **Angourie Point**, but Yamba's beaches have something for everyone else. **Main Beach** is the busiest, with an ocean pool, banana palms and a grassy slope for those who don't want to get sandy.

Convent Beach is a sunbaker's haven and **Turner's**, protected by the breakwater, is ideal for surf lessons. You can sometimes spot dolphins along the long stretch of **Pippi Beach**.

THE DRIVE: Go north up the M1 but turn off through Ballina and then hug the coast, drawing near to Lennox Head's picturesque coastline with some dramatic views from the road. Byron begins a long time before you arrive. Don't miss the excellent bakery in Suffolk Park, at the southern end of Byron's sprawl.

10 Byron Bay

Between its eye-watering property prices, trending eateries and traffic jams regularly stretching to the M1 turnoff, today's Byron Bay is a bit different from the sleepy coastal idyll 'discovered' by surfers in the 1950s, with hippies hot on their sandy heels.

Yet the low-rise (just) holiday hot spot continues to enchant visitors with its natural beauty, famous surf breaks, fabulous food scene and youthful energy. Packed with cafes and boutiques, the compact centre is comfortably walkable. Immediately in front of town, lifesaver-patrolled

> **PHOTO OPPORTUNITY**
>
> Sunset on the beach at Byron Bay.

HYSERB/SHUTTERSTOCK

Byron Bay

Main Beach is busy from sunrise to sunset with local ocean swimmers, holidaying families and hungover backpackers. Buskers often perform in the beachfront park. Tucked below the **Cape Byron Lighthouse** is gorgeous **Wategos Beach**, a thin crescent of white sand fringed by some of the nation's most expensive real estate. To the south, **Tallow Beach** is a wild sandy stretch that extends for 7km south to beautiful Broken Head.

DETOUR

Bangalow & Nimbin

Start: 10 Byron Bay

Before you arrive in Byron (or as a detour from Byron itself), two hinterland communities make for a fascinating detour. First up, surrounded by subtropical forest and rolling green farmland, sophisticated **Bangalow** is home to a small, creative community, a dynamic, sustainable food scene and a range of urbane boutiques.

And then there's **Nimbin**, Australia's alternative-lifestyle capital, an intriguing little town that struggles under the weight of its own clichés. Nimbin was once an unremarkable Northern Rivers dairy village, but that changed forever in May 1973. Thousands of students, hippies and devotees of the back-to-earth movement descended on the town for the Aquarius Festival, with many staying on and creating new communities in the beautiful valleys in an attempt to live out the ideals expressed during the 10-day celebration.

Another landmark in Nimbin's history came in 1979 with the Terania Creek Battle, the first major conservation victory of its kind in Australia, which is often credited with ensuring the survival of NSW's vast tracts of rainforest. Protestor Falls, in what is now Nightcap National Park, is named in its honour.

Today, the old psychedelic murals of the rainbow serpent Dreaming and marijuana bliss that line Nimbin's main street may be a little faded and the dread-locked, beaded locals somewhat weathered, but genuine remnants of that generation remain. A stroll through the centre will bring the optimistic days of peace-and-love flooding back.

STAY AWHILE

PORT STEPHENS

BY SARAH REID

If I had to choose the best coastal viewpoint in New South Wales, the summit of **Tomaree Head** would come close. After slogging up the steep trail, the vistas of the white-sand beaches and lush forested hills of Tomaree National Park stretching south from this 161m-high perch are pure magic – especially during the winter whale migration.

Port Stephens is one of Australia's most genetically blessed peninsulas. On one side are the calm, sapphire waters of an enormous natural harbour where you can board whale-watching boats and swim with wild dolphins. Around the headland, koala-filled **Tomaree National Park** *(nationalparks.nsw.gov.au)* hugs the Pacific coast, with a good handful of beautiful beaches and rainforest trails to explore on foot or by bike.

At the base of the peninsula are the **Worimi Conservation Lands** *(worimiconservationlands.com),* home to the southern hemisphere's largest shifting sand dunes. Adrenaline junkies can learn about their Aboriginal significance atop a quad bike with Worimi-owned **Sand Dune Adventures** *(sanddune adventures.com.au),* or you can access wild beach camp sites in your own 4WD.

There's also plenty of wining and dining to enjoy in the region's relaxed villages and beyond. The **B.Farm** *(bfarm.net.au),* complete with restaurant, bar, winery and distillery, is an obligatory stop on the drive in from the M1. While Port Stephens' proximity to Sydney (2½ hours away) makes it a popular escape for city folk, it can feel blissfully bucolic outside the busy school holidays. With so much to see and do, you'll want to stick around.

LINK YOUR TRIP

A comfortable first stop on a road trip from 06 **Sydney to Byron Bay**.

FROM LEFT: LKONYA/SHUTTERSTOC, BJANKA KADIC/ALAMY

Left: View from Tomaree Head
Right: Bannisters Port Stephens

PLACES TO STAY

Local accommodation options cover all bases, from a collection of beachfront holiday parks including the sublimely situated **Halifax Holiday Park** *(beachsideholidays.com.au)* to posh digs like the new **Marina Resort** *(marinaresort.com.au)*, and **Bannisters Port Stephens** *(bannisters.com.au/port-stephens)*, home to the lauded Rick Stein seafood restaurant. You'll also find a number of midrange hotels and B&Bs. For something different, check your family into a glamping tent or room at the **Port Stephens Koala Sanctuary** *(portstephenskoalasanctuary.com.au)*, where stays include unlimited access to the state-of-the-art sanctuary and an exclusive morning tour before it opens to the general public.

07

NEW SOUTH WALES & THE AUSTRALIAN CAPITAL TERRITORY

SNOWY MOUNTAINS

★ BEST FOR:

OUTDOORS

Kiandra combines evocative scenery with thought-provoking human history.

DURATION: 2–3 DAYS

DISTANCE: 275KM / 171 MILES

GREAT FOR: NATURE

BEST TIME TO GO: SPRING AND AUTUMN. ROADS MAY BE IMPASSABLE WITHOUT CHAINS IN WINTER.

Snowy Hydro hydroelectric infrastructure

From Cooma to Jindabyne, this imagination-firing route traverses the Snowy Mountains' lonesome landscapes. Along the way, as wedge-tailed eagles soar on the thermals, the road passes dense forests, patches of ribbony grass and up-country views you won't find anywhere else in Australia. This meandering mountain drive suits poetic souls and solitude seekers but not nervous drivers or fidgety passengers.

LINK YOUR TRIP

02 Sydney to Melbourne
Drive south from Cooma for 45km, then turn east towards the coast. You enter Trip 2 at Merimbula.

08 Canberra & the South Coast
Take the Monaro Hwy north from Cooma for 116km to Queanbeyan, which lies along Trip 8 between Canberra and Batemans Bay.

01 Cooma

Cooma is a fine place to begin this crossing of Australia's highest terrain. Proximity to the snowfields keeps this little town punching above its weight during winter, while it can be whisper-quiet in summer. Provided you have small-town expectations, Cooma has plenty to intrigue among its friendly cafes and heritage buildings. Spare an hour or two for the **NSW Corrective Services Museum** *(correctiveservices.dcj.nsw.gov.au/about-us/museums-and-galleries.html)*, where inmates of the prison lead engaging (and often darkly humorous) museum tours into correctional history. On the Monaro Hwy, 2km north of the town centre, tap into the town's lifeblood at the **Snowy Hydro Discovery Centre** *(snowyhydro.com.au)* to understand the hydroelectric scheme that is one of Australia's finest feats of engineering. The dams and hydroelectric plant took 25 years and more than 100,000

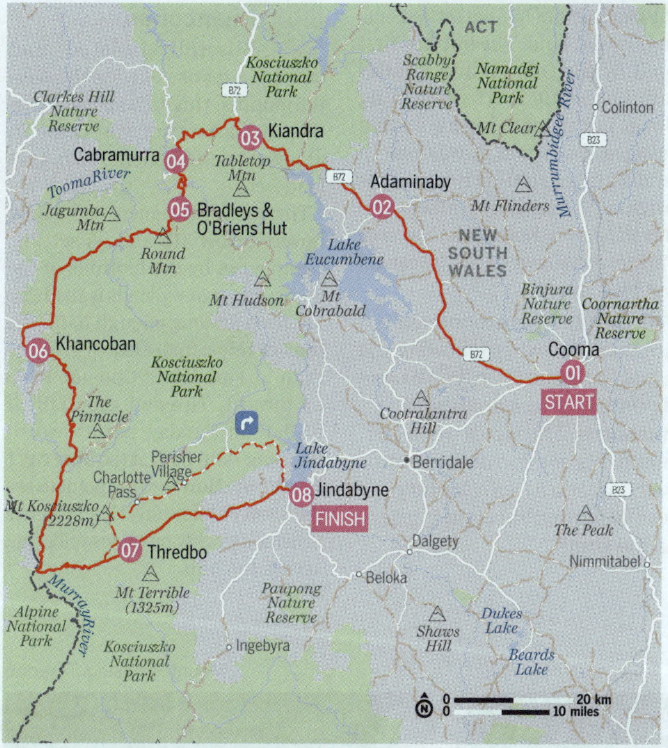

TARAS VYSHNYA/SHUTTERSTOCK

people to build and there's more to come, in the form of 'Snowy 2.0'.

THE DRIVE: To begin, take Sharp St in Cooma west, then take the turnoff to Tumut 7km out of town. From there, it's 44km to Adaminaby, climbing gently through subalpine pastures.

02 Adaminaby

Gloriously named Adaminaby, at an elevation of 1017m, looks like any other sleepy Australian hamlet of widely spaced houses and shady parklands, but looks can be deceptive – old Adaminaby was drowned by the rising waters of Lake Eucumbene when dams were built in the 1950s. In times of drought, when the waters recede, relics of the former town emerge like spectres. The trout fishing is as legendary as the local hospitality, and the town has a respectable record of appearances in literature and film. It was the inspiration for *Happy Valley*, the first novel of Australia's Nobel Prize-winning author Patrick White, while its racecourse has appeared in two Hollywood films: *The Sundowners* (1960) and *Phar Lap* (1983). It's worth stopping here for a view of the lake (or to have a flick – Aussie slang for 'to go fishing') and a fuel top-up, as things get ghostlier from here. And the town's pink-striped Big Trout was made for a selfie.

THE DRIVE: Some 13km beyond Adaminaby, you leave behind rolling grazing country and enter the denser woodlands of Kosciuszko National Park.

03 Kiandra

Covering 6900 sq km, Kosciuszko National Park is the roughest diamond in NSW's considerable national-park crown. In spring and summer, walking trails and camp sites are framed by alpine flowers. It's less a single stop than a series of places where you'll be tempted to pull over, turn off the engine and take in the views in blissful silence. At the 88km mark out of Cooma, at the sign for Kiandra, leave the car by the roadside and climb to the poignant hillside graves of the **Kiandra Cemetery** – from 1891 to 1912, 47 people were buried at this remote gold-mining spot and only six died of old age. The scenery here has a wild and lonely aspect. The long-abandoned town is also the birthplace of recreational skiing in Australia, introduced by Norwegian settlers.

THE DRIVE: The road climbs past the ruins of Kiandra, 1400m above sea level; take the turnoff for Cabramurra soon after at the 89km mark, with another turnoff for Cabramurra at 104km. Cabramurra itself is 4km further on.

04 Cabramurra

At a dizzying elevation (by Australian standards) of 1488m, Cabramurra is Australia's highest settlement. It's a strange place in a stunning setting, custom-built in the 1950s to house workers on the Snowy Mountains Hydroelectric Scheme, then left behind to house those who maintain the dam complex. Its residential community was replaced by contract workers in 2018.

With more than half of Cabramurra's houses razed by the 2020 Black Summer bushfires, along with its school and ski club, there's little to see here now. Stop for lunch at the canteen before continuing on your way.

THE DRIVE: The steep descent from Cabramurra is one of the prettiest on the whole route, with a stunning honour guard of eerie white, fire-scarred trunks before the road drops to the dam itself, then continues through alternating alpine woodlands and grasslands.

05 Bradleys & O'Briens Hut

Around 120km out of Cooma, Bradleys & O'Briens Hut is a timber-framed mountain shack clad in corrugated iron. It's an evocative place – one of those isolated Aussie structures that somehow captures the loneliness of human settlements in this vast land. The hut was first built by the O'Brien and Bradley families in 1952. After burning down in the 2020 bushfires that ravaged the region, it was rebuilt in 2024 in the spitting image of the original. It's used by walkers and day-trippers to Kosciuszko National Park, especially when they're caught out by a storm.

THE DRIVE: As you continue southwest, always following the signs to Khancoban, you'll pass a number of rest areas and trailheads. The views open out along this section of the route, with Victoria's High Country visible across the state border to the south.

06 Khancoban

Blissfully isolated, and quiet as a mouse outside the winter months, tiny Khancoban feels like an oasis after you come in along the long, lonely roads that lead here.

The town's permanent population hovers below 319 and its setting, hemmed in by the foothills of the Snowy Mountains, lends it an idyllic air. Stop for long enough to fill the tank or refuel (more expensive here than in Thredbo or Cooma). Push on towards Thredbo, especially if it's late in the day, but it's worth stopping 7km south at the **Murray 1 Power Station** viewing point to see the Snowy Mountains Hydroelectric Scheme's mighty pipelines spidering across the hills.

Mountain-biking, Thredbo

LIGHTITUP/SHUTTERSTOCK

THE DRIVE: With the trip clock at 192km, pause for fine views at Scammells Lookout, named after a local family who grazed their cattle nearby in the 1860s. You'll pass several riverside rest areas, then after 243km you'll climb to the road's highest point, with a sign that says 'Great Dividing Range 1580m', before dropping down the valley into Thredbo.

07 Thredbo

At 1365m, Thredbo is often lauded as Australia's number-one ski resort, and its narrow valley setting is a dramatic sight as you descend from the Khancoban road. Summertime heralds adventures along 40km of mountain-biking trails, as well as on hiking routes into the raw wilderness that extends from nearby Charlotte Pass. Thredbo also gets soulful in midsummer, with the **Thredbo Blues Festival** *(thredboblues.com.au)* running for three days in January. In winter, Thredbo is all about skiing, and snow-heads arrive en masse to thunder down Australia's longest runs.

THE DRIVE: Although you'll pass through plenty of alpine woodland on the first stretch out of Thredbo, the more picturesque sections of the route are now behind you and it's an easy run through open country for the last few kilometres into Jindabyne.

FILEDIMAGE/SHUTTERSTOCK

Scammells Lookout

PHOTO OPPORTUNITY

Scammells Lookout, a magnificent mountain vantage point amid often-dense gum forest.

DETOUR

Mt Kosciuszko

Start: 07 Thredbo or 08 Jindabyne

It may be a mere hill when compared to mountains around the world, but Mt Kosciuszko (2228m) is the highest mountain on the Australian continent. As mountains go, it's relatively easy to climb, although getting to the top can still be strenuous. There are two possible trailheads and three available routes. The most straightforward is the **Mt Kosciuszko Track** – from Thredbo, take the **Kosciuszko Express Chairlift**; from the top of the lift it's a 13km hike to the summit and back. Gauge your group's fitness before setting out: plenty of kids can be seen skipping ahead of their parents on the trail, but if little legs slow your progress, there's a risk of missing the last lift down.

The other two trails require you to drive to the end of the paved road above Charlotte Pass (40km west of Jindabyne). The easier of the two routes is the **Summit Walk** (18km return, with a thigh-burning final ascent). The other option is the **Main Range Track**, a much tougher 22km loop that crosses minor creeks; ask at the **visitor centre** *(thredbo.com.au)* before setting out, as inclement weather can make it impossible to complete. Be sure to register a trip-intention form.

No park fees for Kosciuszko National Park are payable

if you're just driving straight through. If, however, you're overnighting or driving beyond Jindabyne towards Charlotte Pass, the fee is $17 per vehicle per 24 hours (or $29 in winter).

08 Jindabyne

Jindabyne is the closest town to Kosciuszko National Park's major ski resorts. Though its inky-blue lake is undeniably beautiful, it's a feeder town rather than a destination in its own right – with 2.5 million annual overnight stays in the Snowy Mountains, Jindabyne ends up welcoming a large number of mountain-bound visitors. In summer the town assumes a more peaceful vibe, and fishing and mountain biking are the main pastimes. **Sacred Ride** *(sacredride.com.au)* can kit you out with wheels, helmets and sage trail advice, while the **Snowy Region Visitor Centre** *(nationalparks.nsw.gov.au/things-to-do/visitor-centres/snowy-region-visitor-centre)* offers experienced hiking guidance and tips on kayaking.

SKIING IN THE SNOWY MOUNTAINS

The main ski resorts are Thredbo, on the southern slopes of Kosciuszko, and Perisher, on the eastern side. The much smaller Charlotte Pass resort is approached from the Perisher side and sits higher up the slopes.

Ski season officially lasts from early June to Labour Day (early October). Peak season is June to August, though July and August have the best snow. Snow-making machines ensure that there's usually some cover throughout the season, though you can expect the 'white ribbon of death' – that is, a ski route fashioned from artificial snow with bare earth or muddy ground on either side – at the beginning and end of the season.

Off the slopes there's lively nightlife, good restaurants and a plethora of facilities and activities catering to families. Both Thredbo and Perisher have a designated kids' skiing programme, crèches and day care.

On the downside, resorts tend to be particularly crowded at weekends, and the limited season means that operators have to get their returns quickly, so costs are high.

Perisher ski resort
TARAS VYSHNYA/ALAMY

08

NEW SOUTH WALES & THE AUSTRALIAN CAPITAL TERRITORY

CANBERRA & THE SOUTH COAST

★ BEST FOR:

OUTDOORS

Kangaroo Valley and the road up and over the Great Dividing Range are simply gorgeous.

DURATION: 3-4 DAYS

DISTANCE: 494KM / 307 MILES

GREAT FOR: HISTORY & NATURE

BEST TIME TO GO: NOVEMBER TO MARCH FOR COASTAL AREAS, BUT YEAR-ROUND EVERYWHERE ELSE.

Wollongong botanic garden

While everyone else gets distracted by the big Pacific blue, this itinerary eases you away from the coast and, within no time at all, Kangaroo Valley's wildlife and history will hold you in their thrall. Berrima and Bowral rank among inland NSW's most charming historic towns, while Canberra is the national cultural repository. Then it's down through forests to rejoin the coast at Batemans Bay, for surf lessons and golden sands.

LINK YOUR TRIP

02 Sydney to Melbourne
Stanwell Tops is just south of Royal National Park, at the start of the Sydney-to-Melbourne trip, while Batemans Bay is close to its midpoint.

07 Snowy Mountains
From Queanbeyan, drive 109km south along the Monaro Hwy to Cooma, where the 275km Snowy Mountains loop begins.

01 Stanwell Tops

Bald Hill in Stanwell Park starts the drive with a mesmeric view. Stanwell Beach's crescent of golden sand is utterly photogenic from this lofty lookout; on a good day, you'll see hang-gliders floating on the breeze. Ten kilometres south of Stanwell Tops, stop in the **Scarborough Hotel** *(thescarboroughhotel.com.au)*, which has everything you could possibly want from a pub on the coast: a heritage feel (built 1886), good seafood lunches and a marvellous beer garden with views of the sea.

THE DRIVE: Stick to the coast road south of Stanwell Tops and soar over the dramatic Seacliff Bridge before rejoining the Princes Hwy to zip into Wollongong.

02 Wollongong

Like Sydney on a far more manageable scale, the 'Gong' captures the Aussie ideal of laid-back

MAKJANRUS/SHUTTERSTOCK

coastal living but adds a modest live-music scene, restaurants and excellent bars. There are 17 patrolled beaches in the vicinity – North Beach generally has better surf than Wollongong City Beach, while further north are the surfer magnets of Bulli, Sandon Point, Thirroul (where DH Lawrence lived during his time in Australia) and pretty Austinmer. Other fetching spots are the dreamy **botanic garden** *(wollongongbotanicgarden.com.au)* and the panoramic **lookout** atop Mt Keira.

THE DRIVE: Forsake the truck-heavy M1 for the quieter coastal road, passing Shellharbour, Kiama and Gerringong before rejoining M1 all the way into Berry.

03 Berry

Charming Berry is a popular inland stop on the South Coast, thanks to a slew of National Trust–classified buildings and accompanying antique and homeware stores. Berry's foodie scene jostles happily with the heritage buildings, a lost-in-time pub and nostalgia-steeped shops like **Treat Factory** *(treatfactory.com.au)*. Encouraging an overnight stop, the B&Bs in the rolling countryside nearby are some of the cosiest around.

THE DRIVE: Follow the M1 for around 12km and, just when it seems as though you have no choice but to pass into sprawling, somewhat humdrum Nowra, turn off to the right and journey northwest into Kangaroo Valley.

04 Kangaroo Valley

Here's something special: picturesque Kangaroo Valley is arrayed against a fortress-like backdrop of rainforest-covered cliffs, its valley floor carpeted by sweeping green pasturelands, river gums and gurgling creeks. The slow country town of Kangaroo Valley has an excellent pub, restaurants, and the odd feel-good shop and gallery to satiate wealthy Sydneysiders who populate the town at weekends. The formal entry to the valley is the castellated sandstone-and-iron **Hampden Bridge** (1898), a few kilometres north of town.

The river beach just below the bridge is a good spot for a swim. If you have time to linger, take your pick of cafes on the main drag, and stop in at the **Valley Fudge & Teahouse** for a sampling. Alternatively, **Kangaroo Valley Adventure Co** *(kvac.com.au)* can set you up for hiking and kayaking.

THE DRIVE: The road northwest from Kangaroo Valley is a wonderfully winding ascent of the escarpment, with fine views of hill-flanked plains, before you get lost in the dizzyingly tall trees of the upper montane forest; watch for colourful king parrots in the upper reaches. Stop at Fitzroy Falls for a creek-side ramble, then pass through history-rich Moss Vale on your way into Bowral.

05 Bowral

You could be forgiven for thinking you've taken a wrong turn in the Southern Highlands and ended up in the south of England when you reach Bowral, a pretty area that revels in its Englishness. That feeling will come to seem rather incongruous, however, when you learn that it was here that Sir Donald Bradman, that quintessential Aussie hero and nemesis of English cricket, spent his boyhood. Within the **International Cricket Hall of Fame** complex *(bradman.com.au)* there's a pretty cricket oval, and fans pay homage to Bradman at the **Bradman Museum of Cricket**, which overflows with Ashes memorabilia. The ever-expanding collection showcasing the international game is a must for all sports fans, not just cricket buffs.

THE DRIVE: To reach Berrima, you'll need to loop north and then southwest onto the Hume Hwy ever so briefly. You should be there no more than 15 minutes after leaving Bowral.

PHOTO OPPORTUNITY

CANBERRA

Parliament House.

DETOUR

Wombeyan Caves

Start: 05 Bowral

Southern NSW is riddled with fabulous limestone caves, none more spectacular than the **Wombeyan Caves** *(nationalparks.nsw.gov.au/visit-a-park/parks/wombeyan-karst-conservation-reserve)*. This convoluted network of extraordinary underground caverns lies up a well-signposted, unsealed mountain road (which is passable in a 2WD vehicle but adds a real sense of adventure to the excursion), 70km northwest of Bowral. Nearby are walking trails and plenty of wildlife.

06 Berrima

Heritage-classified Berrima could just be the loveliest town along the Hume Hwy. Founded in 1829 with visions of a future as a major metropolis, Berrima grew into an important inland waystation that was, during its 19th-century peak, home to 14 hotels. It later settled into quiet obscurity, but not before an appealing portfolio of sandstone buildings adorned the streets. These buildings – among them the **Berrima Courthouse** (1838), the **Old Berrima Gaol** (1839), the **Holy Trinity Anglican Church** (1849) and the **St Francis Xavier Catholic Church** (1849) – together speak volumes for the

Parliament House, Canberra

ALEXANDRE.ROSA/SHUTTERSTOCK

preoccupations of early settlement life. That other essential pillar of bijou rural Aussie towns, the secondhand bookshop, finds expression around 3km north in **Berkelouw Book Barn & Café** *(berkelouw.com.au)*, with over 200,000 secondhand tomes. There's also a wide selection of new Australia-themed books. It sits on the historic Bendooley Estate and has an excellent attached restaurant and cellar door.

THE DRIVE: It's possible to avoid the Hume Hwy as far south as sleepy Bundanoon, a gateway to Morton National Park. But thereafter you might as well join the highway, bypassing Goulburn, then following the signs down into Canberra.

07 Canberra

Canberra, Australia's custom-built capital, is a city built for the car, and having one allows you to explore its expansive open spaces and catch a sense of the city's seamless alignment of built and natural elements. Though Canberra seems big on architectural symbolism and low on spontaneity, the city's cultural institutions have lively visitor and social programmes, and there's a cool urban energy in Braddon, New Acton and the Kingston Foreshore. During parliamentary sitting weeks the town hums with the buzz of national politics, but it can be a tad sleepy during university holidays, especially around Christmas and New Year. If you're here at such times, get out and explore its kangaroo-filled parks and its picturesque natural hinterland.

THE DRIVE: From Canberra city centre, follow the signs to Queanbeyan, then take the Kings Hwy up and over the Great Dividing Range on a twisting forest road to the coast. Although it's only 150km from Canberra to Batemans Bay, count on the drive taking well over two hours. Avoid Friday afternoons, when Canberrans head for the coast.

STEVE TRITTON/SHUTTERSTOCK

Hot air balloons, Lake Burley Griffin

LAKE BURLEY GRIFFIN

Though it might seem at first glance that Canberra was built around the sparkling waters of Lake Burley Griffin, the reality is actually the other way around. The concept of an artificial lake was part of the original design of the nation's capital as early as 1909; however it wasn't until 1961, with the excavation of the lake floor and the damming of the Molonglo River at Scrivener Dam, that Lake Burley Griffin finally came into existence. Even then, the final stages of construction were hampered by a prolonged period of drought, which meant that the lake did not reach its planned water level until 1964, when it was officially inaugurated by then Prime Minister Sir Robert Menzies. A statue of Menzies, who championed the lake project throughout his prime ministership, can be seen strolling along the lake shore near Nerang Pool.

08 Batemans Bay

Like any good South Coast beach town worth its sea salt, Batemans Bay promises a decent restaurant strip, good beaches and, in this case, a sparkling estuary. Waterborne activities are diverse, from family-friendly kayaking and fishing to surf lessons amid the crashing waves; for the latter, try **Broulee Surf School** *(brouleesurfschool.com.au)* or **Surf the Bay Surf School** *(surfthebay.com.au)*, which also offers paddleboarding. There are plenty of beaches if all you need is somewhere to lay your towel. Closest to town is **Corrigans Beach**, and longer stretches north of the bridge lead into **Murramarang National Park**. Surfers flock to **Pink Rocks**, **Surf Beach**, **Malua Bay**, **McKenzies Beach** and **Bengello Beach**. Broulee has a wide crescent of sand, but there's a strong rip at the northern end. It's no surprise that Batemans Bay is one of coastal NSW's most popular holiday centres, so book ahead if you're planning to stay in summer or on a weekend.

09

★ BEST FOR:

HISTORY

Coming face-to-face with the Aboriginal past in Bingara.

NEW SOUTH WALES & THE AUSTRALIAN CAPITAL TERRITORY

NEW ENGLAND

DURATION: 5-7 DAYS

DISTANCE: 944KM / 587 MILES

GREAT FOR: HISTORY & NATURE

BEST TIME TO GO: TAMWORTH'S COUNTRY MUSIC FEST IN MID-JANUARY; MARCH TO MAY FOR AUTUMNAL COLOURS.

Coffs Harbour coastline

Leave the coast behind and head for the hills – the drive from Coffs to Armidale is one of New South Wales' prettiest. After Tamworth, that big-hat capital of all things country, the roads empty and a string of national parks and lovely towns (where you can strike it rich in more ways than one) will delight you all the way to Yamba.

LINK YOUR TRIP

06 Sydney to Byron Bay
Coffs Harbour sits roughly at the midpoint between Sydney and Byron Bay, while Yamba is closer to Byron, where Trip 6 ends.

18 Southern Queensland Loop
Drive 180km north of Yamba and you'll end up nudging Coolangatta, part of a loop through the Queensland coast.

01 Coffs Harbour

Coffs Harbour is one of the beach stalwarts of the Aussie coast, a popular if slightly ageing resort with surf schools, fish and chips, and long, golden stretches of sand. It's the sort of place that's as popular with families as it is with backpackers and blue-rinse retirees. Of the beaches, try **Park Beach**, a long, lovely stretch of sand backed by dense shrubbery and sand dunes that conceal the buildings beyond. **Jetty Beach** is somewhat more sheltered. We also love Coffs for the chance to learn to surf at East Coast Surf School, or eat fish and chips from the **Fishermen's Coop** *(coffsfishcoop.com.au)* on the beach. And then there's always the **Big Banana** *(bigbanana.com)*.

THE DRIVE: From Coffs, take the M1 south of town for around 24km, then bid farewell to the coast and head inland (west), bound for Bellingen. Almost

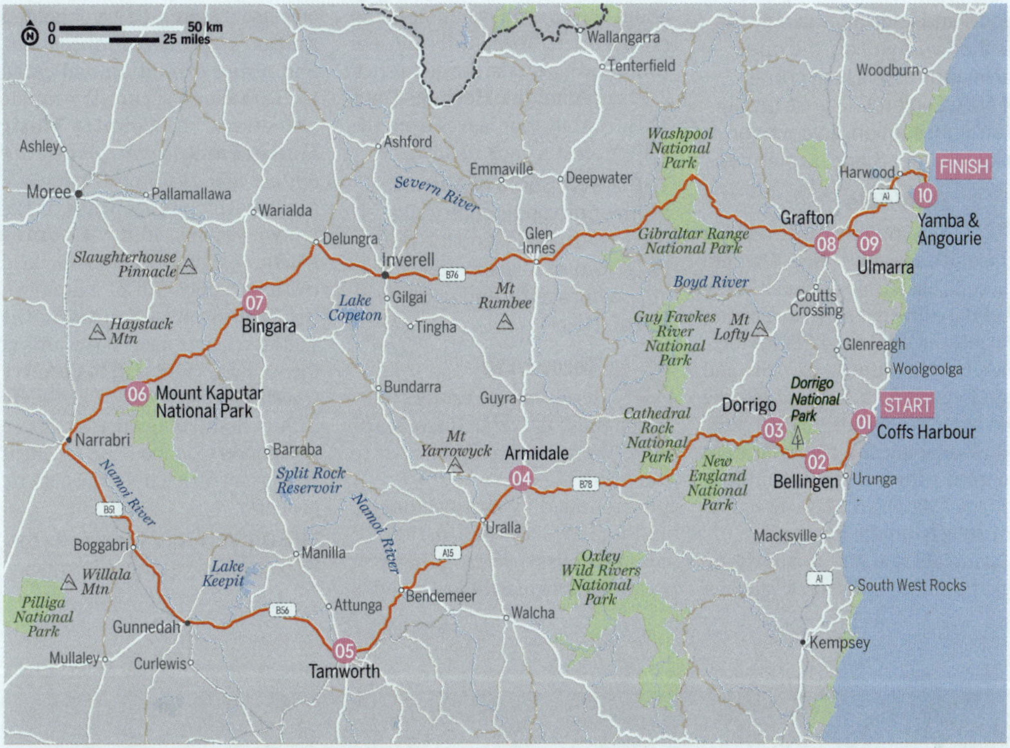

SINCLAIR BLACK/SHUTTERSTOCK

immediately, the world becomes quieter and the hills of the Great Dividing Range rise up ahead of you.

02 Bellingen

Thick with gourmet, organic cuisine and accommodation, 'Bello' is hippie without the dippy. Partly it's the location that catches your eye, but it also has just the right mix of seasonal markets, vintage stores like Retro Bello, and its very own jazz festival, the **Beyond Jazz Weekender** *(beyond jazzweekender.com.au)*. Throw in river canoeing, a huge colony of flying foxes on Bellingen Island and a quirky literary heritage – there's the **Bellingen Readers & Writers Festival** *(bellingenwriters festival.com.au)* and its fame as the setting of Peter Carey's Booker Prize-winning novel *Oscar and Lucinda* – and you'll soon be hooked.

THE DRIVE: The Waterfall Way road from Bellingen runs pancake-flat for a wee while, then climbs the eastern flank of the Great Dividing Range and barely stops doing so until you're in Dorrigo, 27km beyond Bellingen. The views along this drive are splendid.

03 Dorrigo

Amid so much natural beauty, Dorrigo can seem almost incidental, although it's a pretty little place arrayed around the T-junction of two wider-than-wide streets. The town's main attraction is the Dangar Falls, 1.2km north, which dramatically plummets over a rock shelf and into a basin. But even more beautiful attractions await in the nearby **Dorrigo National Park** *(nationalparks.nsw.gov.au/visit-a-park/parks/dorrigo-national-park)*. Covering 119 sq km, this park is part of the Gondwana Rainforests World Heritage Area. The **Dorigo Rainforest Centre**, at the park entrance, has displays and advice on which walk to tackle. It's also home to the **Skywalk**, a viewing platform that juts over the rainforest and provides vistas over the valleys below. Immerse in the greenery on the 3.2km-return **Crystal Shower Falls Walk**.

THE DRIVE: It's a long, lovely drive through forests, light woodland and, increasingly the further west you go, the open farmlands of this lush corner of New England. There's barely a straight section, so count on taking longer than you planned.

04 Armidale

Few places capture that graceful and refined New England air quite like Armidale, and it's here that the entire region's name makes the most sense. Armidale's heritage blue-brick buildings, gardens and moss-covered churches look like the stage set for an English period drama, and it's these facades, coupled with spectacular autumn foliage (March to May), that will live longest in the memory.

Armidale also has an appealing microclimate – set at an elevation of 980m, it enjoys mild summers and crisp winters. To make the most of your time here, take the detail-rich 2½-hour **Armidale Heritage Tour**. This free bus tour leaves from the visitor centre; book in advance.

THE DRIVE: Some of Australia's premier grazing country surrounds Armidale, and the drive to Tamworth takes in green, rolling pasturelands and pockets of forest (111km).

05 Tamworth

If you had to identify a town to epitomise the rural Aussie heartland, Tamworth would be close to the top of the list.

Surrounded by rich farmlands, and a pilgrimage destination for country-music lovers, Tamworth wears its provinciality as a badge of honour. There's the iconic **golden guitar** *(biggoldenguitar.com.au)*, and a fine exhibition dedicated to Tamworth's country-music soundtrack, the **Country Music Hall of Fame** *(countrymusichalloffame.com.au)*. Tamworth's love affair with country peaks at the truly awesome, 10-day **Country Music Festival** *(tcmf.com.au)* held in the second half of January – the biggest music festival in the southern hemisphere. If you miss it, there's always **Hats Off to Country** *(facebook.com/hatsoffTocountry)* in July. South of town, Glasshouse at Goonoo Goonoo is an excellent restaurant on a handsome historic property.

THE DRIVE: From Tamworth, the B56 crosses yet more farmland

Sawn Rocks, Mount Kaputar National Park

BLACKDOGMOTOTRAVELS/SHUTTERSTOCK

on its way to Gunnedah (75km), an agricultural centre and the self-proclaimed 'Koala Capital of the World'. Then it's 95km northwest to Narrabri and on to Mount Kaputar National Park, around 40km northeast.

06 Mount Kaputar National Park

One of New England's most spectacular corners, **Sawn Rocks** *(nationalparks.nsw.gov.au/visit-a-park/parks/mount-kaputar-national-park)*, a pipe-organ formation about 40km northeast of Narrabri (20km unsealed but fine in a 2WD vehicle), is the most accessible and popular part of Mt Kaputar National Park. The southern part of the park has dramatic lookouts, climbing, bushwalking and camping, but it's the organ pipes that most people come here to see.

THE DRIVE: Return to Narrabri, then take the quiet, quiet road running northeast 108km to interesting little Bingara.

07 Bingara

A charming little town by the swift-flowing Gwydir River, Bingara is horse country, and a great place to swap four wheels for four hooves on a trail ride through lush pastures and low forested hills.

In town, don't miss the **Roxy Theatre Greek Museum** *(roxybingara.com.au)*, an art-deco theatre, cafe and museum.

If you need to overnight, the **River House** *(theriverhousebingara.com.au)* is a friendly, well-appointed B&B, while the **Imperial Hotel** *(imperialhotelbingara.com.au)* does classic Aussie pub food. Outside of town, the **Myall Creek Memorial**, on the site where convict stockmen massacred at least 30 Wirrayaraa people in 1838, is a sobering reminder of the often-brutal meeting of Aboriginal and European Australia.

> PHOTO OPPORTUNITY
>
> ### MOUNT KAPUTAR NATIONAL PARK
>
> Mount Kaputar National Park has New England's most dramatic land formations.

THE DRIVE: Bingara to Glen Innes is a 136km drive along the Gwydir Hwy and is one of the least-interesting sections of the route – drive right on through. Later the road bucks and weaves up and over the forested hillsides of the Great Dividing Range, passing tempting national parks en route to Grafton.

08 Grafton

On the flat coastal plain but without the ocean frontage, Grafton's appeal is not immediately obvious. But it's a grand old place once you take a second look. Its grid of gracious streets are adorned with imposing old pubs and some splendid historic houses. In late October the town is awash with the soft lilac rain of jacaranda flowers – a simply wonderful sight – and for two weeks from late October, Australia's longest-running floral festival, the **Jacaranda Festival** *(jacafest.com)*, paints the town a lovely shade of mauve. **Susan Island**, in the middle of the river, is home to a large colony of fruit bats; their evening fly-past is pretty impressive. **The Fitzroy Hotel** *(fitzroymotel.com.au)* is a decent, if unremarkable, place to bed down for the night.

THE DRIVE: The delta between Grafton and the coast is a patchwork of farmland in which the now-sinuous, spreading Clarence River forms more than 100 islands, some very large. Follow the Big River Way northeast to the M1, then drop down to the coast by following the signs into Yamba.

09 Ulmarra

Ulmarra (population 418) is a heritage-listed town with a river port that few travellers know about. Its name comes from an old Aboriginal word that means 'bend in the river' and there's a lazy, subtropical feel to this enchanted little place. The **Ulmarra Hotel** *(ulmarrahotel.com.au)* is a quaint old corner pub with a wrought-iron verandah and a greener-than-green beer garden that stretches down to the river – the perfect place to slow down to the decidedly laid-back Ulmarra pace of life.

10 Yamba & Angourie

Yamba draws creative types and sunseekers to its great beaches and tasty choice of dining spots. Surfing is the draw at nearby Angourie, 5km to the south, a relaxed place that was designated as one of the country's first surfing reserves. Choose whichever of the two appeals, use it as a base to explore the beaches, nature reserves and coastal walking trails in the area and then sit back to rest from the long and winding New England road.

10

NEW SOUTH WALES & THE AUSTRALIAN CAPITAL TERRITORY

OUTBACK NEW SOUTH WALES

★ BEST FOR:

WINE

Mudgee is one of the state's best wine regions.

Bathurst Courthouse

DURATION: 10–14 DAYS

DISTANCE: 2405KM / 1494 MILES

GREAT FOR: NATURE, HISTORY & WINE

BEST TIME TO GO: APRIL TO OCTOBER HAS COLD NIGHTS, BUT IT'S BETTER THAN THE SEARING SUMMER WEATHER.

You've heard about the outback. The only way to get there is via long and empty roads that pass through fascinating, isolated communities whose very names – Bourke, Wilcannia and Broken Hill – carry a whiff of outback legend. Before heading for the 'Back of Bourke', however, take time to sample the culinary and architectural treasures of civilisation in Bathurst, Mudgee and Gulgong.

LINK YOUR TRIP

06 Sydney to Byron Bay
It's 196km from Bathurst to Sydney to start this coastal odyssey, a mere blip on your speedo compared to outback distances.

16 Along the Murray
Although Mungo National Park is actually closer to Mildura, the 299km paved road (Silver City Hwy) connects Mildura with Broken Hill.

01 Bathurst

Australia's oldest inland settlement, Bathurst has historical references strewn across its centre, especially in the beautiful, manicured central square where formidable Victorian buildings transport you to the past; the most impressive of these is the 1880 **Courthouse**, and don't miss the utterly fascinating **Australian Fossil and Mineral Museum** *(museumsbathurst.com.au/afmm)* complete with Australia's only complete skeleton cast of Tyrannosaurus rex. But this is no static open-air architectural museum – Bathurst displays a Sydney sensibility when it comes to enjoying good food and wines. Step back in time in **Annie's Old Fashioned Ice-Cream Parlour** *(facebook.com/anniesbathurst)* for a refreshing break in a kitsch 1950s setting.

In a dramatic change of pace, Bathurst is also the bastion of Australian motorsport: if you're a

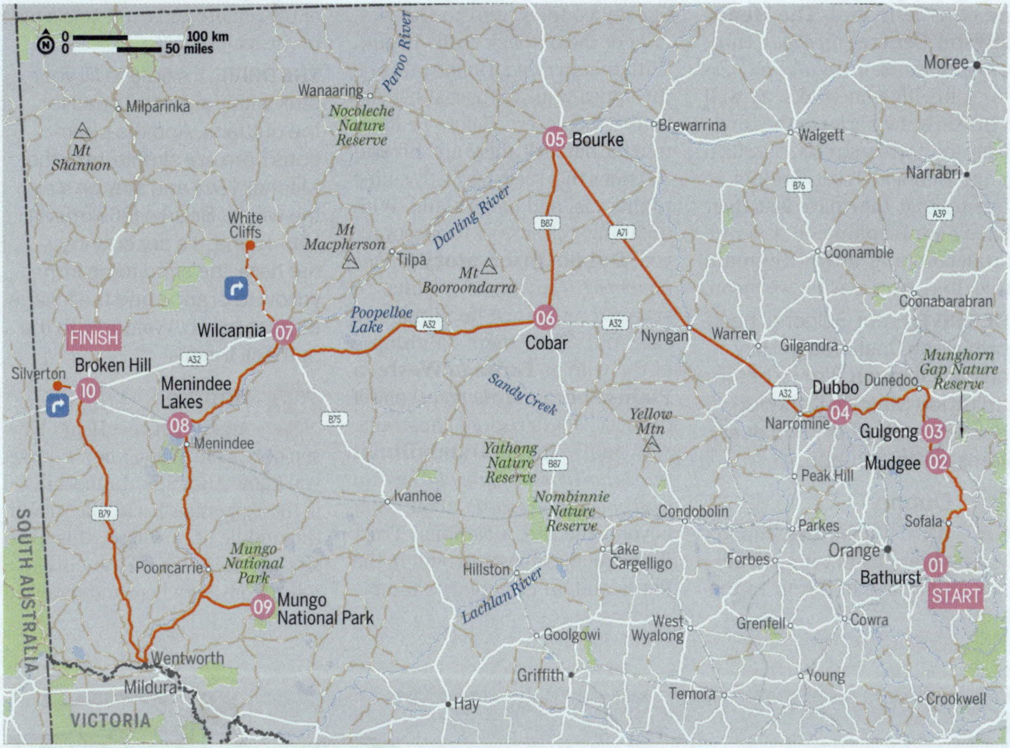

HARLEY KINGSTON/SHUTTERSTOCK

devotee, head to the **Mt Panorama Motor Racing Circuit**, home to the epic Bathurst 1000 V8 race each October, as well as the **National Motor Racing Museum** *(nmrm.com.au)*.

THE DRIVE: Follow the signs towards Lithgow from Bathurst city centre, then take the turnoff for Sofala, before joining the main road to Mudgee (130km from Bathurst).

02 Mudgee

Mudgee is a Wiradjuri word for 'nest in the hills', a fitting name for this pretty town surrounded by vineyards and rolling hills. The wineries come hand-in-hand with excellent food, making Mudgee a popular getaway. Weekends have a buzzy vibe with plenty of people about, while midweek visits have a more relaxed atmosphere. Mudgee's 35 cellar doors are primarily clustered northeast of town – check out *mudgeewine.com.au* for further details. If wine is why you're here, consider taking a guided excursion with **Mudgee Tourist Bus** *(mudgeetouristbus.com.au)*. And stop by Mudgee's best (NSW's oldest) wine bar, **Roth's** *(rothswinebar.com.au)*. Consider dropping everything to be here in September for the two-week **Mudgee Food + Wine Month**. If you're visiting the wineries under your own steam, begin with **Lowe Family Wine Co** *(lowefamilywineco.com.au)* and **Robert Stein Winery & Vineyard** *(robertstein.com.au)*.

THE DRIVE: On the main Ulan road, around 29km after leaving Mudgee, follow the signs for Gulgong, which lies 24km away through rolling valleys.

03 Gulgong

To catch a glimpse of a small, rural, timbered Australian country town as it once was, there's nowhere better than Gulgong. And it's not just us who think so – this sweet, time-warped town once featured alongside author Henry Lawson on the $10 note. Australia's most famous poet, Lawson spent part of his childhood in Gulgong and, suitably, the town celebrates a **Henry Lawson Heritage Festival** during the June long weekend, with concerts at the opera house and other festivities. **The Henry Lawson Centre** *(facebook.com/henrylawsoncentregulgong)* explores his life and works, as well as his early memories of the town. Today the narrow streets, classified by the National Trust, are not so done up that they have lost their charm: we recommend a gentle wander up and down the main street to really see what we mean.

THE DRIVE: From Gulgong, head north along Castlereagh Hwy and pass through Birriwa before turning left (west) at Dunedoo. From there, it's 87 dry and dusty kilometres into Dubbo.

04 Dubbo

It's at Dubbo that you get the first hint of what lies ahead – there's a dryness in the air in this big-sky country, and to the west of here the outback really begins. With that in mind, Dubbo takes on the appearance of the last big city before the desert. Before heading into the outback, there are three attractions that seem perfectly suited to this vast and barren land. With unfailingly clear skies to encourage you, **Dubbo Observatory** *(dubboobservatory.com)* is a place to stargaze; advance bookings are essential. Then there's a glimpse of the wild at **Taronga Western Plains Zoo** *(taronga.org.au)*, one of the best zoos in regional Australia. And finally, there's **Dundullimal** *(nationaltrust.org.au/places/dundullimal-homestead)*, about 2km beyond the zoo, a National Trust timber-slab homestead built in the 1840s and an exemplary example of the remote and rural homestead of Australian lore.

THE DRIVE: It's time to fill your tank with petrol and head for the outback. And the directions here are simple: take the Mitchell Hwy and stay on it all the way to Bourke (369km) via Narromine. It's dry country out here: the sand turns from yellow to orange and the foliage turns to scrub. Welcome to the outback fringe.

05 Bourke

Australian poet Henry Lawson once said, 'If you know Bourke, you know Australia.' Immortalised in the expression 'back of Bourke' (in the middle of nowhere), this town sits on the edge of the outback, miles from anywhere and sprawled

Wilcannia

DARKYDOORS/SHUTTERSTOCK

along the Darling River. The **Back O' Bourke Exhibition Centre** *(visitbourke.com.au)* is an excellent space that follows the legends of the back country (both Aboriginal and settler) through interactive displays – ask about its packages that include a river cruise on the **PV Jandra** and an entertaining outback show (note that the cruise and show operate April to October only). Another option for local knowledge is a walking tour with the **Bourke Aboriginal Art Gallery** *(mgnsw.org.au/organisations/bourke-aboriginal-art-gallery)*, where you can yarn with local artists as they work. Finally, **Bourke's Historic Cemetery** (Kidman Way) is peppered with epitaphs like 'perished in the bush'; Professor Fred Hollows, the renowned eye surgeon, is buried here. If you're keen to explore on your own, ask for the leaflet called *Back O'Bourke Mud Map Tours.*

THE DRIVE: The B87, lined with dull eucalyptus greens and scrubby horizons, runs due south of Bourke for 160km with not a single town to speak of en route. Time to fire up some good music or an interesting podcast or audio book.

06 Cobar

Out here, a town doesn't need to have much to have you dreaming of arriving. It might be just a petrol station, but occasionally a place has a little more to detain you. And on this score, Cobar fits the bill perfectly. It's a bustling mining town with a productive copper mine, and as something of a regional centre, it even has a handful of interesting buildings – true to old colonial form, these include the **old courthouse** and **police station**. And even if you're not the museum type, don't miss the **Great Cobar Museum**: it has sophisticated displays on the environment, local Aboriginal life and the early Europeans. Watch for the Big Beer Can, Cobar's contribution to that strange provincial Australian need to erect oversized and decidedly kitsch monuments to prosaic icons of Aussie life.

THE DRIVE: It's not quite the 90 Mile Straight (Australia's straightest road), but the Barrier Hwy is very long and very straight, all 250km of it into Wilcannia. Long straw-coloured paddocks line the roadside until, all of a sudden, you're crossing the Darling River and its tree-lined riverbanks at the entrance to town.

07 Wilcannia

The majority-Aboriginal community is among the state's most disadvantaged. With this in mind, it shouldn't come as a surprise that **Wilcannia** *(wilcanniatourism.com.au)* doesn't get a lot of love from travellers. But it can be a fascinating, if complicated, place. A good cafe and a shady riverside caravan park make it a worthwhile overnight stop if you're camping. The local motel is forgettable.

THE DRIVE: Double back along the Barrier Hwy for 8km, then turn onto the Wilcannia-Menindee Rd and follow it alongside the Darling River for 144km to Menindee Lakes. This unsealed road is suitable for 2WD vehicles (if it hasn't rained recently), but take care.

DETOUR

White Cliffs

Start: 07 Wilcannia

There are few stranger places in Australia than the tiny pockmarked opal-mining town of **White Cliffs** *(whitecliffsnsw.com.au)*, 93km northwest of Wilcannia along the sealed Opal Miners Way. Surrounded by pretty hostile country and enduring

BATHURST TO MUDGEE DETOURS

The region north of Bathurst is good driving territory, with beautiful scenery, parks and reserves and a handful of quaint little towns. An easy drive through increasingly rolling country dips down into a valley 43km northeast of Bathurst. Just before crossing the bridge, detour along the charming, ramshackle main street of **Sofala**, a pretty hangover from the region's gold-mining days – it's such a perfect evocation of a semi-abandoned mining village that you'll wonder whether it's custom made. From Sofala continue for 28km to Ilford, where you join the main Lithgow–Mudgee road. As you head northwest, you'll pass pretty Lake Windamere before reaching Mudgee. Ignore the town's untidy outskirts and head for the centre, taking Church St, which becomes Ulan Rd, which in turn heads northwest of town past some of the best wineries. Some 11km out of Mudgee, consider a detour to the **Munghorn Gap Nature Reserve**, where there's the popular 8km-return Castle Rock walking trail; the reserve is home to the endangered regent honeyeater.

temperatures that soar well past 40°C in summer, many residents have moved underground, Coober Pedy–style, to escape the heat. You can visit opal showrooms where local miners sell their finds (these are well signed), or try fossicking around the old diggings, where you'll see interpretative signs. Watch your step, as many of the shafts are open and unsigned. If you can't face the long haul back to civilisation, you can stay underground at the **White Cliffs Underground Motel** *(undergroundmotel.com.au)* – custom-built with a tunnelling machine. It has a pool, a lively dining room and simple, cool, silent rooms. There's also good food and motel-style accommodation at the **White Cliffs Hotel** *(whitecliffshotel.com.au)*.

08 Menindee Lakes

The combined impact of drought and poor water management in recent decades severely impacted the size and depth of the nine natural, ephemeral lakes fanning out from the ramshackle town of Menindee. Once-thriving birdlife was severely reduced and the lakes' stocks of native fish like Murray cod were decimated following algal blooms in 2019. Major floods in recent years have seen water levels (and birdlife) recover somewhat, and state-of-the-art fishway technology is being used to help boost fish stocks. Stop in at the **Menindee Visitor Information Centre** *(the darlingriverrun.com.au/directory/menindee-visitor-information-centre)* in town to get the latest information on the area's environmental challenges.

THE DRIVE: Unless it has been raining, which is rare out here, take the unsealed gravel-and-sand road that heads south from Menindee for around 120km, then follow the signs east for 41km into Mungo National Park. This is dry, barren country, deliciously remote and filled with sparse desert flora and fauna.

09 Mungo National Park

One of Australia's most soulful places, this isolated, beautiful and important park covers 278.5 sq km of the Willandra Lakes Region World Heritage Area. It is one of Australia's most accessible slices of the true outback, where big red kangaroos and emus graze the plains and unimpeded winds carve the land into the strangest shapes. Lake Mungo is a dry lake and site of the oldest archaeological finds in Australia. It also embodies the longest continual record of Aboriginal life (the world's oldest recorded cremation site has been found here), dating back around 40,000 years, making the history of European settlement on this continent seem like the mere blink of an eye. The area is the traditional homeland of the Barkandji/Paakantyi, Ngyiampaa and Mutthi Mutthi peoples, and in late 2018 the remains of 105 tribal ancestors – including that of 40,000-year-old 'Mungo Man' – were returned to the park. The undoubted highlight here, aside from the blissful sense of utter remoteness, is the fabulous 33km semicircle ('lunette') of sand dunes known as **Walls of China**, created by the unceasing westerly wind. From the visitor centre, a road leads across the dry lakebed to a car park, then it's a short walk to the viewing platform. For more information on the park, visit *nationalparks.nsw.gov.au/visit-a-park/parks/mungo-national-park*.

> PHOTO OPPORTUNITY
>
> **WALLS OF CHINA**
>
> Walls of China in Mungo National Park is one of NSW's more weird-and-wonderful landforms.

THE DRIVE: Instead of retracing your route from Menindee, take the unsealed Arumpo Rd for 105km to the sealed Silver City Hwy, from where it's 294km to Broken Hill.

10 Broken Hill

The massive silver skimp dump that forms a backdrop for Broken Hill's town centre accentuates the unique character of this desert frontier town somewhere close to the end of the earth. Broken Hill's unique historic value was recognised in 2015, when it became the first Australian city to be included on the National Heritage List. It joins 125 other sites (including the Sydney Opera House and the Great Barrier Reef) as examples of exceptional places that contribute to the national identity.

One of Broken Hill's most memorable experiences is viewing the sunset from the **Living Desert Sculpture Symposium** on the highest hilltop 12km from town. The sculptures are the work of 12 international artists who carved the huge sandstone blocks on-site. Other highlights include: the **Palace Hotel** *(thepalace hotelbrokenhill.com.au)*, the astonishing star of the hit Australian movie *The Adventures of Priscilla, Queen of the Desert*; the **Line of Lode Miners Memorial**, with its poignant stories and memorable

NICK FOX/SHUTTERSTOCK

Walls of China, Mungo National Park

views; the **Pro Hart Gallery** *(prohart.com.au)*; and the **Royal Flying Doctor Service Museum** *(flyingdoctor.org.au)*. After dark, experience the outback's pristine night sky with **Outback Astronomy** *(outbackastronomy.com.au)*.

DETOUR

Silverton

Start: 10 Broken Hill

If you think Broken Hill is remote, try visiting quirky Silverton, an old silver-mining town and now almost a ghost town. Visiting is like walking into a Russell Drysdale painting. Silverton's fortunes peaked in 1885, when it had a population of 3000, but in 1889 the mines closed and the people (and some houses) moved to Broken Hill. It stirs into life every now and then – Silverton is the setting of films such as *Mad Max II* and *A Town Like Alice*. The town's heart and soul is the **Silverton Hotel** *(silvertonhotel.com.au)*, which displays film memorabilia and walls covered with miscellany typifying Australia's peculiar brand of larrikin humour. The 1889 **Silverton Gaol** once housed 14 cells; today the museum is a treasure trove in which room after room is crammed full of a century of local life (wedding dresses, typewriters, mining equipment, photos). The **School Museum** is another history pit stop, tracing the local school from its earliest incarnation, in a tent in 1884. Considerably more offbeat is the **Mad Max 2 Museum** *(facebook.com/MadMaxMuseum)*, the culmination of Englishman Adrian Bennett's lifetime obsession with the film.

Take the A32 out of town where the Silverton road branches off to the northwest – it's 25km from Broken Hill to Silverton. The road beyond Silverton becomes isolated and the horizons vast, but it's worth driving 5km to **Mundi Mundi Lookout** where the view over the plain is so extensive that it reveals the curvature of Earth.

NEW SOUTH WALES
VICTORIA
SOUTH AUSTRALIA
AUSTRALIAN CAPITAL TERRITORY
CANBERRA
Melbourne
Mildura
Wentworth
Hattah
Ouyen
Manangatang
Swan Hill
Kerang
Echuca
Deniliquin
Hay
Narrandera
Wagga Wagga
Gundagai
Yass
Cooma
Bega
Batemans Bay
Mallacoota
Genoa
Cann River
Orbost
Lakes Entrance
Bairnsdale
Sale
Dargo
Omeo
Bright
Beechworth
Wodonga
Albury
Corryong
Yarrawonga
Cobram
Wangaratta
Glenrowan
Shepparton
Seymour
Yea
Eildon
Healesville
Walhalla
Morwell
Leongatha
Tidal River
Sorrento
Torquay
Geelong
Lorne
Apollo Bay
Colac
Port Campbell
Warrnambool
Port Fairy
Portland
Nelson
Mount Gambier
Hamilton
Dunkeld
Lake Bolac
Mortlake
Ballarat
Daylesford
Macedon
Kyneton
Castlemaine
Bendigo
Elmore
Avoca
Ararat
Stawell
Halls Gap
St Arnaud
Charlton
Warracknabeal
Dimboola
Horsham
Nhill
Edenhope
Naracoorte
Linga
Lachlan River
Murrumbidgee River
Murray River
Snowy River
Lake Hindmarsh
Port Phillip
Phillip Island
Bass Strait
King Island
Flinders Island
Hattah-Kulkyne National Park
Murray-Sunset National Park
Wyperfeld National Park
Big Desert National Park
Little Desert National Park
Mt Arapiles
Grampians National Park
Great Otway National Park
Barmah National Park
Alpine National Park
Mt Hotham (1868m)
Mt Buller (1805m)
Snowy River National Park
Mt Kosciuszko (2228m)
Snowy Mountains
Kosciuszko National Park
Wilsons Promontory National Park
11
12
13
14
15
16
A20
A79
B400
B220
B12
20
75
39
58
31
23
1
B23
A1
M39
M31
C543
B500
A300
B75
M79
M8
A200
A8
B240
C240
B160
A300
M1
B100
B440
0
200 km
0
100 miles

PINKCANDY / SHUTTERSTOCK

Great Alpine Road (p122)

VICTORIA

EXPLORE

VICTORIA

Victoria may not typically get the plaudits that its neighbour to the north, New South Wales, receives, but therein lies a large part of its charm. It all begins in marvellous Melbourne, a mature city that rewards those who value the finer things in life. It's also just the starting point for so many easy adventures to first-class attractions. These include the wildlife of Wilsons Prom, the glorious little mining town of Walhalla, the Great Ocean Road, gold-laden historic towns and a river where paddle-steamer boats still draw crowds.

Melbourne

If you want a brash, showy experience that immediately catches the eye, you may be looking for Sydney. But for the kind of city you'll fall in love with and never want to leave, Melbourne is your place. The Victorian capital is an artsy city filled with galleries, museums, sports stadiums and parks, as well as a cafe culture known the world over. Excellent roads radiate out from here to all corners of the state.

Ballarat

A couple of hours west of Melbourne, Ballarat is distinguished by a storied past that lives on in its grand main-street facades and some first-rate attractions tied to the town's mining past. It's also something of a crossroads for the western half of the state, with roads reaching south to the coast, north towards the Murray River and a looping trail between the goldfield towns on which Victoria's prosperity was built.

Echuca

Echuca is one of Victoria's loveliest towns. Its pretty main street nicely complements the historic Murray River frontage where paddle steamers, houseboats and pleasure craft share the waters of what was once an important inland port. Handy for much of Victoria's north, and a

WHEN TO GO

Most Victorian routes are best from November to March. Fine weather in the state is never guaranteed, but these summer months offer your best chance of beach weather. In the goldfields, winters can be bitterly cold by Australian standards, but autumn can be ideal, especially around the Macedon Ranges. Spring (September to November) and autumn (March to May) are best along the Murray.

natural starting point (it's connected to Melbourne by train and good roads) for journeys up and down the river, it's a fine town in which to spend some time. It has great eating and sleeping options, too.

Bairnsdale

Bairnsdale wouldn't win a beauty contest, but it does stand at the intersection between roads to/from the High Country and those along the coast – you'll probably pass through here a few times as you explore Victoria's east. It's a good place to refuel, learn a little about local First Nations history and break up the journey (though the nearby coastal towns such as Lakes Entrance and Metung generally have nicer accommodation).

Lorne

Blessed with a scenic location along the Great Ocean Road and wildly popular in summer when traffic jams rival those in peak-hour Melbourne, Lorne is a Victorian coastal icon. At once a destination where you can eat, sleep and drink well and with considerable choice, Lorne is also a crossroads between the main coastal route and other, smaller roads that wind up into the forested hills of the coastal hinterland. In this sense, it's the perfect hub town, no matter how long you stay.

TRANSPORT

Melbourne is easily the state's most convenient gateway: the city rivals Sydney for excellent international and domestic air connections. Buses tend to cover a greater part of the state than trains, but the V/Line rail network does link Melbourne to Bairnsdale, Ballarat, Warrnambool, Echuca and Albury (and beyond to Yass (for Canberra) and Sydney).

RESOURCES

Parks Victoria
The state's national parks, with hiking maps, bookings for in-demand campsites such as Wilsons Prom, and more. *parks.vic.gov.au*

Visit Melbourne
The best the city has to offer, but also covering the goldfields and other destinations within reach of the city. *visitmelbourne.com*

Visit Victoria
Victoria's attractions in one place, with a good mix of practical information and inspiration. *visitvictoria.com*

WHAT'S ON

Riverboats Music Festival
Australia's best rock, blues and roots bands head to Echuca for music, food and wine in February. *riverboatsmusic.com.au*

Melbourne Food & Wine Festival
March draws food lovers to Melbourne for this celebration of the city's world-class food and wine scene. *melbournefoodandwine.com.au*

Bendigo Easter Festival
Multicultural festival of fireworks and Chinese dragons. *bendigoeasterfestival.org.au*

WHERE TO STAY

Melbourne has excellent hotels across all budgets, with the largest concentration in the city centre. The neighbouring regions of the Mornington Peninsula and the Great Ocean Road are also particularly well-served, thanks to their summer role as holiday destinations for people from Melbourne – there are resorts and B&Bs to supplement the usual proliferation of motels. For accommodation with character and a nod to the past (B&Bs, historic pubs and the like), the goldfields region has the widest collection of options. As always in Australia, national park and other campgrounds are popular and often scenically located.

11

VICTORIA

GREAT OCEAN ROAD

★ BEST FOR:

WILDLIFE

Koalas at Cape Otway, seals at Cape Bridgewater, kangaroos at Anglesea, a bit of everything at Tower Hill and whales off Warrnambool.

DURATION: 5–7 DAYS

DISTANCE: 535KM / 332 MILES

GREAT FOR: NATURE

BEST TIME TO GO: YEAR-ROUND, BUT OCTOBER TO MARCH HAS THE BEST WEATHER.

Surfer, Bells Beach

The Great Ocean Road begins in Australia's surf capital of Torquay, swings past Bells Beach and then winds along the coast to the wild and windswept koala haven of Cape Otway. The Twelve Apostles and Loch Ard Gorge are obligatory stops before the road sweeps on towards Warrnambool, with its whales, and Port Fairy, with its fine buildings and folk festival, before the natural drama peaks again close to the South Australian border.

LINK YOUR TRIP

02 Sydney to Melbourne
From Melbourne take the Princes Hwy (A1) towards Geelong, then follow the signs to Torquay.

14 Victoria's Goldfields
From where the goldfields trip ends in Ballarat it's an 87km drive down the Midland Hwy to the Geelong bypass, and then around 30km to Torquay.

01 Torquay

The undisputed surfing capital of Australia is a brilliant place to start your journey. The town's proximity to world-famous Bells Beach and its status as the home of two iconic surf brands – Rip Curl and Quiksilver – have assured Torquay's place at the pinnacle of mainstream surf culture. Its beaches lure everyone from kids in floaties to backpacker surf-school pupils. **Fisherman's Beach**, protected from ocean swells, is the family favourite. Ringed by shady pines and sloping lawns, **Front Beach** beckons lazy bums, while surf lifesavers patrol the frothing **Back Beach** during summer. Famous surf beaches include nearby **Jan Juc** and **Winki Pop**. Visit the **Surf World Museum** *(australiannationalsurfingmuseum.com.au)*, home to Australia's Surfing Hall of Fame, then start working on your legend by taking

FILEDIMAGE/SHUTTERSTOCK

lessons with **Sea Earth Adventures** *(seaearthadventures.com.au)* or **Torquay Surf Academy** *(torquaysurf.com.au)*.

THE DRIVE: Pass the turnoff to Jan Juc, then take the next left (C132) and follow the signs to Bells Beach.

02 Bells Beach

A slight detour off the Great Ocean Road takes you to famous **Bells Beach**, the powerful point break that's part of international surfing folklore (it was here, albeit in name only, that Keanu Reeves and Patrick Swayze had their ultimate showdown in the film *Point Break*). When the right-hander is working, it's one of the longest rides in the country. If you're here just to look, park in the car park and head for the lookout, from where stairs lead down to the beach (not for swimming).

THE DRIVE: Return to the Great Ocean Road (B100), and soon after consider taking the turnoff to spectacular Point Addis, a vast sweep of pristine beach. Anglesea is a further 10km down the Great Ocean Road, with forested national park lining the road as you descend into town.

03 Anglesea

Mix sheer orange cliffs falling into the ocean with hilly, tree-filled 'burbs and a population that booms in summer and you've got Anglesea, where sharing fish and chips with seagulls by the Anglesea River is a decades-long family tradition for many. **Main Beach** is good for surfers, while sheltered **Point Roadknight Beach** is made for families.

In addition to such quintessentially Australian summer pastimes, Anglesea is famous for those seeking to spy their first kangaroo – at **Anglesea Golf Club** *(angleseagolfclub.com.au)* you can watch them graze on the fairways.

THE DRIVE: The B100 follows the coast for 11km to Aireys Inlet, with its historic lighthouse, and to Fairhaven for wonderful beaches. From Aireys it's 18km of glorious coast-hugging road into Lorne – stop for photos at the Great Ocean Road memorial archway in Eastern View.

EASTVILLAGE IMAGES/SHUTTERSTOCK

Gog and Magog

PHOTO OPPORTUNITY

The Twelve Apostles are one of Australia's most spectacular sights.

04 Lorne

There's something about Lorne. For a start, this is a place of incredible natural beauty, something you see vividly as you drive into town from Aireys Inlet: tall old gum trees line its hilly streets, and Louttit Bay gleams irresistibly. Kids will love **Live Wire Park** *(livewire park.com.au)* and the beachside swimming pool and trampolines, and there's more than 50km of bush-walking tracks around the town. Up in the hilly hinterland, seek out lovely **Erskine Falls**; it's an easy walk to the viewing platform, or 250 (often slippery) steps down to its base. Back in town, the **Great Ocean Road Story** recounts the history of the road's construction.

THE DRIVE: Although the winding nature of the road makes it feel longer – by now you know the deal: dense forests to your right, uninterrupted sea views to your left – it's just 20km from Lorne to Kennett River.

DETOUR

Brae at Birregurra
Start: 04 Lorne

Dan Hunter is one of Australia's most celebrated chefs and these days his restaurant **Brae** *(brae restaurant.com)* – a regular in the World's Best 100 Restaurants list – is synonymous with Birregurra, the tiny historic township where it's located. The restaurant uses whatever is growing in its 12 hectares of organic gardens to create its highly innovative, ever-changing degustation menu, where Aboriginal ingredients feature prominently. Reservations well in advance are essential. It also has stylish, informal luxury accommodation on-site. Brae is a 36km drive from Lorne on the way to Colac.

05 Kennett River

Kennett River is one of the easiest places in Australia to see koalas (although they have headed up into the surrounding forest a little more in recent years). In the trees immediately west of the general store and around the excellent caravan park, koalas pose (well, they're often asleep) in the tree forks, sometimes at eye level. Local parrots and lorikeets are also known to swoop down and perch on heads and outstretched arms if you stay still enough – but it's important that you don't feed them.

THE DRIVE: The road could hardly get closer to the coast for the 21km from Kennett River into Apollo Bay.

06 Apollo Bay

At Apollo Bay, one of the Great Ocean Road's largest towns, rolling hills provide a postcard backdrop, while broad, white-sand beaches dominate the foreground. Local boy Mark Brack, son of the Cape Otway lighthouse keeper, knows this stretch of coast better than anyone around – both of his **walking tours** *(greatoceanwalk.asn.au/marks-tours)* are outstanding. Another worthwhile excursion is the **Apollo Bay Surf & Kayak** *(apollobaysurfkayak.com.au)* expedition out to an Australian fur-seal colony in a double kayak.

THE DRIVE: The turnoff for Cape Otway (Lighthouse Rd), which leads 12km down to the lighthouse, is 20km from Apollo Bay. That 12km stretch is through dense, scenic rainforest pretty much all the way.

07 Cape Otway

Cape Otway is the second-most-southerly point of mainland Australia (after Wilsons Promontory), and this coastline is particularly beautiful and rugged – and historically treacherous for passing ships, despite the best efforts of the **Cape Otway Lightstation** *(lightstation.com)*. The oldest surviving lighthouse on mainland Australia, it was built in 1848 by more than 40 stonemasons without mortar or cement. The forested road leading to Cape Otway is terrific for koala sightings. Where are they? Look for cars parked on the side of the road and tourists peering up into the trees.

THE DRIVE: The road levels out after leaving the Otways and enters narrow, flat, scrubby escarpment that falls away to sheer, 70m-high cliffs along the coast between Princetown and Peterborough – a distinct change of scene. The Twelve Apostles are after Princetown.

08 Twelve Apostles

The most enduring image for most visitors to the Great Ocean Road, the Twelve Apostles jut from the ocean in spectacular fashion. There they stand, as if abandoned to the waves by the retreating headland, all seven of them. Just for the record, there never were 12, and they were called the 'Sow and Piglets' until some bright spark in the 1960s thought they might attract tourists with a more venerable name. The two stacks on the eastern (Otway) side of the viewing platform are not technically Apostles – they're Gog and Magog. And the soft limestone cliffs are dynamic and changeable, suffering constant erosion from the tides: one 70m-high stack collapsed into the sea in July 2005 and the Island Archway lost its archway in June 2009.

The best time to visit is just before sunset, partly to beat the tour buses and also to see little penguins returning ashore.

For the best views, take a chopper tour with **12 Apostles Helicopters** *(12apostleshelicopters.com.au)*.

THE DRIVE: When you can finally tear yourself away, continue northwest along the Great Ocean Road and in no time at all you'll see the signpost to Loch Ard Gorge.

09 Loch Ard Gorge

Loch Ard Gorge is a gorgeous U-shaped canyon of high cliffs, a sandy beach and deep, blue waters. It was here that the Shipwreck Coast's most famous and haunting tale unfolded: the iron-hulled clipper *Loch Ard* foundered off Mutton Bird Island at 4am on the final night of its voyage from England in 1878. Of its 37 crew and 19 passengers, only two survived. Eva Carmichael, a non-swimmer, clung to wreckage and was washed into a gorge where apprentice officer Tom Pearce rescued her. Despite rumours of a romance, they never saw each other again and Eva soon returned to Ireland. Several walks in the area take you down to the cave where the shipwreck survivors took shelter, and also to a cemetery and a rugged beach.

THE DRIVE: It's around 6km along the B100 from Loch Ard Gorge to Port Campbell.

> ♥ WHY I LOVE THIS TRIP
>
> **ANTHONY HAM, WRITER**
>
> 
>
> Whenever I have visitors from overseas, the first place I take them is the Great Ocean Road. What makes it a classic is the winning combination of stunning natural beauty and world-famous attractions lined up along the roadside like a string of pearls – Bells Beach, koalas at Cape Otway, the Twelve Apostles, Loch Ard Gorge – and they're just the beginning.

10 Port Campbell

Strung out around a tiny bay, this laid-back town is the ideal base for the Twelve Apostles and Loch Ard Gorge. It has a lovely, sandy, sheltered beach, one of the few safe places for swimming along this tempestuous coast.

THE DRIVE: There's a feeling of crossing a clifftop plateau on the first stretch out of Port Campbell. After the Bay of Islands, the road turns inland through an agricultural landscape.

11 Warrnambool

Warrnambool means whales, at least between May and September, when the mammals frolic offshore during their migration. Southern right whales (so named due to being the 'right' whales to hunt) are the most common to head to these temperate waters from Antarctica. Undoubtedly the best place to see them is at Warrnambool's **Logan's Beach**

whale-watching platform – they use the waters here as a nursery. Call ahead to the **visitor centre** to check if whales are about, or see *visitwarrnambool.com.au* for the latest sightings. Take the time to visit top-notch **Flagstaff Hill Maritime Village** *(flagstaffhill.com)*, with its shipwreck museum, heritage-listed lighthouses and garrison, and reproduction of a historical Victorian port town. It also has the nightly **Tales of the Shipwreck Coast**, an engaging 70-minute sound-and-laser show telling the *Loch Ard* wreck story.

THE DRIVE: The road – the Princes Hwy (A1), and no longer the Great Ocean Road – loops around to Port Fairy, just 29km from Warrnambool.

DETOUR

Tower Hill Reserve
Start: 11 Warrnambool

A 16km drive from Warrnambool, en route to Port Fairy, is the stunning Tower Hill Reserve, the crater of a dormant volcano that last erupted some 35,000 years ago. It's a significant site for the Aboriginal Worn Gundidj people, who operate the reserve today and offer nature walks where you can learn about their culture. There are some wonderful wildlife encounters, including with emus, koalas, wallabies and kangaroos.

12 Port Fairy

Settled in 1833 as a whaling and sealing station, Port Fairy retains its 19th-century charm, with a relaxed, salty feel, heritage bluestone and sandstone buildings, whitewashed cottages, colourful fishing boats and wide, tree-lined streets; in 2012 it was voted the world's most liveable community.

To guide your steps through the town, pick up a copy of the popular *Maritime & Shipwreck Heritage Walk* from the visitor centre. There's a growing foodie scene here, too, and don't miss **Basalt Wines** *(basaltwines.com.au)*, a family-run biodynamic winery that offers tastings in its shed.

THE DRIVE: The road hugs the coast into Portland (75km) and then the traffic lessens as you leave the main highway and drive northwest along the C192 for 67km into Nelson.

DETOUR

Cape Bridgewater
Start: 12 Port Fairy

Cape Bridgewater is an essential 21km detour off the Portland–Nelson Rd. The stunning 4km arc of **Bridgewater Bay** is perhaps one of Australia's finest stretches of white-sand surf beach. The road continues to **Cape Duquesne**, where walking tracks lead to a spectacular **blowhole** and the eerie **petrified forest** on the clifftop. A longer two-hour return walk takes you to a **seal colony** where you can see dozens of fur seals sunning themselves on the rocks.

13 Nelson

Tiny Nelson is the last settlement before the South Australian border – just a general store, a pub and a handful of accommodation places.

Its appeal lies in its proximity to the mouth of the **Glenelg River**, which flows through **Lower Glenelg National Park**.

Leisurely 3½-hour trips run by **Nelson River Cruises** *(glenelgrivercruises.com.au)* head along the Glenelg and include the impressive **Princess Margaret Rose Cave**, with its gleaming underground formations – along this coastline of towering formations, the ones at journey's end are surely the most surprising.

If you prefer to explore under your own steam, contact **Nelson Boat Hire**.

PORT CAMPBELL TO WARRNAMBOOL

The Great Ocean Road continues west from Port Campbell, passing **London Bridge**, which has indeed fallen down. Now sometimes called London Arch, it was once linked to the mainland by a narrow natural bridge. In January 1990 the bridge collapsed, leaving two terrified tourists marooned on the world's newest island – they were eventually rescued by helicopter.

The **Bay of Islands** is 8km west of tiny **Peterborough**, where a short walk from the car park takes you to magnificent lookout points. The Great Ocean Road officially ends near here, where it meets the Princes Hwy (A1).

Port Fairy
LKONYA/SHUTTERSTOCK

12

★ BEST FOR:

OUTDOORS

Take a sea-kayaking tour to spot dolphins and seals.

VICTORIA

MORNINGTON PENINSULA

DURATION: 3–4 DAYS

DISTANCE: 146KM / 91 MILES

GREAT FOR: WINE

BEST TIME TO GO: OCTOBER TO MARCH; WINTER MONTHS CAN BE COLD AND THE TOWNS EMPTY.

Bathing boxes, Mornington Peninsula

To fully appreciate Melbourne's privileged bayside suburbs, take the long drive south to where the bay meets the ocean, passing the historic seaside towns of Mornington, Sorrento and Portsea en route. This fairly sedate coastline takes on a whole new personality in the wave-lashed Mornington Peninsula National Park, while Flinders is a tranquil haven on Western Port Bay.

LINK YOUR TRIP

11 Great Ocean Road
Take the car ferry from Sorrento to Queenscliff and then head to Torquay, the gateway to Victoria's most famous coastal road.

13 Gippsland & Wilsons Prom
Phillip Island is easily reached from the Mornington Peninsula; take the back road to Koo Wee Rup and down to the island (127km).

01 Mornington

Known for its photogenic bathing boxes and delightful swimming beaches, this suburb just beyond the reaches of Melbourne's urban sprawl is the gateway to the peninsula's holiday coastal strip. Originally part of the lands of the Boonwurrung people, it was founded as a European township in 1854. Echoes of those days remain. Grand old buildings around Main St include the 1892 **Grand Hotel**, the 1860 **Old Court House** on the corner of Main St and the Esplanade, and the 1862 **Police Lock-Up** behind it. On the opposite corner is the 1863 **post office building**. For views over the harbour, take a walk along the 1850s **pier** and around the **Schnapper Point** foreshore boardwalk past the **Matthew Flinders monument** that commemorates his 1802 landing. **Mothers Beach** is the main swimming option, while at **Fossil Beach** there are remains

NORMAN ALLCHIN/SHUTTERSTOCK

of a lime-burning kiln; fossils found here date back 25 million years. And it's at **Mills Beach** where you can see the colourful bathing boxes.

THE DRIVE: From Mornington, the Esplanade heads south on the gorgeous scenic drive towards Sorrento, skirting the rocky Port Phillip Bay foreshore; if you're travelling with kids, be sure to stop for a gelato at Vulcano in Rye en route. Inland, the Nepean Hwy (B110) takes a less scenic route and again becomes the Mornington Peninsula Fwy.

02 Sorrento

Historic Sorrento, the site of Victoria's first official European settlement in 1803, is the prettiest town on the Mornington Peninsula. The town has loads going for it – beautiful limestone buildings, ocean and bay beaches, and a buzzing seaside summer atmosphere – so it should come as no surprise that it has become one of Victoria's most popular resort towns. Some of the grandest old buildings, among them **Sorrento Hotel** (1871), **Continental Hotel** (1875) and **Koonya Hotel** (1878), were built to serve well-to-do 19th-century visitors from Melbourne. These days, its main street is lined with alluring boutiques, cafes and restaurants.

THE DRIVE: The short, 4km hop from Sorrento to Portsea follows the coast – look out for glimpses of the bay on the Portsea approach.

DETOUR

Queenscliff
Start: 02 Sorrento

Historic Queenscliff, across the water from Sorrento on the Bellarine Peninsula, is one of coastal Victoria's loveliest towns. It's a place of heritage streetscapes, the formidable **Fort Queenscliff** *(fortqueenscliff.com.au)* and parkland sweeping down to the beach. From some areas, particularly from the lookout at the southern end of Hesse St (next to the bowling club), the views across Port Phillip Heads and Bass Strait are glorious. And getting here couldn't be easier – the **Queenscliff–Sorrento Ferry** *(searoad.com.au)* crosses the bay in 40 minutes throughout the day.

03 Portsea

If you thought Sorrento was classy, wait until you see Portsea. The last village on the peninsula, it's where many of Melbourne's wealthiest families have built seaside mansions. You can walk the **Farnsworth Track** (1.5km, 30 minutes) out to scenic London Bridge, a natural rock formation, and spot middens of the Boonwurrung people who once called this area home. Diving and sea-kayaking are both possible through **Bayplay** *(bayplay.com.au)*, while **Portsea Surf Beach** is where the sheer power of the ocean never fails to impress. Back in town, Portsea's pulse can be taken at the iconic **Portsea Hotel**, an enormous pub with a sea-facing beer garden.

THE DRIVE: Your next destination, Mornington Peninsula National Park, extends into the Portsea hinterland and there are numerous access points – Portsea Surf Beach, along the back road between Portsea and Rye, at Gunnamatta Beach and, perhaps most memorably, at Cape Schanck.

> PHOTO OPPORTUNITY
>
> **CAPE SCHANCK LIGHTHOUSE**
>
> The view from Cape Schanck Lighthouse.

04 Mornington Peninsula National Park

Stretching from Portsea's sliver of coastline to Cape Schanck and inland to the Greens Bush area, this national park showcases the peninsula's most beautiful and rugged ocean beaches. Along here are the cliffs, bluffs and crashing surf beaches of Portsea, Sorrento, Blairgowrie, Rye, St Andrews, Gunnamatta and Cape Schanck; swimming and surfing are dangerous at these beaches, so swim only between the flags at Gunnamatta and Portsea during the summer patrol season. Built in 1859, **Cape Schanck Lighthouse** is a photogenic working lighthouse; from the lighthouse, descend the steps of the boardwalk that leads to the craggy cape for outstanding views. Longer walks are also possible.

THE DRIVE: From Cape Schanck Lighthouse, return to the C777 and follow it for 11km east along the coast to Flinders. Watch

Cape Schanck Lighthouse

CJSAERIALPHOTOGRAPHY/SHUTTERSTOCK

FILEDIMAGE/SHUTTERSTOCK

Flinders Golf Club

THE GOLF TRAIL

- **The Dunes** *thedunes.com.au*
- **Flinders Golf Club** *flindersgolfclub.com.au*
- **Moonah Links** *moonahlinks.com.au*
- **Portsea Golf Club** *portseagolf.com.au*
- **Cape Schanck** *racv.com.au/travel-experiences/resorts/cape-schanck/golf.html*

for sweeping ocean views, especially in the middle section of the route.

05 Flinders

From Cape Schanck Lighthouse, return to the C777 and follow it for 11km east along the coast to Flinders. Watch for sweeping ocean views, especially in the middle section of the route.

THE DRIVE: Follow the C777 along the Western Port Bay coast northeast to Balnarring. After a further 7km, turn off southeast to Stony Point (7km from the turnoff). Leave your car and take the ferry from Stony Point to French Island's Tankerton Jetty.

06 French Island

Exposed, windswept and wonderfully isolated, French Island is two-thirds national park and retains a real sense of tranquility – you can only get here by passenger ferry, so it's virtually traffic-free. The main attractions are bushwalking and cycling, taking in wetlands, checking out one of Australia's largest koala colonies and observing a huge variety of birds. All roads on the island are unsealed and some are quite sandy. From the jetty it's around 2km to the licensed **French Island General Store** *(figsfrenchisland.com.au)*, which also serves as post office, provider of tourist information and bike-hire centre.

THE DRIVE: Take the ferry back to Stony Point, return the 17km to Shoreham, then cut inland to Red Hill.

07 Red Hill

The undulating hills of the peninsula's interior around Red Hill and Main Ridge is a lovely tree-covered region where you can spend a sublime afternoon visiting winery cellar doors. It can be difficult to choose (and pity the poor designated driver who'll be unable to drink), but we'd pick **Pt. Leo Estate** *(ptleoestate.com.au)*, **Montalto** *(montalto.com.au)*, **Port Phillip Estate** *(portphillipestate.com.au)* and **Ten Minutes by Tractor** *(tenminutesbytractor.com.au)*. If you happen upon Red Hill on the first Saturday of the month (except in winter), the **Red Hill Market** *(craftmarkets.com.au)* is well worth the effort, although its future is uncertain and may need a change of venue; check the website for the latest. Families will enjoy exploring **Ashcombe Maze & Lavender Gardens** *(ashcombemaze.com.au)*. Whenever you're here, allow time to take the 16km round-trip detour to **Arthurs Seat**, which, at 305m, is the highest point on the Port Phillip Bay coast. Jump on the cable car to enjoy views over the bay and territory that you've just explored.

13

★ BEST FOR:

WILDLIFE

Wilsons Prom for wallabies, roos, emus and wombats.

VICTORIA

GIPPSLAND & WILSONS PROM

DURATION: 6-7 DAYS

DISTANCE: 495KM / 308 MILES

GREAT FOR: NATURE & HISTORY

BEST TIME TO GO: OCTOBER TO APRIL, WHEN THE WEATHER IS WARM.

The Nobbies, Phillip Island

Traversing one of Australia's most underrated corners, this journey southeast and east of Melbourne takes in the wildlife and wild landscapes of Phillip Island and Wilsons Prom, and engaging rural towns such as Inverloch, Koonwarra and Port Albert, before almost falling off the map in the ghost town of Walhalla on your way back to Melbourne.

LINK YOUR TRIP

02 Sydney to Melbourne
If you were doing this trip in reverse (ie from Melbourne), you'd miss nothing by driving from Walhalla to Paynesville and starting from there.

12 Mornington Peninsula
The road from Phillip Island to Red Hill (127km) connects you to the end point of the trip around the Mornington Peninsula.

01 Phillip Island

It may cover barely 100 sq km, but Phillip Island sure crams a lot in. For most visitors, the island is synonymous with the nightly arrival of the penguins at the **Penguin Parade** *(penguins.org.au)*, one of Australia's great wildlife spectacles. It doesn't happen until sunset, so wildlife-lovers will want to fill in the afternoon with a visit to **Seal Rocks & the Nobbies**, home to the country's largest colony of fur seals, and the **Koala Conservation Centre** *(penguins.org.au)*. The island's coast is the domain of swimmers and surfers, with world-class breaks at **Woolamai**, **Smiths Beach**, **Summerland Beach** and **Cat Bay**. And just to prove that there's something for everyone, Phillip Island has its **Motorcycle Grand Prix racing circuit** and attached **History of Motorsport Museum** *(phillipislandcircuit.com.au)*.

CHARLESTONDAVID/SHUTTERSTOCK

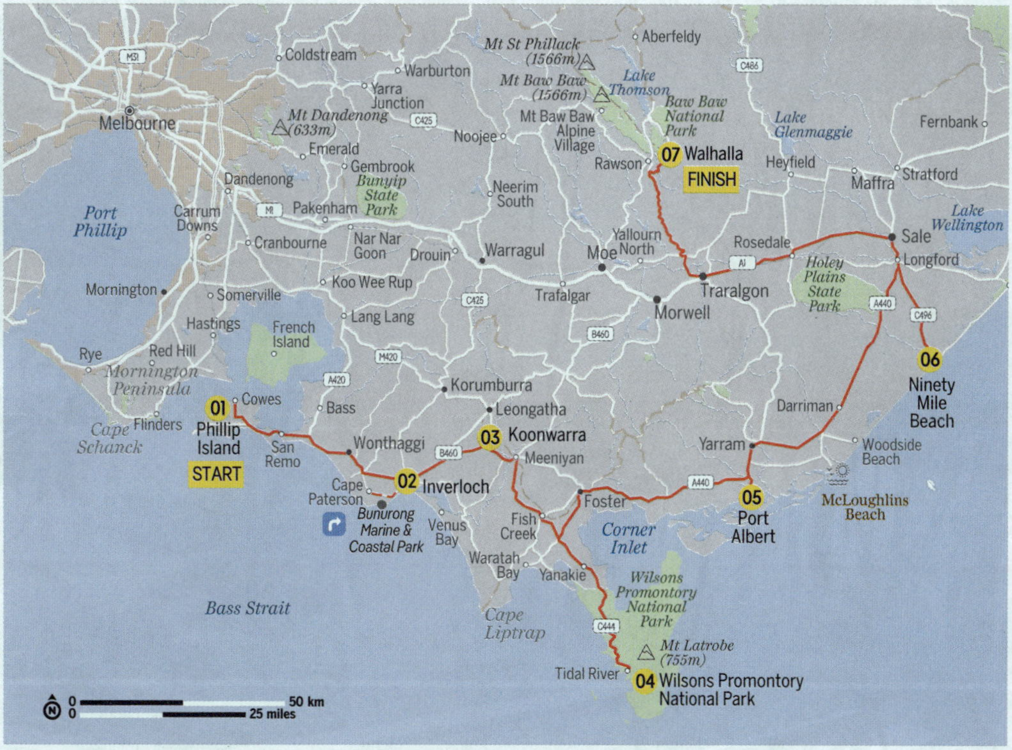

THE DRIVE: Leave the island via the causeway at Newhaven, then cruise along the pancake-flat Bass Hwy (B460), through Wonthaggi, and on to Inverloch, just 50km from where your day's journey began.

02 Inverloch

Inverloch is just far enough off main roads to feel like a secret – most visitors to Phillip Island are day-trippers who never make it this far, while those heading for Wilsons Promontory cross Gippsland further north. And at the heart of this secret locals like to keep to themselves are fabulous surf, calm inlet beaches and outstanding diving and snorkelling; try **Offshore Surf School** *(offshoresurfschool.com.au)* if you feel inspired to learn how to catch a wave. Add in some good eating options and you, too, will soon want to keep the secret all to yourself.

THE DRIVE: You could take the quiet and narrow back roads along the coast to Wilsons Prom, but it's more enjoyable to zip northeast from Inverloch along the B460 for 10km before taking the turnoff to Koonwarra, a further 11km through rolling dairy country away to the northeast.

DETOUR

Bunurong Marine & Coastal Park

Start: 02 Inverloch

The inland route to Inverloch may be singularly lacking in drama, but the same can't be said for the 13km detour southwest to Cape Paterson. This stunning cliff-hugging drive looks out upon the **Bunurong Marine & Coastal Park** which offers some of Australia's best snorkelling and diving – contact **SEAL Diving Services** *(facebook.com/sealdiving services)* to line up gear and guides. If you're going it alone and have the equipment to hand, **Eagles Nest**, **Shack Bay**, the **Caves** and **Twin Reefs** are great for snorkelling. **The Oaks** is the locals' favourite surf beach. The Caves took the archaeological world by storm in the early 1990s when dinosaur remains dating back 120 million years were discovered here; remarkably, you can see a dinosaur footprint at low tide.

03 Koonwarra

Blink and you could very easily miss Koonwarra, tucked away as it is in rolling dairy country along the South Gippsland Hwy. But this is one tiny township worth seeking out, having built itself a reputation as something of a niche foodie destination. Much of the appeal centres on **Milly & Romeo's Artisan Bakery & Cooking School** *(millyandromeos.com.au)*, Victoria's first organic-certified cooking school, which offers short courses in making cakes, bread, traditional pastries, French classics and pasta, and runs cooking classes for kids. But wait, there's more: if you happen upon Koonwarra on the first Saturday morning of the month, the **farmers market** *(facebook.com/producemarket)* will be on, with organic everything (fruit, vegetables, berries, coffee), plus hormone-free beef and chemical-free cheeses. There's even a nearby winery where you can rest your head for the night.

THE DRIVE: From Koonwarra the C444 sweeps down through cafe-studded Meeniyan, artsy Fish Creek and Yanakie, bound for the Prom. The further you go, the wilder the land becomes, and the dramatic forested outcrops of the Prom's headlands soon come into view. As you reach the park, slow down and watch for wildlife and, at regular intervals, fine little trails down to wonderful beaches.

04 Wilsons Promontory National Park

The southernmost tip of mainland Australia, Wilsons Promontory ('The Prom') is a wild and wonderful place. Its dense woodland shelters a rich portfolio of native Australian wildlife and its combination of stirring coastal scenery and secluded white-sand beaches has made it one of the most popular national parks in the country. The **Lilly Pilly Gully Nature Walk**, **Mt Oberon Summit** and **Squeaky Beach Nature Walk** will give you a chance to stretch your legs and get a taste of the Prom's appeal. Even if you don't stray beyond Tidal River (where there's no fuel to be had), you'll catch a sense of the Prom's magic, with car-park access off the Tidal River road leading to gorgeous beaches and lookouts, and tame wildlife everywhere. Swimming is generally safe at the wonderful beaches at **Norman Bay** (Tidal River), but be aware of rips and undertows. Don't miss the beautiful **Squeaky Beach**, too – the ultra-fine quartz sand here really does squeak beneath your feet.

THE DRIVE: Retrace your route northwest back up the C444 for 45km, then turn northeast towards Foster (a further 14km). From Foster, it's 50km to Port Albert along the A440, with a signed turnoff 6km before the town. En route, there are fine Prom views away to the south.

TOP PROM DAY HIKES

Lilly Pilly Gully Nature Walk
An easy 5km (two-hour) walk through heathland and eucalypt forest, with lots of wildlife.

Mt Oberon Summit
Starting from the Telegraph Saddle car park, this moderate-to-hard 7km-return walk is an ideal introduction to the Prom, with panoramic views from the summit.

Little Oberon Bay
A moderate 19km (six-hour) walk over sand dunes covered in coastal tea trees, with beautiful views over Little Oberon Bay.

Squeaky Beach Nature Walk
An easy 5km return stroll (two hours) from Tidal River through coastal tea trees and banksias to a sensational white-sand beach.

Prom Wildlife Walk
In the north of the park, this short 2.3km (45-minute) loop trail yields good kangaroo, wallaby and emu sightings. It's located off the main road about 14km south of the park entrance.

Sealers Cove
This popular 19km hike (six hours return) takes you through pristine forest and along boardwalks that lead to a beautiful sandy cove. There's a campsite here if you want to spend the night.

Lilly Pilly Gully Nature Walk
BOSSA ART/SHUTTERSTOCK

05 Port Albert

Port Albert looks out over serene waters and has developed a reputation as a trendy stopover for boating, fishing and sampling the local seafood, which has been a mainstay of this place for more than 150 years. The town proudly pronounces itself Gippsland's first established port, and the many historic timber buildings in the main street dating from the busy 1850s bear a brass plaque detailing their age and previous use.

THE DRIVE: Return to the A440, pass through Yarram, then wind down the window and breathe in the salty sea air. Around 66km from Yarram, take the C496 turnoff southeast to Seaspray (27km).

06 Ninety Mile Beach

Quiet little Seaspray, a low-key, low-rise seaside village of prefab houses, feels stuck in a 1950s time warp, but the town itself plays second fiddle to what stretches out from its doorstep. To paraphrase the immortal words of Crocodile Dundee – that's not a beach, this is a beach. Isolated Ninety Mile Beach, a narrow strip of dune-backed sand punctuated by lagoons, stretches unbroken for more or less 90 miles (150km) from near McLoughlins Beach to the channel at Lakes Entrance. Stand on the sand and watch the beach unfurl to the northeast while waves curl and crash along its length, and you'll likely be rendered silent by the vast emptiness and sheer beauty of it all.

THE DRIVE: With a last, longing look over your shoulder, steel yourself for the least interesting stretch of the journey, the 127km to Walhalla that goes something like this: take the C496 for 27km, then the A440 for 6km into Sale. From there it's 55 downright dull kilometres to Traralgon, before the final 42km through rich forest to Walhalla.

07 Walhalla

Tiny, charming Walhalla lies hidden high in the green hills and forests of West Gippsland. It's a postcard-pretty collection of sepia-toned period cottages and other timber buildings (some original, most reconstructed). The setting, too, is lovely: the township's strung out along a deep, forested valley, with Stringers Creek running through its centre. In its gold-mining heyday in the 1860s, Walhalla had a population of 5000. That fell to just 10 people in 1998 (when mains electricity arrived in the town); today it's booming at around 20. Like all great ghost towns, the dead – buried in a stunningly sited cemetery – vastly outnumber the living. The best way to see the town is on foot: take the tramline walk (45 minutes), which begins from opposite the general store soon after you enter town. A tour of the **Long Tunnel Extended Gold Mine** *(walhallaboard.org.au)* offers insights into why Walhalla existed at all, while the **Walhalla Goldfields Railway** *(walhallarail.com.au)* is a fine adjunct to your visit, snaking along Stringers Creek Gorge, passing lovely, forested country and crossing a number of trestle bridges en route.

Ninety Mile Beach
EJM1807/SHUTTERSTOCK

PHOTO OPPORTUNITY

Ninety Mile Beach stretching out to eternity.

14

VICTORIA

VICTORIA'S GOLDFIELDS

DURATION: 4–5 DAYS

DISTANCE: 201KM / 125 MILES

GREAT FOR: HISTORY

BEST TIME TO GO: SOUTHERN SECTIONS CAN BE BITTERLY COLD IN WINTER. AUTUMN IS WONDERFUL.

★ BEST FOR:

HISTORY

Ballarat has some monumental gold-rush architecture and a palpable sense of the past.

Hanging Rock

The Macedon Ranges are the perfect place to begin, home to haunting Hanging Rock and some lovely little towns that capture the essence of rural Victoria. From then on, it's stately, historic gold-mining towns all the way to Ballarat, which wears the region's gold-mining heritage like a glittering badge of honour. En route, stop by pretty little Kyneton, arty Castlemaine, time-worn Maryborough and Victoria's premier book town, Clunes.

LINK YOUR TRIP

02 Sydney to Melbourne
Join this epic route in reverse by driving south along the Calder Hwy to Melbourne and then taking the Princes Hwy east.

11 Great Ocean Road
From Macedon take the Calder Hwy south, then the Western Ring Rd to the Princes Hwy to join one of Australia's great road trips.

01 Macedon

Less than an hour northwest of Melbourne, quiet, unassuming Macedon nonetheless seems a world away. It may lack the historical streetscapes of other towns along the route, but its green parklands serve as an agreeable prelude to the Macedon Ranges, a beautiful area of low mountains, native forest, excellent regional produce and wineries. Charming at any time of year, these hills can be enveloped in suggestive clouds in winter but are at their best when bathed in golden autumnal shades. The scenic drive up **Mt Macedon**, a 1010m-high extinct volcano, passes grand mansions and gardens, taking you to picnic areas, walking trails, lookouts and a huge memorial cross near the summit car park. If you're keen to linger, there are some great **wineries** *(visitmacedonranges.com/eat-drink/wineries)* in the area;

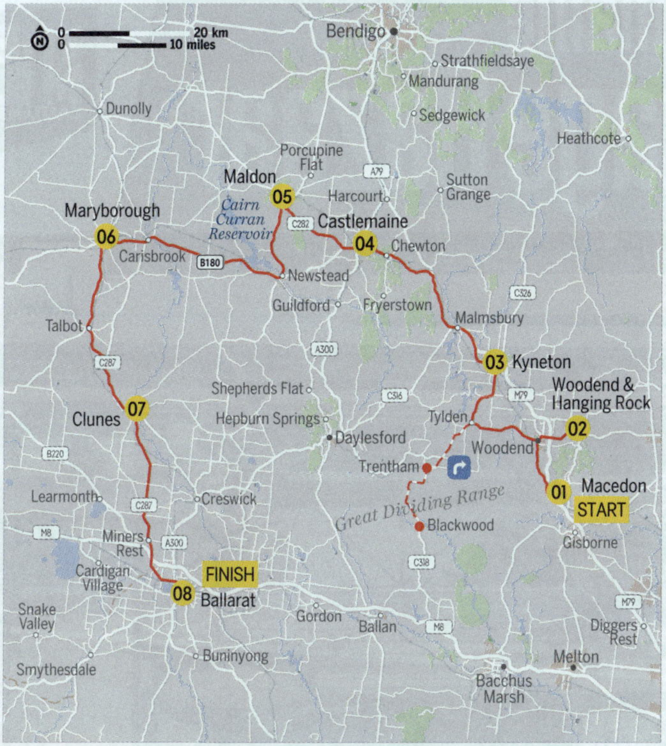

FILEDIMAGE/SHUTTERSTOCK

THE DRIVE: It's only 7km from Macedon north to Woodend, but forsake the Calder Fwy (M79) and take the quieter back road that runs parallel.

02 Woodend & Hanging Rock

Pleasant little Woodend has a certain bucolic appeal – the wide streets, the free-standing clock tower, the smattering of heritage buildings with wide verandahs and wrought-ironwork. But it's the setting that truly beguiles, amid rolling hills and expansive woodlands latticed by vineyards. East of town lies **Hanging Rock**, an ancient and captivating place made famous by the unsettling Joan Lindsay novel (and the subsequent film) *Picnic at Hanging Rock*. The volcanic rock formations are the sacred site of the traditional owners, the Wurundjeri people. They also once served as a hideout for bushrangers, and many mysteries and legends surround them; an eerie energy is said to be felt by many who climb among the boulders. From the summit, a 20-minute climb, splendid views of Mt Macedon and beyond open up. Spreading out below the rock is its famous **racecourse** *(country.racing.com/hanging-rock)*, which hosts two excellent picnic race meetings on New Year's Day and Australia Day, and kangaroos the rest of the time.

THE DRIVE: From Woodend, head west 12km to Tylden, from where the road branches southwest to the Trentham–Blackwood detour or north to Kyneton. Whichever route you choose, it's a pretty drive through farmland and light eucalyptus woodlands.

DETOUR

Trentham & Blackwood
Start: 02 Woodend

The historic township of Trentham (population 764) sits at the top of the Great Dividing Range midway between Woodend and Daylesford. At an elevation of 700m, it's noticeably cooler than the surrounding areas. A stroll of its quaint streetscape is well worthwhile, with the quality **Annie Smithers** *(anniesmithers.com.au)* and long-time local-favourite watering hole the **Cosmo** *(thecosmopolitanhotel.com.au)*. Although it's growing in popularity, visit on a weekday and you're likely to have the place all to yourself. Trentham is a 20-minute drive from Woodend via the Woodend–Tylden Rd.

A mere 16km away to the south and surrounded by state forest, tiny **Blackwood** is a lesser-known, even-smaller version of Trentham, with the same charm. On the main strip is **Martin St Coffee** *(martinstreetcoffee.com)*, a sleek, Melbourne-style cafe doing good java and contemporary dishes. Its back patio has lovely forest views. On the corner is the historic **Blackwood Hotel**, established in 1868, and there's also the quaint **Garden of St Erth** *(diggers.com.au/pages/st-erth)*, a nursery and garden centred on an 1860 sandstone cottage, with a cafe serving produce grown on-site.

03 Kyneton

Kyneton's existence predates the gold rush by a year, and it's the first of the gold-mining towns

Castlemaine
Vintage Bazaar
THE MILL
CASTLEMAINE
OPEN
← Beer
→ Bread
→ Cheese
→ Chocolate
→ Coffee
→ Icecream
← Offices
→ Smallgoods
→ Wine
→ Workshops

you'll reach on this trip. It was the main coach stop between Melbourne and Bendigo, and the centre for the farmers who supplied the diggings with fresh produce. These days, Kyneton serves a similar purpose as a regional centre set amid prosperous farming country. It's filled with the kinds of attractions that are a staple of the gold-era towns, but it's a whole lot quieter, too often overlooked on the rush to the regional centres of Daylesford, Bendigo or Castlemaine. Piper St is a historic precinct lined with bluestone buildings that have been transformed into fine-dining restaurants, a gin distillery, pubs and antique shops. If you're keen to see what many of these buildings used to look like on the inside, visit the **Kyneton Historical Museum**, decked out in period furnishings. The town's **Botanic Gardens** *(kynetonbotanicgardensfriends.org)* occupy a lovely spot beside the Campaspe River.

THE DRIVE: The well-worn trail from Melbourne to Castlemaine passes right by Kyneton, but if you take the quieter parallel roads that shadow the Calder Fwy, you'll get to see Malmsbury and lovely little Chewton on your way into Castlemaine.

04 Castlemaine

In the heart of the central Victorian goldfields, Castlemaine is one of the most happening places in Victoria, where a growing community of artists and tree-changers (rural relocators) live amid some inspiring architecture and gardens. It all stems from the mid-19th century, when Castlemaine was the thriving marketplace for the goldfields. Even after the gold rush subsided, the town built a reputation for industry and innovation – this was the birthplace of the Castlemaine XXXX beer-brewing company (now based in Queensland). Historic buildings include the Roman-basilica facade of the old **Castlemaine Market** (1862) on Mostyn St; the **Theatre Royal** (1856) on Hargreaves St; the **post office** (1894); and the original **courthouse building** (1851) on Goldsmith Cres. For a good view over town, head to **Castlemaine Gaol**, now a contemporary art gallery. And to see why the buzz around Castlemaine never abates, enjoy a glass of wine or a feed at the reborn **Theatre Royal** *(theatreroyalcastlemaine.com.au),* now also one of regional Victoria's best live-music venues.

THE DRIVE: The C282 from Castlemaine to Maldon (16km) passes through the box-ironbark forests of Victoria's gold country. It's a lovely drive to a lovely place.

Castlemaine

PAUL HARDING 00/SHUTTERSTOCK

PAUL HARDING 00/SHUTTERSTOCK

Historic building, Maldon

PHOTO OPPORTUNITY

Maldon's main street is lined with heritage buildings and small-town perfection.

05 Maldon

Like a pop-up folk museum, the whole of tiny Maldon is a well-preserved relic of the gold-rush era, with many fine buildings constructed from local stone. The population is significantly lower than the 20,000 who used to work the local goldfields, but this is still a living, working town – packed with tourists on weekends but reverting to its sleepy self during the week. Evidence of those heady mining days can be seen around town – you can't miss the 24m-high **Beehive Chimney**, just east of Main St, while the **Old Post Office**, built in 1870, was the childhood home of writer Henry Handel Richardson. A short trip south along High St reveals the remains of the **North British Mine**, once one of the world's richest mines.

THE DRIVE: On the way out of town, don't miss the 3km drive up to Mt Tarrengower for panoramic views from the poppet-head lookout. Once you're ready to leave, head due south towards Newstead, then west along the B180 through Joyces Creek and Carisbrook to Maryborough.

06 Maryborough

Maryborough is an essential part of central Victoria's 'Golden Triangle' experience, but it's sufficiently far west to miss out on the day-trippers that flock to Castlemaine and Maldon. Those who do make it this far are rewarded with some splendid Victorian-era buildings, but **Maryborough Railway Station** leaves them all for dead. Built in 1892, the inordinately large station, complete with clock tower, was described by Mark Twain as 'a train station with a town attached'. Today it houses a cafe and gift shop. Prospectors still find a nugget or two here. If you're interested in finding your own nuggets, **Coiltek Gold Centre** *(thegoldcentre.com.au)* offers full-day prospecting courses with state-of-the-art metal detectors. It also sells and hires out prospecting gear.

THE DRIVE: The C287 runs south and then southeast for 32km to Clunes. It's an attractive, quiet road with stands of forest interspersed with open farmland; watch for Mt Beckworth rising away to the southwest as you near Clunes.

07 Clunes

Clunes may be small, but this is where it all began. In June 1851 a find here, roughly halfway between Maryborough and Ballarat, sparked the gold rush that transformed Victoria's fortunes. Today the small town is a quintessential gold-mining relic, with gorgeous 19th-century porticoed buildings whose grandeur seems out of proportion to the town's current size. Clunes has another claim to fame. The town hosts the annual **Book Town Festival** *(clunesbooktown.org.au)* in early March and is home to no fewer than eight bookstores, with a focus on the secondhand trade.

THE DRIVE: There are two possible routes to Ballarat, although we prefer the quieter C287. All along its 24km, there's a growing sense of accumulating clamour as the flat yellow farm-lands south of Clunes yield to the outskirts of Ballarat when you pass under the Western Hwy.

08 Ballarat

Ballarat is one of the greatest gold-mining towns on Earth, and the mineral continues to provide most of the town's major attractions, long after the end of the gold rush. That heritage partly survives in the grand buildings scattered around the town centre – in particular Lydiard St, one of Australia's finest streetscapes for Victorian-era architecture. Impressive buildings include **Her Majesty's Theatre**, **Craig's Royal Hotel**, the **George Hotel** and the **Art Gallery** *(artgalleryofballarat.com.au)*, which also houses a wonderful collection of early colonial paintings. But Ballarat's story is most stirringly told in two museums that hark back to the town's glory days in the fabulous recreated village at **Sovereign Hill** *(sovereignhill.com.au)* and the impressive **Eureka Centre** *(eurekacentreballarat.com.au)*.

VICTORIA'S GOLD RUSH

When gold was discovered in New South Wales in February 1851, a reward was offered to anyone who could find gold within 300km of Melbourne, amid fears that Victoria would be left behind. They needn't have worried. By June, a significant discovery had been made at Clunes, 32km north of Ballarat, and prospectors flooded into central Victoria. Over the next few months, several more deposits were found at Ballarat, Bendigo, Mt Alexander and many other places. By the end of 1851, hopeful miners were coming from England, Ireland, Europe, China and the failing goldfields of California.

The gold rush ushered in a fantastic era of growth and prosperity for Victoria. Within 12 years, the population had increased from 77,000 to 540,000. Mining companies invested heavily in the region, the development of roads and railways accelerated, and huge shanty towns were replaced by Victoria's modern provincial cities, most notably Ballarat, Bendigo and Castlemaine, which reached the height of their splendour in the 1880s.

Sovereign Hill, Ballarat

FRITZ16/SHUTTERSTOCK

15

VICTORIA

GREAT ALPINE ROAD

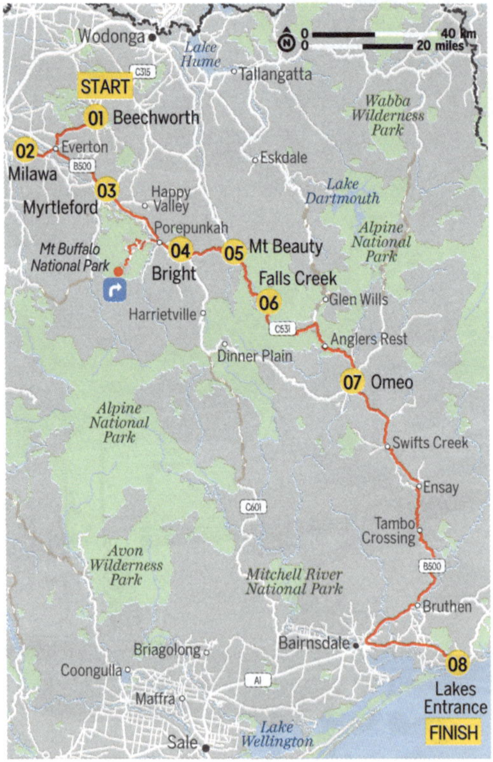

DURATION: 7 DAYS

DISTANCE: 375KM / 233 MILES

GREAT FOR: WINE, NATURE & HISTORY

BEST TIME TO GO: NOVEMBER TO APRIL; THE STUNNING AUTUMNAL COLOURS CAN PERSIST INTO MAY.

The High Country of Victoria's northeast is one of the state's favourite playgrounds, from the culinary excursions to Beechworth (one of Victoria's best-preserved historic relics), Milawa and Myrtleford to the ski slopes of Falls Creek. And either side of a stirring up-and-over mountain drive, Bright and Lakes Entrance are ideal getaways for putting your feet up surrounded by superb natural beauty.

LINK YOUR TRIP

02 Sydney to Melbourne
Lakes Entrance is Stop 11 on this classic route, but you could just as easily begin here and do it in reverse.

16 Along the Murray
Beechworth lies 203km southwest of the starting point of Echuca – drive via Wangaratta, Benalla and Shepparton.

01 Beechworth

There is a danger in beginning your journey in Beechworth: you may never want to leave. Few regional Victorian towns have such a diverse array of disparate but somehow complementary charms. The most obvious of these is the town's open-air museum of historic, honey-coloured granite buildings. Take a **walking tour** that takes in such architectural luminaries as the **Beechworth Courthouse** *(explore beechworth.com.au)*, where the trials of many key historical figures took place (including bushranger Ned Kelly and his mother), the **Telegraph Station**, the **Town Hall** and the **Burke Museum** – Burke (of the ill-fated explorers Burke and Wills fame) was the police superintendent at Beechworth from 1854 to 1858. But for foodies, such fine facades also serve as a backdrop to the wonderful gourmet temptations for which the town is famed.

THE DRIVE: It's a short hop from Beechworth to Milawa, passing

PHILIP GAME/ALAMY

★ BEST FOR:

FOODIES

Milawa Gourmet Region has wine, cheese, mustard and more.

Milawa Mustard

through Everton and arid farmlands and stands of light eucalyptus woodlands – count on no more than 20 minutes.

02 Milawa

If Beechworth is where the end product most often appears on restaurant tables, the Milawa Gourmet Region is where so much of the produce comes from. In **Brown Brothers** *(brownbrothers.com.au)*, Milawa has one of Victoria's best-known and most-respected wineries, going strong since 1899. As well as the tasting room, there's the superb Epicurean Centre restaurant, a gorgeous garden, kids' play equipment and picnic and barbecue facilities. What Brown Brothers is to wine, the **Milawa Cheese Company** *(milawacheese.com.au)* is to cheese. About 2km north of Milawa, it excels at soft farmhouse brie (from goat or cow) and pungent washed-rind cheeses. There's a bakery here and an excellent restaurant where the speciality is a variety of pizzas using Milawa cheese. And on no account miss **Milawa Mustard** *(milawamustards.com.au)*, offering up handmade seeded mustards, herbed vinegars and preserves along the town's main street. For road-tripping picnics, pick up ham and gourmet sausages at **Gamze Smokehouse** *(gamzesmokehouse.com.au)*.

THE DRIVE: Return to Everton, then drive southeast along the B500 until, barely half an hour after leaving Milawa, you reach Myrtleford. Depending on the season, mountains, possibly snow-capped, rise up ahead and red-orange leaves set fire to the landscape in autumn.

03 Myrtleford

Near the foothills of Mt Buffalo, Myrtleford is noteworthy for two main reasons. First, this is the 'Gateway to the Alps', the first town of note along the Great Alpine Rd (B500).

Join a Rolling Gnocchi tour combining cycling, pasta making and vineyard visits with the **Myrtleford Cycle Centre** *(myrtlefordcycle.com)*. American-style smoked meats and Victorian craft beers merge at the **Old Factory** *(facebook.com/theoldfactorymyrtleford)*, a welcoming destination with occasional live music on Saturday nights from 6pm.

THE DRIVE: One of the loveliest sections of the entire drive, the 31km from Myrtleford to Bright meanders through green farmlands with steeply forested hillsides lining the roadside and the Victorian Alps away to the north and east. Around Myrtleford look out for the telltale profile of former tobacco kilns.

04 Bright

Ask many Victorians for their favourite country town and the chances are that most of them will say Bright.

The town itself has little in the way of architectural appeal, but its location (spread across the valleys that preview the Alps), glorious autumn colours, fine foods and a range of activities all add up to a real rural gem. Skiers who have tired of the off-piste scene up at Falls Creek or Mt Hotham often use it as a quieter, more sophisticated base in the winter.

Thrill seekers love it for its adrenaline rush of activities, from paragliding (enthusiasts catch the thermals from the nearby Mystic Mountain) to mountain biking.

After the active adventure of kayaking, subterranean river caving or abseiling with **Bright Adventure Company** *(brightadventurecompany.com.au)*, enjoy a High Country craft beer (or two!) at **Bright Brewery** *(brightbrewery.com.au)*.

THE DRIVE: From Bright to Mt Beauty (30km), the road becomes lonelier, green fields rise gently into the alpine foothills, and there is the accumulating sense that very big mountains lie up ahead. As you draw near to Mt Beauty, the road becomes steeper with some lovely alpine views.

DETOUR

Mt Buffalo National Park
Start: 04 Bright

Beautiful Mt Buffalo is an easily accessible year-round destination – in winter it functions as a snowplay area with tobogganing and cross-country ski trails suitable for families and children, and in summer it's a great spot for bushwalking, mountain biking and rock climbing. This is a world of granite outcrops, lookouts, streams, waterfalls, wildflowers and wildlife. Hook up with **Bright Adventure Company** or **Adventure Guides Australia** *(adventureguidesaustralia.com)* for action-packed outings. A road leads to just below the summit of the Horn (1723m), the highest point on the massif. On the way, the views from the car park of the defunct Mt Buffalo Chalet are simply splendid, and activities are a year-round prospect, from 14km of groomed cross-country ski trails and tobogganing to summer hang-gliding and rock climbing. If a short stroll to a lookout is the most you can muster, **Mt Buffalo Olives**, on the road up to Mt Buffalo from Porepunkah, might be more to your taste.

To get here from Bright, return 6km northwest up the B500 to Porepunkah, from where the signposted road climbs steeply up Mt Buffalo.

05 Mt Beauty

The mountain air just feels cleaner in Mt Beauty, a quiet pre-alpine village huddled at the foot of Victoria's highest mountain, Mt Bogong (1986m), on the Kiewa River. Mt Beauty and its twin villages of Tawonga and Tawonga South are the gateways to Falls Creek ski resort,

Bright Brewery
WIRESTOCK CREATORS/SHUTTERSTOCK

BRIGHT BREWERY
Twelve days of partridges?!
Please. Give the gift of
BEER instead!

but it's also a worthwhile stop in its own right, not least for the pleasing short walks in the vicinity: the 2km **Tree Fern Walk** and the longer **Peppermint Walk** both start from Mountain Creek Picnic and Camping Ground, on Mountain Creek Rd, off the Kiewa Valley Hwy (C531). Located about 1km south of Bogong Village (towards Falls Creek), the 1.5km return **Fainter Falls Walk** takes you to a pretty cascade.

GREG BRAVE/SHUTTERSTOCK

Bright (p124) in autumn

PHOTO OPPORTUNITY

The town of Bright in autumn.

THE DRIVE: From Mt Beauty the road really begins to climb, bucking and weaving along valley walls scarred by a devastating 2013 bushfire. In winter you'll need chains. For the rest of the year, count on pulling over often to take in the view. Before leaving Mt Beauty, check if the road past Falls Creek to Omeo is open (usually from early November to April). Mt Beauty to Falls Creek is 31km (around 40 minutes).

06 Falls Creek

Part of the appeal of Falls Creek resides in its deserved reputation as one of Australia's premier winter ski resorts. In that guise, Victoria's glitziest, most fashion-conscious resort combines a picturesque alpine setting with impressive skiing and infamous après-ski entertainment. The Summit chairlift also operates during the summer school holidays and mountain biking is popular here in the green season. But for all this, we also love Falls for its location along one of the country's prettiest mountain traverses accessible by road.

THE DRIVE: With most of the ski action and ski-station approaches concentrated west of Falls Creek, the slow descent down to Omeo (first along the C531, then south along the C543) is every bit as beautiful but a whole lot quieter. Note this road is usually only open from early November to April. Falls Creek to Omeo is 76km (around 85 minutes).

Fainter Falls, Mt Beauty

DANNY.C IMAGES/SHUTTERSTOCK

07 Omeo

High in the hills, and not really on the road to anywhere, historic Omeo is the main town on the eastern section of the Great Alpine Rd. There's not much to see here, but Omeo is a place to simply enjoy the view, safe in the knowledge that a pretty road awaits in whichever direction you're travelling.

THE DRIVE: The descent from Omeo down the B500 to the coast is a really lovely drive. The first 95km twist and turn gently, following narrow river valleys and running alongside rushing rapids for at least part of the way. From Bruthen to Lakes Entrance, go via Sarsfield, Lucknow and Swan Reach for the fine ocean views on the final approach. Omeo to Lakes Entrance is 120km.

08 Lakes Entrance

Architecturally, Lakes Entrance is a graceless strip of motels, caravan parks, mini-golf courses and souvenir shops lining the Esplanade. But you're not here for the architecture. Instead it's about the fine vantage points such as **Jemmy's Point Lookout** and **Kalimna Lookout**, where the drama of this watery prelude to the vast Tasman Sea becomes apparent. It's also about dining on some of Victoria's freshest seafood, all the while accompanied by a sea breeze. Or it's about cruising the lakes that sit just back from the marvellous Ninety Mile Beach – **Peels Cruises** *(lakesentrance.com/cruises/charter-cruise/item/peels-cruises/)* is a respected operator of long standing. And behind it all, there's the satisfaction and sense of completion that comes from following mountain valleys down to the sea.

16

VICTORIA

ALONG THE MURRAY

★ BEST FOR:

OUTDOORS

Hattah-Kulkyne National Park has stirring Murray River woodland and great birdwatching.

DURATION: 5 DAYS

DISTANCE: 460KM / 286 MILES

GREAT FOR: WINE, HISTORY & NATURE

BEST TIME TO GO: SPRING AND AUTUMN HAVE THE MILDEST WEATHER, OFTEN COMBINED WITH CLEAR SKIES.

River red gum, Barmah National Park

The Murray has one of Australia's most evocative inland shores. River red gums, that icon of the Aussie bush, line the riverbank, drawing cockatoos, corellas and cormorants, while some of Victoria's older and more appealing towns – Echuca, Swan Hill and Mildura – watch over the water, harking back in architecture and atmosphere to the days when the Murray was the lifeblood for the river's remote hinterland.

LINK YOUR TRIP

10 Outback New South Wales
The New South Wales trip swings south to Mungo National Park before heading north to Broken Hill – either is a few hours' drive from Mildura.

15 Great Alpine Road
Echuca lies 203km northwest of Beechworth, the starting point of this mountains-to-the-sea route – drive via Shepparton, Benalla and Wangaratta.

01 Echuca

Echuca is one of the grand old dames of inland Australia. While the modern town sprawls away from the water's edge, historic buildings cluster around the old wharf that climbs several storeys above the water level. Unpaved Murray Esplanade runs along behind the wharf, an appealing movie set of facades and horse-drawn carriages, and from where access to the wharf is via the outstanding **Port of Echuca Discovery Centre** *(portofechuca.org.au)*, a swish interpretation centre with museum-standard displays and boardwalks that lead you past old machinery and derelict riverboats, not to mention the best river views in town. This is also the place to arrange your excursion aboard one of Echuca's early-20th-century steam-powered riverboats: the **PS Pevensey** *(echucapaddle steamers.net.au)* is one of the most

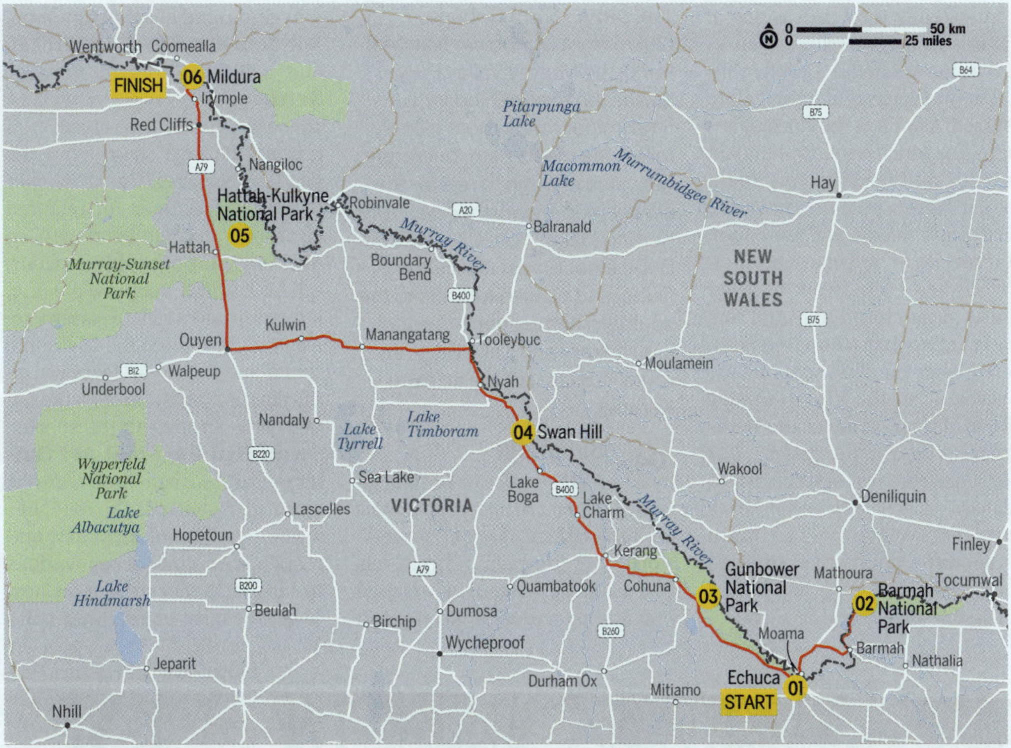

ICONSAUSTRALIA/ALAMY

atmospheric, and cruises are also offered on the gracious **PS Emmylou** *(murrayriverpaddlesteamers.com.au)*. A block back from the river, along Echuca's attractive High St, covered verandahs shelter stores selling local wines, charcuterie and cheeses, fine restaurants and a gin distillery.

THE DRIVE: Pass the turnoff to Jan Juc, then take the next left (C132) and follow the signs to Bells Beach.

02 Barmah National Park

Barmah is one of the prettiest corners of the Murray River floodplain and the largest remaining red gum forest in Australia. It's a place where the swampy understorey usually floods and the sight of these hardy gum trees half submerged in water is an instantly recognisable emblem of the Australian bush – the red hued trunks, the muted eucalyptus greens, the slow-moving muddy brown of the Murray's waters. The area is also an important breeding area for many species of fish and birds: it's one of few places in Victoria to see the superb parrot. On your way into the park, stop off at the Barmah pub for a park map and head for the Barmah Lakes camping area, which has picnic tables, barbecue areas and tracks (mostly accessible by 2WD) that lead alongside the gums.

THE DRIVE: Return to Echuca (40km) via the Cobb Hwy, then take the Murray Valley Hwy (B400) that shadows the Murray northwest of Echuca – aside from the occasional glimpse, the long line of trees to the north is all you'll see of the river. At Gunbower, 40km from Echuca, turn right (north); the road loops through Gunbower National Park and rejoins the B400 at Cohuna.

03 Gunbower National Park

Gunbower Island, formed between the Murray River and Gunbower Creek, is one of the least-known highlights of the Murray traverse. In 2010, Parks Victoria created the 88-sq-km Gunbower National Park (previously a state forest) to protect its beautiful river red gum forests from logging; the result is one of Victoria's most accessible expanses of riverine woodland. Despite this, you may be lucky and have it all to yourself. As well as the glorious red gums, the park is home to abundant animals and birdlife: you might see kangaroos, possums, goannas, turtles and snakes, and more than 200 species of birds have been recorded here. A network of 'river tracks' criss-cross the island and lead to more than a hundred numbered bush-camping spots by the riverbank on the Victorian side of the Murray. Some of the roads are dirt and a bit rough, but are passable to conventional vehicles when it's dry – after heavy rain it's 4WD-only. The main Gunbower–Cohuna road through the park is, however, sealed and accessible year-round in a 2WD.

THE DRIVE: From Cohuna, (20km from Gunbower National Park), the Murray Valley Hwy leaves the river behind for a time; minor roads more closely follow the river's path, but rarely get close enough to render the slower journey worthwhile. From Kerang (32km from Cohuna), the B400 bisects vast agricultural fields, and passes turnoffs to the southern hemisphere's largest ibis rookery and Lake Boga en route to Swan Hill (59km from Kerang).

04 Swan Hill

A classic Aussie provincial centre, Swan Hill possesses little obvious charm on first impressions – its long main street has the usual newsagent, porticoed pub and purveyors of gelato, fish and chips, and cheap Asian food. But drop down to the riverbank and you'll find the terrific **Pioneer Settlement** *(pioneersettlement.com.au)*, an artful re-creation of a riverside port town from the paddle-steamer era. In the manner of such places, look for restored riverboats and old carriages, an old-time photographic parlour, an Aboriginal keeping place, a lolly shop and a school classroom. Every night at dusk, the 45-minute sound-and-light show takes you on a dramatic journey through the settlement in an open-air transporter. **Swan Hill Regional Art Gallery** *(swanhillregionalartgallery.com.au)*, just across the road, has a fine portfolio of local art, and reopened after major renovations in late 2025. For advice on how to get the most out of Swan Hill's

Hattah-Kulkyne National Park

IMOGEN WARREN/SHUTTERSTOCK

riverside walks, visit the **Swan Hill Region Information Centre** *(visitswanhill.com.au)*.

THE DRIVE: Some 46km northwest of Swan Hill, head due west along the Mallee Hwy, a long, lonely stretch of road where the land turns yellow and big horizons evoke the coming outback. After 100km on the Mallee Hwy, at Ouyen, turn north on the Calder Hwy, then follow the signs to the Hattah-Kulkyne National Park from the barely discernible hamlet of Hattah, 35km north of Ouyen.

05 Hattah-Kulkyne National Park

Northwestern Victoria has numerous big-sky national parks, but Hattah-Kulkyne may be the best of them, and is certainly the most easily reached. The park is classic Murray country and the vegetation here ranges from dry, sandy mallee scrub to the fertile riverside areas closer to the Murray, which are lined with red gum, black box, wattle and bottlebrush. The Hattah Lakes system fills when the Murray floods, which is great for waterbirds. The many hollow trees here are perfect for nesting, and more than 200 species of birds have been recorded in the area – watch in particular for the rare and really rather beautiful Regent's parrot or the even rarer Mallee fowl. Even if you're not here to bushwalk or drive off-road, there are two nature drives, the Hattah and the Kulkyne, that are accessible in a 2WD vehicle. **Hattah-Kulkyne National Park Visitor Centre** *(parks.vic.gov.au)* is a terrific place to begin exploring.

P. J. HICKOX/SHUTTERSTOCK

Echuca (p128)

PHOTO OPPORTUNITY

A riverboat setting out from Echuca's historic wharf.

THE DRIVE: Return to the Calder Hwy and its 70 uncomplicated kilometres into Mildura. En route, the surrounding landscape turns greener by degrees, as the arid Mallee yields to the fertile floodplains which support vineyards and fruit orchards.

06 Mildura

Sunny, sultry Mildura is something of an oasis amid some really dry country, a modern town with its roots firmly in the grand old pastoralist era. Its other calling cards include art-deco buildings and some of the best dining in provincial Victoria. In town, paddle-steamer cruises depart from historic Mildura Wharf, while the **Old Mildura Station Homestead** evokes the days of prosperous riverborne trade. The hinterland, too, is worth exploring with abundant Murray River activities that include fishing, swimming, canoeing, waterskiing, houseboating, taking a paddle-steamer cruise or playing on riverside golf courses. Mildura also just happens to be one of Australia's most prolific wine-producing areas: pick up a copy of the *Mildura Wines* brochure from the **visitor information centre** *(visitmildura.com.au)* or visit *mildurawines.com.au*. For a taste of the region's excellent food scene, visit Saturday morning's **Sunraysia Farmers Market** *(sunraysiafarmersmarket.com.au)*.

STAY AWHILE

ECHUCA

BY ANTHONY HAM

Draped along the banks of the Murray River in Victoria's central north, Echuca is a classic riverbank town that's ideal for resting from the rigours of life on the road. Its central location, too, puts you within reach of so many routes through the state.

No matter how many times I've explored the Port of Echuca and gone for a ride upriver on one of the old-world paddle steamers, I never tire of the experience. More than a tour, it's the stories of old Victoria, of a time when rivers were roads connecting the towns of the interior. Learn some of those stories by lantern light, with a few ghostly versions on the **Port After Dark Guided Tour**, booked through the **Port of Echuca** *(portofechuca.com.au)*.

But Echuca is just as much a chance to follow the parklands along the riverbank, or enjoy the signature pit stops of the main street, a stand-in for every historic country town in the state. Second-hand bookshops and gourmet delis, one of Victoria's most celebrated fish-and-chip shops, and the view of the Campaspe River on the back terrace of the **Beechworth Bakery** *(beechworthbakery.com.au)* – each on its own is a quiet and simple pleasure. Strung together, they're enough to fill a couple of days winding down to a slower pace of life.

And in the languid, late-summer days of mid-February, the town is transformed by the **Riverboats Music Festival** *(riverboatsmusic.com.au)*, one of Victoria's best musical celebrations.

LINK YOUR TRIP

Kick off your trip 16 **Along the Murray** from Echuca.

Left: Paddleboarding, Murray River; Right: Paddle-steamers, Murray River

FROM LEFT: P.J.HICKOX/SHUTTERSTOCK, ALEX CIMBAL/SHUTTERSTOCK

PLACES TO STAY

Near Echuca train station, **Caledonian Hotel-Motel** *(thecal.com.au/accommodation)* has spacious, well-appointed rooms which are delightfully more hotel than motel for the price point. **CocknBull Boutique Hotel** *(cocknbullechuca.com.au)* has luxury apartments that add a touch of class to Echuca's central motel-style options. The building's older section (once a bustling pub from the 1870s) looks out over the Campaspe River. The excellent, self-contained **Elinike Guest Cottages** are set in rambling gardens on the Murray River around 5km northwest of town. They blend old-world style with modern conveniences such as double spas, and the lilac cottage has a glass-roofed garden room.

0 500 km
0 250 miles
PAPUA NEW GUINEA
Cape York
Jardine River National Park
Weipa
Coen
Gulf of Carpentaria
CORAL SEA
Laura
Cooktown
21
20
Mossman
Port Douglas
Cairns
Mornington Island
Staaten River National Park
Chillagoe
Karumba
Burketown
Normanton
Croydon
Innisfail
Tully
Mission Beach
Cardwell
Ingham
22
Boodjamulla (Lawn Hill) National Park
Flinders River
A1
Townsville
A7
Whitsundays Islands
Bowen
Charters Towers
A2
Airlie Beach
Mt Isa
Cloncurry
A5
Hughenden
Mackay
Moranbah
17
Winton
A2
Boulia
Clermont
A1
Yeppoon
Diamantina National Park
Diamantina River
Longreach
Barcaldine
Emerald
Rockhampton
A4
Gladstone
Bedourie
A2
Town of 1770
Biloela
Barcoo River
Idalia National Park
Carnarvon National Park
Simpson Desert National Park
Bundaberg
K'gari
Birdsville
Hervey Bay
Maryborough
A39
19
Charleville
Quilpie
Gympie
Roma
A2
Kingaroy
Cooper Creek
Maroochydore
SOUTH AUSTRALIA
A71
Caloundra
Dalby
BRISBANE
Cunnamulla
Toowoomba
St George
18
Currawinya National Park
Goondiwindi
Stanthorpe
Coolangatta
NEW SOUTH WALES

MATHIAS BERLIN/SHUTTERSTOCK

Mission Beach (p143)

QUEENSLAND

EXPLORE

QUEENSLAND

Queensland offers a real touch of the exotic. The coastline north of Brisbane traces Australia's transition from East Coast playgrounds in the south, where year-round tourism is possible, to the sultry climes of Tropical North Queensland. Along the way, you'll encounter gorgeous beaches, the glorious Great Barrier Reef, croc-filled rivers and rainforest. You don't have to stray far from the main road to end up in some pretty remote country, from Cape York to the outback. Going on a road trip is the perfect way to discover this diverse and remarkable state.

Brisbane

For what it lacks in surf beaches, Queensland's capital makes up for in just about every other way. With some 300 days of sunshine a year, it's a city best enjoyed outdoors, from lush parks to rooftop bars and cruising the serpentine Brisbane River. When you need a break from the sun, choose from plenty of cultural and foodie diversions. With a fresh buzz about Brisbane as it gears up to host the 2032 Summer Olympics, it's an excellent time to experience it.

Cairns

One of Australia's northernmost cities, Cairns is a laid-back, languid tropical place where the temperature rarely drops below balmy and shorts are like a uniform year-round. Although travel in these parts becomes complicated in the November-to-April wet season (known by locals simply as 'the Wet'), it's the gateway to just about every journey in Tropical North Queensland, including Cape York, the Daintree, the Great Barrier Reef and the Atherton Tablelands.

Townsville & Magnetic Island

Larger than Cairns, Townsville presents a more local experience. It's less touristy, so you're more likely to share the waterfront cafes

WHEN TO GO

In Tropical North Queensland, the wet season (November to March or April) is best avoided; it coincides also with the October-to-April cyclone season. In the tropics and the outback, May to September are undoubtedly best. In Queensland's southeast, around Brisbane and its nearby areas, year-round visits are possible.

with locals than travellers. With its own collection of offshore reefs and islands, including koala-filled Magnetic Island, Townsville also offers a number of different ways to experience the Great Barrier Reef. As such, it makes a worthwhile stopover as you travel along the coast.

Rockhampton

You could pick almost any medium-sized town along the Queensland coast and consider it a hub: distances are huge in these parts, and most can feel like an oasis as you pull in from the long road. In tropical, humid Rockhampton, the hats, boots and utes are big, and the bulls are even bigger. It also has fine Victorian buildings, a walkable centre, a pleasant riverfront promenade, some great dining and a host of top-ticket attractions nearby, among them Great Keppel Island and Byfield National Park.

TRANSPORT

Except for those road trips where the journey is the thing, consider flying a leg or two, as distances in Queensland are vast; beware of one-way car-rental charges, however. Brisbane has the best flight connections, Cairns is well served by domestic flights and the occasional international flight, and Townsville has some interstate links. **Rex** *(rex.com.au)* flies a loop through outback Queensland.

Mt Isa

A world (and thousands of kilometres) away from the coast, Mt Isa is a place of rodeos, mining smokestacks and pubs filled with character. Good museums and a real sense of being on the cusp of the outback add to the appeal of being here. Given the distances at play, numerous outback attractions aren't so much nearby as accessible from here and the big-sky country of far western Queensland starts right on the edge of town.

WHERE TO STAY

Brisbane easily has the widest range of accommodation, with something to suit most budgets. That said, towns all along the Queensland coast offer some of the most varied accommodation in Australia beyond the main cities. Beach resorts (from midrange to high-end exclusivity), rainforest retreats, B&Bs, buzzing backpacker lodges and even the occasional treehouse hideaway are possible. National park campsites are a bargain at $7.50 per person or $30 per family per night, while the outback is more the domain of pubs (called hotels, with rooms above the bar area) and motels, which remain the workhorses of Queensland's rural tourist industry.

RESOURCES

- **Great Barrier Reef**
  Distils all the info on the world's best reef into a single site. *greatbarrierreef.org*
- **Outback Queensland**
  Brings the state's remote interior into focus. *outbackqueensland.com.au*
- **Queensland National Parks**
  Dive into the wonderful world of Queensland's national parks. *parks.des.qld.gov.au*
- **Tourism and Events Queensland**
  Will have you licking your lips in anticipation. *queensland.com*

WHAT'S ON

- **Noosa Eat & Drink Festival**
  One of Australia's best regional culinary fests, over three days in May. *noosaeatdrink.com.au*
- **Cairns Indigenous Arts Fair**
  Celebrates Aboriginal art, dance, song, theatre, fashion and food in July. *ciaf.com.au*
- **Gympie Music Muster**
  In August, Gympie descends into country and western madness, alongside a celebration of the 'ute'. *muster.com.au*

17

QUEENSLAND

QUEENSLAND COASTAL CRUISE

DURATION: 10–14 DAYS

DISTANCE: 1680KM / 1044 MILES

GREAT FOR: NATURE & FAMILIES

BEST TIME TO GO: APRIL TO SEPTEMBER – THE FURTHER NORTH YOU GO, THE WETTER IT GETS.

Taking in more than 1600km of prime coastal Queensland, this classic sun-soaked sojourn wraps together many of the state's most compelling attractions. Stretching the length of the Bruce Hwy, the drive takes in all the major centres between Brisbane and Cairns, shifting from subtropical to tropical climes, and offers endless opportunities to deviate and linger in rainforests and on islands and beaches along the way.

LINK YOUR TRIP

18 Southern Queensland Loop
This trip also begins in Brisbane, and offers a great prelude to to the long drive north.

20 Cairns & the Daintree
If you want to continue beyond Cairns, this 195km add-on gets you out onto the reef and deep into the rainforest.

01 Brisbane

While Brisbane merely marks the beginning of this epic drive, it's a vibrant, artsy, fast-evolving city that merits as much attention as you can give it. If you're in town for a few days before hitting the highway, the **Gallery of Modern Art** (GOMA; *qagoma.qld.gov.au*) and **Museum of Brisbane** (*museumofbrisbane.com.au*) are among its best sights.

THE DRIVE: Take the M1 north of Brisbane, ignoring the siren call of Sunshine Coast resorts from Moroochydore to Noosa, and you'll be in Maryborough in around three hours.

02 Maryborough

The extraordinary coastline may be the ultimate lure, but it's well worth pulling into the grand old river port of Maryborough, one of Queensland's oldest towns. Heritage oozes from its broad, Victorian streets, its former eminence reflected in beautifully restored colonial-era buildings and gracious

CHAMELEONSEYE/SHUTTERSTOCK

★ BEST FOR:

OUTDOORS

Snorkelling the reef in all its technicolour glory.

Snorkelling, Great Barrier Reef

Queenslander homes. Stroll to the Mary River along historic Quay St, admiring lattice-wrapped buildings and the museums of **Portside Heritage Precinct**; see how country commerce looked in the 1890s at **Brennan and Geraghty's Store** *(naturaltrustqld.org.au)* and hear tales of the past at the 1864 **Bond Store** *(ourfrasercoast.com.au/bond-store)* while shopping for quality port. Mary Poppins fans may treat this visit as a pilgrimage – Maryborough is the birthplace of Pamela Lyndon (PL) Travers, creator of the famous nanny. There's a life-sized **statue** of Ms Poppins on the corner of Richmond and Wharf Sts; **Tea With Mary** offers tours of the historic precinct with a Mary Poppins–bedecked guide; and the **Mary Poppins Festival** *(marypoppinsfestival.com.au)* unfolds over nine days in June/July.

THE DRIVE: Drive northeast from town on Rte 57 (Hervey Bay–Maryborough Rd). After around 30km you'll enter the outskirts of Hervey Bay, with the ocean dead ahead and kilometres of built-up beachfront to your right.

03 Hervey Bay & K'gari

Hervey Bay is attractive simply for its broad beaches, holiday atmosphere and restaurants such as Coast. But throw in the chance to see migrating humpback whales in its waters between July and October, and its convenient access to the UNESCO-listed K'gari (Fraser Island), and an enticement becomes a compulsion. **MV Tasman Venture** *(tasmanventure.com.au)*, **Freedom Whale Watch** *(freedomwhalewatch.com.au)* and **Blue Dolphin Marine Tours** *(bluedolphintours.com.au)* can all take you out to see the whales in season, while the **Hervey Bay Whale Festival** *(herveybaywhalefestival.com.au)* celebrates the gentle giants of the deep on several dates in July and August.

Thirty minutes by barge offshore, K'gari, formerly known as Fraser Island, is the largest sand island in the world, and the only known place where rainforest grows on sand. It's home to a profusion of birdlife and wildlife (most famously the dingo), while its waters teem with all manner of marine life including sharks and migrating humpback whales.

THE DRIVE: Head west of Hervey Bay on the Pialba–Burrum Heads Rd, then take the Old Toogoom Rd southwest to rejoin the Bruce Hwy. Pass through Childers, heading north until, at Miriam Vale, you turn east off the Bruce Hwy. From here it's 56km to Agnes Water and a further 8km to the Town of 1770.

04 Agnes Water & Town of 1770

Surrounded by national parks and the Pacific Ocean, the twin coastal towns of Agnes Water and Town of 1770 (which marks Captain Cook's first landing in the state) are among Queensland's loveliest. Tiny Agnes Water has the East Coast's most northerly surf beach – you can learn in its long, gentle breaks with the highly acclaimed **Reef 2 Beach Surf School** *(reef2beachsurf.com.au)*, and make new friends at exemplary hostels such as **Backpackers @ 1770** *(backpackers1770.com.au)*. If you'd rather cast a line, **Hooked on 1770** *(1770tours.com)* and several other outfits take fishers out on the reef. Back on land, 8km south of Agnes Water you'll find **Deepwater National Park** *(parks.des.qld.gov.au/parks/deepwater)*, an unspoiled coastal landscape with long sandy beaches, walking trails, freshwater creeks and good fishing spots. Practically inaccessible except on foot, by boat or in a 4WD, it's a major breeding ground for loggerhead turtles, which lay eggs on the beaches between November and February – the hatchlings emerge at night between January and April.

THE DRIVE: Track back to Miriam Vale to rejoin the Bruce Hwy north. On the southern outskirts of Rockhampton you'll cross into the tropics by passing the Tropic of Capricorn, an obligatory photo stop marked by a huge spire. Mackay is 334km northwest of Rockhampton, with the best sea views along a 20km stretch north of Clairview.

DETOUR

Byfield National Park

Start: 04 Agnes Water

When people driving this stretch of coast see signs to Yeppoon, most start dreaming of Great Keppel Island, 13km offshore. While the island's charms are well known, we recommend taking the road north from Yeppoon, through Byfield to the beautiful Byfield National Park, a diverse playground of mammoth sand dunes, thick semitropical rainforest, wetlands and rocky pinnacles. It's superb 4WDing terrain, with enough hiking paths and isolated beaches to warrant a longer stay.

To get here, take the Yeppoon Rd turnoff just north of Rockhampton. From Yeppoon, Byfield town is around 40km north.

WHY I LOVE THIS TRIP

ANTHONY HAM, WRITER

What could be more suited to a classic road trip than a highway that stays within sight of the Great Barrier Reef, Australia's top natural attraction, for almost 2000km? It's a drive that connects two worlds – the subtropical south with the steamy tropics of the tropical north. It's the elemental combinations of land and sea, and the world-famous and the little-known, that most defines this wonderful journey.

05 Mackay

Despite a good dining scene, broad tropical streets, art-deco buildings, tangled mangroves and a welcoming populace, Mackay doesn't quite make the tourist hit list, which is precisely why we like it. If you arrive feeling peckish, Southeast Asian restaurants are a notch above, while the impressive art-deco architecture sprinkled around the centre owes much to a devastating 1918 cyclone – flattened timber buildings had to be replaced in sturdier form. Most of the facades are at their finest on the second storey – noteworthy examples include **Chaseley House**, the **Australian Hotel** and the **Ambassador Hotel**. Pick up a copy of *Art Deco in Mackay* from the **Mackay Visitor Centre** *(mackayisaac.com)* if you want to spot more. The redeveloped marina entices with al-fresco restaurants and cafes along its picturesque promenade, and there are plenty of beaches, the best of which are 16km north of town: **Bucasia** is the most undeveloped, and arguably the prettiest.

THE DRIVE: Cape Hillsborough National Park lies 50km north of Mackay, well signposted along the Yakapari–Seaforth road, off the Bruce Hwy.

06 Cape Hillsborough National Park

Despite being so accessible, this small **coastal park** *(parks.des.qld.gov.au/parks/cape-hillsborough)* feels like it's at the end of the Earth. Ruggedly beautiful, it takes in the rocky, 300m-high Cape Hillsborough, and Andrews Point and Wedge Island, which are joined by a cause-

JAKUB MACULEWICZ/SHUTTERSTOCK

Deepwater National Park

way at low tide. The park features rough cliffs, a broad beach, rocky headlands, sand dunes, mangroves, hoop pines and rainforest. Kangaroos, wallabies, sugar gliders and turtles are common, and the roos are likely to be seen on the beach in the evening and early morning. There are also the remains of Aboriginal middens and stone fish traps, accessible by good walking tracks. On the approach to the foreshore area you'll find an interesting boardwalk leading out through a tidal mangrove forest.

THE DRIVE: Return via the Cape Hillsborough and Mount Ossa–Seaforth roads to the Bruce Hwy, which tracks relentlessly northwest. At Proserpine, take the Airlie Beach turnoff – Airlie is 34km away, with good Whitsunday Islands views for much of the second half of the approach.

07 Airlie Beach

Airlie perhaps owes its prominence to the proximity of the splendid Whitsunday Islands and to its place on the backpacker circuit, but once here you may appreciate its charming location, not to mention the chance to eat, drink and make merry in its many bars and restaurants. A sundowner at **Northerlies** *(northerlies.com.au)*, wander in **Conway National Park** *(parks.des.qld.gov.au/parks/conway)* or beachward plunge with **Airlie Beach Skydivers** *(airliebeachskydivers.com.au)* are all good reasons to linger, depending on what floats your boat. And speaking of boats, this natural jumping-off point for the diadem of glorious islands just offshore is the harbour not only for myriad bareboating vessels, but for top-notch tour operators such as **Red Cat Adventures** *(redcatadventures.com.au)*.

THE DRIVE: Head southwest of Airlie along Shute Harbour Rd, then dead west along Gregory Cannon Valley Rd, then resume your northward journey on the Bruce Hwy. Pass through Bowen, and continue 202km to Townsville, via Ayr and the delta of the mighty Burdekin River, with sugar-cane fields all around.

DETOUR

Whitsunday Islands

Start: 07 Airlie Beach

Paradise may be an overused cliché, but here it might just be true. **Whitehaven Beach**, on **Whitsunday Island**, is a pristine

7km-long stretch of blinding sand that's central to most day trips (and longer excursions) leaving from Airlie. **Hamilton Island**, the group's main tourist hub, doesn't really do budget hospitality, but if you're okay with the price tag, **Qualia** *(qualia.com.au)* is the best it can offer.

Formed when the Pacific swamped a volcanic mountain range on Queensland's prehistoric coast, there are numerous ways to see these fabled tropical jewels: take a scenic helicopter flight with **HeliReef** *(helireef.com.au)*, a scenic-flight-and-snorkel excursion with **Air Whitsunday** *(airwhitsunday.com.au)*, or sail with **Illusions 2**, a 12m catamaran offering excellent, inexpensive day trips.

Cruise Whitsundays *(cruisewhitsundays.com)* also offers trips to Hardy Reef and **Daydream** and Long Islands, or day-long catamaran cruises aboard the *Camira*. If you like it zippy, **Ocean Rafting** *(oceanrafting.com.au)* offers a range of tours in semi-rigid inflatable speedboats.

08 Townsville

Sprawling between a brooding red hill and a sparkling blue ocean, Townsville is a tidy and relatively modern-feeling city with a lot to offer: good museums, great diving, vibrant nightlife and a major new aquarium on the way. It's a pedestrian-friendly city and its grand, refurbished 19th-century buildings feature loads of landmarks. Townsville also has a lively, young populace, with thousands of students and armed forces members intermingling with old-school locals, fly-in/fly-out mine workers, and sun seekers lapping up the average 320 days of sunshine per year.

THE DRIVE: For all but a small stretch between Mutarnee and the far side of Ingham, the road hugs the coastline on this 235km leg of the journey. You'll want to pull over often to take in the view, or divert your course to the beach.

DETOUR

Magnetic Island

Start: 08 Townsville

With dozens of daily passenger and car ferries to 'Maggie' from Townsville, it's one of the easiest island escapes on the Queensland coast. Koalas were introduced to the 52-sq-km granite island in 1930s and the population continues to thrive, making it an excellent place to see these furry creatures in the wild. The island served as a critical defensive outpost in WWII, with the remnants of structures now part of the popular Forts Walk. Lovely beaches and snorkelling trails round out the key draws.

09 Mission Beach

Less than 30km east of the sugar-cane and banana plantations that line the Bruce Hwy, Mission Beach is hidden among stunning heritage-listed rainforest, which rolls down to meet a 14km-long stretch of secluded inlets and quiet beaches. Really a sequence of sequestered towns, 'Mission' comprises **Bingil Bay**, 4.8km north of **Mission Beach** proper; **Wongaling Beach**, 5km to the south; and **South Mission Beach**, 5.5km further south again. Rustic as these places are, they nonetheless harbour delightful cafes and restaurants such as **Bingil Bay Cafe** *(bingilbaycafe.com.au)*. And remember – while Mission's waters look pure and appealing, you can't just fling yourself in any old where: stick to the swimming enclosures, lest you have a nasty encounter with a marine stinger – or saltwater crocodile. Walking tracks fan out through the surrounding rainforest, which harbours Australia's highest density of cassowaries.

THE DRIVE: The road north from Mission Beach rejoins the Bruce Hwy at El Arish, from where it's a straight shot north to Cairns (although you may be tempted by turnoffs to beach communities such as exquisite Etty Bay, with its wandering cassowaries, rocky headlands and rainforest). Once you pass Innisfail, it's 88km to Cairns.

10 Cairns

Last stop is Cairns, contender for the capital of Tropical North Queensland, and jumping-off point for further exploration of the Great Barrier Reef and the steamy attractions of Queensland's tropical north. But it would be unfair to treat this 'metropolis' merely as a hub for access to greater pleasures – dining options such as **Ochre** *(ochrerestaurant.com.au)*, sights including the **Cairns Aquarium** *(cairnsaquarium.com.au)*, and the tropical fruit-fest of **Rusty's Markets** *(rustysmarkets.com.au)* are only the tip of the iceberg that is this tourist-pleasing town.

PHOTO OPPORTUNITY

WHITEHAVEN BEACH

One of the world's most photogenic stretches of silica.

Whitehaven Beach, Whitsunday Island

MARTIN VALIGURSKY/SHUTTERSTOCK

STAY AWHILE

MAGNETIC ISLAND

BY SARAH REID

Just 40 minutes on the car ferry from Townsville, 'Maggie' offers a unique Great Barrier Reef island experience. One of my favourite detours along the Queensland coast, the 52-sq-km island has some lovely beaches and great wildlife spotting, namely northern Australia's largest population of wild koalas, easily seen on the popular **Forts Walk**. Also showcasing Maggie's WWII relics and superb views, this 4km trail is one of many to explore in **Magnetic Island National Park** *(parks.qld.gov.au)*, which covers more than 75% of the island. Another local icon is the adorable allied rock wallaby, which I spotted in the rocky coastal terrain of Geoffrey Bay in Arcadia.

The snorkelling is good, too, particularly along the snorkel trails in Nelly Bay and Geoffrey Bay. Nelly Bay is known for its textural corals; on the Geoffrey Bay trail, the wreck of the *Moltke*, a German ship scuttled here in 1911, attracts an array of marine life. If you're snorkelling independently, be mindful that stinger season applies.

Despite its proximity to Townsville, Maggie is wonderfully low-key. 'Relaxed' is the default dining mode – you won't find fancy restaurants, spas or boutiques here. With return ferry transfers for cars costing $236, it's worth staying on the island for at least a few days to get more bang for buck. Alternatively, leave your car at the terminal and rent one on the island, or use the local bus that runs the length of the island between Picnic Bay (where the ferry arrives) and Horseshoe Bay every 45 minutes.

LINK YOUR TRIP

Magnetic Island is a great detour from the 17 **Queensland Coastal Cruise**.

Left: Wallabies, Magnetic Island
Right: WWII Bunker, Forts Walk

FROM LEFT: FRANK FICHTMUELLER/SHUTTERSTOCK, KRYPTOTHEON/SHUTTERSTOCK

PLACES TO STAY

Maggie's accommodation is centred in its four main villages: Picnic Bay, Nelly Bay and Arcadia on the east coast and Horseshoe Bay on the northeast coast. Holiday apartments rule, but there are also a couple of resorts including **Peppers Blue on Blue Resort** *(all.accor.com)* in Arcadia. Hands-down the best option for budget travellers is **Bounce** *(staybounce.com)* in Horseshoe Bay, which has dorms, rooms and camping (including powered sites) in a wild koala habitat. If you don't spot the furry icons snoozing in the trees above your tent, you can see more at the on-site Magnetic Island Koala Park.

18

QUEENSLAND

SOUTHERN QUEENSLAND LOOP

DURATION: 7 DAYS

DISTANCE: 374KM / 232 MILES

GREAT FOR: NATURE, FAMILIES & WINE

BEST TIME TO GO: APRIL TO OCTOBER IS BEST; AVOID THE NOVEMBER SCHOOLIE SEASON.

The journey from Brisbane to Lamington National Park confirms that there is more to southern Queensland than the wham-bam thrills of the Gold Coast's famous theme parks. North and South Stradbroke Islands and Burleigh Heads serve as reminders of why this coast is so coveted, while Springbrook and Lamington National Parks soothe mind and soul with their lush, world-famous rainforests.

LINK YOUR TRIP

17 Queensland Coastal Cruise
This route along the length of the Queensland coast to Cairns (1680km) also begins in Brisbane.

19 Brisbane's Hinterland
Another road trip that begins in Brisbane: this 457km trip loops north and west then south as far as Toowoomba.

01 Brisbane

Brisbane's selling points are many: polished cafes, bars and microbreweries; thriving music and art scenes; unique Queenslander architecture; and that near-perfect climate. But perhaps it's the Brisbane River itself that gives the city its edge. The river's organic convolutions carve the city into a patchwork of urban villages, each with a distinct style and topography: bohemian, low-lying West End; upwardly mobile, hilltop Paddington; boutique, peninsular New Farm. Flanking this massive waterway are some of the city's most celebrated assets, from **South Bank** cultural institutions to **Brisbane Riverwalk** and the always-buzzing dining and leisure precinct **Howard Smith Wharves** *(howardsmithwharves.com)*. The latter encapsulates the city's growing confidence as it transforms into a serious, sophisticated rival for Melbourne and Sydney. Even Melbourne's famous laneway culture is being adapted and celebrated,

TOBY ROBINSON/SHUTTERSTOCK

★ BEST FOR:

FAMILIES

Movie World is the pick of the many kid-friendly theme parks in the area.

Humpback whale, North Stradbroke Island (Minjerribah)

in Fish Lane which harbours top-tier places to wine and dine, and smashing street art murals.

THE DRIVE: From inner Brisbane, Old Cleveland Rd heads east through the city's eastern suburbs. Follow the signs all the way to Cleveland. From here, the vehicle ferry sets out for an easy 30-minute sail across to North Stradbroke Island.

02 North Stradbroke Island (Minjerribah)

Unpretentious 'Straddie' has a string of glorious powdery white beaches, great surf and some quality places to stay. It's also a hot spot for spying dolphins, turtles, manta rays and, between June and November, humpback whales. **Naree Budjong Djara National Park** *(parks.des.qld.gov.au/parks/naree-budjong-djara)* is the island's heartland, home to the glittering Kaboora (Blue Lake). Keep an eye out for forest birds, skittish lizards and swamp wallabies, and there's a wooden viewing platform at the lake, encircled by a forest of paperbarks, eucalyptuses and banksias. To learn about the island's rich Aboriginal culture, take a tour with **Yura Tours** *(yuratours.com.au)*, catch an exhibition at **Salt Water Murris Quandamooka Art Gallery** *(saltwatermurris.com.au)* or chat with Aboriginal artist Delvene Cockatoo-Collins at her gallery-shop **Cockatoo-Collins Studio** *(cockatoocollins.com)*. There are only a few small settlements on the island, with a handful of accommodation and eating options – mostly near Point Lookout in the northeast.

THE DRIVE: Take the ferry back to Cleveland, then wind your way inland, and as long as you're heading west, you'll hit the Pacific Mwy (M1). Head south, taking the Smith St exit, which loops up around Southport. At the T-junction, turn right onto Gold Coast Hwy, which leads to Surfers Paradise.

03 Surfers Paradise

Some may mumble that paradise has been lost, but there's no denying that Surfers' buzzing streets, skyscraping apartments and glorious strip of sand attract a phenomenal number of visitors. This is the pounding heart of the Gold Coast, a booming, hedonistic sprawl of buff bodies, blue skies and aqua-coloured waves. To get your bearings, check out **SkyPoint Observation Deck** *(skypoint.com.au)* on the 77th floor of Q1 tower (322.5m), currently the second-tallest building in the southern hemisphere. The panoramic views of the nation's sixth-largest city take in coast and hinterland. Those seeking added thrill factor can book the SkyPoint Climb, the country's highest external building ascent. Within easy driving are a string of blockbuster theme parks. Coomera claims **Dreamworld** *(dreamworld.com.au)*, Australia's biggest theme park. Admission includes neighbouring **WhiteWater World** *(dreamworld.com.au/our-worlds/whitewater-world)*, with water activities and slides both tame and thrilling. Across in Oxenford lies **Warner Bros. Movie World** *(movieworld.com.au)*, with shows and rides inspired by the silver screen.

THE DRIVE: The high-rise jungle of Surfers Paradise slowly spaces out on the short hop south along the Gold Coast Hwy to Burleigh Heads, with leafy Currumbin barely separated from Palm Beach by the turquoise Tallebudgera Creek.

04 Burleigh Heads & Currumbin

Surf, hipster and bohemian cultures entwine in Burleigh Heads, famed for its right-hand point break, lovely beach and chilled-out vibe. Food lovers soak up dreamy surf-and-skyline views from **Rick Shores** *(rickshores.com.au)*, a beachside bistro-bar with an Asian-fusion menu. Vietnamese flavours and Aussie creativity conspire at easier-on-the-wallet **Jimmy Wah's** *(jimmywahs.com.au)*, a few blocks from the waves. Both are indicative of the city's rapidly evolving food scene. Burleigh also has a great after-dark scene. Begin a night out with Australiana cocktails at **Rosella's** *(rosellasbar.com.au)* and end it with a sophisticated nightcap at clandestine **Lockwood Bar** *(instagram.com/lockwood.bar)*. For a natural high, take a walk around the headland through **Burleigh Head National Park** *(parks.des.qld.gov.au/parks/burleigh-head)*, a 27-hectare rainforest reserve teeming with birdlife and fine views of the surf en route. Three kilometres further inland, **David Fleay Wildlife Park** *(parks.des.qld.gov.au/parks/david-fleay)* has mangroves, rainforest and informative native wildlife shows. There's also **Currumbin Wildlife Sanctuary** *(cws.org.au)*, with Australia's biggest rainforest aviary, crocodile feeding and shows that include an Aboriginal dance display.

THE DRIVE: The Gold Coast Hwy arcs around to the southeast to Coolangatta, a mere 8km skip from Currumbin.

05 Coolangatta

At the southern end of the Gold Coast, 'Cooly' is renowned among surfers for the Superbank, an artificial sandbank that creates perfect barrels when the swell, wind and tides align. Not surprisingly, the break plays host to the annual World Surf Leagues' Quiksilver and Roxy Pros. Film fans might recognise the place from the last scene in '90s cult hit *Muriel's Wedding*, in which it moonlights as the fictional Porpoise Spit. The best and most challenging break is Snapper Rocks, at Cooly's

Currumbin Wildlife Sanctuary

HYSERB/SHUTTERSTOCK

PHOTO OPPORTUNITY

Take a selfie with a rainbow lorikeet at Currumbin Wildlife Sanctuary.

eastern tip. Heading west, Rainbow Bay and Greenmount beaches are better for beginners. And Kirra often has waves for all levels. At **Gold Coast Surfing Centre** *(goldcoast surfingcentre.com)*, former professional surfer and Australian surfing team coach Dave Davidson promises to get you up and surfing in your first lesson. Alternatively, from around mid-June to the end of October, **Blue Seafaris** *(blueseafaris.com)* runs 2½-hour whale-watching cruises.

THE DRIVE: Double back up the western fringe of the Gold Coast via the M1 and take the exit for Rte 99 towards Springbrook National Park. The drive becomes windier, but prettier, as it climbs towards the park.

06 Springbrook National Park

Springbrook National Park *(parks.des.qld.gov.au/parks/springbrook)* is a steep remnant of the huge Tweed Shield volcano that centred on nearby Wollumbin (formerly Mt Warning) in NSW more than 20 million years ago. It's treasured among hikers, with excellent trails through cool-temperate, subtropical and eucalypt forests offering a mosaic of gorges, cliffs and waterfalls. The park is divided into four sections. The 1000m-plus-high Springbrook Plateau section houses the strung-out township of Springbrook along Springbrook Rd, and receives the most visitors: it's punctuated with waterfalls, trails and eye-popping lookouts. The scenic Natural Bridge section, off the Nerang–Murwillumbah road, has a 1km walking circuit leading to a huge rock arch spanning a water-formed cave – home to a luminous colony of glow-worms. Guided tours of the cave are available. The Mt Cougal section, accessed via Currumbin Creek Rd, has several waterfalls and swimming holes (watch out for submerged logs and slippery rocks); while the heavily forested Numinbah section to the north is the fourth section of the park.

THE DRIVE: Wherever you are in the park, return to Rte 97 and head north. Before you reach Nerang, head west on Rte 90 (Mt Nathan Rd) to Canungra and then south on Lamington National Park Rd up to the Green Mountains section of the park.

07 Lamington National Park

Australia's largest remnant of subtropical rainforest cloaks the valleys and cliffs of the McPherson Range, reaching elevations of 1100m on the Lamington Plateau. Here, the World Heritage–listed **Lamington National Park** *(parks.des.qld.gov.au/parks/lamington)* offers over 160km of walking trails. The two most accessible sections are the **Binna Burra** and **Green Mountains** sections. The Green Mountains (O'Reilly's) section can be reached via the long, narrow, winding Lamington National Park Rd from Canungra (not advisable for campervans). Binna Burra can be accessed using the Beechmont or Binna Burra roads via Nerang (from the Gold Coast) or Canungra (from Brisbane), both suitable for campervans. Bushwalks within the park include everything from short jaunts to multiday epics. For experienced hikers, the **Gold Coast Hinterland Great Walk** is a three-day trip along a 54km path from the Green Mountains section to the Springbrook Plateau. Another favourite is the excellent **Tree Top Canopy Walk** along a series of rope-and-plank suspension bridges at Green Mountains.

Lamington National Park
ZSTOCK/SHUTTERSTOCK

19

QUEENSLAND

BRISBANE'S HINTERLAND

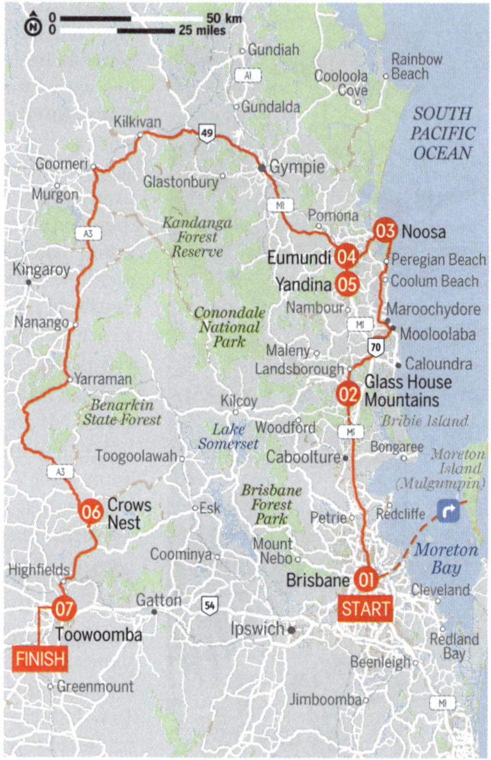

DURATION: 3-4 DAYS

DISTANCE: 457KM / 284 MILES

GREAT FOR: NATURE, HISTORY & FAMILIES

BEST TIME TO GO: YEAR-ROUND IS FINE, BUT GOOD WEATHER IS MORE LIKELY FROM MAY TO OCTOBER.

While you could visit many of these places as day trips from Brisbane, you'd lose that dual sense of the open road and the escape from the big city. The Glass House Mountains seem otherworldly this close to Brisbane's urbanity, and the lushness of Spirit House evokes sultry Bali. Throw in languid Noosa, free-spirited Eumundi and the nostalgia of Crows Nest and Toowoomba, and you'll understand exactly what we mean.

LINK YOUR TRIP

17 Queensland Coastal Cruise
This trip runs the length of the Queensland coast, beginning in Brisbane and finishing in Cairns a mere 1680km later.

18 Southern Queensland Loop
This trip takes in the clamour of south coast Queensland and the tranquil rainforested hinterland.

01 Brisbane

Increasingly sophisticated Brisbane still manages to retain a wonderfully laid-back vibe that's missing from its larger, more frazzled southern rivals. The city's riverside **Gallery of Modern Art** *(qagoma.qld.gov.au)* is a heavyweight on the Australian art scene, while venues like **The Triffid** *(thetriffid.com.au)* and **Fortitude Music Hall** *(thefortitude.com.au)* have helped rocket Brisbane's booming live-music scene. While new, on-trend wine bars, microbreweries and eateries seem to open every week, the city is also a great spot for families, with draws including **South Bank** *(visitsouthbank.com.au)*, a waterfront park with a free, lagoon-style swimming beach with skyline views. For your purposes, however, Brisbane is the launching pad for a journey out into some of the weekend escapes much loved by Brisbanites. Keep a day free for a trip to Moreton Island (Mulgumpin).

ZSTOCK/SHUTTERSTOCK

★ BEST FOR:

FAMILIES

Seeing the crocs in action at Australia Zoo.

Moreton Island (Mulgumpin)

THE DRIVE: From the city, take the M3 motorway north, following signs for the Sunshine Coast. The motorway funnels out of the city, becoming the M1 (Bruce Hwy). Stay on it only as far as the Beerwah turnoff; once the signs start pointing to Caboolture, start moving over towards the left-hand lane in readiness.

DETOUR

Moreton Island (Mulgumpin)
Start: 01 Brisbane

If you're not going any further north in Queensland (and perhaps even if you are), slip over to refreshing Moreton Island (Mulgumpin). Separated from the mainland by Moreton Bay – famous for its Moreton Bay bugs (a type of slipper lobster that's absolutely delicious), which are beloved by those who value strange-looking-and-found-nowhere-else seafood – the island has a cache of sweeping sandy shores, bushland, birdlife, dunes and glorious lagoons. A remarkable 95% of the island is protected as part of the **Gheebulum Kunungai (Moreton Island) National Park** *(parks.des.qld.gov.au/parks/gheebulum-kunungai-moreton-island)*. Shell middens and bone scatters speak of the island's original inhabitants, the Ngugi people, a clan belonging to the Quandamooka group. Moreton Island (Mulgumpin) is also home to Queensland's oldest operating lighthouse, built in 1857 and a great spot for whale watching, which generally takes place between June and October. Off the island's west coast are the rusty, hulking Tangalooma Wrecks, a popular spot for diving and snorkelling. Apart from a few rocky headlands, the island is all sand. In fact, Moreton Island (Mulgumpin) is the third-largest sand island in the world, and its coastal sand hill Mt Tempest (280m) the highest in the southern hemisphere.

To go exploring both on land and sea, book a day trip with **Australian Sunset Safaris** *(sunsetsafaris.com.au)*, which will have you sand tobogganing, snorkelling and kayaking in transparent kayaks.

02 Glass House Mountains

The ancient volcanic plugs of the Glass House Mountains rise abruptly from the subtropical plains 20km northwest of Caboolture. In Aboriginal Dreaming, these rocky peaks belong to a family of mountain spirits. To British explorer James Cook, their shapes recalled the industrial, conical glass-making furnaces of his native Yorkshire. Over the years, their surreal shapes and magnetic presence have inspired many prolific Australian creatives, including poet Judith Wright, painter Fred Williams and Brisbane-born writer David Malouf. Exiting the Bruce Hwy, slower Steve Irwin Way leads to the **Glass House Mountains Visitor & Interpretive Centre** *(visitsunshinecoast.com.au),* where you'll find a plethora of information (including maps) on the Glass House Mountains and its network of walking trails. Options include the 2.8km Mt Ngungun (253m) summit walking track, a moderate-grade trail with spectacular close-up views of Mt Tibrogargan, Mt Coonowrin and Mt Beerwah. Steve Irwin Way also leads to **Australia Zoo** *(australiazoo.com.au),* a fitting homage to its founder, the late, larger-than-life wildlife enthusiast Steve Irwin.

THE DRIVE: Drive east, follow the signs to Caloundra and then turn north through a string of coastal resorts – Maroochydore, Mudjimba and Coolum Beach. Find out which part of Noosa you're headed to: Noosa Heads (around Laguna Bay and Hastings St), Noosaville (along the Noosa River) or Noosa Junction (the administrative centre).

03 Noosa

One of the most famous beach towns in Australia, low-rise Noosa is a fashionable resort town with crystalline beaches and lush subtropical rainforests. While the designer boutiques and smart restaurants draw cash-splashing sophisticates, the wonderful beaches and bush are free, leading to a healthy intermingling of urbanites, laid-back surfers and beach bods in thongs (flip flops). All manner of activities and tours are possible from Noosa, from kayaking and surf schools to 4WD adventures on Fraser Island – the **Noosa Visitor Information Centre** *(visitnoosa.com.au)* has a full list. One of the

View of Glass House Mountains

ALEX CIMBAL/SHUTTERSTOCK

attractions is best explored under your own steam – **Noosa National Park** *(parks.qld.gov.au/parks/noosa)* covers the headland, and has soothing walks, arresting coastal scenery and a string of bays with great swimming and surfing. The most scenic way to access the national park is to follow the boardwalk along the coast from town. **Laguna Lookout** also has fabulous views – walk or drive up to it from Viewland Dr in Noosa Junction.

THE DRIVE: Head out of Noosa on Eumundi–Noosa Rd (Rte 12), following the signs to Eumundi and the Bruce Hwy. Just before the Bruce Hwy, at the roundabout, turn right into Caplick Way, which leads directly into the heart of Eumundi. The town is close enough to Noosa that many people visit as a day trip from there.

04 Eumundi

Timber pubs, broad verandahs and tin-roof cottages line sweet Eumundi's main street, a scene that seems pulled straight out of a Russell Drysdale painting. Here, weathered faces and XXXX schooners mingle with artists, yoga teachers and tree-change urbanites.

The highland township is best known for its eponymous **markets** *(eumundimarkets.com.au)*, their 600-plus stalls attracting over 1 million visitors a year.

It's a magical place, with roaming street performers, musicians, global street food and artisans selling everything from hand-crafted furniture and jewellery to homemade clothes, artisan food products and alternative healing.

Sample the Eumundi Brewery beers brewed on-site at the **Imperial Hotel** *(imperialhoteleumundi.com.au)*, down the street.

PHOTO OPPORTUNITY

GLASS HOUSE MOUNTAINS

Sweeping views of ancient volcanic plugs from Glass House Mountains Lookout.

THE DRIVE: Return to the Bruce Hwy for 11km, then take the turnoff for (and follow the signs to) Yandina. At the first roundabout, take the Coulson Rd exit. After about 500m, the road ends at a T Junction with Ninderry Rd. Turn right and Spirit House is around 50m along on the right.

05 Yandina

One of the greatest culinary excursions anywhere in the state, **Spirit House** *(spirithouse.com.au)* is as much an experience as a lauded restaurant. A path winds from the car park amid flowering greenery, past lily ponds and discreet Buddhist shrines. Almost immediately, it's as if the outside world has ceased to exist and you've been transported to a Southeast Asian Shangri-La, imbued with peace and understated sophistication. Set on two hectares of lush gardens, the complex includes a **cooking school** and the sleek **Hong Sa Bar**, the latter serving impeccable cocktails and beautiful sharing plates. The pièce de résistance, however, is the main, open-sided restaurant, which features tables arranged around a tranquil pool.

THE DRIVE: Return to the Bruce Hwy, follow the signs north to Gympie, then turn left onto Wide Bay Hwy (Rte 49), looping up and over the Coast Range of green hills, travelling via Kilkivan, Nanango, Yarraman and Wutul to Crows Nest.

06 Crows Nest

Arrayed across a broad green valley on the gentle downslopes of the Great Dividing Range, sleepy Crows Nest (population 2212) surrounds a village green with porticoed pub, the odd antique shop, rustic **historical village** *(cnhs.com.au)* and kooky local festival – Crows Nest hosts the **World Worm Races** as part of the Crows Nest Festival every October. Just 6km east of town, **Crows Nest National Park** *(parks.qld.gov.au/parks/crows-nest)* has a clutch of lovely walking trails, waterfalls and lookouts. If it's the first Sunday of the month, browse the stalls at the crafty **Crows Nest Village Markets** *(facebook.com/crowsnestqldmarkets)*.

THE DRIVE: The sense of civilisation comes gently but unmistakably on the 50km run south to Toowoomba via Highfields on the New England Hwy (A3).

07 Toowoomba

Squatting on the edge of the Great Dividing Range, 700m above sea level, Toowoomba is a sprawling country hub with wide tree-lined streets, stately homes and brisk winters made for red wine and crackling fires. Attractions include Australia's largest traditional **Japanese Garden** *(unisq.edu.au/about-unisq/locations/toowoomba/japanese-garden)*, the **Cobb & Co Museum** *(museum.qld.gov.au/cobb-and-co)*, and a small regional **art gallery** *(tr.qld.gov.au/facilities-recreation/theatres-galleries/galleries)*. The biggest surprise, however, is Toowoomba's burgeoning cool factor, reflected in its growing number of hip cafes, bars and eateries (try **Host** for spot-on mod Oz dining; *hostdinewine.com)*, not to mention a slew of street art by nationally and globally recognised talent.

20

QUEENSLAND

CAIRNS & THE DAINTREE

DURATION: 7 DAYS

DISTANCE: 195KM / 121 MILES

GREAT FOR: NATURE & HISTORY

BEST TIME TO GO: MAY TO NOVEMBER; SUMMER IS WET AND CYCLONES ARE AN EVER-PRESENT DANGER.

Languid Cairns is a gateway to some of the best bits of Tropical North Queensland: diving or snorkelling the Great Barrier Reef is de rigueur from Cairns and Port Douglas; the wildlife-rich rainforests of Daintree National Park beckon exploration; and the beaches from Palm Cove to Cape Tribulation have the unmistakable whiff of paradise. This region lies on the traditional lands of numerous Aboriginal groups including the Yirrganydji of the Cairns area and the Kuku Yalanji of the Daintree region.

LINK YOUR TRIP

17 Queensland Coastal Cruise
Cairns is where this classic route ends after having traversed the Queensland coast north from Brisbane.

21 Towards Cape York: Cairns to Cooktown
If Cairns isn't far enough north for you, go a little further – our journey to Cooktown via the Cape York fringe begins in Cairns.

01 Cairns

Gateway to the Great Barrier Reef and the Daintree Rainforest, Cairns is an important regional centre, but it's more board shorts than briefcases.

Sun- and fun-lovers flock to the spectacular, lifeguard-patrolled, artificial, sandy-edged lagoon pool at **Cairns Esplanade** *(cairns.qld.gov.au/esplanade)* on the city's reclaimed foreshore or head to nearby **Barron Gorge National Park** and take the 1.6km-return Din Din Barron Falls Lookout Track to gaze at the spectacular waterfall.

Dozens of operators will get you out to the reef for a day of snorkelling or diving. Gain fascinating insights into Indigenous connections to the reef on a day trip with **Dreamtime Dive & Snorkel** *(dreamtimedive.com)*.

THE DRIVE: Drive for 13km north of Cairns, past the airport turnoff, and then take the left-branching road, following the signs another 14km up to Kuranda village.

SOPHIE COSTELLO/SHUTTERSTOCK

Mossman Gorge (p158)

02 Kuranda

Arty Kuranda is one of Cairns' most popular day trips. Even this close to Cairns, it's rainforest and art at every turn here. Most people head straight to the **Kuranda Markets** *(kurandaoriginalrainforestmarket.com.au)* for a browse but don't miss **Rainforestation** *(rainforest.com.au)*, with a wildlife section, rainforest/river tours and interactive Aboriginal experience. Not surprisingly, wildlife is a recurring theme here, with **Kuranda Koala Gardens** *(koalagardens.com)*, **Birdworld** *(birdworldkuranda.com)* and the **Australian Butterfly Sanctuary** *(australianbutterflies.com)* all in the vicinity. The **Kuranda Riverboat** *(kurandariverboat.com.au)* will take you for a cruise on the Barron River, or walk or drive the 3km to see impressive Barron Falls.

THE DRIVE: It's 14km back down the road to the Cook Hwy. Turn left, then follow the signs to Palm Cove, located 15km further on.

03 Palm Cove

Surprisingly, Cairns doesn't have its own beach but the sands start about a 15-minute drive north and culminate in the most beautiful beach of all at Palm Cove. More intimate than Port Douglas and more upmarket than its southern neighbours, Palm Cove is a cloistered coastal community with a beautiful promenade along the paperbark-lined Williams Esplanade, a gorgeous stretch of white-sand beach and a procession of fancy restaurants. Palm Cove is a place for kayaking or standup paddleboarding by day and enjoying a romantic candlelit dinner by night.

THE DRIVE: Head back onto the Cook Hwy, drive north, and then sit back and enjoy the 44km ride to Port Douglas. Dramatic sections of coastline open up at various points along the way and the region's boast of this being where the rainforest meets the sea is frequently evident along this stretch. Port Douglas is well signposted, 5km northeast of the Cook Hwy.

04 Port Douglas

The traditional home of the Kuku Yalanji people, **Port Douglas** developed from a sleepy fishing village in the 1960s to a sophisticated alternative to Cairns' hectic tourist scene. With the outer Great Barrier Reef 90 minutes offshore, the Daintree Rainforest practically in the backyard, and dozens of resorts, restaurants and shops on a compact peninsula, Port Douglas has so much going for it that many visitors choose it as their Tropical North Queensland base, leaving Cairns at the airport. The town's main attraction is **Four Mile Beach**, a pristine strip of palm-fringed, white sand that begins at the eastern end of Macrossan St, the main drag for shopping, wining and dining. Climb to **Trinity Bay Lookout** for sensational views, then head to the **Crystalbrook Superyacht Marina** *(portdouglasmarina.com)* on Dickson Inlet to see what trips are heading out to the reef (there are many) or to book a sunset sail.

PHOTO OPPORTUNITY

Trinity Bay Lookout, Port Douglas.

THE DRIVE: Return to the Cook Hwy, then follow it northwest into Mossman, 14km after rejoining the highway.

05 Mossman Gorge

Around 5km west of Mossman, in the southeast corner of Daintree National Park, **Mossman Gorge** *(mossmangorge.com.au)* also forms part of the traditional lands of the Kuku Yalanji people. Carved by the Mossman River, the gorge is a boulder-strewn valley where sparkling water washes over ancient rocks. From the fantastic **Mossman Gorge Cultural Centre**, which houses an art gallery and a bush-tucker restaurant, walking tracks loop along the river to a refreshing swimming hole – take care, as the currents can be swift. A shuttle bus runs from the visitor centre into the heart of the gorge. Better still, book the unforgettable 1½-hour Indigenous-guided **Ngadiku Dreamtime Walk** through the cultural centre – it's an intimate experience getting to know the rainforest, and you'll come away with a head full of anecdotes and soulful stories that centre on Kuku Yalanji relationships to the land.

THE DRIVE: Travelling north from Mossman, it's 26km

Trinity Bay Lookout, Port Douglas

ADRIANOK/SHUTTERSTOCK

through cane fields and farmland before the crossroads to either Daintree Village or the Daintree River Ferry. It's a lovely 10km winding drive through lush country to Daintree Village, with the final stretch offering a hint of the forests that lie up ahead.

06 Daintree Village

Daintree is essentially a one-street town with some heritage buildings, cafes and a pub, plus a pleasant sense of isolation. But most people are here for a cruise on the Daintree River – the best place in North Queensland to search for saltwater crocs. There are numerous operators, some offering specialist birdwatching or photography trips. Try **Daintree River Wild Watch** *(daintreeriverwildwatch.com.au)*, which has informative sunrise birdwatching cruises.

THE DRIVE: Return back down the (only) road and continue north along the highway to the Daintree River Ferry, the only way to cross the river by vehicle. From the other side, it's 40 wonderful, rainforested kilometres to the beach at Cape Tribulation (Kulki), where the paved road, and this journey, ends. Watch out for cassowaries en route.

07 Cape Tribulation

Part of the Wet Tropics World Heritage Area, the spectacular region from the Daintree River north to **Cape Tribulation (Kulki)** features ancient rainforest, sandy beaches and rugged mountains.

This isolated piece of paradise retains a frontier quality, with road signs alerting drivers to cassowary crossings, croc warnings along the beaches and a tangible sense of having left civilisation back on the other side of the Daintree River.

The rainforest tumbles right down to magnificent **Myall** and **Cape Tribulation** beaches, which are separated by a knobby cape, and there are numerous ways to explore: **Ocean Safari** *(oceansafari.com.au)* leads small groups on snorkelling cruises to the Great Barrier Reef, just half an hour offshore.

On the way to Cape Trib, don't miss the **Daintree Discovery Centre** *(discoverthedaintree.com)* at Cow Bay, with its rainforest education and aerial walkway. Numerous walking tracks, including wheelchair-accessible boardwalks, lace the Cape Trib section of **Daintree National Park** *(parks.qld.gov.au/parks/daintree)*.

ADAM CALAITZIS/SHUTTERSTOCK

Vinegar station for treating jellyfish stings

BEWARE OF STINGERS

Australia's formidable portfolio of deadly and otherwise dangerous creatures can seem endless. The risks in most cases are way overblown, but you should definitely be careful of venturing out into the ocean here. Jellyfish – including the potentially deadly box jellyfish and Irukandji – live in Australia's tropical waters. It's unwise to swim north of Agnes Water (which lies well south of Cairns) between November and May unless there's a stinger net. 'Stinger suits' (full-body Lycra swimsuits) prevent stinging, as do wetsuits. Swimming and snorkelling are usually safe around Queensland's reef islands throughout the year; however, the rare (and tiny) Irukandji has been recorded on the outer reef and islands. Wash stings with vinegar (or, failing that, with seawater) to prevent further discharge of remaining stinging cells and remove the tentacles with a tool such as tweezers or the edge of a credit card. Then proceed directly to a hospital.

21

Esplanade, Cairns

★ BEST FOR:

CULTURE

Quinkan Rock Art Sites are one of Australia's premier Aboriginal rock-art sites.

QUEENSLAND

TOWARDS CAPE YORK: CAIRNS TO COOKTOWN

DURATION: 5–7 DAYS

DISTANCE: 506KM / 314 MILES

GREAT FOR: NATURE & HISTORY

BEST TIME TO GO: THE DRY (APRIL TO OCTOBER); OTHERWISE IT'S IMPOSSIBLY HUMID OR RAINING.

From Cairns to Cooktown, this trip transports you to the very cusp of Cape York, almost as close as you can safely get in a 2WD vehicle. Cairns and Mareeba provide a gentle introduction, but from then on there are detours to remote settlements such as Laura and Wujal Wujal, fabulous Aboriginal rock art, and the frontier charm of Cooktown.

LINK YOUR TRIP

20 Cairns & the Daintree
Cairns is the starting point for many journeys through the tropical north – this one heads north and offshore in search of rainforest and reef.

22 Outback Queensland
Return to Cairns for this route from tropical coast deep into the Gulf Country and the vast outback.

01 Cairns

Cairns, where so many journeys in Tropical North Queensland begin and end, is where you leave the coast behind. Enjoy its fine choice of restaurants, go for a swim at the lagoon pool along the **Esplanade**, take a lazy 3km walk along the foreshore boardwalk, and brush up on arts and culture at the **Cairns Art Gallery** *(cairnsregionalgallery.com.au)* and the **Cairns Museum** *(cairnsmuseum.org.au)*. Browse the **Night Markets** *(nightmarkets.com.au)* before finding a suitable bar in which to start enjoying Cairns' legendary nightlife.

THE DRIVE: Take the Cook Hwy north for 13km, take the left turn up to Kuranda, then follow the Kennedy Hwy southwest all the way into Mareeba for a total trip clock of 64km for the day. Watch for rolling, rainforested hills along the way, and the views back down to Cairns.

MARTIN VALIGURSKY/SHUTTERSTOCK

INDIGENOUS PEOPLES

More than 70 Aboriginal and Torres Strait Islander groups have cultural and spiritual connections to the Great Barrier Reef.

02 Mareeba

Mareeba revels in an unashamed Wild West atmosphere, with local merchants selling leather saddles, handcrafted bush hats and oversized belt buckles in readiness for the annual **Mareeba Rodeo** *(mareebarodeo.com.au)*.

The land around Mareeba is largely farming country, with one of the biggest crops being coffee. You can visit **Jaques Coffee Plantation** *(jaquescoffee.com.au)* or **Coffee Works** *(coffeeworks.com.au)* to see what all the fuss over beans is about. Or try the tropical sweet mango wine of **Golden Drop Mango** *(goldendrop.com.au)* or spirits at **Mt Uncle Distillery** *(mtuncle.com)*. For local history, don't miss the **Mareeba Heritage Museum** *(mareebaheritagecentre.com.au)*.

THE DRIVE: Some 42km north of Mareeba, just after tiny Mt Molloy, the Mulligan Hwy arcs away to the northwest and then north, passing roadhouse and pub pit stops at Mt Carbine and Palmer River and crossing the Bryerstown Range. From the road junction at tiny Lakeland, the Peninsula Developmental Rd heads northwest for another 60km to remote Laura. Total drive is an easy 250km with little traffic.

03 Laura & Quinkan Rock Art Sites

The road is sealed to Laura, where you enter Quinkan Country, so named for the Aboriginal spirits depicted at the rock-art sites scattered throughout this area. UNESCO lists Quinkan Country in the world's top 10 rock-art regions. The **Split Rock Gallery** is the only rock-art site open to the public without a guide. Entrance is by donation at the car park. The sandstone escarpments here are covered with paintings dating back 14,000 years. Depending on when you come, it can be quite a surreal experience to walk the path up the hillside in silence, solitude and isolation, before coming upon the various otherworldly galleries in the rock faces. There's a real sense of the sacred at Split Rock: it's both eerie and breathtaking. Visit the **Quinkan & Regional Cultural Centre** *(cooktownandcapeyork.com/do/museums/quinkan_centre)* in Laura, which can organise guided trips to more remote rock-art sites.

Laura, with a pub, store and roadhouse, marks the start of an epic journey into the Cape York Peninsula. The Peninsula Developmental Rd is progressively being sealed beyond here, but for now you'll need a 4WD and a sense of adventure if you want to continue north.

THE DRIVE: The Split Rock Gallery is only 12km south of Laura. It's around 140km from Laura to Cooktown. The Peninsula Developmental Rd back to Lakeland is flat and mostly straight, before it joins the Mulligan Hwy. From here the landscape begins to twist and undulate until you reach the turnoff for Bloomfield Rd, about 25km before Cooktown.

04 Wujal Wujal & Bloomfield Falls

Take the 45km Bloomfield Rd from the iconic Lion's Den Hotel to the Aboriginal community of Wujal Wujal on the Bloomfield River. The scenic drive (sealed) winds through Rossville and Cedar Range National Park. Highlights include the **Black Cockatoo Gallery** *(blackcockatoo gallery.com.au)*, walks on the beach at Ayton and the **Bana Yirriji Art Centre** *(banayirrijiart.com.au)* in Wujal Wujal. Don't miss photogenic **Bloomfield Falls**; book ahead for a tour of the falls with the local Aboriginal Walker family *(0475 837 489)*. Don't even think of swimming in the **Bloomfield River** – it's home to some very large crocs. Beyond here, the road is 4WD-only to Cape Tribulation.

THE DRIVE: Return back along Bloomfield Rd for the 70km drive to Cooktown. Stop in at the Lion's Den Hotel for a beer on the verandah and a swim in the croc-free creek.

05 Cooktown

Cooktown, the most northerly town on Queensland's coast, is a spirited place at the southeastern edge of Cape York Peninsula. This is a small town with a big history: for thousands of years, Waymbuurr was a meeting ground for Aboriginal communities, and it was here on 17 June 1770 that Lieutenant Cook (not yet a captain) beached the *Endeavour*, which had earlier struck a reef offshore from Cape Tribulation. Cook's crew spent 48 days here, making Cooktown Australia's first non-Aboriginal settlement. Do as Cook did and climb 162m-high **Grassy Hill Lookout** for awesome 360-degree views of the town, river and ocean. Cooktown still has some beautiful 19th-century buildings, among them the excellent **Cooktown Museum** *(national trustqld.org.au/visitor-sites/cook town-museum)*, with well-preserved relics from the *Endeavour*. For an Aboriginal perspective on the land, join **Maaramaka Walkabout Tours** *(cooktownandcapeyork.com/tours/local-tours/maaramaka tours)*.

CAPE YORK PENINSULA

Rugged, remote Cape York Peninsula has one of the wildest tropical environments on the planet. The Great Dividing Range forms the spine of the Cape: tropical rainforests and palm-fringed beaches flank its eastern side; sweeping savannah woodlands, eucalyptus forests and coastal mangroves its west. This untamed landscape undergoes a spectacular transformation each year when the torrential rains of the monsoonal wet season set in: rough, dry earth turns to rich, red mud; quenched, the tinder-dry bush awakens in vibrant greens, and trickling creek beds swell to raging rivers teeming with barramundi.

Generally impossible in the Wet, the overland pilgrimage to the Tip is a 4WD trek into one of Australia's last great frontiers, and not for the uninitiated. Rough, corrugated roads and challenging croc-infested river crossings are par for the course on the Old Telegraph Track, though newer bypass roads make the journey doable for anyone with the right vehicle. For 4WD journeys beyond Laura, the end of the sealed road, you must carry spare tyres, tools, winching equipment, food and plenty of water, which is scarce along the main track. Roadhouses can be more than 100km apart and stock only basic supplies. Be sure to check **RACQ road reports** *(racq.com.au)* before you depart. Mobile phone service is limited to the Telstra network and is sketchy at best – take a sat phone. Do not attempt the journey alone.

All of Cape York's **terrestrial national parks** *(parks.qld.gov.au/parks/cape-york/about)* are located on Aboriginal land and are jointly managed by the Queensland Parks & Wildlife Service. Camping fees apply in all parks (book online in advance), with free camping generally allowed outside national parks. There are also a handful of **private camping grounds** on the cape including the camping ground beside the Jardine River ferry; both the camping ground and pricey ferry are operated by the Northern Peninsula Area Regional Council. In Bamaga, the **Cape York Peninsula Lodge** *(capeyorklodge.au)* offers more creature comforts.

Bloomfield Falls
ATTEM/SHUTTERSTOCK

PHOTO OPPORTUNITY

Bloomfield Falls at Wujal Wujal.

22

★ BEST FOR:

OUTDOORS

Karumba is the most accessible corner of the Gulf of Carpentaria.

QUEENSLAND

OUTBACK QUEENSLAND

DURATION: 7–10 DAYS

DISTANCE: 1219KM / 758 MILES

GREAT FOR: OUTDOORS & CULTURE

BEST TIME TO GO: APRIL TO OCTOBER – THE REST OF THE YEAR IS VERY HOT AND/OR VERY WET.

Historic Village Herberton

The outback may seem like the preserve of hardened 4WD adventurers, but this 2WD traverse crosses stirring outback country and has all the ingredients for a fine adventure without leaving the tarmac. It all begins in the lush, tropical surroundings of Cairns and the Atherton Tablelands, with Undara Volcanic National Park offering drama before the parched outback of Croydon, Normanton, Cloncurry and Mt Isa, each getting remoter by degrees.

LINK YOUR TRIP

17 Queensland Coastal Cruise
Travel the Queensland coast ending (or beginning) in Cairns, which is also where your journey into the outback begins.

20 Cairns & the Daintree
Reef and rainforest are the highlights on this journey from Cairns to Cape Tribulation.

01 Cairns

Cairns is an unlikely gateway to the outback, but therein lies its charm. Above all else, swim in the ocean (you won't see it again for a while), stock up on your favourite snacks for the long drive ahead (most shops from here on in will stock only the basics) and dive into the culinary scene (it's pub food and not much else until Mt Isa).

THE DRIVE: Follow the coastal Bruce Hwy for 24km south to Gordonvale, then veer inland at the Gillies Hwy. The road bucks and weaves southwest through rainforested hillsides and rocky outcrops to Yungaburra, idyllic twin lakes of **Crater Lakes National Park** *(parks.qld.gov.au/parks/crater-lakes)*, 12km before reaching Atherton. It's then 18km southwest to Herberton.

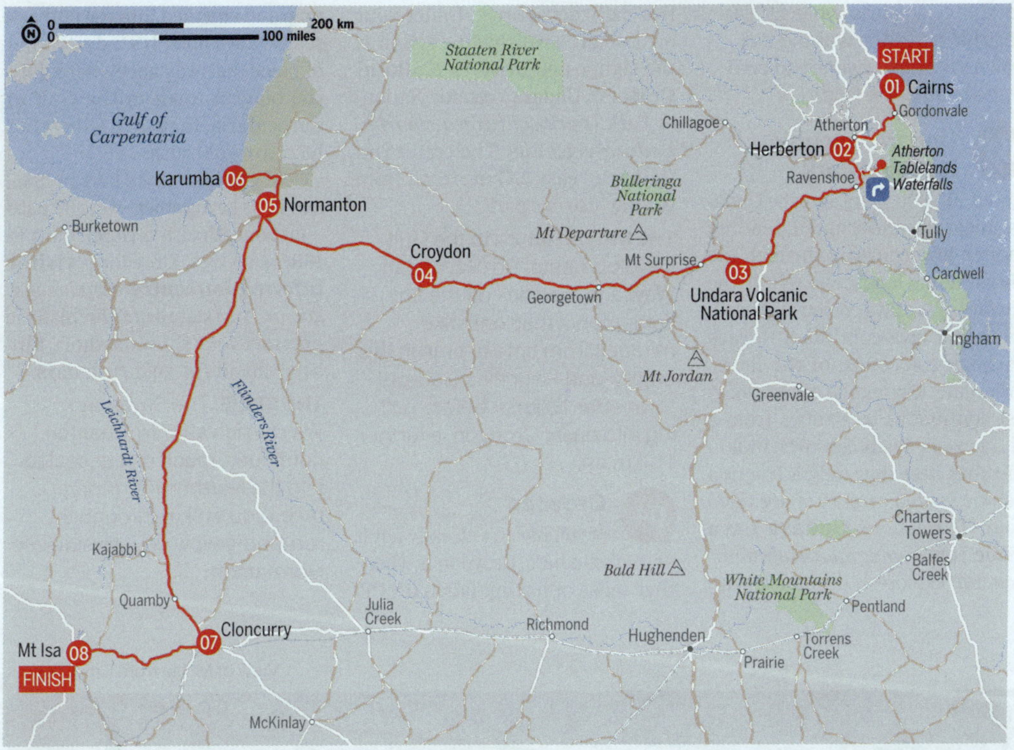

AUSTRALIANCAMERA/SHUTTERSTOCK

02 Herberton

A must-see on any comprehensive trip into the tableland is the fascinating, fun and unique **Historic Village Herberton** *(historicvillageherberton.com.au)*, which comprises over 50 heritage buildings, restored and relocated to this sweet, sleepy tableland town. Exhibits range from the school to the sawmill, the bank to the bishop's house, the coach house to the camera shop and everything in between. It all feels like a rather cutesy museum, but that's the point and there's nothing quite like it anywhere else in Australia.

THE DRIVE: It's 18km back to the Kennedy Hwy, a further 19km south to Ravenshoe, then 142km to Undara Volcanic National Park, with the views either side of the road getting drier with each passing kilometre. Undara is 15km south off the Gulf Developmental Rd, via a sealed road.

DETOUR

Atherton Tablelands Waterfalls

Start: 02 Herberton

Climbing back from the coast between Innisfail and Cairns is the fertile food bowl of the tropical north, the Atherton Tablelands. Quaint country towns, eco-lodges and luxurious B&Bs dot greener-than-green hills between patchwork fields, pockets of rainforest, spectacular lakes and waterfalls, and Queensland's highest mountains, Bartle Frere (1622m) and Bellenden Ker (1593m).

From Herberton it's 39km to Millaa Millaa, which lies along the Palmerston Hwy; 1km east of Millaa Millaa, turn north on to Theresa Creek Rd. Surrounded by tree ferns and flowers, the Millaa Millaa Falls, 1.5km along, are easily the best for swimming and have a grassy picnic area. Almost ridiculously picturesque, the spectacular 12m falls are reputed to be the most photographed in Australia. Zillie Falls, 8km further on, are reached by a short walking trail that leads to a lookout peering down (with some vertigo) on the falls, while Ellinjaa Falls have a 200m walking trail down to a rocky swimming hole at the base of the falls.

03 Undara Volcanic National Park

About 190,000 years ago, the Undara shield volcano erupted, sending molten lava coursing through the surrounding landscape. While the surface of the lava cooled and hardened, hot lava continued to race through the centre of the flows, eventually leaving the world's longest continuous lava tubes from a single vent. There are over 160km of tubes here, but only a fraction can be visited as part of a guided tour. Three-hour **Undara Lava Tube Tours** *(undaralavatubetours.com.au)* explore four tunnels, with two daily departures. Under your own steam, a worthwhile detour is the signposted drive to **Kalkani Crater** in Undara Volcanic National Park *(parks.qld.gov.au/parks/undara-volcanic)*. The crater rim walk is an easy 2.5km circuit from the day-use car park.

THE DRIVE: Return to the Gulf Developmental Rd (Savannah Way) and then tick off the tiny settlements that loom like mirages from time to time in this empty land – such as Georgetown after 127km – before pulling into dusty Crodyon, a further 149km on.

04 Croydon

If you haven't already felt it on the road here, Croydon is where that sense of having fallen off the map and emerged into the outback really takes hold. It's a dusty kind of place that was once, incredibly, the biggest town in the Gulf of Carpentaria, thanks to a short but lucrative gold rush.

Gold was discovered here in 1885, and in its heyday there were 30 pubs – just one, the Club Hotel, built in 1887, survives. Croydon's **visitor information centre** *(croydon.qld.gov.au)* has details of the historic precinct and shows a short film (free) about the gold-rush days.

THE DRIVE: The Savannah Way (which after Normanton continues, much of it unsealed, into the Northern Territory) takes you 148km through the red-and-yellow countryside into Normanton.

View of Mt Isa from City Lookout

ROB WALLS/ALAMY

05 Normanton

The port for Croydon's gold rush, Normanton has a broad and rather long main street lined with colourful old buildings. These days it's a quiet place that occasionally springs into life: every Easter the **Barra Classic** lures big crowds, as do the **Normanton Rodeo & Campdraft** (mid-June) and the **Normanton Races** (September). In the historic Burns Philp building, Normanton's excellent **visitor information and heritage centre** *(carpentaria.qld.gov.au)* has historical displays and lots of regional info.

Everyone takes a photo of **Krys the Crocodile** on Landsborough St. It's a supposedly life-size statue of an 8.64m saltie shot by croc hunter Krystina Pawloski on the Norman River in 1958 – the largest recorded croc in the world.

THE DRIVE: As the crow flies, Karumba, on the shores of the Gulf, is a short distance away across the Mutton Wetlands, but by road you'll need to travel around 74km to reach the town.

06 Karumba

When the sun sinks into the Gulf of Carpentaria in a fiery ball of burnt ochre, Karumba is transformed into a little piece of outback paradise. This is the only town accessible by sealed road on the entire gulf coast, and it's a great place to kick back for a few days. The actual town is on the Norman River, while Karumba Point, about 6km away by road, is on a gulf beach.

PHOTO OPPORTUNITY

SUNSET FROM MT ISA

Sunset from City Lookout, Mt Isa, for its mine lights and smokestacks.

Karumba's **visitor information centre** *(carpentaria.qld.gov.au)* has details of fishing charters and cruises; **Ferryman** *(ferryman.net.au)* operates regular sunset cruises and fishing charters in the Dry, while **Karumba Cruises** *(karumbacruises.com.au)* runs excellent half-day tours including crab-catching and croc-spotting on the Norman River.

THE DRIVE: When you can bring yourself to leave the gulf behind, return to Normanton. From here the Burke Developmental Rd is a seriously quiet outback road, crossing the dry gulf hinterland. After 192km, pause for some company at the Burke & Wills Roadhouse, and then it's 181 lonely kilometres south to Cloncurry.

07 Cloncurry

Compared with where you're coming from, Cloncurry (population 3167) will seem like the height of civilisation. Known to its friends as 'the Curry', it's renowned as one of the hottest places in Australia and the birthplace of the Royal Flying Doctor Service (RFDS); today it's a busy pastoral centre. The outstanding **John Flynn Place** *(experiencecloncurry.com)* celebrates Dr John Flynn's work setting up the invaluable and groundbreaking RFDS, which gives hope, help and health services to people across the remote outback.

THE DRIVE: You're almost there and, having come so far, you'll barely notice the final 122km along the slightly (but only slightly) more heavily trafficked Barkly Hwy.

08 Mt Isa

You can't miss the smokestacks as you drive into Mt Isa, one of Queensland's longest-running mining towns and a travel and lifestyle hub for Queensland. The sunset view from the **City Lookout** of the twinkling mine lights and silhouetted smokestacks is strangely pretty and very Mt Isa. Strange rock formations – padded with olive-green spinifex – line the perimeter of town, and deep-blue sunsets eclipse all unnatural light. Try to visit in mid-August for Australia's largest **rodeo** *(mountisarodeo.com.au)*. Don't miss the award-winning **Outback at Isa** *(outbackatisa.com.au)*, which includes the **Hard Times Mine**, an underground tour guided by ex-miners; the **Isa Experience Heritage Display**, a hands-on museum providing a colourful and articulate overview of local history; and the fascinating **Riversleigh Fossil Centre**.

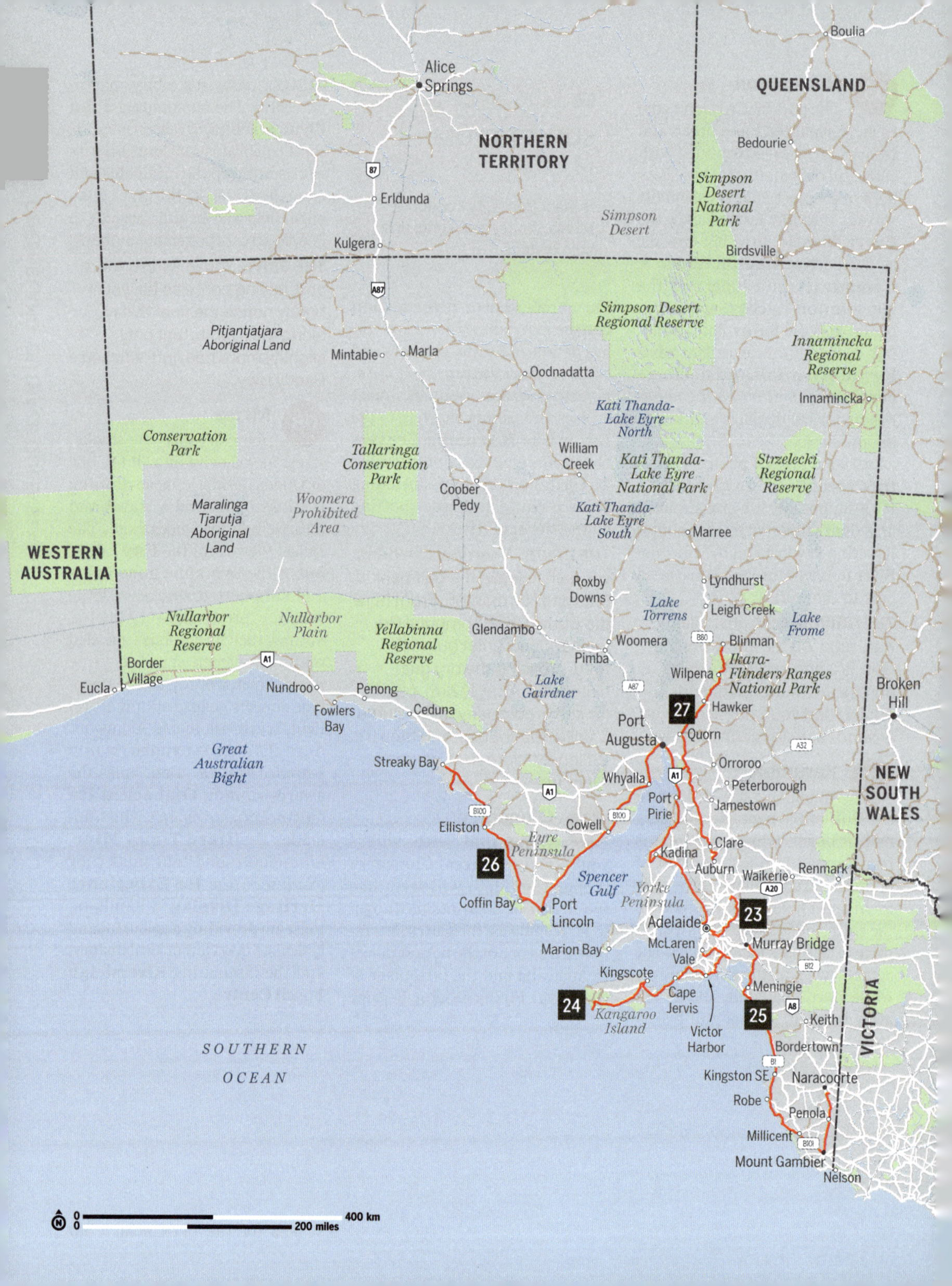

Alice Springs
NORTHERN TERRITORY
QUEENSLAND
Boulia
Bedourie
Simpson Desert National Park
Simpson Desert
Erldunda
Kulgera
Birdsville
87
A87
Simpson Desert Regional Reserve
Pitjantjatjara Aboriginal Land
Mintabie
Marla
Oodnadatta
Innamincka Regional Reserve
Innamincka
Kati Thanda-Lake Eyre North
Conservation Park
Tallaringa Conservation Park
William Creek
Kati Thanda-Lake Eyre National Park
Strzelecki Regional Reserve
Coober Pedy
Maralinga Tjarutja Aboriginal Land
Woomera Prohibited Area
Kati Thanda-Lake Eyre South
Marree
WESTERN AUSTRALIA
Roxby Downs
Lyndhurst
Lake Torrens
Leigh Creek
Lake Frome
Nullarbor Regional Reserve
Nullarbor Plain
Yellabinna Regional Reserve
Glendambo
Woomera
B80
Blinman
Pimba
Ikara-Flinders Ranges National Park
Wilpena
Border Village
A1
Eucla
Nundroo
Penong
Lake Gairdner
A87
Broken Hill
Fowlers Bay
Ceduna
27
Hawker
Port Augusta
Quorn
A32
Great Australian Bight
Streaky Bay
Whyalla
Orroroo
A1
Peterborough
NEW SOUTH WALES
Port Pirie
Jamestown
B100
Elliston
Cowell
B100
Clare
Eyre Peninsula
Kadina
26
Auburn
Waikerie
Renmark
Spencer Gulf
Yorke Peninsula
A20
Coffin Bay
Port Lincoln
Adelaide
23
Murray Bridge
Marion Bay
McLaren Vale
B12
Kingscote
Cape Jervis
Meningie
24
Kangaroo Island
A8
25
Keith
Victor Harbor
VICTORIA
SOUTHERN OCEAN
Bordertown
B1
Kingston SE
Naracoorte
Robe
Penola
Millicent
B101
Mount Gambier
Nelson
0 400 km
0 200 miles
N

HDDIGITAL/SHUTTERSTOCK

Barossa Valley vineyard (p175)

SOUTH AUSTRALIA

EXPLORE SOUTH AUSTRALIA

Often underestimated as a traveller destination, South Australia is quite happy to fly under the radar. Its coastline is wild and simply superb (nowhere more so than on Kangaroo Island). The Flinders Ranges may well be one of the most beautiful outback mountain ranges Australia has to offer. And the state's many wine regions – the Barossa Valley, Coonawarra, McLaren Vale, Clare Valley – are widely regarded as some of Australia's finest. At the start and end point of so many road trips, Adelaide is a green and cultured city filled with festivals.

Adelaide

One of Australia's quieter state capitals, Adelaide can feel like a large country town with a refreshing lack of big-city brashness. Parklands ripple out from the centre, and the city is well known for its fine festivals and pretty architecture. By far the state's biggest city, it also has SA's best choice of accommodation and dining options. Perhaps more than any other state capital, Adelaide's location puts it at the centre of so many journeys: whichever direction you're heading, chances are you'll pass through this place. Plan to spend some time enjoying its charms.

Port Augusta

The Spencer Gulf cuts deep into the South Australian interior, bringing the sea within sight of the outback. Where that happens, Port Augusta sits as the quintessential crossroads town – roads from here fan out to Alice Springs (and beyond to Darwin), Perth, Adelaide and elsewhere. There's a pleasant waterside park and a fabulous botanical garden dedicated to outback flora. Otherwise, Port Augusta is a place to refuel, restock your supplies in its supermarkets, rest from life on the road (there are lots of motels, but not a lot of variety) and grab a quick meal and/or beer.

WHEN TO GO

Most of SA is fine to visit year-round, although winters (June to August) in the southeast can be cold and unappealing and many places close across the Yorke and Eyre peninsulas. Autumn (March to May) can be glorious in the Adelaide Hills and Barossa Valley, while spring wildflowers (September to November) are a highlight from Clare Valley heading north.

Mt Gambier

If you're coming from Victoria, or otherwise journeying around the state's southeast, Mt Gambier is the main hub. Victoria's Great Ocean Road lies just across the border, while on the SA side you're close to Naracoorte Caves and Coonawarra wine region. Historic buildings line its town centre while the astonishing Blue Lake vividly lives up to its name in summer. Accommodation consists mostly of pubs and motels, with the occasional B&B thrown in, and for meals there's a decent choice of cafes, restaurants, burger joints and pub meals.

Coober Pedy

There's one paved road into Coober Pedy and another (actually, the continuation of the same road) heading out. And there are no other towns of any size for hundreds of kilometres in any direction. This important outback centre and opal-mining town, where a significant proportion of the population lives underground, also happens to be an important crossroads where dozens of outback trails – many of them unsealed and best traversed in a 4WD – converge and fan out into the desert. It's a remarkable place where you can get a much-needed meal, stock up on supplies and find a place to sleep (also underground if you want).

TRANSPORT

Adelaide is South Australia's main transport hub, with a decent roster of flights connecting the city to the rest of the country. Distances are vast, so fly where you can: **Rex** *(rex.com.au)* connects Adelaide with Coober Pedy, Mt Gambier, Ceduna and Port Lincoln. Buses run along a handful of major and interstate routes. Otherwise, roads are generally in excellent condition.

WHERE TO STAY

South Australia generally has less variety in its accommodation than other Australian states. Exceptions include Adelaide, which has some charming historic hotels and B&Bs; the plentiful B&Bs that appear throughout the wine regions, especially in the Barossa Valley, McLaren Vale and Clare Valley; and Kangaroo Island, which has a small but great mix of accommodation, with epic coastal views a recurring theme. Elsewhere, finding somewhere to stay usually means resorts (along the coast and in the Flinders Ranges), national park campgrounds (in remote areas) or motels and caravan parks (just about everywhere).

RESOURCES

- **Experience Adelaide**
  The lowdown on Australia's most underrated city. *experienceadelaide.com.au*
- **National Parks and Wildlife Service South Australia**
  Explore South Australia's wild places. *parks.sa.gov.au*
- **South Australian Tourism Commission**
  Online info for practical planning and inspirational dreaming. *southaustralia.com*

WHAT'S ON

- **Adelaide Fringe**
  This annual independent arts festival in February and March is second on the world stage after the Edinburgh Fringe. *adelaidefringe.com.au*
- **Barossa Vintage Festival**
  Music, maypole dancing, tug-of-war contests etc; around Easter (harvest time) in odd-numbered years. Combines with SA's top foodie gatherings through the year. *barossavintagefestival.com.au*
- **WOMADelaide**
  Among Australia's best live-music events, attracting more than 300 performers from around the globe in March. *womadelaide.com.au*

23

SOUTH AUSTRALIA

ADELAIDE HILLS & THE BAROSSA VALLEY

DURATION: 3–4 DAYS

DISTANCE: 130KM / 80 MILES

GREAT FOR: WINE & HISTORY

BEST TIME TO GO: MARCH TO MAY, WHEN THE VINE LEAVES ARE AT THEIR AUTUMNAL BEST.

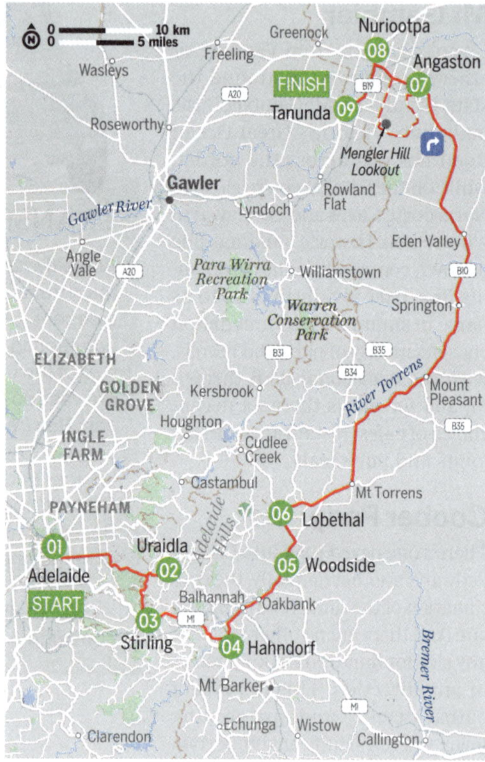

When the Adelaide plains are desert-hot in summer, the Adelaide Hills (technically the Mt Lofty Ranges – the traditional lands of the Peramangk people) are always a few degrees cooler, with crisp air and labyrinthine valleys. Early colonists built stately summer houses around Stirling and Aldgate, and German settlers infused towns with European architecture. Further north, the Barossa Valley's wineries are truly world-class.

LINK YOUR TRIP

04 Alice Springs to Adelaide
From the outback to South Australia's urbane capital (1500km), this trip is an exercise in contrasts.

26 Yorke & Eyre Peninsulas
Adelaide is the start of the 701km trip to Streaky Bay before crossing two vast peninsulas, joined by a ferry.

01 Adelaide

Adelaide these days has moved on from its pious, hokey 'City of Churches' tag, with hip laneway bars and a reputation for world-class cultural fiestas. While this trip offers plenty of opportunities for a drink, let's sidestep the booze for a moment and find a laid-back spot to chill out. Beachy **Glenelg** fits the bill perfectly. 'The Bay' – the site of SA's first colonial incursion into Kaurna country – is Adelaide at its most LA. Glenelg's lovely beach faces west, and as the sun sinks into the sea, the fish-and-chip shops fill up with surfies, backpackers and sun-tanned sexagenarians. The tram rumbles in from the city, past the Jetty Rd shopping strip to the al-fresco cafes around Moseley Sq. The **Glenelg Visitor Information Centre** has the local low-down: pick up the *Kaurna yarta-ana* cultural map for some insights into Aboriginal heritage in the area.

THE DRIVE: From the city centre, the quickest route into the

DARREN TIERNEY/SHUTTERSTOCK

★ BEST FOR:

WINE

Tanunda's big reds and the Adelaide Hills' cool-climate whites are truly world-class.

Vineyard, Barossa Valley (p175)

Adelaide Hills is the South-eastern Fwy (M1) to Stirling. But take Greenhill Rd from the southern edge of the Adelaide Park Lands instead – a very straight then very wiggly 17km Hills mainline that deposits you in endearing little Uraidla.

02 Uraidla

Just a few short years ago, the town of **Uraidla** (and neighbouring **Summertown**) were neglected, overlooked, bypassed and forgotten (we could think of plenty more grim adjectives, but you get the picture). Then, the old pub was smartened up and started brewing craft beer out the back of the cafe next door. A pizza joint opened up in the old church across the road, and a bistro started making 'Top 100 Restaurants' lists around the country. Now there are few more pleasant places in the Hills to while away an afternoon. The **Uraidla Hotel** *(uraidlahotel.com.au)* is the epicentre of proceedings here: don't miss it.

THE DRIVE: From Uraidla, the drive to Stirling is convoluted and poorly signed – but basically you want to backtrack a kilometre or so to Summertown, turn south onto Piccadilly Rd, left onto Old Mt Barker Rd, cross the freeway, take a right into Pomona Rd and you're there. It's a very scenic 8km drive.

03 Stirling

The photogenic little village of **Stirling** (population 2970) is famed for its bedazzling autumn colours, thanks to the deciduous trees the first white residents saw fit to seed – it's one of the most spectacular autumnal shows in the country. In late April, the resident doctor-and-lawyer types are positively brimming with civic pride. There are some great cafes here these days and the brilliant **Stirling Hotel** *(stirlinghotel.com.au)* – but a more constructive use of your time might be a visit to **Mt Lofty Summit** *(parks.sa.gov.au)* which, at a surprising 727m, has show-stopping views across the Adelaide plains to the shimmering Gulf St Vincent.

Mt Lofty Summit Visitor Information Centre has info on local attractions and walking tracks, including the steep Waterfall Gully Track (8km return, 2½ hours) and **Mt Lofty Botanic Garden** *(botanicgardens.sa.gov.au)* Loop Trail (7km loop, two hours). There's a decent **cafe** here too. Afterwards, if you've yet to spy a koala on your travels, you can hug one at **Cleland Wildlife Park** *(clelandwildlifepark.sa.gov.au)*, just below the summit. Backtrack into Stirling and ferret out one of the best little wineries in the Adelaide Hills, **Deviation Road** *(deviationroad.com)*. There's nothing deviant about the wines here: sublime pinot noir, substantial shiraz, zingy pinot gris and a very decent bubbly. Put a couple of bottles in your bag for later on. Not far away, one-horse **Aldgate** (population 3350) has been home to both Bon Scott and Mel Gibson over the years.

THE DRIVE: From Aldgate, forsake the fast-paced M1 and change down a gear: the quieter, prettier Mt Barker Rd through Bridgewater (is the waterwheel on the old Bridgewater Mill spinning today?) is a much nicer drive. It's about eight very wiggly kilometres from Aldgate up over Germantown Hill and down into Hahndorf, the oldest German settlement in Australia.

04 Hahndorf

Like the Rocks in Sydney, and Richmond near Hobart, **Hahndorf** is a 'ye olde worlde' colonial enclave that trades ruthlessly on its history: it's something of a kitsch parody of itself. That said, Hahndorf (population 2670) is undeniably pretty, with Teutonic sandstone architecture, European trees, and flowers overflowing from half wine barrels. And it is interesting: Australia's oldest surviving German settlement (1839), founded by 50 Lutheran families fleeing religious persecution in Prussia, Hahndorf was placed under martial law during WWI, and its name changed to 'Ambleside' (renamed Hahndorf in 1935). It's also slowly becoming less kitsch and more cool: there are a few interesting cafes and bars, and on a sunny day the main street is positively pumping. For an informed taste of what it's all about, try **Hahndorf Walking**

Hahndorf Inn, Hahndorf

MYPHOTOBANK.COM.AU/SHUTTERSTOCK

Tours *(hahndorfwalkingtours.com.au)*, or duck into one of the town's old stone pubs for a *wurst* (sausage), a Löwenbräu and some sauerkraut – we like the **Hahndorf Inn** *(hahndorfinn.com)*. The town's history assumes a more artistic shape at the **Hahndorf Academy** *(hahndorfacademy.org.au)*, but if your journey is all about good food and wine, you're in luck. Three of the Hills' best wineries are on the outskirts of town: **Nepenthe Wines** *(nepenthe.com.au)*, **Shaw & Smith** *(shawandsmith.com)* and **The Lane** *(thelane.com.au)* – the last of these three also has superb views over rolling vine-striped hillsides. On the opposite side of Hahndorf, you can pick your own strawberries between November and May from the famous, family-run **Beerenberg Strawberry Farm** *(beerenberg.com.au)*.

THE DRIVE: From Hahndorf, return northwest along Mt Barker Rd, then turn north (right) along Ambleside Rd. Where it ends, take Onkaparinga Valley Rd (B34) to the right through Balhannah and Oakbank to Woodside – it's a picturesque 12km drive.

05 Woodside

Workaday **Woodside** (population 2610 – founded in the early 1850s) has a few enticements for galloping gourmands – it's here that the foodie character of your classic SA trip begins to show itself. In an old redbrick industrial complex behind the main street, **Woodside Cheese Wrights** *(woodsidecheese.com.au)* is a passionate and unpretentious gem, producing classic, artisan and experimental cheeses (soft styles a speciality) from locally grazing sheep and cows. Our pick is the lemon myrtle chevre. Just next door, stock up on rocky road, scorched almonds and appallingly realistic chocolate cow pats at **Melba's Chocolate & Confectionery Factory** *(melbaschocolates.com)*, a long-running Hills institution. If you're in more of a wine frame of mind, check out **Bird in Hand** *(birdinhand.com.au)* just north of town. Expect brilliant pinot rosé plus shiraz, merlot and blends, and an olive-oil press. Regular concerts happen in summer and there's the upmarket Galley restaurant for lunch.

BAROSSA VALLEY WINES

Thanks to hot, dry summers and cool, moderate winters, the Barossa is one of the world's great wine regions – an absolute must for anyone with even the slightest interest in a good drop. It's a compact valley – just 25km long – yet it produces 21% of Australia's wine. The local towns have a distinctly German heritage, dating back to 1842. Fleeing religious persecution in Prussia and Silesia, settlers (bringing their vine cuttings with them) created a Lutheran heartland where German traditions persist today. The physical remnants of colonisation – Gothic church steeples and stone cottages – are everywhere. Cultural legacies of the early days include a dubious passion for oom-pah bands, and an appetite for *wurst* (sausage), pretzels and sauerkraut.

The Barossa is best known for shiraz, with riesling the dominant white. There are 80-plus vineyards here and around 60 cellar doors, ranging from boutique wine rooms to monstrous complexes. The long-established 'Barossa Barons' hold sway – big and brassy – while spritely young boutique wineries are harder to sniff out.

These are the pick of the bunch:

Rockford Wines
Boutique 1850s cellar door with small-range wines, including sparkling reds.
rockfordwines.com.au

Henschke
Old-school Henschke (1860s) is known for its iconic Hill of Grace red.
henschke.com.au

Peter Lehmann
The shiraz and riesling vintages here are probably the most consistent, affordable and widely distributed wines in the Barossa.
peterlehmannwines.com

Seppeltsfield
Atmospheric, bluestone Seppeltsfield estate started life in 1851 when Joe Seppelt established one of Australia's most esteemed wine brands.
seppeltsfield.com.au

Penfolds
A Barossa legend. Book ahead for the Make Your Own Blend tour ($65) or the Taste of Grange tour ($150).
penfolds.com

THE DRIVE: Continue northeast along the B34 for 3km, then take the Lobethal turnoff to the left. Bisect a few paddocks and you'll be in Lobethal in a quickfire 3km.

06 Lobethal

In the 'Valley of Praise', Lobethal (population 2530) was established by Lutheran Pastor Fritzsche and his followers in 1842. Like Hahndorf, Lobethal was renamed during WWI – 'Tweedale' was the unfortunate choice. It's still a pious town: church life plays a leading role in many locals' day-to-day lives, though some excellent wineries in the surrounding hills demand reverence of a different kind. Lobethal's main street has the usual complement of soporific pubs and hardware stores, but the town really hits its stride during December's **Lights of Lobethal festival** *(lightsoflobethal.com.au)* – a blaze of Christmas lights bringing in sightseers. Check out the town, then head to the streetside terrace at the **Lobethal Bierhaus** *(bierhaus.com.au)* for some serious craft-beer concoctions. The Red Truck Porter will put hairs on your chest, whether you want them or not. Up in the hills behind town, seek out **Pike & Joyce** *(pikeandjoyce.com.au)* winery for some sublime chardonnay and mesmerising views.

THE DRIVE: From Lobethal, get your skates on and make the physical and psychological shift from the Adelaide Hills to the Barossa Valley. Angaston is 60km away via the B34, then the B10.

07 Angaston

An agricultural vibe persists in photo-worthy Angaston, named after George Fife Angas, a pioneering Barossa pastoralist. There are relatively few wineries on the town's doorstep: cows graze in paddocks at the end of the streets. Along the main drag are two pubs, some terrific eateries and a few B&Bs in old stone cottages. Don't miss the hearty Germanic offerings, local produce and questionable buskers at the weekly **Barossa Farmers Market** *(barossafarmersmarket.com)* and the excellent **Barossa Valley Cheese Company** *(barossacheese.com.au)* on the main street (it's unlikely you'll leave without buying a wedge of the Washington Washed Rind).

To get the whole wine thing happening, about 10km southeast of Angaston in the Eden Valley, old-school **Henschke** is known for its iconic Hill of Grace red, but most of the wines here are classics. If you don't have the time, energy, or petrol to visit Henschke, duck into **Taste Eden Valley** in the middle of Angaston to sample the valley's best offerings. Also in Angaston, **Yalumba** *(yalumba.com)* is one of the Barossa's (and Australia's) major players, making big bucks at the budget end of the wine spectrum. But there's nothing budget about the gorgeous 1850s estate. The cellar door here offers tastes of the good stuff that doesn't end up in cardboard casks. Check out the old brick chimney – the Leaning Tower of Angaston?

THE DRIVE: Nuriootpa lies just 7km northwest of Angaston along the B10. You're now deep in the dark heart of the Barossa Valley.

DETOUR

Mengler Hill Lookout

Start: 07 Angaston

From Angaston, rise above the boozy goings-on down on the valley floor with a detour up to **Mengler Hill Lookout**, from where hazy views extend across the vine stripes and the church spires (just ignore the tacky sculptures in the foreground). Studded with huge eucalyptus trees, Mengler Hill Rd tracks through beautiful rural country between the two towns. To rejoin the main route, continue down the other side of the hill and head for Nuriootpa via Light Pass Rd, turning left onto Siegersdorf Rd, then right onto Murray St.

08 Nuriootpa

Along an endless main street at the northern end of the valley, Nuriootpa is the Barossa's commercial centre. It's not as endearing as Tanunda or Angaston, but it has a certain agrarian simplicity. There's a big new supermarket

---

♥ WHY I LOVE THIS TRIP

CHARLES RAWLINGS-WAY, WRITER

Any visitor to South Australia who's into wine will want to check out the Barossa Valley – the region is a true icon of SA. But it's a desperately dull drive up a series of freeways from Adelaide. Instead, take the superscenic (and only slightly longer) route through the old towns of the Adelaide Hills – a South Australian history lesson and a mighty pretty wine region in its own right.

ROBERTHARDING/ALAMY

Mengler Hill Lookout, Barossa Valley

complex here too, and unlike many South Australian towns, the population in 'Nuri' is actually growing. Perhaps it has something to do with Lutheran spirit: a sign says, 'God has invested in you – are you showing any interest?' Don't miss a drive along **Seppeltsfield Rd** *(seppeltsfieldroad.com)*, an incongruous avenue of huge palm trees meandering through the vineyards behind Nuri. Beyond Marananga, the palm rows veer off the roadside and track up a hill to the **Seppelt Family Mausoleum** – a Grecian tomb fronted by chunky Doric columns. If wine is why you're here, **Seppeltsfield** *(seppeltsfield.com.au)* itself is one of Australia's most esteemed wineries, founded in 1851 when Joe Seppelt stuck some vines in the Barossa dirt and came up trumps. It's famous for its 100-year-old Para Tawny. Back closer to town, **Penfolds** *(penfolds.com)* is a Barossa institution and one of Australia's best-known wineries. Book ahead for the Make Your Own Blend tour, or the Taste of Grange tour, which allows you to slide some Grange Hermitage across your lips (if you want to buy a bottle, prices kick off at around $900).

PHOTO OPPORTUNITY

MENGLER HILL LOOKOUT

Across the Barossa from atop Mengler Hill Lookout.

THE DRIVE: Take the B19 southwest from Nuriootpa and after 7km you'll find yourself in busy Tanunda.

09 Tanunda

At the centre of the valley both geographically and socially, Tanunda is the Barossa's main tourist town. It's a place which manages to combine the practicality of Nuriootpa with the charm of Angaston without a sniff of self-importance. The wineries are what you're here for and it's very much worth the wait. Tanunda is flush with historic buildings, including the cottages around **Goat Square**. Enjoy a stroll to take them in, then get down to the seriously pleasurable business of indulging in the region's wines.

24

★ BEST FOR:

FOODIES

Shuffling between cellar doors in the McLaren Vale Wine Region.

SOUTH AUSTRALIA

MCLAREN VALE & KANGAROO ISLAND

d'Arenberg Cube, McLaren Vale

DURATION: 7 DAYS

DISTANCE: 381KM / 237 MILES

GREAT FOR: WINE & NATURE

BEST TIME TO GO: YEAR-ROUND

Patterned with vineyards running down to the turquoise sea, the Fleurieu Peninsula is home to the world-renowned McLaren Vale Wine Region, best known for its bottles of blood-red shiraz. Further east, the Fleurieu's Encounter Coast is an engaging mix of surf beaches, low-key historic towns and whales cavorting in the water. Wildlife-rich Kangaroo Island is a vast, untouristed land mass 13km offshore – the perfect place to chill at your journey's end.

LINK YOUR TRIP

04 Alice Springs to Adelaide
Head for Australia's Red Centre – our journey may begin in Alice Springs, but there's no reason you can't drive it in reverse.

23 Adelaide Hills & the Barossa Valley
This trip into the not-so-lofty Mt Lofty Ranges and beyond to the famed Barossa Valley begins in Adelaide.

01 McLaren Vale

Flanked by the wheat-coloured Willunga Scarp and striated with vines, McLaren Vale is just 40 minutes south of Adelaide. Servicing the famed McLaren Vale Wine Region, it's a businesslike, utilitarian town that's not much to look at – but it has some top eating options and offers easy access to some truly excellent winery cellar doors. To make the most of your time here (and to neatly sidestep the possibility of losing your driving licence), sign up for a tour and tick a few cellar doors off your list. Operators include **Cellar Door Tours** *(cellardoorwinetours.com.au)*, **Chook's Little Winery Tours** *(chookstours.com.au)* and **Adelaide's Top Food & Wine Tours** *(topfoodandwinetours.com.au)*. Don't miss the amazing **d'Arenberg Cube** *(darenberg.com.au/darenberg-cube-restaurant)* at d'Arenberg winery, a huge Rubik's

TRABANTOS/SHUTTERSTOCK

Cube-like restaurant/cellar door/museum that's fast becoming a regional icon. To mix it all up without straying too close to sobriety, check out family-run **Goodieson Brewery** *(goodiesonbrewery.com.au)* and imbibe a few pale ales, or **McLaren Vale Distillery** *(mvdistillery.com.au)* for a weekend whisky.

THE DRIVE: The cute heritage town of Willunga is a quick 6km drive south of McLaren Vale. You'll pass by well-tended vineyards along the way, owned by some big-name SA wine producers, including Leconfield and Penny's Hill.

02 Willunga

A one-horse town with three pubs and two craft-beer breweries, arty Willunga took off in 1840 when large quantities of high-quality slate were discovered here, mined, then exported across Australia. Willunga slate was used for everything from flagstones to street gutter linings and billiard tables. Today, the town's early buildings along sloping High St are occupied by some excellent eateries, B&B accommodation and galleries. There's also the terrific **Willunga Farmers Market** *(willungafarmersmarket.com.au)* here every Saturday morning, heavy on the organic, the bespoke and the locally sourced – don't miss it. For an insight into the town's slate-mining history (and the Cornish miners who did all the dirty work), check out the **Willunga Slate Museum** *(nationaltrust.org.au/places/willunga-slate-museum)* at the top of the main street. You can also pick up the *Willunga Slate Trail & Museum* brochure and tour the town's top slate spots.

THE DRIVE: The drive from Willunga to Langhorne Creek (59km) climbs over the Mt Lofty Ranges, a photogenic ridge along the spine of the Fleurieu Peninsula. Alternating between densely forested slopes and rolling farm country, this same range becomes the Adelaide Hills further north, cradling the city like a giant croissant. Pass through country-town Meadows and Strathalbyn en route.

03 Langhorne Creek

Around 16km east of Strathalbyn, **Langhorne Creek** *(langhornecreek.com)* is a rather disparate congregation of buildings, but it's one of Australia's oldest wine-growing regions. There are 20-plus wineries here, producing brilliant shiraz, cabernet sauvignon and chardonnay. **Bleasdale Winery** *(bleasdale.com.au)* was the district's first, and has a wide range, historic cellars and an old red-gum lever press (don't get your fingers stuck). Run by two savvy sisters, **Bremerton Wines** *(bremerton.com.au)* is an innovative operator in an old-school region, producing top chardonnay and shiraz. For a solid Langhorne Creek wine overview, try the **Winehouse** *(thewinehouse.com.au)*, a collective cellar door for five wineries. Allow yourself a good long afternoon to nose your way around.

THE DRIVE: Return the way you came 16km to Strathalbyn, but then jag south on the B37 for 28km to Currency Creek, another off-the-beaten-track SA wine region. It's a little hard to believe, but this tiny town was once slated as the future capital of South Australia. From Currency Creek it's a further 8km into Goolwa on the mighty Murray River.

04 Goolwa

Goolwa is a historic port on the Murray River, near where Australia's biggest waterway empties into the sea. It's hard to imagine now, but in 1875 there were 127 riverboats plying the river between here and NSW. Beyond the town's engaging main street is a fantastic beach with ranks of Southern Ocean breakers rolling in. If you feel like braving the waves, book a lesson with **Ocean Living Surf School** *(olsurfschool.com.au)*. Down on the riverfront, a slew of cruise operators vie for your attention, taking you upriver and into the fertile **Coorong National Park**. Try **Canoe the Coorong** *(canoethecoorong.com)* for a water-level perspective, or **Spirit of the Coorong** *(spiritofthecoorong.com.au)*, who can take you down to the Murray River mouth. Back on dry land, **Fleurieu Distillery** *(fleurieudistillery.com.au)* is another of SA's very few whisky distillers (gin is more the thing here). Nearby, the **Wharf Barrel Shed** *(90milewines.com)* zeroes

Coriole vineyard

FILEDIMAGE/SHUTTERSTOCK

MCLAREN VALE WINERIES

If the Barossa Valley is SA wine's old school, then McLaren Vale is the upstart teenager smoking cigarettes behind the shed and stealing nips from mum's sherry bottle. These luscious vineyards have a Tuscan haze in summer, rippling down to a calm coastline that's similarly Ligurian. This is shiraz country – solid, punchy and seriously good. There are 80-plus wineries here: pick up a winery map at the **McLaren Vale & Fleurieu Visitor Information Centre** *(mclarenvale.info)* and go exploring. Some tastings are free; others are pricey, but often redeemable if you buy a bottle. Five of the Vale's finest:

★ Alpha Box & Dice
This refreshing little gambler wins top billing for interesting blends, funky retro furnishings, quirky labels and laid-back staff. *alphaboxdice.com*

★ Coriole
Duck into the Farm Shop at this beautiful stone-cottage cellar door (1860) and assemble a regional tasting platter to share on the lawns, with Redstone shiraz or the flagship chenin blanc. *coriole.com*

★ d'Arenberg
'd'Arry's' relaxes atop a hillside with mighty fine views; the Dead Arm shiraz and the Broken Fishplate sauvignon blanc are our faves. *darenberg.com.au*

★ Wirra Wirra
This barnlike, 1894 cellar door has a grassy picnic area – or a roaring fire inside in winter. Whites include a citrusy viognier and an aromatic riesling. Tasting fees apply. *wirrawirra.com*

★ SC Pannell
With one of the best views in the business, SC Pannell produces excellent reds you can drink young. *pannell.com.au*

in on quality Fleurieu wines (not a difficult task).

THE DRIVE: The drive from Goolwa to its kissing cousin, Victor Harbor, is just 17 coastal kilometres, with views of Encounter Bay away to the south for much of the trip. You'll pass through the affluent enclave of Port Elliot along the way: stop at the town's famous bakery if you're feeling peckish.

05 Victor Harbor

The biggest town on the Encounter Coast is **Victor Harbor** (yes, that's the correct spelling: blame one of SA's poorly schooled early Surveyor Generals) – a raggedy, brawling holiday destination with three huge pubs. Just offshore is the boulder-strewn Granite Island, connected to the mainland by an 1875 causeway. A ride out there on the 1894 double-decker **Horse-Drawn Tram** *(horsedrawntram.com.au)* is the quintessential 'Victor' experience. Victor Harbor is also on the migratory path of southern right whales (May to October). The multilevel **South Australian Whale Centre** *(sawhalecentre.com.au)* has impressive displays and can give you the lowdown on where to see them. For sightings info, call **Whale Information Hotline**.

THE DRIVE: From Victor Harbor, cruise across the southern end of the Fleurieu Peninsula through Inman Valley and Yankalilla, headed for Cape Jervis and the Kangaroo Island ferry terminal. It's 60km from Victor Harbor to the terminal, then a 13km chug across the (sometimes rough) Backstairs Passage to Penneshaw.

06 Penneshaw

Looking across Backstairs Passage to the Fleurieu Peninsula, **Penneshaw** (population 300), on the north shore of the Dudley Peninsula, is the ferry arrival point and Kangaroo Island's second-biggest town. The passing tourist trade, including thousands of wandering cruise-ship passengers in summer, lends a certain transience to the businesses here, but the pub and the backpacker joint remain authentically grounded.

If you're in Penneshaw on the first Sunday of the month, browse the **Kangaroo Island Farmers Market**. Baked goods, chutneys, seafood, olive oil, honey, eggs, cheese, yoghurt, wine, buskers – it's all here, and all good (well, the buskers can be a bit hit-and-miss).

THE DRIVE: From Penneshaw heading west, the road climbs over a steep rise, then returns to sea level for the 61km run to Kingscote. Along the way you'll pass lagoons, dunes, beaches and the turnoff to American

River, named after a crew of American sealers who built a trading schooner here in 1803. Pennington Bay is also en route, KI's best surf beach.

07 Kingscote

Another town once mooted as the future capital of South Australia, snoozy seaside **Kingscote** (kings-coat; population 1830) is the main settlement on KI, and the hub of island life. It's a photogenic town with swaying Norfolk Island pines, a couple of pubs and some decent dining choices – but even in peak summer season it can be deathly (or pleasantly) quiet. There are some interesting foodie haunts around town, however, including **Island Beehive** *(kangarooislandbeeco.com.au),* where factory tours deliver the lowdown on the island's hard-working Ligurian bees. By-products include delicious organic honey and honeycomb ice cream. On the booze front there's craft beer at **Kangaroo Island Brewery** *(kibeer.com.au),* small-batch gin made with native KI juniper berries at **Kangaroo Island Spirits** *(kangarooislandspirits.com.au)* – pray the organic honey-and-walnut version hasn't sold out – and impressive pinot gris and island tasting platters at **Bay of Shoals Wines** *(bayofshoalswines.com.au).* Don't miss dinner at the historic **Ozone Hotel** *(ozonehotelki.com.au)* on the waterfront, or perhaps a pizza at good-fun **Amadio Wines** *(amadiowines.com/kangarooisland)* on the main street.

FLINDERS & BAUDIN IN THE NEW WORLD

As the 1700s drew to a close, British and French navigators were exploring the globe in search of fertile new terrain. Englishman Matthew Flinders made three voyages to the land he later named 'Australia' between 1791 and 1810, bumping into French explorer Nicolas Baudin off Victor Harbor in 1802 and amicably exchanging notes. Baudin surveyed much of the Kangaroo Island coastline, leaving KI's many French place names in his wake. After stepping ashore in 1803 at what is now Penneshaw's Hog Bay, Baudin left his mark: under a white concrete dome on the shoreline is a replica of KI's first piece of graffiti – a rock engraved with *'Expedition De Decouverte par le Commendant Baudin sur Le Geographe 1803'* ('Expedition of discovery by Commander Baudin on Le Geographe 1803'). The original rock can be seen safely preserved at the **Gateway Visitor Information Centre** *(tourkangarooisland.com.au)* nearby. For more on Flinders, Baudin and Penneshaw's history, swing into the Penneshaw **Maritime & Folk Museum** *(nationaltrustsa.org.au).* Inside a 1922 stone school house, this sea-salty collection includes artefacts from local shipwrecks and early white settlement (check out those girthsome millstones), plus endearingly geeky models of Flinders' Investigator and Baudin's *Le Geographe.*

THE DRIVE: It's a straightforward 115km from Kingscote to the outer reaches of Flinders Chase National Park, but it's a drive to cherish as you cross the island from one end to the other. A visit to see the Australian fur seals at Seal Bay Conservation park is a worthwhile detour en route.

08 Flinders Chase National Park

Occupying KI's southwestern corner, **Flinders Chase National Park** *(parks.sa.gov.au)* is one of SA's top national parks. Wildlife is rampant here: kangaroos, wallabies, bandicoots, echidnas and possums, plus koalas and platypuses introduced in the 1920s when it was feared they would become extinct elsewhere. Much of the park is mallee scrub, and there are also some beautiful, tall sugar-gum forests around wildlife-rich **Rocky River** near the park **visitor centre**, and the **Ravine des Casoars** in the park's northern reaches. From Rocky River, a road runs south to the remote 1906 **Cape du Couedic Lighthouse** atop its wild namesake cape. A boardwalk weaves down to **Admirals Arch**, a huge archway eroded by heavy seas, passing a colony of New Zealand fur seals (sweet smelling they ain't). A few kilometres east of Cape du Couedic, the much-photographed **Remarkable Rocks** are a cluster of hefty, weather-gouged granite boulders atop a rocky dome that arcs 75m down to the sea. A remarkable spot to complete your journey.

Remarkable Rocks, Flinders Chase National Park, Kangaroo Island
ADWO/SHUTTERSTOCK

PHOTO OPPORTUNITY

The wind-sculpted Remarkable Rocks on Kangaroo Island.

25

SOUTH AUSTRALIA

LIMESTONE COAST & COONAWARRA

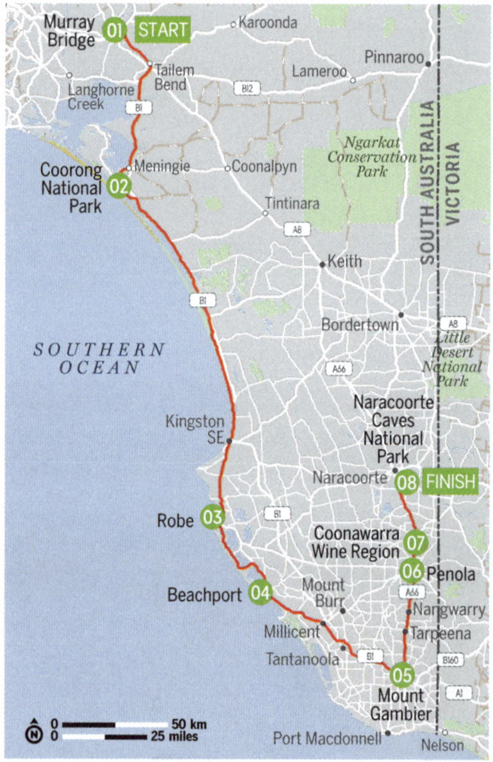

DURATION: 5–7 DAYS

DISTANCE: 493KM / 306 MILES

GREAT FOR: NATURE & WINE

BEST TIME TO GO: YEAR-ROUND, BUT SA'S SOUTHEAST CAN BE COLD AND MISERABLE JUNE TO AUGUST.

It wouldn't be a South Australian road trip without wine involved, but there's plenty to experience here other than dazzling bottles in the Coonawarra Wine Region. Where the Murray River empties into the sea, add the amazing Coorong to your list; plus historic seaside towns like Beachport and Robe; a luminous blue lake; and South Australia's only World Heritage–listed sight, the David Attenborough-endorsed Naracoorte Caves.

LINK YOUR TRIP

23 Adelaide Hills & the Barossa Valley
Murray Bridge is only 76km from Adelaide, and even closer to the gorgeous Adelaide Hills.

24 McLaren Vale & Kangaroo Island
This journey skirts the western side of the Coorong; to get to McLaren Vale, head west and then southwest from Murray Bridge.

01 Murray Bridge

Your journey begins at Murray Bridge on the mighty Murray River – a rambling regional hub (population 14,560; the fifth-biggest town in SA) with charms more subtle than obvious. There's not a whole lot to keep you here, other than the impressive **Murray Bridge Regional Gallery** *(murraybridgegallery.com.au)*, so head down to the muddy riverbanks and shift your mindset into the chilled-out, slow-roaming mode required for the rest of your road trip.

THE DRIVE: Drive 24km southeast of Murray Bridge; at Tailem Bend, take the turnoff south towards Meningie. Roll your windows down and smell the sea-salty air as you approach Coorong National Park.

02 Coorong National Park

The amazing **Coorong National Park** *(parks.sa.gov.au)* is a fecund

★ BEST FOR:

FOODIES

Hopping between tasting rooms in the Coonawarra Wine Region.

CEZARY WOJTKOWSKI/SHUTTERSTOCK

Australian pelicans, Coorong National Park

lagoon landscape curving along the coast for 145km southeast of Lake Alexandrina. A complex series of soaks and salt pans, it's separated from the sea by the chunky dunes of the Younghusband Peninsula. More than 200 waterbird species live here. In the 1860s when white settlers arrived, the Coorong's bountiful resources supported a large Ngarrindjeri population. The Ngarrindjeri are still closely connected to the Coorong, and many remain here. Moving into the 20th century, *Storm Boy*, an endearing 1976 film about a young boy's friendship with a pelican, was filmed here (re-made in 2019). The Princes Hwy scuttles through the Coorong, but you can't see much from the road. Instead, take the 13km, unsealed **Coorong Scenic Drive**. Signed as Seven Mile Rd, it starts 10km southwest of Meningie off the Narrung Rd and takes you right into the landscape, with its stinky lagoons, sea mists, fishing shanties, formation-flying pelicans, black swans and wild emus. The road rejoins the Princes Hwy 10km south of Meningie.

THE DRIVE: From Kingston SE, beyond the Coorong, leave the Princes Hwy and follow the signs towards Robe along the coast. A detour to Cape Jaffa and its endless Southern Ocean views is worthwhile, especially if you stop at Cape Jaffa Wines. Cape Jaffa itself (population 390) is a rather odd place, dominated by a huge artificial anchorage almost completely devoid of yachts.

03 Robe

Poll 100 South Australians for their favourite holiday town and 90 of them will say Robe (the other 10 probably haven't been there). It's a cherubic little fishing port that's become a getaway for Adelaidians and Melburnians alike. The sign saying 'Drain L Outlet' as you roll into town doesn't promise much, but along the main street you'll find quality eateries and boundless accommodation. There are some magic beaches, surf breaks and lakes around town, and myriad heritage-listed buildings dating from the late 1840s to the 1870s. Don't miss the **Obelisk**, an iconic clifftop pre-lighthouse from early colonial days (there were 30 shipwrecks here in 1835 alone), and a visit to raffish **Robe Town Brewery** *(robetownbrewery.com.au)* to sample the local product. Built in 1858, the atmospheric stone **Caledonian Inn** *(caledonianinnrobe.com.au)* is the place to be as the sun sets on another Robe beach day.

THE DRIVE: Swing southeast from Robe along the coast to unpretentious Beachport (46km), a little town with a big jetty.

04 Beachport

'See and be seen: headlights 24 hours!' say signs around this stretch of the Limestone Coast. Is Beachport desperate to be noticed? A plaintive cry for attention? We like it the way it is: low-key and beachy, with aqua-marine surf, the famous 772m-long jetty, staunch stone buildings and rows of Norfolk Island pines. Forget about being seen – your time here will be perfectly anonymous. Beachport's impressive-looking **pub** *(beachporthotel.com)* is the most reliable place for a meal around this neck of the coast, or book yourself in for a meaty treat at **Mayura Station** *(mayurastation.com/dining)*, home to Australia's best Wagyu beef. Not far away are the amazing **Tantanoola Caves** *(parks.sa.gov.au)*, with stalactites and stalagmites aplenty, plus shell and bone remnants from eons ago when the beach was much closer than Beachport.

THE DRIVE: From Beachport, head inland along the easy 85km highway stretch to Mount Gambier.

05 Mount Gambier

Strung out along the flatlands below an extinct volcano, **Mount Gambier** (population 28,670; SA's second city) is the Limestone Coast's service hub. 'The Mount' can sometimes seem a little short on urban virtues, but it's not what's above the streets that makes Mount Gambier special – it's the deep Blue Lake and the caves that worm their way though the limestone beneath the town. For a taster, **Cave Gardens**

THE LONG WALK TO BALLARAT

Robe set up shop as a fishing port in 1846 – one of SA's earliest settlements. During the 1850s gold rush in Victoria, Robe came into its own when the Victorian government whacked a £10-per-head tax on Chinese gold miners arriving to work the goldfields. Thousands of Chinese miners dodged the tax by landing at Robe in SA, then walking the 400-odd kilometres to Bendigo and Ballarat in Victoria; 16,500 arrived between 1856 and 1858 and 10,000 in 1857 alone! But the flood stalled as quickly as it started when the SA government instituted its own tax on the Chinese. The 'Chinamen's wells' along their route (including one in the Coorong) can still be seen today, as can a memorial to the Chinese arrivals on the Robe foreshore.

Blue Lake (p189), Mount Gambier
GAGLIARDIPHOTOGRAPHY/SHUTTERSTOCK

PHOTO OPPORTUNITY

Looking down on Mount Gambier's iridescent Blue Lake.

(mountgambierpoint.com.au/attractions/cave-gardens) is a 50m-deep sinkhole right in the middle of town; you can walk down into it. But Mount Gambier's big-ticket item is the luminous, 75m-deep **Blue Lake** *(mountgambierpoint.com.au/attractions/blue-lake)*, which turns an insane hue of blue during summer. Perplexed scientists think it has to do with calcite crystals suspended in the water, which form at a faster rate during the warmer months. Consequently, if you visit between April and November, the lake will look much like any other – a steely grey. **Aquifer Tours** *(aquifertours.com)* can take you down to the lake's surface.

THE DRIVE: Penola is a 51km shot north of Mount Gambier along the Riddoch Hwy.

06 Penola

A rural town on the way up, **Penola** (population 1600) is the kind of place where you walk down the main street and three people say 'Hello!' to you before you reach the pub. The town itself has some historic corners – **Petticoat Lane** *(nationaltrust.org.au/places/petticoat-lane)* was one of Penola's first streets, and although most of the original buildings have been razed, there are still a few old timber-slab houses, red-gum kerbs and gnarly trees to see. Otherwise, the town is famous for two things: first, for its association with the Sisters of St Joseph of the Sacred Heart, cofounded in 1867 by Australia's first saint, Mary MacKillop; and secondly, for being smack bang in the middle of the **Coonawarra Wine Region** (killer cabernets). If you're here for the former, head straight to the **Mary MacKillop Interpretive Centre** *(mackilloppenola.org.au)*. Otherwise, it's wine time.

THE DRIVE: Tiny Coonawarra township is just 10km north of Penola via the Riddoch Hwy: in between the two (and just beyond Coonawarra), the wineries of the Coonawarra Wine Region include some of the most recognisable brands in the Australian wine biz.

07 Coonawarra Wine Region

When it comes to spicy cabernet sauvignon, it's just plain foolish to dispute the virtues of the **Coonawarra Wine Region** *(coonawarra.org)*. The *terra rossa* (red earth) soils here also produce irresistible shiraz and chardonnay: wine devotees should dedicate a couple of days to ease from one cellar door to the next. Where to start? How about **Balnaves of Coonawarra** *(balnaves.com.au)*, where the tasting notes ooze florid wine speak (dark seaweed, anyone?). But even if your nosing skills aren't that subtle, you'll enjoy the cab sav and chardonnay. Nearby, traditional **Zema Estate** *(zema.com.au)* captures the Coonawarra's essence with fine shiraz and cab sav, while **Rymill Coonawarra** *(rymill.com.au)* mixes it up with some of the best sauvignon blanc you'll ever taste. Return to Coonawarra's roots at **Wynns Coonawarra Estate** *(wynns.com.au)*, the oldest winery and internationally known for its top-shelf shiraz, fragrant riesling and golden chardonnay. **Bellwether Wines** *(bellwetherwines.com.au)* takes a more rebellious tack, with its arty cellar door in a stone 1868 shearing shed (and glamping).

THE DRIVE: It's 50km north, then northwest through vineyard country from Coonawarra to Naracoorte, where the focus shifts from what's above the earth to what lies beneath. Access to the national park is 10km south of town.

08 Naracoorte Caves National Park

Naracoorte Caves National Park *(naracoortecaves.sa.gov.au)* is the only World Heritage–listed site in SA. The discovery of an ancient fossilised marsupial in these limestone caves raised palaeontological eyebrows around the world, and featured in the David Attenborough 1979 BBC series *Life on Earth*. The 28 limestone caves here, including **Alexandra Cave**, curiously named **Stick-Tomato Cave** and **Victoria Fossil Cave**, have bizarre stalactite and stalagmite formations. The park visitor centre doubles as the impressive **Wonambi Fossil Centre** – a re-creation of the rainforest (and its inhabitants) that covered this area 200,000 years ago.

Stick-Tomato Cave, Naracoorte Caves National Park

ALEXANDRE.ROSA/SHUTTERSTOCK

STAY AWHILE

ROBE

BY ANTHONY HAM

It's easy on a road trip through South Australia to become addicted to the rhythm of life on the road, to the need to keep moving from one extraordinary stop to another. Robe has long been my antidote to that impulse.

Rich in history and quite simply the cutest little seaside town in a state of many, Robe is the kind of place where I always stop and look wistfully in the windows of real estate agents selling houses and wonder what it might be like to live in such a magical place. Staying for a couple of days is, at least, a start.

Built from local limestone and largely dating from the mid-1800s, the main street's facades tell stories of ancient adventures. The 1863 **Customs House** *(nationaltrust.org.au)* is now a maritime museum. Robe's self-guided **Town Heritage Trail** strings together 31 of these landmarks across 3km of walkable backstreets. Grab a free map from the **Robe Visitor Information Centre** *(robe.com.au)*.

Admire the heritage buildings, by all means, but these are no museum pieces. Overlooking the Southern Ocean, **Robe Hotel** *(robehotel.com.au)* has been around since 1847, and is a classic Aussie pub with counter meals and Coopers on tap.

And whenever I feel the need to walk off the great meals and fine pubs, I head for the well-signed, wheelchair-friendly 6km **Robe Scenic Trail**. It's at its best when waves roll in, lashing the frayed limestone shoreline and surging into Guichen Bay.

LINK YOUR TRIP

Robe is a great stop on the 25 **Limestone Coast & Coonawarra** road trip.

Left: Customs House
Right: View over Robe

FROM LEFT: DAVID SOUTH/ALAMY, FILEDIMAGE/SHUTTERSTOCK

PLACES TO STAY

Robe has some great accommodation options which retain the town's heritage feel. The stately **Caledonian Inn** *(caledonianinnrobe.com.au)*, established in 1858, has bright upstairs rooms with doors salvaged from shipwrecks. Right on Lake Fellmongery, at boutique **Lakeside Tourist Park** *(lakesiderobe.com.au)*, you'll find heritage-listed pine trees and reception building (132-year-old former stables), plenty of grass, basic cabins and flashy villas. At the quiet end of town (a five-minute walk from the action), the well-run **Harbour View Motel** *(robeharbourview.com.au)* has namesake harbour views from the best half-dozen rooms at the front. Expect nice linen, subtle colours, friendly hosts and vamped-up bathrooms.

26

★ BEST FOR:

FOODIES

Slurping down oysters in Coffin Bay or Ceduna.

SOUTH AUSTRALIA

YORKE & EYRE PENINSULAS

Port Adelaide Lighthouse

DURATION: 5–7 DAYS

DISTANCE: 701KM / 436 MILES

GREAT FOR: NATURE, HISTORY & WINE

BEST TIME TO GO: YEAR-ROUND, BUT MANY BUSINESSES REDUCE OPERATIONS DURING CHILLY WINTER.

The northwestern end of boot-shaped 'Yorkes' has a trio of old towns called the Copper Triangle: Moonta (the mine), Wallaroo (the smelter) and Kadina (the service town). Innes National Park is remote but definitely worth the detour (mining ruins, surf beaches, ospreys and emus), before you cross to the vast, wheat-coloured wedge of Eyre Peninsula. The coastline between Port Lincoln and Streaky Bay is seafood-rich and unfailingly dramatic.

LINK YOUR TRIP

03 Across the Nullarbor
This trip ends at Streaky Bay, but it's just 110km to Ceduna from here – an essential stop on the epic 2493km Nullarbor Crossing.

23 Adelaide Hills & the Barossa Valley
Before you head into SA's western frontier, indulge in some fine wine and food in the Adelaide Hills and Barossa Valley.

01 Port Adelaide

If you've been in Adelaide any length of time, you may be looking for a new corner of the city to explore, and considering that you're heading north from the city, Port Adelaide might just be that place. Mired in the economic doldrums for decades, Port Adelaide – 15km northwest of the city centre – is slowly gentrifying, morphing its old stone warehouses into art spaces and museums, and its brawl-house pubs into craft-beer emporia. Things are on the up. The helpful **Port Adelaide Visitor Information Centre** *(visitpae.com.au)* stocks brochures on self-guided history, heritage-pub and dolphin-spotting walks and drives, plus the enticements of neighbouring **Semaphore**, a very bohemian beach 'burb. Fill in a day around the Port with a dolphin-spotting cruise, some kayaking through nearby mangroves and the 'Ships' Graveyard', and a visit to the excellent **South Australian Maritime Museum** *(maritime.*

MYPHOTOBANK.COM.AU/SHUTTERSTOCK

history.sa.gov.au), looking at the history of Port Adelaide through a maritime lens. Highlights include the iconic red-and-white **Port Adelaide Lighthouse**, busty figureheads made everywhere from Londonderry to Québec, shipwreck and explorer displays, and a computer register of early migrants. Along similar nautical lines, wander down to the end of Divett St for a look at the oldest clipper ship in the world (1864). The high-and-dry hulk of the **City of Adelaide** *(cityofadelaide.org.au)* was transported here from Scotland in 2013. Take a tour to get the most of the boat.

THE DRIVE: You've got a lot of tarmac ahead of you, so take the A1 (Port Wakefield Hwy) northwest out of the city to get some miles under your belt. After Port Wakefield, at the head of Gulf St Vincent, the traffic thins as you peel off the A1 and continue northwest on the B85 (Copper Coast Hwy) for 51km to Kadina.

02 Kadina

The largest of the three towns that make up the Yorke Peninsula's 'Copper Triangle', Kadina is a long way inland – without the benefit of a sea breeze, it really bakes under the summer sun. If you can stand the heat, it's worth exploring a little on foot to check out the town's impressive copper-era buildings (many of them are cavernous old pubs – there'll be plenty of opportunities for liquid refreshments). To aid your navigations, pick up the *Kadina Historical Walking Trail* map from the **Copper Coast Visitor Information Centre** *(yorkepeninsula.com.au)* – the peninsula's main visitor centre, and an essential stop for planning ahead. Behind the centre is an amazing collection of old farming, mining and domestic bits and pieces at the **Farm Shed Museum** *(visitcoppercoast.com.au/farm-shed-museum)* – well worth an hour or two of today spent thinking about yesterday. And who doesn't love a miniature railway? Toot-toot.

THE DRIVE: Moonta lies 17km southwest of Kadina – an easy, flat, unremarkable drive through a band of wheat country, as one town's outskirts fade momentarily before the next one's commence. This is about as close as any two towns get on this epic road trip – enjoy the sense of proximity while it lasts.

03 Moonta

In the late 19th century, the Moonta copper mine was the richest in Australia and attracted fortune-seekers from around the globe, including many from Cornwall. The legacy of those boom years bequeathed Moonta its fine streetscapes and weathered crop of squat miners' cottages. The town, which calls itself 'Australia's Little Cornwall', maintains a faded glory and a couple of decent pubs and places to bite into a Cornish pasty; try the famous **Cornish Kitchen**. **Moonta Visitor Information Centre** *(visitcoppercoast.com.au/moonta-vic)* has details on the **Moonta Heritage Site** 1.5km east of town. The site includes the excellent **Moonta Mines Museum**, an impressive 1878 stone edifice that was once the Moonta Mines Model School and had 1100 students. The museum captures mining life – at work and at home – in intimately preserved detail. A little **tourist train** chugs out of the museum car park occasionally – ask at the visitor centre to see if it's running. Across the road from the museum, the 1846 **Old Sweet Shop** has also served as a post office, and it still sells sweets. The faithfully restored **Miner's Cottage** is an 1870 mud-and-grass house and garden, typical of the compact living arrangements of the time (perhaps miners were used to cramped conditions). But for all that history, Moonta is a pretty sleepy place, where fishing seems to be the main preoccupation.

Shallow Moonta Bay is 3km west of the town centre, with good fishing from the jetty and a netted swimming area.

THE DRIVE: It's a short, 18km hop up the road from Moonta to Wallaroo, through yet more wheat and barley fields. Fine views of Wallaroo Bay enter the picture on the last few kilometres into town, along with Wallaroo's huge concrete grain silos down by the jetty – a feature that defines the town both aesthetically and economically.

DETOUR

Dhilba Guuranda-Innes National Park

Start: 03 Moonta

The Yorke Peninsula has a shape that vaguely resembles Italy's famous boot (though it's a lot smaller, and doesn't have a stiletto heel). The peninsula's south coast is largely sheltered from the Southern Ocean's fury by Kangaroo Island, so there are some great swimming beaches along here. The surf finds its way through around Troubridge Point and Cape Spencer. The latter, at the extreme southwest of the peninsula, in the toe, is part of one of South Australia's least-visited national parks, **Dhilba Guuranda-Innes National Park** *(parks.sa.gov.au/parks/dhilba-guuranda-innes-national-park)*. Here, sheer cliffs plunge into indigo waters and rocky offshore islands hide small coves and sandy beaches. **Marion Bay**, just outside the park, and **Stenhouse Bay** and **Pondalowie Bay**, both within the park, are the main local settlements. Pondalowie Bay has a bobbing lobster-fishing fleet and a gnarly surf beach. The rusty ribs of the

Ethel shipwreck, Dhilba Guuranda-Innes National Park

ANNE-MARIE HARTMAN/SHUTTERSTOCK

711-tonne steel barque *Ethel*, which foundered in 1904, arc forlornly from the sands just south of Pondalowie Bay. Follow the sign past the Cape Spencer turnoff to the ghost-town ruins of **Inneston**, a gypsum-mining community abandoned in 1930. There's quirky self-contained accommodation here in old houses around the mine site, plus plenty of camping spots along the coastline, where ospreys, sea eagles and emus abound. There's a park office at the Stenhouse Bay entrance, but opening hours are unpredictable: it's best to pay entry and camping/accommodation fees online before you arrive.

To get to Dhilba Guuranda-Innes National Park, head 82km south from Moonta to Minlaton via Maitland. For refreshments, stop in at Maitland's **Barley Stacks Wines** *(barleystackswines.com)*, then **Minlaton's Watsacowie Brewing Company** *(watsacowie.com.au)* for a quick craft beer. From Minlaton, it's a further 89km southwest to the park entrance at Stenhouse Bay.

04 Wallaroo

Still a major grain port and fishing town, **Wallaroo** is on its way up: there's a huge new subdivision north of town, a new shopping complex, and the shiny **Copper Cove Marina** is home to expensive boats. The town is full of pubs, and the pubs are full of drinkers. The (temporarily suspended) vehicle ferry to cross Spencer Gulf to Lucky Bay on the Eyre Peninsula leaves from here, too – a shortcut that shaves 350km and several hours off the drive around the top of the gulf via the industrial cities of Port Pirie, Port Augusta and Whyalla. Before you leave Wallaroo, don't miss the stoic 1865 post office, which now houses the **Heritage & Nautical Museum** *(nationaltrust.org.au)*. There are several of these little National Trust museums around Yorke Peninsula – in Port Victoria, in Ardrossan, in Milaton, in Edithburgh – but this is the best of them, with tales of square-rigged English ships, the Tipara Reef Lighthouse and George the pickled giant squid. In the shadow of the silos, the **old town** area retains a romantic 'seen-better-days' vibe: wander around the compact alleys and raggedy cottages and soak up the atmosphere. For more on local history, pick up the *Wallaroo Historical Walking Trail* (or driving trail) brochure from the **Copper Coast Visitor Information Centre**. A cold beer and a waterside seafood dinner at the **Coopers Alehouse** *(coopersalehouse.com.au)* on the marina is the perfect end to your Wallaroo day.

THE DRIVE: With the **Spencer Gulf ferry** crossing suspended indefinitely (check for updates at *spencergulfsearoad.com*), the long-haul drive via Whyalla is your sole option from Wallaroo. It's 194km north via Spencer Hwy (B89) and A1 to Port Augusta, then 77km south via A1 and Lincoln Hwy (B100) to Whyalla and another 267km further south to Port Lincoln.

05 Port Lincoln

Prosperous **Port Lincoln**, the 'Tuna Capital of the World', overlooks broad Boston Bay on the southern end of Eyre Peninsula. It's a raffish fishing town a long way from anywhere, but the vibe here is progressive and energetic. This innate energy almost saw the town anointed the South Australian capital in the 1830s – a possibility eventually quashed by a lack of fresh water. These days it's salt water (and the tuna therein) that keeps the town ticking over – there are purportedly more millionaires per capita here than anywhere else in Australia. The grassy foreshore is a busy promenade, and there are some good pubs, eating options and aquatic activities here to keep you out of trouble. To get a feel for the place, tag along on a 90-minute **Port Lincoln Walk & Talk History Tour** *(facebook.com/portlincoln walkandtalktours)* along the foreshore with a fifth-generation local who knows the town backwards. Don't miss a visit to the **Fresh Fish Place** to sample the local product. For a look at the sea-battered coastline around Port Lincoln, visit sea-salty **Lincoln National Park** *(parks.sa.gov.au)*, 13km south of town. You'll find roaming emus, roos and brush-tailed bettongs, safe swimming coves, vast dunes and pounding surf beaches. On private land, **Whalers Way** *(portlincoln.com.au/what-to-do-port-lincoln/whalers-way)* is a super-scenic 14km coastal drive featuring blowholes, cliffs and crevasses on a remote spit, starting 32km southwest of Port Lincoln (ever seen a 2642-million-year-old rock?). Contact the **Port Lincoln Visitor Information Centre** *(portlincoln.com.au)* for permits.

THE DRIVE: Next stop is the oyster-farming capital of Coffin Bay, barely 50km across the southern tip of the Eyre Peninsula from Port Lincoln – you'll be there in less than an hour. The road continues beyond Coffin Bay town to Point Avoid, a wild and wind-blown vantage point for the Southern Ocean in all its cold fury.

F O R M E

06 Coffin Bay

Deathly sounding **Coffin Bay** (named by Matthew Flinders after his buddy Sir Isaac Coffin) is a sleepy fishing village that basks languidly in the warm sun – until a 4000-strong holiday horde arrives every January. The town is also the oyster capital of Australia – salty Coffin Bay oysters from the nearby beds are exported worldwide, but you shouldn't pay more than a dollar or two per oyster around town. Get a feel for the industry's inner workings on a tour with **Oyster Farm Tours** *(oysterfarmtours.com.au)* or **Pure Coffin Bay Oysters** *(experiencecoffinbay.com.au)*, with plenty of tastings. Beyond the strung-out town centre there's some wild coastal scenery, most of which is part of **Coffin Bay National Park** *(parks.sa.gov.au)*, overrun with roos, emus and fat goannas. In a 2WD you can get to picturesque **Point Avoid** (coastal lookouts, rocky cliffs, good surf and whales passing between May and October) and **Yangie Bay** (arid-looking rocky landscapes and walking trails). In a 4WD, check out some of the park's remote campsites.

THE DRIVE: The Flinders Hwy (A1) plays hide-and-seek with this fabulous, wild coast for 135km northwest of Coffin Bay to Elliston. Detour down dirt roads to see broken limestone cliffs and isolated beaches, famous for surfing (try Greenly Beach just south of Coulta, 40km north of Coffin Bay) and fishing (some of the salmon hooked around here are record-breakingly big).

Oysters, Coffin Bay

BLAZE LOPES/@BAREFOOT.BLAZE

DARRYL LEACH/SHUTTERSTOCK

Makybe Diva statue, Port Lincoln

LOCAL KNOWLEDGE: CHAMPIONS OF PORT LINCOLN

A guaranteed friend-maker in Port Lincoln is to slip Dean Lukin's name into every conversation. Straight off the tuna boats, big Dean won the Super Heavyweight weightlifting gold medal at the 1984 Olympics in LA – what a champ! If you follow this up with a mention of freestylin' local swim-king Kyle Chalmers, who won the 100m gold at the Rio Olympics in 2016, you'll be invited home for dinner and introduced to the town's eligible bachelors/bachelorettes. Another Port Lincoln champ is the legendary racehorse Makybe Diva, who won three back-to-back Melbourne Cups between 2003 and 2005. Owned by a local tuna fisherman, Makybe Diva was actually born in the UK, but was trained here in Port Lincoln. There's a sculpture of her down on the town waterfront, looking appropriately noble.

07 Elliston

Tiny **Elliston** (population 380) is a fishing town on soporific Waterloo Bay, with a beautiful swimming beach (paddle out to the pontoon), free seaside barbecues and a fishing jetty (hope the whiting are hungry). Bakery, country pub, caravan park – it has all the essentials. **Elliston Visitor Information Centre** *(elliston.com.au)* can direct you towards the **Great Ocean**

Tourist Drive just north of town – a 10km detour to **Anxious Bay** via some anxiety-relieving ocean scenery (or inducing, if you get too close to the cliffs). En route you'll pass **Blackfellows** that has some of the west coast's best surf. Further north is **Venus Bay** (population 140) sustaining a gaggle of pelicans, a caravan park, the obligatory fishing jetty and sheltered beaches (and the not-so-sheltered **Mt Camel Beach**). **Locks Well** has good salmon fishing and a long, steep stairway called the **Staircase to Heaven** (283 steps? Count 'em!) leading from the car park down to an awesome surf beach.

THE DRIVE: Follow the A1 northwest as it arcs around the eastern reaches of the Great Australian Bight. Some 25km beyond Port Kenny, a series of narrow back roads heads off the main highway towards Baird Bay and Point Labatt. This is remote terrain – you'll be lucky if you pass anyone else on these roads.

08 Point Labatt & Baird Bay

This wild corner of the country may contain some of SA's smaller settlements, but attractions come thick and fast out here. At diminutive Baird Bay, 30km west of the Flinders Hwy, **Baird Bay Ocean Eco Experience** *(bairdbay.com)* runs boat trips where you can swim with sea lions and dolphins. The approach is very 'hands-off' and unintrusive, though research suggests that human interaction with sea mammals does potentially alter behavioural and breeding patterns. Accommodation is also available. If you'd rather stay high and dry, the road to Point Labatt, 43km south of Streaky Bay, takes you to one of the few permanent **sea-lion colonies** on the Australian mainland; ogle them from the clifftops (with binoculars). A few kilometres down the Point Labatt road are the globular **Murphy's Haystacks**, an improbable congregation of 'inselbergs' – colourful, weather-sculpted granite outcrops that are an estimated 1500 million years old (not much chance of them eroding while you prep your camera – take your time).

THE DRIVE: You could easily spend a pleasurable hour or two losing yourself on the back roads running north to Streaky Bay. It's difficult to get truly lost here – head far enough east and you'll hit the A1; turn west and you're in the Southern Ocean. Sticking to the A1, it's an easy 39km run from the Point Labatt turnoff to Streaky Bay.

09 Streaky Bay

Sheltered from the Southern Ocean by a sturdy headland, there's something almost reassuring about this endearing little seasider, which takes its name from the streaks of seaweed Matt Flinders spied in the bay as he sailed by in 1802. Visible at low tide, the seagrass attracts ocean critters and the bigger critters that eat them – which means first-class fishing. The little **Streaky Bay Museum** *(nationaltrust.org.au/places/streaky-bay-museum)* occupies a 1901 schoolhouse. On site you'll find a fully furnished pug-and-pine hut, bird eggs and shell collections, an old iron lung (the Both Iron Lung artificial respirator, built by Edward Thomas Both of Adelaide in 1837 – one for the medical nerds among us) and plenty of pioneering history. More recently (1990), a 5m-long, 1.5-tonne **white pointer shark** was reeled in off Streaky Bay: check out the unnervingly large life-size replica in the little room out the back of the **Streaky Bay Roadhouse** *(streakybay.com.au/categories/fuel)*. Beyond town, drive north past wheat fields to the rugged dune country around **Cape Bauer** *(streakybay.com.au/explore/scenic-drives-trails)* – a 38km dirt-road loop that makes a superscenic detour. Islands, beaches, reefs, blowholes, eroding limestone cliffs and the endless ocean grinding into shore: this is isolated, end-of-the-world terrain, and a chance to redress your urban overload. Look for ospreys, kangaroos and circling sea eagles. Back in town, sit on the broad deck of the affable **Streaky Bay Hotel** *(streakybayhotel.com.au)*, sip something cold and celebratory, and ponder the many miles you've covered.

Murphy's Haystacks, Point Labatt
DALLASETTA/SHUTTERSTOCK

PHOTO OPPORTUNITY

Sunset at Murphy's Haystacks.

27

SOUTH AUSTRALIA

CLARE VALLEY & THE FLINDERS RANGES

DURATION: 7–10 DAYS

DISTANCE: 420KM / 261 MILES

GREAT FOR: WINE & NATURE

BEST TIME TO GO: SEPTEMBER TO NOVEMBER FOR A CARPET OF SPRING WILDFLOWERS.

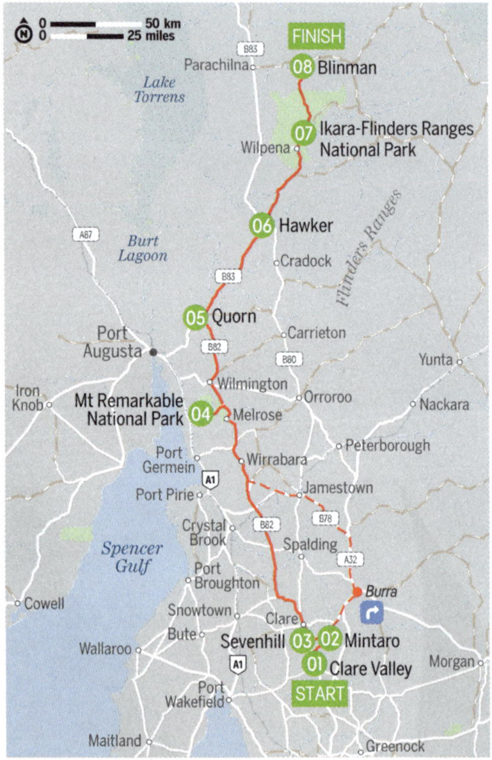

Clare Valley has plenty of competition, but it has always been one of South Australia's top wine regions. Vineyards carpet valleys that radiate out from lovely little townships like Mintaro and Sevenhill. Before reaching the outback, there's the aptly named Mt Remarkable, then it's arid landscapes and remote settlements all the way into the peerless Flinders Ranges.

LINK YOUR TRIP

03 Across the Nullarbor
Port Augusta, close to Quorn, is the crossroads for many journeys, including the epic Nullarbor crossing to Perth.

04 Alice Springs to Adelaide
This trip from the Alice heads south – the routes intersect close to Port Augusta.

01 Clare Valley

At the centre of the fertile Mid North agricultural district, two hours north of Adelaide, the wine-bottle-slender Clare Valley produces world-class, sweet scented rieslings and mineral-rich reds. This is gorgeous countryside – Ngadjuri Aboriginal homelands – with open skies, rounded hills, stands of large gums and wind rippling over wheat fields. Towns here date from the 1840s; many were built to service the Burra copper mines further north. Auburn marks the southern end of the valley; Clare itself marks the northern end, 25km north of Auburn. Sleepy **Auburn** (founded 1849) is a leave-the-back-door-open-and-the-keys-in-the-ignition kinda town, with a time-warp atmosphere that makes you feel like you're in an old black-and-white photograph. The streets are defined by beautifully preserved stone buildings, and cottage gardens overflow with untidy blooms. Pick

ALEX CIMBAL/SHUTTERSTOCK

★ BEST FOR:

OUTDOORS

Mt Remarkable National Park lives up to its name – and don't miss Melrose.

Alligator Gorge (p203), Mt Remarkable National Park

up a copy of the *Walk with History at Auburn* brochure in shops.

THE DRIVE: More an adjunct to Clare Valley than anything else, little Mintaro lies 18km northeast of Auburn, via Horrocks Hwy, then a turnoff to the right 7km north of Auburn. Follow the signs.

02 Mintaro

A little way off the main Clare Valley wine-touring route, heritage-listed **Mintaro** (min-*tair*-oh, founded 1849) is a lovely stone village that could have been lifted out of the Cotswolds and plonked into the Australian bush – a distinct shift from the Germanic echoes of the Barossa and the Adelaide Hills. There are very few architectural intrusions from the 1900s here; let the *Historic Mintaro* pamphlet (you'll find it at various places around the valley) guide your explorations. Don't miss **Martindale Hall** *(martindale hall.com.au),* an astonishing 1880 manor 3km south of Mintaro town centre. Built for young pastoralist Edmund Bowman Jnr, who subsequently partied away the family fortune, the manor features original furnishings, a magnificent blackwood staircase, Mintaro-slate billiard table (Mintaro slate is used around the world for the production of same) and an opulent, museum-like smoking room. The hall starred as Appleyard College in the 1975 film *Picnic at Hanging Rock,* directed by Peter Weir. If you're hungry/thirsty, Mintaro has a classic country pub, the endearingly named **Magpie & Stump** *(magpieandstump.com.au)*; and the excellent **Reilly's** *(reillys wines.com.au),* which started life as a cobbler's shop in 1856. These days it's a cellar door for Reilly's Wines and has a lovely restaurant, decorated with local art and serving creative, seasonal Mod Oz food (antipasti, rabbit terrine, platters) and the house wines.

THE DRIVE: Head 15km northwest from Mintaro to Sevenhill, via the hilly Jolly Way. This route passes through Polish Hill River – a subregion of the broader Clare Valley wine region.

03 Sevenhill

Between Auburn and Clare along the main highway, a string of tiny towns unfolds: Leasingham, Watervale, Pentwortham and Sevenhill – most of which you'll bypass if you divert to Mintaro. But the Mintaro road spits you out again at Sevenhill, the busiest of these towns, with a good bakery, a pub, the impressive **Clare Valley Brewing Co** *(facebook.com/clarevalleybrewing)* and some of the best wineries in the Clare Valley; our favourite is **Skillogalee** *(skillogalee.com.au)*. Sevenhill was founded in 1850 by wandering Jesuit priests, who got the name from Rome's famous seven hills.

THE DRIVE: Continuing north from Sevenhill, you'll hit Clare itself after just 7km – the valley's main administrative, business and population hub. Truck on through – you're headed for Melrose, 132km away via Bungaree, Gladstone, Laura and Stone Hut on the Horrocks Hwy.

DETOUR

Burra

Start: 03 Sevenhill

Bursting with historic sites, Burra, 47km northeast of Clare, was a copper-mining boom town between 1847 and 1877, with a Cornish community. Towns like Mintaro and Auburn serviced miners travelling between Burra and Port Wakefield, from where the copper was shipped. The miners had it tough here, excavating earth dugouts for themselves and their families to live in. **Burra Visitor Information Centre** *(visitburra.com.au)* sells the self-guided Burra Heritage Passport which provides access to nine sights and two museums along an 11km driving route. Many of the old mining sites are in a state of thorough dereliction, but this only adds to the sense of historic intrigue. The museums are in slightly better condition, but still atmospheric and appropriately musty. For commentary along the way, go to *daytrippa.com.au/burra*.

Also of interest here (for music fans at least) is the **Midnight Oil House** *(clarevalley.com.au/directory/midnight-oil-house)*. A legendary Australian rock band, 'The Oils' sold millions of albums in the late 1980s – and more than

Midnight Oil House, Burra

OZITRAVELER/SHUTTERSTOCK

a few of them had a photo of this derelict stone farmhouse on the front sleeve. *Diesel and Dust* was released in 1987 and went straight to number one on the Australian charts, thanks in no small part to this poignant image, questioning whether or not white Australia had any business at all trying to tame this wild country. It's 3km north of Burra town centre. Also worth a look is the **Burra Scrumpy Cumpany** just south of town: sip your way through some trad farmhouse ciders.

To pick up the main trip route, continue north on the Barrier Hwy 32m to Hallett, turn left onto the Wilkins Hwy, drive for 69km and rejoin the route just north of Stone Hut.

CLARE VALLEY WINERIES

The Clare Valley's moderate microclimate noticeably affects the local wines, enabling white grapes to be laid down for long periods and still be brilliant. The valley produces some of the world's best riesling, plus grand semillon and some challengingly flinty shiraz. For an interactive map of the valley's many winery cellar doors, see *clarevalley.com.au/wine/cellar-doors*. The **Clare Valley Wine, Food & Tourism Centre** *(clarevalley.com.au)* can also help with suggestions and maps, and features a local winery every Friday evening.

Skillogalee
This small family outfit is known for its spicy shiraz. *skillogalee.com.au*

Sevenhill Cellars
Established by Jesuits in 1851, this is the oldest winery in the Clare Valley. *sevenhill.com.au*

Pikes
The industrious Pike family set up shop in the Polish Hill River subregion of the Clare Valley in 1984. *pikeswines.com.au*

Mr Mick
Occupies a noble former distillery down a quiet Clare street. *mrmick.com.au*

Jeanneret Wines
Some of the loveliest rosé you're ever likely to taste. *jeanneretwines.com*

04 Mt Remarkable National Park

Bush-boffins-in-the-know rave about the steep, jagged **Mt Remarkable National Park** *(parks.sa.gov.au)*, which straddles a hidden cache of isolated gorges in the Southern Ranges. The park has three main access points: Alligator Gorge to the north, Mambray Creek in the west, and Melrose in the east. From the **Alligator Gorge** car park, take the short, steep walk (2km, two hours) down into the **craggy gorge** (no sign of any 'gators), the **ring route** (9km, four hours), or the walk to **Hidden Gorge** (18km, seven hours) or **Mambray Creek** (13km, seven hours). Or you can sweat up the track to the 960m-high summit of **Mt Remarkable** (12km, five hours); the trail starts behind Melrose Caravan Park. The oldest town in the Flinders (1853), **Melrose** itself sits snug in the elbow of Mt Remarkable. It has the perfect mix of well-preserved architecture, a cracking good pub, quality accommodation and parks with actual grass (you won't see a whole lot of that where you're heading). It is also a **mountain-biking** hub, with a section of the 900km Mawson Trail tracking through town, and a web of challenging single-track trails in the surrounding forests. See *bikesa.asn.au/ridemapslist* for more, or hire a bike from **Over the Edge** *(otesports.com.au)* and go exploring. Afterwards, enjoy some liquid refreshments and a meal at the excellent **North Star Hotel** *(northstarhotel.com.au)*, presiding over the top end of Melrose's main street. As welcome as summer rain, this noble 1854 pub has been renovated in city-meets-woolshed style.

THE DRIVE: From Melrose, head north 52km along the Horrocks Hwy to Quorn, via Wilmington. Along the way you'll cross Goyder's Line, an invisible east–west boundary established in 1865 between arable southern lands and dry country to the north, where less than 250mm of annual rainfall was deemed to be too little to support crops. Where would Goyder draw his line today?

05 Quorn

Is Quorn a film set after the crew has gone home? With more jeering crows than people, it's a cinematographic little outback town with a pub-lined main street. Wheat farming took off here in 1875, and the town prospered with the arrival of the Great Northern Railway from Port Augusta. Quorn (pronounced 'corn') remained an important railroad junction until trains into the Flinders were cut in 1970. Its historic streetscapes have featured in iconic Australian films such as *Gallipoli* and *Sunday Too Far Away*.

Pick up the *Quorn Historic Buildings Walk* brochure from the visitor info centre. Out of town, derelict ruins litter the Quorn–Hawker road, the most impressive of which is **Kanyaka**, a once-thriving sheep station founded in 1851. From the ruins (41km from Quorn), it's a 20-minute walk to a waterhole loomed over by the massive **Death Rock**. Local Aboriginal people once placed their dying kinfolk here to see out their last hours (be respectful).

THE DRIVE: From Quorn, hit the highway and head northeast – it's a straight 66km dash to Hawker, the next town on the Flinders Ranges Way.

06 Hawker

Hawker is the last outpost of civilisation before Ikara (Wilpena Pound), 59km to the north. Much like Quorn, Hawker has seen better days, most of which were when the old *Ghan* train stopped here en route to Alice Springs. These days it's a pancake-flat, pit-stop town with an ATM, a general store, a pub, the impressive **Flinders Food Co cafe** *(flindersfoodco.com.au)* and the world's most helpful petrol station.

THE DRIVE: Exit Hawker on the east side of town: it's an easy 55km north to Wilpena on the Flinders Ranges Way.

07 Ikara-Flinders Ranges National Park

One of SA's most treasured parks, **Ikara-Flinders Ranges National Park** *(parks.sa.gov.au)* is laced with craggy gorges, saw-toothed ranges, abandoned homesteads, Adnyamathanha Aboriginal sites, native wildlife and, after it rains, colourful wildflowers. The park's big-ticket drawcard is the 80-sq-km natural basin **Ikara (Wilpena Pound)** – a sunken elliptical valley ringed by gnarled ridges (don't let anyone tell you it's a meteorite crater). The only vehicular access to the Pound is via the Wilpena Pound Resort's shuttle bus, which drops you about 1km from the old **Hills Homestead**, from where you can walk to **Lookout** (another steep 500m). Pick up the Bushwalking in Flinders Ranges National Park brochure from the visitors information centre if you're keen to explore further.

To look down on it all, both **Wilpena Pound Resort** *(discoveryholidayparks.com.au)* and **Rawnsley Park Station** *(rawnsleypark.com.au)* offer scenic flights.

THE DRIVE: Truck north from Wilpena on the sealed road to Blinman. It's a wiggly, 59km drive, with some scenic lookouts along the way (keep an eye out for road washouts after heavy rains).

08 Blinman

About an hour north of Wilpena, supercute **Blinman** (population 30) owes its existence to the copper ore discovered here in 1859 and the smelter built in 1903. But the boom went bust and 1500 folks left town.

Today Blinman's main claim to fame is as SA's highest town (610m above sea level). Toast the end of your road trip at the old **North Blinman Hotel** *(northblinmanhotel.com.au)*.

PHOTO OPPORTUNITY

FLINDERS RANGES

At sunrise or sunset.

Ikara (Wilpena Pound), Ikara-Flinders Ranges National Park

TARAS VYSHNYA/SHUTTERSTOCK

0 400 km
0 200 miles
ARAFURA SEA
TIMOR SEA
Cobourg Peninsula
Melville Island
Wessel Islands
Nguiu
Gunbalanya (Oenpelli)
Nhulunbuy
Yirrkala
Darwin
Jabiru
31
Adelaide River
Kakadu National Park
Arnhem Land
Arnhem Land Aboriginal Land
Litchfield National Park
30
Daly River
Pine Creek
Cape Londonderry
Joseph Bonaparte Gulf
Nitmiluk National Park
Groote Eylandt
Numbulwar
Daly River/Port Keats Aboriginal Land
Barunga
Katherine
Beswick
Gulf of Carpentaria
Ngukurr
Mataranka
Limmen National Park
Sir Edward Pellew Group
Timber Creek
Wyndham
Larrimah
Kununurra
Victoria River Crossing
Lake Argyle
Judbarra/Gregory National Park
Daly Waters
Borroloola
Dunmarra
Top Springs
Cape Crawford
Victoria River
Newcastle Waters
Kalkarindji
Elliott
Purnululu National Park
Renner Springs
Halls Creek
Lajamanu
Waanyi/Garawa Aboriginal Land
29
Karlantijpa North Aboriginal Land
Tennant Creek
Great Sandy Desert
Camooweal
Central Desert Aboriginal Land
Wakaya Aboriginal Land
Karlantijpa South Aboriginal Land
Anurrete Aboriginal Land
Central Australia Aboriginal Land
Lake Mackay Aboriginal Land
Ti Tree
Yuendumu
Aileron
Lake Mackay
Tjoritja/ West MacDonnell National Park
Alice Springs
Gibson Desert
Haasts Bluff Aboriginal Land
Atnetye Aboriginal Land
Hermannsburg
Watarrka National Park
Pmere Nyente Aboriginal Land
QUEENSLAND
Petermann Aboriginal Land
28
Simpson Desert
Yulara
Kata Tjuṯa
Erldunda
Uluṟu
Mt Conner
Finke (Aputula)
Kulgera
WESTERN AUSTRALIA
SOUTH AUSTRALIA
Simpson Desert Regional Reserve

BENNY MARTY/SHUTTERSTOCK

Ellery Creek Big Hole (p213)

NORTHERN TERRITORY

EXPLORE

NORTHERN TERRITORY

If you're looking for a classic Australian road trip through the outback, the NT will have what you're looking for. Sealed roads aren't the norm in these parts: beyond the Stuart Hwy and roads to Uluṟu, Kings Canyon, the West MacDonnell Ranges and Kakadu, you'll need a 4WD. But the sealed roads will provide adventure enough for most visitors, taking you to some of the most soul-stirring landmarks in Australia. Opportunities to experience Aboriginal culture abound in the NT, from community-run art centres in major towns and remote communities to the storytelling wonder of Aboriginal-led tours into the heart of wildly beautiful landscapes.

Alice Springs

In the very heart of the country, Alice (or Mparntwe, as it's known to its Arrernte traditional owners) bakes under the desert sun. It also draws a fascinating mix of tourists, Aboriginal people from desert communities and a motley mix of people from all walks of life. It's an eclectic combination of cafes, fabulous art galleries, decent restaurants and accommodation to suit every budget.

Darwin

Like no other city in Australia, Darwin is a fascinating tropical outpost clinging to the country's northern shore. It's a frontier town with a devil-may-care attitude about what the rest of the world thinks. It's also a fun place with top museums, restaurants and hotels, to go with a regular roster of markets, a storied outdoor cinema, First Nations art galleries and a laid-back charm that moves between the welcoming and the rather rough at the edges.

Tennant Creek

Marooned like an island in an outback sea, Tennant Creek is one of Australia's most isolated towns – it's 988km from Darwin and 508km

WHEN TO GO

For most of the NT, April to October are the best months to visit. In the south, this is when you can expect milder temperatures and generally fine weather. Up north, in the tropics, this is the dry season: travel can be difficult during the humid November-to-March wet season, when even sealed roads are sometimes closed by flooding.

from Alice Springs. There's just a handful of restaurants and motels here, but you can stock up on most things, rest from life on the road and visit an Aboriginal cultural centre or mining museum as you get ready for what comes next. By outback standards, the wonderful Karlu Karlu / Devils Marbles are just around the corner (95km away).

Jabiru

The main service town for Kakadu National Park, Jabiru has a delightfully laid-back air and its transformation from a mining town to a tourism hub is only just beginning. It has a small but excellent number of places to stay, a scattering of decent meal options, a supermarket and an art centre. Best of all, it's a convenient base for exploring the park.

Yulara

A relatively recent creation in the desert, Yulara serves one purpose: it's the service town for visiting Uluru-Kata Tjuta National Park. Aside from its airport (called Ayers Rock Airport), it's filled with hotels, a campground, restaurants, a supermarket, art galleries, shops and tour operators that run all manner of adventures. Its shallow roots in the soil (it only opened in 1976) mean it can feel a little artificial, but it has all the comforts and services you could possibly want or need in such a remote place.

TRANSPORT

Unless you like long, straight roads (ie the 1500km Stuart Hwy between Alice Springs and Darwin), it makes sense to build your road trips from Darwin and/or Alice Springs, and then fly between the two. Apart from regular flights, there are interminable bus rides or a high-end rail journey aboard *The Ghan* (*journeybeyondrail.com.au*).

WHERE TO STAY

Alice Springs and Darwin have by far the widest range of accommodation, with decent choices also possible around Yulara (near Uluru), Kings Canyon, Kakadu and Litchfield National Park. Everywhere else, you'll need to take what you find, which will rarely extend beyond roadside motels, outback roadhouses with a few cabins, and the occasional glamping experience in Arnhem Land or around Uluru or Alice Springs. Camping in the NT can be excellent, though it's a highly seasonal proposition (ie only recommended from April to October).

RESOURCES

- **Desart**
  A fine resource of Aboriginal art centres across the NT. *desart.com.au*
- **Discover Central Australia**
  Uluru, Kings Canyon, Alice Springs and so much more. *discovercentralaustralia.com*
- **Northern Territory**
  Covers the Territory in vivid, bold colours. *northernterritory.com*
- **NT Parks & Reserves**
  Learn about NT's fabulous national parks. *nt.gov.au/parks*

WHAT'S ON

- **Parrtjima**
  This fine First Nations–led sound-and-light festival illuminates Alice in April. *parrtjimaaustralia.com.au*
- **Camel Cup**
  Held in the cool of mid-July in Alice, these camel races date back to 1970, when two mates first challenged each other to a race.
- **Henley-on-Todd Regatta**
  On the 3rd Saturday in August, bottomless boats take to the dry Todd River. *henleyontodd.com.au*
- **Darwin Festival**
  Over 18 August days, this outdoor arts and culture festival is the Territory's best. *darwinfestival.org.au*

28

★ BEST FOR:

OUTDOORS

Walk through the Valley of the Winds for true outback magic.

NORTHERN TERRITORY

ULURU & THE RED CENTRE

DURATION: 10–14 DAYS

DISTANCE: 1180KM / 733 MILES

GREAT FOR: NATURE & HISTORY

BEST TIME TO GO: APRIL TO OCTOBER HAS COOLER TEMPERATURES; IT'S FIERCELY HOT NOVEMBER TO MARCH.

Glen Helen Gorge (p213)

If you make one trip through the Australian outback, make it this one. Uluṟu is an extraordinary, soulful place where nature and culture are deeply intertwined. Nearby, Kata Tjuṯa and Kings Canyon leave spellbound all who visit, while the West MacDonnell Ranges capture the essence of the Red Centre – red earth, red rocks and ghostly gums in a spiritually charged landscape.

LINK YOUR TRIP

29 Alice Springs to Darwin
Alice Springs is Stop 4 on the Uluṟu & the Red Centre trip, and it's also where the Alice Springs to Darwin route (1493km) begins.

04 Alice Springs to Adelaide
From Alice Springs, the other choice is to head south to Adelaide (1500km).

01 Uluṟu

Uluṟu: nothing can really prepare you for the immensity, grandeur, changing colour and stillness of 'the Rock'. The first sight of Uluṟu on the horizon invariably astounds even the most jaded traveller. Before arriving, visit the **Uluṟu-Kata Tjuṯa Cultural Centre** *(uluru.gov.au/things-do/cultural-centre)*, 1km away. Uluṟu itself is 3.6km long and rises a towering 348m from the surrounding sandy scrubland (867m above sea level). Closer inspection reveals a wondrous contoured surface concealing numerous sacred sites of particular significance to the Anangu. If your first sight of Uluṟu is during the afternoon, it appears as an ochre-brown colour, scored and pitted by dark shadows. As the sun sets, it illuminates the rock in burnished orange, then a series of deeper reds before it fades into charcoal. A performance in reverse, with marginally fewer spectators, is given at dawn. There's plenty to

BILL BACHMAN/ALAMY

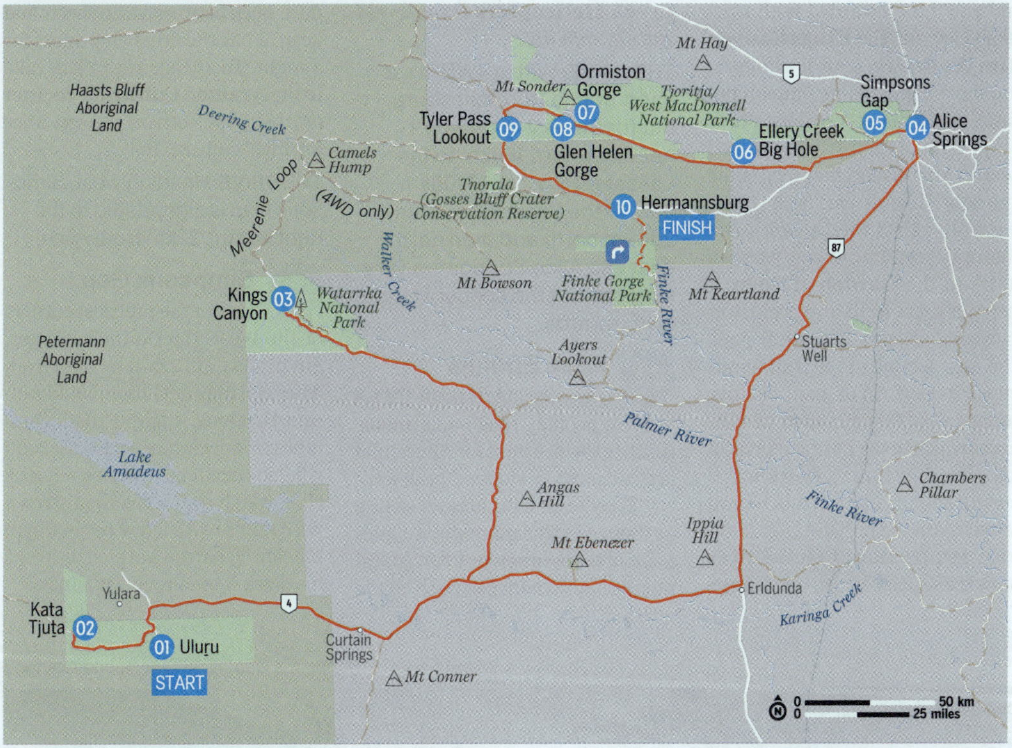

see and do: meandering walks, bike rides, guided tours, desert culture and simply contemplating the many changing colours and moods of the great monolith itself.

THE DRIVE: The road from Uluṟu to Kata Tjuṯa (40km) is sealed, as is the 20km road between Uluṟu and Yulara (where all of the accommodation for both places is). There are no other roads out here: you can't get lost.

02 Kata Tjuṯa

No journey to Uluṟu is complete without a visit to Kata Tjuṯa, a striking group of domed rocks huddled together about 40km west of Uluṟu and part of **Uluṟu-Kata Tjuṯa National Park** *(uluru.gov.au)*. There are 36 boulders shoulder to shoulder forming deep valleys and steep-sided gorges. Many visitors find them even more captivating than their prominent neighbour. The tallest rock, **Mt Olga** (546m, 1066m above sea level), is approximately 200m higher than Uluṟu. Kata Tjuṯa means 'many heads' and is deeply significant to Tjukurpa (the foundation of Anangu culture), so stick to the tracks. The 7.4km **Valley of the Winds** loop (two to four hours) winds through the gorges, giving excellent views of the surreal domes. The short signposted track beneath towering rock walls into pretty **Walpa Gorge** (2.6km return, 45 minutes) is especially beautiful in the afternoon. Like Uluṟu, Kata Tjuṯa is at its glorious, blood-red best at sunset.

THE DRIVE: From Kata Tjuṯa, make the 40km return drive to Uluṟu, then 20km more to Yulara, before the long road really begins. The Lasseter Hwy runs east; watch for Mt Conner, the large mesa (table-top mountain) that looms 350m out of the desert away to the south. Some 137km from Yulara, take the Kings Canyon turnoff, from where you've 169km to go.

03 Kings Canyon

The yawning chasm of Kings Canyon in **Watarrka National Park** *(nt.gov.au/parks/find-a-park/watarrka-national-park)* is one of the most spectacular sights in central Australia. This is one place where it pays to get out and walk, and you'll be rewarded with awesome views on the **Kings Canyon Rim Walk** *(6km loop, four hours*; you must begin before 9am on hot days), which many travellers rate as a highlight of their trip to the Red Centre. After a short but steep climb (the only 'difficult' part of the trail), the walk skirts the canyon's rim before descending down wooden stairs to the **Garden of Eden**: a lush pocket of ferns and prehistoric cycads around a tranquil pool. The next section of the trail winds through a swarm of giant beehive domes: weathered sandstone outcrops, which to the Luritja represent the men of the Kuniya Dreaming. If that all sounds like too much hard work, take a scenic helicopter flight with **Professional Helicopter Services** *(phs.com.au)* or **Kings Creek Helicopters** *(kingscreekstation.com.au)*.

THE DRIVE: With a 4WD, it's a short hop to Hermannsburg, but for the rest of us, you'll need to return 169km to the Lasseter Hwy, travel 108km east to the Stuart Hwy, then 200km north and then northeast into Alice Springs – a very long day but the scenery has its own rewards.

04 Alice Springs

Alice Springs is many things to many people – rough-and-tumble frontier town, centre for Aboriginal arts, set amid glorious outback scenery. They're all true, and yet sitting as it does in the approximate midpoint of this journey, its main appeal may lie in the chance to wash off the dust, sleep between clean sheets and keep at bay the great emptiness for a night. To anchor your visit, take in the **Araluen Cultural Precinct** *(araluenartscentre.nt.gov.au)*, Alice Springs' cultural hub.

THE DRIVE: Heading west, Simpsons Gap is signposted to the right (north), 22km from Alice.

05 Simpsons Gap

One of the prettiest corners of the West MacDonnell Ranges, Simpsons Gap, 22km by road from Alice Springs and 8km off Larapinta Dr along a paved road, combines wonderful scenery with good wildlife-watching. Towering red-rock cliffs watch over a riverbed strewn with gums, with a few pools where the canyon narrows. Watch the rocks for black-footed rock wallabies.

Simpsons Gap, West MacDonnell Ranges

THOSGRA/SHUTTERSTOCK

THE DRIVE: Return to the main road and continue to the fork: turn right onto Namatjira Dr. Ellery Creek Big Hole is 51km after this turnoff (91km from Alice Springs).

06 Ellery Creek Big Hole

Ellery Creek Big Hole has a large permanent waterhole and is a beautiful spot. It's also a popular place for a swim on a hot day (the water is usually freezing), but be very careful – numerous swimmers have drowned here. If you're really lucky, you might see a dingo coming down to drink.

THE DRIVE: About 11km further, a rough gravel track leads to narrow, ochre-red Serpentine Gorge, with a lovely waterhole, a lookout and ancient cycads. The Ochre Pits line a dry creek bed 11km west of Serpentine and are a source of pigment for Arrernte people. Ormiston Gorge is 25km beyond the Ochre Pits, signposted off the sealed road.

07 Ormiston Gorge

Majestic Ormiston Gorge is the most impressive chasm in the West Macs. There's a waterhole shaded with ghost gums, and the gorge curls around to the enclosed Ormiston Pound. It's a haven for wildlife and you can expect to see some critters among the spinifex slopes and mulga woodland. There are walking tracks, including to the **Ghost Gum Lookout** (20 minutes), which affords brilliant views down the gorge, and the excellent, circuitous **Pound Walk** (8.5km, three hours). There's a visitor centre, a kiosk and an enduring sense of peace whenever the tourist buses move on.

THE DRIVE: About 2km beyond Ormiston Gorge is the turnoff to Glen Helen Gorge.

MPH_PHOTOGRAPHY/SHUTTERSTOCK

Gardens of Eden, Kings Canyon

08 Glen Helen Gorge

Glen Helen Gorge is where the Finke River cuts its way through the MacDonnells.

Wander down to the gorge, which doesn't quite match Ormiston, but is quite dramatic nonetheless.

♥ WHY I LOVE THIS TRIP

ANTHONY HAM, WRITER

By the end of this trip you'll have experienced the magic of the outback through its most enduring symbols: Uluru, Kata Tjuta, Kings Canyon, the West Macs and a town called Alice. It's a well-worn trail and one that it's hard not to love, especially if, like me, you find yourself enchanted by desert silences and yearn for its long empty roads.

Only 1km past Glen Helen is a good **lookout over Mt Sonder** (1380m), one of the highest peaks in the entire range; sunrise and sunset here are particularly impressive.

THE DRIVE: If you continue northwest for 25km beyond Glen Helen you'll reach the turnoff (4WD only) to multihued, cathedral-like Redbank Gorge. Tyler Pass Lookout is well signposted before the road descends to the southwest.

09 Tyler Pass Lookout

There's something impossibly romantic (in a desert sense, at least) about finding a vantage point from which you can gaze out into eternity.

Seeing the desert stretch out to the red horizon evokes both a sense of breathless freedom and a profound sense of one's own smallness.

Tyler Pass Lookout provides a dramatic view of Tnorala (Grosse Bluff), the legacy of an earth-shattering comet impact, but it's the end-of-the-earth, end-of-the-road sense that you'll remember most, long after you've returned home.

THE DRIVE: With the completion of the tarmac along the West MacDonnell Ranges road, it is now possible for 2WD vehicles to complete the loop back to Alice Springs via Hermannsburg.

DORLING KINDERSLEY LTD/ALAMY

10 Hermannsburg

The Aboriginal community of **Hermannsburg** (Ntaria), about 125km from Alice Springs, is famous as the one-time home of artist Albert Namatjira and as the site of the **Hermannsburg Mission** *(hermannsburg.com.au)*, whose whitewashed walls are shaded by majestic river gums and date palms. This fascinating monument to the Territory's early Lutheran missionaries includes a school, a church and various outbuildings. The 'Manse' houses an art gallery and a history of the life and times of Albert Namatjira, as well as works of Hermannsburg artists. Just west of Hermannsburg is **Namatjira's House**.

DETOUR

Finke Gorge National Park

Start: 10 Hermannsburg

With its primordial landscape, the 4WD-only Finke Gorge National Park, south of Hermannsburg, is one of central Australia's premier wilderness reserves. The top attraction is **Palm Valley**, famous for its red cabbage palms which exist nowhere else in the world. These relics from prehistoric times give the valley the feel of a picture-book oasis. Tracks include the **Arankaia Walk** (2km loop, one hour), which traverses the valley, returning via the sandstone plateau; the **Mpulungkinya Walk** (5km loop, two hours), heading down the gorge before joining the Arankaia Walk; and the **Mpaara Walk** (5km loop, two hours), taking in the Finke River, Palm Bend and a rugged natural amphitheatre.

Access to the park follows the sandy bed of the Finke River and rocky tracks, so a high-clearance 4WD is essential.

Hermannsburg Mission

ALFOTOKUNST/SHUTTERSTOCK

4WD, Mereenie Loop Rd

THE RED CENTRE WAY

The Red Centre Way is the 'back road' from Alice to Uluru. It incorporates an 'inner loop' comprising Namatjira and Larapinta Drs, plus the rugged Mereenie Loop Rd, the short cut to Kings Canyon. This dusty, heavily corrugated road is not to be taken lightly. There can be deep sandy patches and countless corrugations, depending on the time of year and how recently it's been graded. It's best travelled in a high-clearance vehicle, preferably a 4WD. Be aware that hire car companies won't permit their 2WDs to be driven on this road, and such vehicles will not be covered by insurance.

To travel along this route, which passes through Aboriginal land, you need a permit ($5), which is valid for one day and includes a booklet with details about the local Aboriginal culture and a route map. The pass is issued on the spot (usually only on the day of travel) at the visitor information centre in Alice Springs, Glen Helen Resort, Kings Canyon Resort and Hermannsburg service station.

29

NORTHERN TERRITORY

ALICE SPRINGS TO DARWIN

DURATION: 5–7 DAYS

DISTANCE: 1493KM / 928 MILES

GREAT FOR: NATURE & HISTORY

BEST TIME TO GO: APRIL TO OCTOBER – THE WET PRESENTS CHALLENGES THE REST OF THE YEAR.

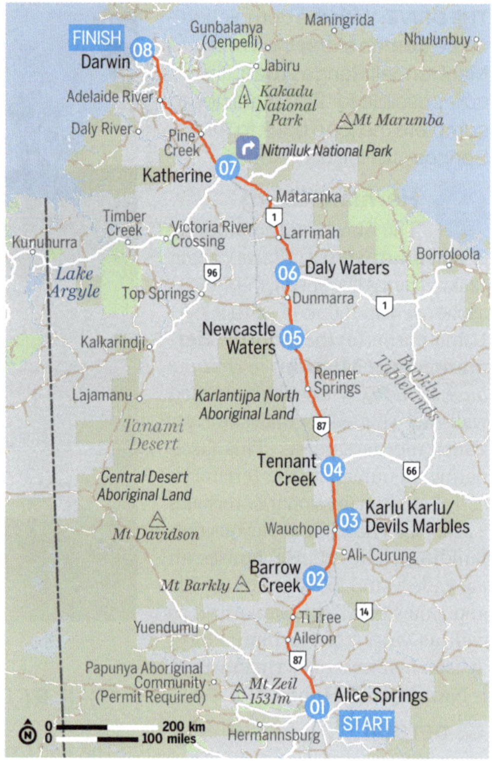

All the monotony and magnificence of the outback is on show on this long, lonely desert crossing. From Alice Springs north the air is tinder-dry and the colour cast shifts from red to yellow to green the further north you travel. By Katherine, you're in a different world, where the outback meets the tropics, and the latter very much takes hold by the time you pull into Darwin.

LINK YOUR TRIP

04 Alice Springs to Adelaide
Instead of heading north, head south. Works only if you've done this trip in reverse and began in Darwin.

30 Darwin & Kakadu
After a few days' rest in Darwin, start your next journey there and make for sublime Kakadu.

01 Alice Springs

There's no town quite like Alice, marooned in the heart of the outback. This ruggedly beautiful town is shaped by its storied landscapes. The mesmerising MacDonnell Ranges stretch east and west from the town centre, and you don't have to venture far to find yourself among crimson gorges, pastel-hued hills and ghostly white gum trees. As much as the terrain, it's the character of Alice that sets it apart. An excellent place to start your exploration of Aboriginal culture is the **Araluen Cultural Precinct** *(araluenartscentre.nt.gov.au)*, as well as countless Aboriginal art galleries.

THE DRIVE: You have a very long road ahead of you, so getting an early start helps. Watch for fine views of the MacDonnell Ranges as you leave town, then barrel on up the dry and dusty highway for 135km to tiny Aileron – don't blink or you might just miss it – with another 149km into Barrow Creek.

ARTIE PHOTOGRAPHY (ARTIE NG)/GETTY IMAGES

Nitmiluk National Park (p219)

02 Barrow Creek

The outback does a fine line in wonderfully offbeat personalities forged in the isolation afforded by this vast and sparsely populated land. At times it's a person, at others a building. But just as often it's the sum total of these and all manner of passing wanderers. One such place is the rustic **Barrow Creek Hotel** *(barrowcreekhotel.com),* one of the highway's truly eccentric outback pubs. In the tradition of shearers who'd write their name on a banknote and pin it to the wall to ensure they could afford a drink when next they passed through, travellers continue to leave notes and photos, and the result is a priceless collage of outback life. Food and fuel are available (though note that the pub had its liquor licence suspended in January 2026) and next door is one of the original telegraph stations on the Overland Telegraph Line. There ain't a whole lot more here, but you'll soon get used to that sensation in these parts.

THE DRIVE: It's 118km from Barrow Creek to the Karlu Karlu / Devils Marbles. At the kooky Wycliffe Well Roadhouse & Holiday Park, you can fill up with fuel and food, or stay and spot the UFOs that apparently fly over with astonishing regularity. At Wauchope (war-kup), 10km south of the Devils Marbles, you'll pass the Wauchope Hotel, where you can stay if need be, with a better-than-average restaurant.

03 Karlu Karlu / Devils Marbles

The gigantic granite boulders arrayed in precarious piles beside the Stuart Hwy, 105km south of Tennant Creek, are known as the Karlu Karlu (Devils Marbles; Karlu Karlu means 'round boulders' in the local Warumugu language) and they're one of the more beautiful sights along this road. The Marbles are a sacred site to the traditional Aboriginal owners of the land, for whom the rocks are, according to one story, the eggs of the Rainbow Serpent. Such are the extremes of temperature out here that the boulders undergo a constant 24-hour cycle of expansion and contraction, hence the large cracks in many of them. There are five signposted walks around the Devils Marbles, from the 20-minute 400m Karlu Karlu Walk, departing from the day-use area, to the 1½-hour, 4km Nurrku Walk, which takes you away from the crowds. If you've only time for one walk, make it the 30-minute, 800m Mayijangu Walk from the day-use area to the campground, with a 20-minute, 350m add-on up to Nyanjiki Lookout. Unless specifically permitted to do so by signposts pointing you in that direction, please respect local beliefs by not climbing on the rocks.

THE DRIVE: Unless you've slept somewhere along the way, the final 105km into Tennant Creek, 511km north of Alice, can't come quick enough. And after so long on the road, arriving even in Tennant Creek feels like paradise.

04 Tennant Creek

Tennant Creek is the only town of any size between Katherine, 680km to the north, and Alice Springs, 511km to the south, although it's all relative: just 3080 people lived here the last time the census-takers passed through. Fortunately there's more than just a good meal, petrol and clean sheets to keep you occupied. Tennant Creek is known as Jurnkurakurr to the local Warumungu people (almost half of the town's population identifies as Aboriginal) and the innovative **Nyinkka Nyunyu** *(julalikari.org.au/project/nyinkka-nyunyu-art-culture-centre)* museum and gallery highlights their dynamic art and culture; learn about bush tucker and Dreaming stories with your personal guide. Don't miss **Battery Hill Mining Centre** *(visit batteryhill.com)*, and to really get a personal experience of the area, take a **Kelly's Ranch** two-hour horse trail ride with local Warumungu man Jerry Kelly.

THE DRIVE: Just 26km north of Tennant Creek you'll pass Three Ways, the junction of the Stuart and Barkly Hwys. Banka Banka, 100km north of Tennant Creek, has a mudbrick bar, while Renner Springs is generally accepted as the dividing line between the seasonally wet Top End and the dry Red Centre; there's a decent roadhouse. Newcastle Waters is a couple of kilometres off the road.

Karlu Karlu / Devils Marbles (p217)

TOTAJLA/SHUTTERSTOCK

05 Newcastle Waters

Most small outback settlements lead a fairly precarious existence and the line between survival and abandonment can be pretty tenuous. Many make it, but **Newcastle Waters** is an eerie example of those that don't. The surrounding station of the same name was (and remains) an important cattle station, but the town's role as a drovers' way station was doomed once road and rail took over as the primary means of transport in the 1960s. These days it's a veritable ghost town, with atmospheric, historic timber-and-corrugated-iron buildings, including the Junction Hotel, cobbled together from abandoned windmills in 1932.

THE DRIVE: From Newcastle Waters to Daly Waters, it's 132 dry and dusty kilometres. Just before Daly Waters, the sealed Carpentaria Hwy branches off to the east, bound for the Gulf of Carpentaria at Eadangula some 376km away. Daly Waters lies a few kilometres off the Stuart Hwy.

06 Daly Waters

Most outback towns of any reasonable size have some unusual claim to fame; Daly Waters, about 3km off the highway, is no exception. This place was an important staging post in the early days of aviation – Amy Johnson landed here on her epic flight from England to Australia in 1930. Just about everyone stops at the famous **Daly Waters Pub** *(dalywaterspub.com.au)*. Decorated with business cards, bras, banknotes and memorabilia from passing travellers, the pub claims to be the oldest in the Territory (its liquor licence has been valid since 1938).

> PHOTO OPPORTUNITY
>
> **KARLU KARLU**
>
> Karlu Karlu / Devils Marbles at sunrise for their sacred stories and sheer beauty.

THE DRIVE: Point the car north along the Stuart Hwy and 160km later you'll arrive in Mataranka. En route, watch for tiny Larrimah, where the candy-pink-hued Larrimah Hotel was immortalised in the 2023 true crime series *Last Stop Larrimah*.

07 Katherine

Katherine is probably best known for Nitmiluk National Park to the east, and the town makes an obvious base, with plenty of accommodation and good opportunities to immerse yourself in the picturesque surroundings and local Aboriginal culture. By day, spend your time exploring the burgeoning world of Aboriginal art at **Top Didj Cultural Experience & Art Gallery** *(topdidj.com)*, and see Aboriginal artists at work at the stunning **Godinymayin Yijard Rivers Arts & Culture Centre** *(gyracc.org.au)* and Aboriginal-owned **Mimi Aboriginal Art & Craft** *(mimiarts.com)*. And don't miss Katherine Hot Springs, a gin-clear natural spring on the banks of the Katherine River.

THE DRIVE: On the final, steamy 314km into Darwin, namecheck the tiny towns of Pine Creek and Adelaide River before the urban sprawl of Darwin leaves you longing for the space and solitude of the deep outback.

> **DETOUR**
>
> **Nitmiluk National Park**
>
> **Start: 07 Katherine**
>
> Spectacular **Nitmiluk (Katherine Gorge)** forms the backbone of the 2920-sq-km **Nitmiluk National Park** *(nt.gov.au/parks/find-a-park/nitmiluk-national-park)*, about 30km from Katherine. A series of 13 deep sandstone gorges have been carved out by the Katherine River on its journey from Arnhem Land to the Timor Sea. It is a hauntingly beautiful place – though it can get crowded in peak season – and a must-do from Katherine. In the Dry, the tranquil river is perfect for a paddle, but in the Wet the deep still waters and dividing rapids are engulfed by an awesome torrent that churns through the gorge. Plan to spend at least a full day canoeing or cruising on the river and bushwalking. The traditional owners are the Jawoyn people, who jointly manage Nitmiluk with Parks & Wildlife. **Nitmiluk Tours** *(nitmiluktours.com.au)* operates accommodation, cruises and activities within the park.

08 Darwin

Australia's only tropical capital city, Darwin gazes out confidently across the Timor Sea. It's closer to Bali than Bondi and can certainly feel far removed from the rest of the country. Aboriginal art centres, markets, excellent museums and good food are all highlights here.

STAY AWHILE

ALICE SPRINGS

BY SARAH REID

After the dusty drive down from Darwin or up from Uluru, the creature comforts of Alice (including a good range of restaurants and places to stay) are the first reason to pause here. But there's more going on in this desert hub – also known by its Arrernte name, Mparntwe – than you might expect, beginning with its vibrant arts scene.

I began my visit at the **Araluen Cultural Precinct** *(araluenarts centre.nt.gov.au)* to marvel at its collection of Albert Namatjira's rich watercolour landscapes. And while Alice wouldn't usually win a beauty contest, April's **Parrtjima** *(parrtjimaaustralia.com.au)* lights festival is a spectacle to behold. Another Alice festival worth dropping by for is **fabALICE** *(fabalice.com)* in March. Celebrating the diversity of the desert with a showcase of drag, family and cabaret events, it's a great example of Alice's quirky – if complex – character.

While Alice makes an excellent base for exploring Tjoritja/West MacDonnell National Park, there are more outdoor adventures to be had closer to town on Alice's excellent network of mountain-biking trails. I hired a bike in town and cycled out to the **Old Telegraph Station** *(alicespringstelegraph station.com.au)* to learn about Alice's role in the establishment of the Overland Telegraph Line in 1872 before hitting one of the handful of MTB trails that begin here. On my ride, I spotted several black-footed rock wallabies and even a couple of dingoes. You can see more outback creatures at the **Alice Springs Desert Park** *(alicespringsdesertpark.com.au)*, which plays an important role in safeguarding endangered species from extinction.

LINK YOUR TRIP

Alice is a great stop along the 28 **Uluru & the Red Centre** trip as well as the kick-off point for the long trek from 29 **Alice Springs to Darwin**.

Left: View over Alice Springs
Right: Old Telegraph Station

FROM LEFT: JOHN WHITE PHOTOS/GETTY IMAGES, JON ARNOLD IMAGES LTD/ALAMY

PLACES TO STAY

With its spacious resort-style facilities, the **Doubletree by Hilton Hotel Alice Springs** *(hilton.com)* is widely considered to be one of Alice's top hotels. There's a good pool and spa, a well-equipped gym and sauna, tennis courts and a resident peacock. One of Alice's best restaurants, Hanuman, is in the reception area. **Alice's Secret Traveller's Inn** *(asecret.com.au)* is arguably the pick of the town's hostels, with private rooms and a pool. Or stay on the edge of the West Macs in glamping-style en suite tents at **Squeaky Windmill** *(thesqueakywindmill.com.au)*; you're out in the bush but also just a 15-minute drive to town.

30

★ BEST FOR:

FAMILIES

Crocs and kangaroos bring Kakadu to life.

NORTHERN TERRITORY

DARWIN & KAKADU

Great egret

DURATION: 5–7 DAYS

DISTANCE: 459KM / 285 MILES

GREAT FOR: NATURE, HISTORY & FAMILIES

BEST TIME TO GO: APRIL TO OCTOBER; MUCH OF THE PARK IS IMPASSABLE THE REST OF THE YEAR.

For lovers of wilderness, it's hard to beat this circular loop through the best Kakadu National Park has to offer. Steamy Darwin and the watery world of Mary River National Park are mere preludes to this extraordinary place that's as rich in wildlife as it is in dramatic landforms, soulful and ancient rock art and a blissful sense of a wild and untamed landscape.

LINK YOUR TRIP

29 Alice Springs to Darwin
This journey from the Red Centre to the high Tropics ends in Darwin, but it could just as easily turn around and begin here.

31 Darwin to Daly River
This trip through Litchfield National Park begins in Darwin; from Pine Creek, drive northwest to Adelaide River (112km) and join it there.

01 Darwin

This trip is all about dramatic, wildlife-rich country, inhabited by its traditional owners for millennia, so what better way to begin than by getting a taste for such things before even leaving Darwin. Head to the superb **Museum & Art Gallery of the Northern Territory** *(magnt.net.au)*, which has an exceptional collection of carvings from the Tiwi Islands, bark paintings from Arnhem Land and dot paintings from the desert. Right in the middle of Mitchell St, **Crocosaurus Cove** *(crocosauruscove.com)* is as close as you'll ever want to get to these amazing creatures, with six of the largest crocs in captivity in state-of-the-art aquariums and pools. And for a slice of nature, enjoy the wetlands of **Charles Darwin National Park** *(nt.gov.au/parks/find-a-park/charles-darwin-national-park)*, which sneak right inside city limits.

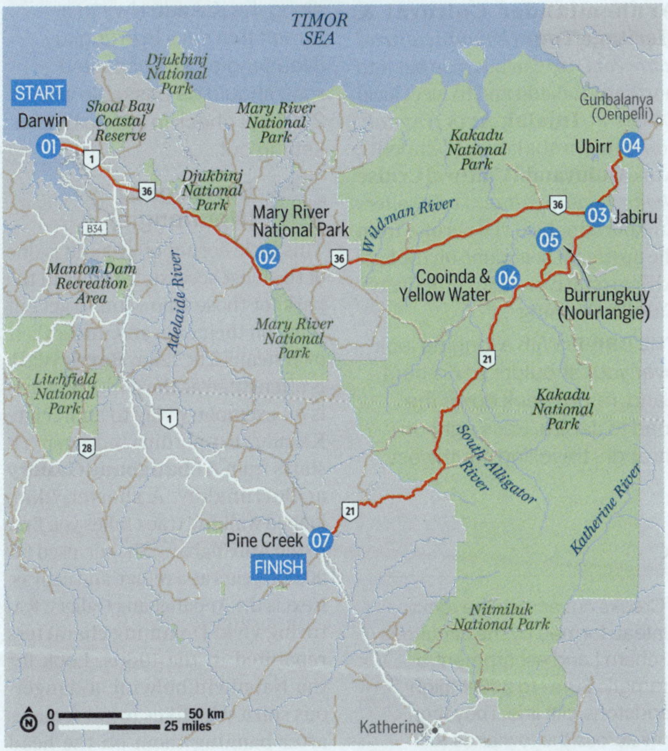

DANIELA CONSTANTINESCU/SHUTTERSTOCK

THE DRIVE: There's only one main road out of Darwin. Follow it for 35km, then take the left-branching (east) Arnhem Hwy, ignoring the signs to Humpty Doo. From where the Arnhem Hwy begins, it's around 80km to the Mary River turnoff.

02 Mary River National Park

The Mary River region is one of the Top End's richest collections of wetlands and wildlife, and it all centres on the **Mary River National Park** *(nt.gov.au/parks/find-a-park/mary-river-national-park),* which begins by the Arnhem Hwy and extends to the north. For a taste of what the park is all about, **Bird Billabong**, just off the highway a few kilometres before **Mary River Crossing**, is a back-flow billabong, filled by creeks flowing off nearby Mt Bundy Hill during the Wet. It's 4km off the highway and accessible by 2WD year-round. The scenic **loop walk** (4.5km, two hours) passes through **tropical woodlands**, with a backdrop of the granite hills of Mt Bundey. Back in the car, about another 2km along the same road, is the emerald-green **Mary River Billabong**, with a BBQ area. From here the 4WD-only Hardies Track leads deeper into the national park to **Corroboree Billabong** (25km) and **Couzens Lookout** (37km).

THE DRIVE: Back on the Arnhem Hwy, you'll enter Kakadu National Park and all the joys that brings. For much of the way, the road passes hardy woodland growing from low red-sand hills and fine escarpments. You'll want to pause for photos where the road crosses the South Alligator River.

03 Jabiru

You may be in the wilderness but Jabiru serves as a reminder that Kakadu is a fragile paradise. The town, with a population of 755 people, exists because of the nearby Ranger uranium mine, but for your purposes, it's more noteworthy as a base for explorations out into the park – this is Kakadu's major service centre, with a bank, newsagent, medical centre, supermarket, bakery and service station. You can even play a round of golf here. To get a sense of what all the fuss is about, we recommended taking a scenic (fixed-wing or helicopter) flight with **Kakadu Air** *(kakaduair.com.au)*; note that flight paths change between seasons, with flights over Jim Jim Falls conducted in the Wet when the falls are at their thundering best.

THE DRIVE: North of Jabiru, the paved road battles on bravely for 39km towards Arnhem Land before petering out at East Alligator River, where you'll find Ubirr and, on the river's far bank, Arnhem Land in all its 4WD-accessible glory.

04 Ubirr

It may get busy with busloads of visitors in the Dry, but they do little to disturb Ubirr's inherent majesty and grace. Layers of **rock-art paintings**, in various styles and from various millennia, command a mesmerising stillness. The main gallery is astonishingly rich with images of kangaroos, tortoises, fish and even a thylacine, many of them painted in X-ray, which became the dominant style about 8000 years ago. Pre-dating these are the paintings of Mimi spirits (cheeky, dynamic figures who, it's believed, were the first of the Creation Ancestors to paint on rock) and the Rainbow Serpent. The magnificent **Nardab Lookout** is a 250m scramble from the main gallery. Surveying the billiard-table-green floodplain and watching the sun set and the moon rise, like they're on an invisible set of scales, is glorious, to say the least. If you're tempted to venture beyond, Aboriginal-owned and operated **Arnhemlander Cultural & Heritage Tour** *(kakaduculturaltours.com.au)* can take you out into northern Kakadu and to meet local artists at **Injalak Arts** *(injalak.com)* in Gunbalanya (Oenpelli), while **Guluyambi Cultural Cruise** *(kakaduculturaltours.com)* offers an Aboriginal-led river cruise from the upstream boat ramp on the East Alligator River near croc-heavy Cahill's Crossing.

THE DRIVE: With a longing look over your shoulder at Arnhem Land, return back down the road to Jabiru. Pass right on through, travelling southwest along the Kakadu Hwy to a turnoff that says Burrungkuy (Nourlangie). The unsealed road should be passable in a 2WD but check in Jabiru before setting out.

KAKADU NATIONAL PARK

Kakadu is a whole lot more than a national park. It's also a vibrant, living acknowledgment of the elemental link between the Aboriginal custodians and the country they have nurtured, endured and respected for thousands of generations. Encompassing almost 20,000 sq km (about 200km north–south and 100km east–west), it holds in its boundaries a spectacular ecosystem and a mind-blowing concentration of ancient **rock art**. The landscape is an ever-changing tapestry – periodically scorched and flooded, apparently desolate or obviously abundant, depending on the season. In just a few days you can cruise on billabongs bursting with **wildlife**, examine 25,000-year-old rock paintings with the help of an Aboriginal guide, swim in pools at the foot of tumbling **waterfalls** and hike through ancient sandstone escarpment country.

Creeks cut across the rocky plateau formed by the circuitous Arnhem Land escarpment, a dramatic 30m- to 200m-high sandstone cliff line. They then flow across the lowlands to swamp Kakadu's vast northern flood plains. The coastal zone has long stretches of mangrove swamp, important for halting erosion and as a breeding ground for bird and marine life. More than 80% of Kakadu is savannah woodland. It has more than 1000 plant species, many still used by Aboriginal people for food and medicinal purposes.

Kakadu also has more than 60 species of mammals, more than 280 bird species, 120 recorded species of reptile, 25 species of frog, 55 freshwater fish species and at least 10,000 different kinds of insect. Most visitors see only a fraction of these creatures (except the insects), since many of them are shy, nocturnal or scarce.

05 Burrungkuy (Nourlangie)

This little corner of Kakadu is one of the most accessible places in the park for those who want to get out there on their own and under their own steam. The 12km **Barrk Walk** is often rated as the park's best and is an exemplary way to appreciate Kakadu's extraordinary diversity; it starts from **Anbangbang Gallery** at Burrungkuy. A shorter, 2km, looped walking track takes you first to the Anbangbang Shelter, used for 20,000 years as a refuge and canvas. Next is the Anbangbang Gallery, featuring vivid Dreaming characters repainted in the 1960s. Look for the Nabulwinjbulwinj, a dangerous spirit who likes to eat females after banging them on the head with a yam. From here it's a short, steep walk to **Gunwarddehwarde Lookout**, with views of the Arnhem Land escarpment.

Another option is **Nawurlandja Lookout Walk**, which begins 1km north of Burrungkuy car park – the 600m, 30-minute walk takes you up to a fine vantage point overlooking the woodlands. Yet another possibility is the Anbangbang Billabong Walk, a 2.5km loop around a picturesque, lily-filled billabong and through paperbark swamp. And don't miss **Nanguluwur Gallery**, an outstanding rock gallery that sees far fewer visitors than Nourlangie simply because it's further to walk (3.5km return, 1½ hours, easy).

THE DRIVE: Return to the Kakadu Hwy, then continue southwest for around 10km to Cooinda. If you're coming

SLJONES/SHUTTERSTOCK

Sunset, Ubirr (p223)

directly from Jabiru, the turnoff to the Cooinda accommodation complex and Yellow Water wetlands is 47km down the Kakadu Hwy from the Arnhem Hwy intersection.

06 Cooinda & Yellow Water

Tiny Cooinda is the gateway to all that's good about the central Kakadu region. Before setting out on one of the tours that are the main reason to come to these parts, stop by the **Warradjan Aboriginal Cultural Centre** *(warradjanculturalcentre.com)*, around 1km from the resort. The centre depicts Creation stories and has a great permanent exhibition that includes clap sticks, sugar-bag holders and rock-art samples, plus there's a mini theatre with a huge selection of films. As soon as you can, get out on to the waters of the South Alligator River and Yellow Water Billabong with **Yellow Water Cruises** *(kakadutourism.com)* – a fabulous wildlife-watching experience. For something a little different, **Kakadu Animal Tracks** *(animaltracks.com.au)* runs seven-hour tours with an Aboriginal guide combining a wildlife safari and Aboriginal cultural tour. You'll see thousands of birds, get to hunt, gather, prepare and consume bush tucker, and crunch on some green ants.

THE DRIVE: Red Kakadu sand and scrubby woodland edge road verges along the Kakadu Hwy as it meanders southwest through the park. Traffic is light, but becomes less so as you near Pine Creek (158km from Cooinda) and the main Stuart Hwy.

> PHOTO OPPORTUNITY
>
> UBIRR
>
> Sunset at Ubirr is a classic image of Australia.

07 Pine Creek

Pine Creek, where the Kakadu and Stuart Hwys meet, is a small, dusty settlement and an anti-climax at the best of times, even though it was once the scene of a frantic gold rush. If nothing else, this is where you reconnect with the main road and start dreaming of where your next adventure may take you.

31

NORTHERN TERRITORY

DARWIN TO DALY RIVER

DURATION: 4 DAYS

DISTANCE: 340KM / 211 MILES

GREAT FOR: NATURE

BEST TIME TO GO: APRIL TO OCTOBER (THE DRY SEASON)

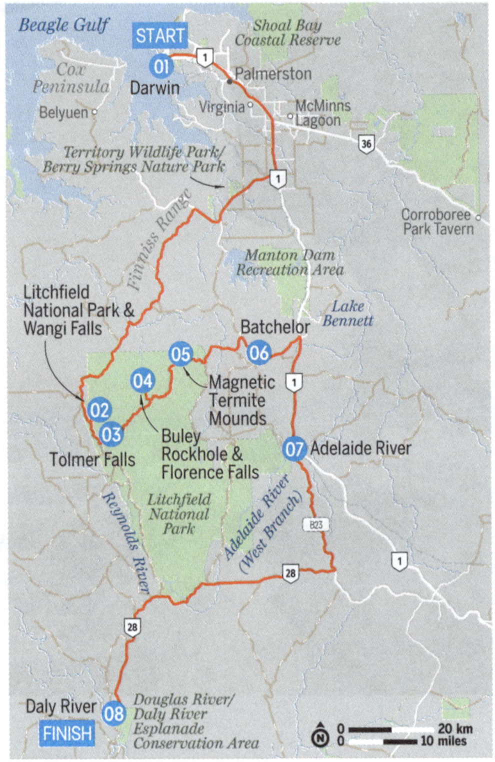

Litchfield National Park may be in danger of being overrun by day-trippers from Darwin, but there's a reason for its popularity. The attractions here are different, although (like in Kakadu) there are picturesque waterfalls and strange landforms in abundance, not to mention a palpable sense of passing through a remote, red-earthed tropical wilderness. Get there early to avoid the crowds, bring your swimwear and you'll never forget this classic Top End park. Continue past the park to discover several classic Territory towns.

LINK YOUR TRIP

29 Alice Springs to Darwin
This trip shares the Stuart Hwy; if you're coming from the south, skip Darwin and join at the Cox Peninsula Rd turnoff.

30 Darwin & Kakadu
Both trips begin in Darwin. If you don't wish to backtrack, drive north from Pine Creek to the Cox Peninsula Rd turnoff and begin this trip there.

01 Darwin

Darwin, where so many journeys in the Top End begin, stands on the cusp of some pretty spectacular country, but it's also the last place before you set out where you can get a choice of meals, a glass of fine wine and have all the attractions and comforts of a big city. Exploring Darwin's WWII heritage is a highlight for many. At the **Darwin Military Museum** *(darwinmilitarymuseum.au)*, the multimedia Defence of Darwin Experience immerses you in the 1942 bombing of Darwin and the lived experiences of those present. Don a VR headset at the **Royal Flying Doctor Service Darwin Tourist Facility** *(rfdsdarwin.com.au)* to experience the Japanese air raid on the harbour as if you were there. And a trip to Darwin wouldn't be complete without a visit to the **Museum and Art Gallery of the Northern Territory** *(magnt.net.au)* with its

NINEFIVER MEDIA/SHUTTERSTOCK

Wangi Falls, Litchfield National Park

poignant Cyclone Tracy exhibition, rich Indigenous art collection and 5.1m taxidermied croc, Sweetheart.

THE DRIVE: Head south on the Stuart Hwy for 46km and turn right (west) onto Cox Peninsula Rd. Pause for a dip in the croc-free (in the Dry) turquoise pools of Berry Springs Nature Park, just off the main road, or continue on and turn left onto the paved Litchfield Park Rd for 64.5km to the Wangi Falls turnoff.

02 Litchfield National Park & Wangi Falls

Litchfield *(nt.gov.au/parks)* is certainly one of the best places in the Top End for bushwalking, camping and especially swimming, with waterfalls plunging into gorgeous, safe (usually) swimming holes. What gives this 1500-sq-km national park its drama is that the park boundaries enclose much of the spectacular Tabletop Range, a wide sandstone plateau mostly surrounded by cliffs. The waterfalls that pour off the edge of this plateau are a highlight of the park, feeding crystal-clear cascades and seasonally croc-free plunge pools. Litchfield's big-ticket attraction is Wangi Falls (pronounced 'wong-guy'). Just 1.5km from Litchfield Park Rd, the falls flow year-round, spilling either side of a huge orange-rock outcrop and filling an enormous swimming hole bordered by rainforest and palm trees. It's particularly impressive in the wet season, when the waters thunder and are wonderfully deep at the base, but they can be dangerous as a result. The falls may be rather modest if you come near the end of the Dry. Then again, they're also at their most popular during the Dry (when there's a refreshment kiosk here and free public wi-fi).

THE DRIVE: The paved road continues through the park. From the Wangi Falls turnoff, it's 10km further on to the Tolmer Falls turnoff. The car park is 600m beyond.

03 Tolmer Falls

Spectacular Tolmer Falls are for looking at only, but goodness it's a lovely view. The trickle of water that approaches the falls from above is barely visible through the dense greenery and rocky landscape of

PHOTO OPPORTUNITY

Magnetic termite mounds look for all the world like outback apparitions.

♥ WHY I LOVE THIS TRIP

SARAH REID, WRITER

As someone who can get a bit restless on long drives, I love how this trip deposits you deep in Litchfield within 90 minutes. Most of its attractions are just a few kilometres apart, meaning you spend more time out of the car than inside it. And if you're camping, you can begin and end the day with a dip in any number of idyllic waterfalls framed by scarlet cliffs. Floating in the pandanus-framed pool at Wangi Falls as the cliffs glowed scarlet at sunset was pure magic.

the plateau until it emerges, settling ever-so-briefly in a pool just above the rim, before plunging down off the cliff. Below, there's a hint of partially submerged caves, and the whole scene looks for all the world like the quintessential Top End waterfall, worthy of the Kimberley or Kakadu.

THE DRIVE: Back on the main road, it's just under 15km to the turnoff to Buley Rockhole (3km) and Florence Falls (5km). En route you'll pass the turnoff to the surreal rock formations of the Lost City, accessed via a 4WD-only dirt road.

04 Buley Rockhole & Florence Falls

At Buley Rockhole, the water cascades through a series of rock pools big enough to swim in. Anywhere else in this part of the world you'd be keeping a careful eye out for crocs, but here it's just crystalline water funnelling through a forest of green, and it couldn't be more tempting. If you find the right spot (ideally before the crowds arrive), the waters crashing over the rocks have a massaging, pummelling effect, without being strong enough to dislodge you from your perch. From the Rockhole, a walking track (1.7km, 45 minutes) follows Florence Creek all the way to Florence Falls, where a 15-minute, 135-step descent leads to a deep, beautiful pool surrounded by monsoon forest. Alternatively, you can see the falls from a lookout, 120m from the car park. Either way, it's a gorgeous spot.

THE DRIVE: Back on the main road, it's only 6km to the magnetic termite mounds, right beside the road.

Magnetic Termite Mounds (p230)
PIOTR GATLIK/SHUTTERSTOCK

ANDREW BAIN/ALAMY

Tabletop Track, Litchfield National Park

☑ TOP TIP

EXPLORING LITCHFIELD ON FOOT

If you've been beguiled by Litchfield and have the kind of schedule (and equipment) that allows for an extended walk through the bush, consider the Tabletop Track (39km) to really see all that Litchfield has to offer. This circuit of the park takes three to five days to complete, depending on how many side tracks you follow. You can access the track at Florence Falls, Wangi Falls and Walker Creek. You must carry a topographic map of the area, available from tourist and retail outlets in Batchelor. The track is closed from late September to March.

05 Magnetic Termite Mounds

Looking for all the world like a cross between an abandoned cemetery and a Top End Stonehenge, the otherworldly and entirely natural magnetic termite mounds are one of the region's more curious apparitions. They may resemble tombstones, but only the very tip of these magnetic termite mounds is used to bury the dead; at the bottom are the king and queen termites, magnetic termite mounds with workers in between. They're perfectly aligned to regulate temperature, catching the morning sun, then allowing the residents to dodge the midday heat. Nearby are some giant, red-hued mounds made by the aptly named cathedral termites – they're impressive and tower impossibly high.

THE DRIVE: Signs of civilisation begin to appear shortly after exiting the park, halfway to Batchelor. It's a 35km drive in total.

06 Batchelor

Sleepy little Batchelor is the gateway town to Litchfield if entering from the south, with an interesting **museum** *(batchelormuseum.org.au)* and a **butterfly farm** *(butterflyfarm.net.au)*. It has a handful of accommodation options (you will have clocked a few more on the road in from the park), but the only place to eat in the township is the Litchfield Outback Resort's **Lil' Ripper Cafe, Bar & Bistro** *(litchfieldoutbackresort.com.au)*.

THE DRIVE: It's 12.5km back to the Stuart Hwy, then a further 28km south to Adelaide River.

07 Adelaide River

With its broad tree-lined streets and riverside setting, Adelaide River could be any Australian country town were it not for the crocs in the river and the knowledge that this is one of the last settlements on the long, lonely road to Katherine and beyond. Other than the roadhouse and petrol station (obligatory in these parts), don't miss the **Adelaide River War Cemetery** *(cwgc.org)*, a poignant and important legacy with a sea of little brass plaques commemorating those killed in the 1942–43 air raids on northern Australia.

THE DRIVE: Leave the Stuart Hwy and head south of town along the Victoria Hwy for 32km. A hard right (to the west) takes you onto narrow Rte 28 (Daly River Rd), which skirts along the southern boundary of Litchfield National Park, before swinging south to Daly River, which you reach after 77km.

08 Daly River

One of the most remote settlements you can reach in the Territory by paved road, tiny Daly River (population 116) sits on the river of the same name and is known for some of the best barramundi fishing in the NT. The town itself has an end-of-the road charm, but it's the river that's the real draw – even if you're not into fishing, it's a pretty place (no swimming) and a little exploring by boat will take you within sight of some choice spots. There's a shop and fuel here, and visitors are welcome without a fishing permit, but note that this is a dry community – no alcohol. Other than fishing, the main attraction is **Merrepen Arts** *(merrepenarts.com.au)*, a gallery displaying locally made arts and crafts including etchings, screen prints, acrylic paintings, carvings and weaving; the quality varies, but it lacks the 'scene' of other Territory arts complexes.

SWIMMING LITCHFIELD

As a general rule, Litchfield's many plunge pools are croc-free during the dry season (always check official advice before swimming), but off-limits in the Wet. Each of the following is accessible in a 2WD vehicle, and each offers a different experience.

Buley Rockhole
A beautiful series of pools; they're also just a short walk from the car park and, as such, they're always very crowded.

Florence Falls
The climb down means that it doesn't get quite as busy as Buley or Wangi, although you'll certainly have plenty of company. The pool is surrounded by cliffs on three sides, making for a dramatic swim.

Wangi Falls
With a wonderful backdrop, this is the most easily accessible of all the swimming holes and draws tour buses as the day wears on.

Walker Creek
A little-known gem with far fewer visitors than elsewhere. It's a bit like better-known Buley, but without the crowds.

Cascade Pools
Another lesser-frequented series of pools surrounded by woodland.

Swimmers at Florence Falls, Litchfield National Park
DAVID WALL/ALAMY

0 500 km
0 250 miles
INDIAN OCEAN
Cape Londonderry
Cape Bougainville
Joseph Bonaparte Gulf
Kalumburu
Prince Regent Nature Reserve
Wyndham
Collier Bay
Kununurra
Cape Leveque
The Kimberley
Lake Argyle
Dampier Peninsula
Derby
Broome
Fitzroy Crossing
Purnululu National Park
Halls Creek
Port Smith
Billiluna
Great Sandy Desert
Port Hedland
Dampier
Karratha
Marble Bar
Balgo Aboriginal Land
Onslow
Millstream-Chichester National Park
Exmouth
Karlamilyi National Park
Tom Price
Karijini National Park
34
Coral Bay
Paraburdoo
Newman
Lake Disappointment
Lake Macleod
Collier Range National Park
Little Sandy Desert
NORTHERN TERRITORY
Gascoyne Junction
Carnarvon
Shark Bay
Peak Hill
Lake Carnegie
Denham
Warburton
Warburton Aboriginal Land
Meekatharra
Wiluna
Steep Point
Toolonga Nature Reserve
Lake Wells
Great Victoria Desert
SOUTH AUSTRALIA
Cue
Sandstone
Leinster
Cosmo Newberry Aboriginal Land
Kalbarri
Mt Magnet
Neale Junction Nature Reserve
Northampton
Mullewa
Laverton
Leonora
Geraldton
Perenjori
Dongara - Port Denison
Karroun Hill Nature Reserve
Goongarrie National Park
Great Victoria Desert Nature Reserve
Nambung National Park
Wubin
Cervantes
Moora
Southern Cross
Coolgardie
Kalgoorlie-Boulder
Nullarbor Plain
Nullarbor Regional Reserve
Kambalda
Northam
Merredin
Perth
Eucla
Cocklebiddy
Madura
INDIAN OCEAN
Fremantle
Norseman
Mandurah
Hyden
Dundas Lake
Balladonia
Israelite Bay
Great Australian Bight
Bunbury
Ravensthorpe
Esperance
Busselton
Katanning
Cape Arid National Park
Hopetoun
33
32
Cape Le Grand National Park
Cape Leeuwin
Augusta
Mt Barker
Bremer Bay
Denmark
Albany
SOUTHERN OCEAN

GAGLIARDIPHOTOGRAPHY/SHUTTERSTOCK

Nature's Window (p250), Kalbarri National Park

WESTERN AUSTRALIA

EXPLORE

WESTERN AUSTRALIA

When you visit Western Australia, you'll wonder why it's not busier or more famous. This vast state is an astonishing destination, from sunny Perth to laid-back Broome and beyond. In the south, there are wine regions, ancient forests and dramatic coastlines. Up north, there are the brooding red-rock escarpments of the Kimberley and otherworldly Purnululu National Park. For much of the journey between the two, there are stirring national parks, a world-renowned reef, UNESCO World Heritage–listed areas and some of Australia's best beaches. Yes, distances can be long, but the drive is always worth it.

Perth

Don't tell Sydney, but many travellers rate Perth's beaches as the best of any Australian city. The sun always seems to shine in Perth, which is one of the world's most remote cities and a place where the cultural and culinary scenes are exploding into life. Great hotels and a transport network that can take you to attractions near and far make this the ultimate gateway city to the west.

Bunbury

Quieter than Perth and blessed with so many activities on land and out to sea, Bunbury offers the best of many worlds. Aside from its wonderful timber jetty, built in 1864 and stretching a remarkable 1.8km into the ocean, Bunbury boasts an excellent food scene and great accommodation. Roads from here fan out across the south, including to the Margaret River gourmet region, the wild southwest coast and the wine regions, forests, beaches and wildlife-watching opportunities of the less visited (yet exceptional) south coast.

Albany

The oldest continuously settled town in Western Australia, Albany is an important crossroads settlement along the state's south coast. Close to wineries, national parks

WHEN TO GO

In WA's south, you could come upon fine weather year-round, but summer (December to February) offers the best weather. Around Ningaloo Reef, whale sharks are present from March to August. Visit the north during the Dry (April to October); the Wet can bring torrential rain and flooding – watch for cyclones from the central coast north from November to April.

and some extraordinarily beautiful stretches of coastline, Albany is where so many adventures begin. These include everything from whale watching to long-haul road trips along the south coast (including the longer back road).

Carnarvon

Any town on the long coastal road from Perth to Broome could qualify as a hub, as roads peel away to and from the coast, to national parks such as Kalbarri (to the south) and Karijini (inland, to the northeast) and to World Heritage-listed Shark Bay and Ningaloo Reef. Carnarvon is the pick of the towns, thanks to a good mix of attractions (a space museum, a cactus farm, Aboriginal tours and a cultural centre), good places to eat and stay, and the possibilities for detours not far from town.

Broome

Clinging to a narrow strip of pindan (red-soil country) on Australia's outer northwestern rim, Broome is at once oasis and frontier. The town has an agreeable tropical feel, with a fascinating history, and it's a fab place to eat, drink and stay. Nothing happens in a hurry in Broome, and it can be such an adventure just getting here that it's worth lingering for a few days before you move on. And when you're done with Broome, the Dampier Peninsula and wider Kimberley region are made for exploration.

TRANSPORT

If WA was a country, it would be the 10th largest on the planet. If you restrict yourself to Perth and the southwest, you can keep the driving distances down and still see a lot. But from Perth north, we're talking days of driving, so you may want to fly (to Broome, for example) to save time.

RESOURCES

- **Australia's Northwest** Your online guide to the Kimberley. *australiasnorthwest.com/explore/kimberley*
- **Explore Parks WA** Get to know WA's amazing national parks. *exploreparks.dbca.wa.gov.au*
- **Tourism Western Australia** Distils this massive state into tempting online morsels. *westernaustralia.com/au/home*

WHERE TO STAY

Perth has excellent accommodation across most budgets and styles. The Margaret River region and much of the southwest and, increasingly, the south coast has lots of variety, including atmospheric B&Bs and hotels both historic and contemporary. The further north you go, the less choice you'll have beyond motels, campgrounds and caravan parks. Notable exceptions include Shark Bay, Exmouth and Broome. There's also a handful of glamping and wilderness-retreat ecotourism resorts along remote coastal stretches and inland at Karijini National Park.

WHAT'S ON

- **Fringe World Festival** Australia's cheekiest arts festival begins in January with boundary-pushing live performances. *fringeworld.com.au*
- **Boab Festival** Concerts, mud footy, mud-crab races, street parades and the Long Table dinner out on the mudflats; held in July. *derbyboabfestival.org.au*
- **Gourmet Escape** International celebrity chefs and food lovers descend on Margaret River in late November for tastings, events and more. *gourmetescape.com.au*
- **Mango Festival** Three days of mango madness in Broome in late November.

32

> ★ BEST FOR:
> FAMILIES
> Wading alongside the dolphins at the Dolphin Discovery Centre, Bunbury.

WESTERN AUSTRALIA

WESTERN AUSTRALIA'S SOUTHWEST COAST

DURATION: 7 DAYS

DISTANCE: 877KM / 545 MILES

GREAT FOR: WINE & NATURE

BEST TIME TO GO: DECEMBER TO FEBRUARY; JULY TO SEPTEMBER FOR WHALE WATCHING.

Dolphin Discovery Centre, Bunbury

Most visitors to Western Australia's southwest make a beeline for Margaret River, but there's so much more to explore. Whale watching is one of the more memorable highlights of this wild and dramatic shore, where beaches stretch to eternity and dolphins draw near in the shallows. Best of all, large swathes of the coast have been protected from development, leaving beaches and forests rich with nature and wildlife to explore.

LINK YOUR TRIP

03 Across the Nullarbor
You could join this route either in Perth, or by driving 202km north from Esperance to Norseman.

33 Margaret River Wine Region
Bunbury is a feature of both itineraries and it would be mad not to loop through the Margaret River area and return to the southwest coast.

01 Bunbury

Once purely industrial, Bunbury is now a seaside destination. The waterfront area has been redeveloped with modern accommodation and restaurants, and downtown has cafes and cocktail bars complemented by colourful street art and an entertainment centre. The real stars are the roughly 60 bottlenose dolphins that live in Bunbury's Koombana Bay; their numbers swell to more than 250 in summer. The **Dolphin Discovery Centre** *(dolphindiscovery.com.au)* has a learning centre pitched for kids and adults alike, plus a beachside zone where dolphins regularly come into the shallows to interact with the tourists. A close encounter with this pod is more likely in the early mornings between November and April. Note there is considerable debate about whether these wild encounters are harmful to the dolphins.

GARY BLAKE/ALAMY

THE DRIVE: From Bunbury, the main route south branches to the Bussell Hwy (for Margaret River), and the South Western Hwy (to the southern forests and south coast). Take the latter, passing through Donnybrook and Greenbushes in the 96km run into Bridgetown.

02 Bridgetown

Lovely little Bridgetown is a quintessential rural Aussie town, surrounded by karri forests and rolling farmland with some lovely Blackwood River frontage that turns yellow, red and orange in autumn. It's garnering something of a reputation as a popular weekender destination and the town comes alive from Friday evening to Sunday lunch. Wander its historic main street for cafes, shops and an artists' collective. Note the occasional art deco building, then retire to the **Cidery** *(thecidery.com.au)* for a tasting session or live music.

THE DRIVE: Thick forest crowds the roadside south of Bridgetown, particularly around the truffle-and-timber town of Manjimup (36km). Around 15km south of Manjimup, take the turnoff right (southwest) for the last 19km into Pemberton.

03 Pemberton

It's hard not to fall in love with misty little Pemberton, hidden deep in the karri forests that are such a feature of this corner of the country. To get out among the tall timbers, aim to spend a day or two driving the well-marked **Karri Forest Explorer** tracks, walking the trails and perhaps swimming in a local waterhole; check in at the **visitor centre** *(pembertonvisitor.com.au)* in town for maps and advice. Wineries, too, are a part of Pemberton's star appeal. If Margaret River is WA's Bordeaux, Pemberton is its Burgundy, producing excellent chardonnay and pinot noir, among other varietals. One option is to visit **Mountford** *(mountfordwines.com.au)*, where the wines and ciders produced are all certified organic. Climb the Gloucester Tree if you dare, and check out the crafts at the **Pemberton Fine Woodcraft Gallery** with its excellent garden cafe, **Holy Smoke**.

THE DRIVE: Return 19km northeast through the forests to the South Western Hwy, where you turn right. From here, the road angles southeast through more wonderfully dense forests. From the turnoff, it's 103km into the tiny seaside hamlet of Walpole; watch for big ocean views opening up on the final approach.

04 Valley of the Giants

The undoubted (and most accessible) highlight of this fabulously wild corner is the **Valley of the Giants** *(valleyofthegiants.com.au)* and its irresistible Tree Top Walk. Here, a 600m-long ramp rises from the valley, allowing visitors access high into the canopy of the giant tingle trees. Good free walking tracks in the Walpole Wilderness Area through jarrah, tingle and karri forests include the long distance **Bibbulmun Track**, which passes through Walpole to Coalmine Beach. Scenic drives include the **Knoll Drive**, 3km east of Walpole.

THE DRIVE: At Walpole, the South Western Hwy (Rte 1) becomes the South Coast Hwy. It occasionally emerges from the forests soon after passing the turnoff to Peaceful Bay, with some wonderful ocean views away to the south as you near Denmark, 66km from Walpole.

05 Denmark

The first reasonably sized town you come to along WA's south coast, Denmark is blessed with long sandy beaches and sheltered inlets to the southwest of the town and forests hard up against its back on the inland side. Detour to get some pictures of the beautiful **Elephant Rocks** and take a swim in the natural shallows at Greens Pool. Denmark has a reputation as something of a sustainable lifestyle and artsy town with a strong surfing community. It's the best place to base yourself in this area for accommodation, dining out and a spot of shopping.

THE DRIVE: It's just 50km from Denmark to Albany and you know the deal – forests to the left of you, ocean to the right, and it's all really rather beautiful.

06 Albany

Albany is WA's oldest town, a bustling commercial centre with a stately and genteel decaying

Elephant Rocks, Denmark

BRAD RUSSELL/SHUTTERSTOCK

colonial quarter and a waterfront in the midst of redevelopment. The story of the Anzacs is sensitively commemorated here among old forts. Southern right and humpback whales gather near the bays and coves of King George Sound from July to mid-October. You can sometimes spot them from the beach, but getting out on the water on a tour will increase your chances. Diving and snorkelling is another Albany speciality, thanks to the 2001 scuttling of the warship HMAS *Perth* to create an artificial reef for divers; contact **Southcoast Diving Supplies** *(divealbany.com.au)*. For lovers of drama, head to The Gap in Torndirrup National Park for spectacular ocean views.

THE DRIVE: The road and the coastline turn northeast, arcing up and over the Great Australian Bight. It's 292km to the Hopetoun turnoff, from where it's another 49km down to the coast.

DETOUR

Bremer Bay & Fitzgerald River National Park

Start: 06 Albany

Far enough off the main road to remain a secret, sleepy **Bremer Bay** is fringed with brilliant white sand and translucent green waters. It's quiet and very beautiful. From July to November the bay is a cetacean maternity ward for southern right whales, while the town also serves as a gateway to **Fitzgerald River National Park**. Walkers will discover beautiful coastline, sand plains, rugged coastal hills (known as 'the Barrens') and deep, wide river valleys. In season, you'll almost certainly see whales and their calves from the shore at Point Ann, where there's a lookout and a heritage walk that follows a short stretch of the 1164km No 2 rabbit-proof fence, one of the longest fences on earth. Entry to the park from Bremer Bay is via Swamp and Murray Rds, and all roads are gravel and passable in 2WD vehicle except after rains – check locally before you set out.

To get here, drive 117km northwest of Albany along Rte 1 to Boxwood Hill. Bremer Bay lies 62km due east of Boxwood Hill.

ADWO/SHUTTERSTOCK

Tree Top Walk, Valley of the Giants

PHOTO OPPORTUNITY

In the tops of really tall trees at the Valley of the Giants.

07 Esperance

Framed by turquoise waters and pristine white beaches, Esperance sits in solitary splendour on the Bay of Isles. It's such an appealing place that families still travel from Perth or Kalgoorlie just to plug into the easygoing vibe and great beach life. Picture-perfect beaches dot the even more remote national parks to the town's southeast, and the pristine environment of the 105 islands of the offshore Recherche Archipelago are home to fur seals, penguins and sea birds. A tour to Woody Island is highly recommended; ask at the visitor centre in Esperance for details. Wreck-diving is also possible with **Esperance Diving & Fishing** *(esperancediving andfishing.com.au)*.

THE DRIVE: Take the Condingup road that runs northeast, then follow the signs along sealed roads first to Gerbryn, then Cape Le Grand National Park.

08 Cape Le Grand National Park

Starting 60km east of Esperance, Cape Le Grand National Park has spectacular coastal scenery, dazzling beaches and excellent walking tracks. There's good fishing, swimming and camping at Lucky Bay and Le Grand Beach, and day-use facilities at gorgeous Hellfire Bay. Make the effort to climb Frenchman Peak (a steep 3km return, allow two hours), as the views from the top and through the rocky 'eye', especially during the late afternoon, are superb. To explore further, your best bet is a 4WD tour along the sand and two-hour circuits of Great Ocean Dr with **Eco-Discovery Tours**.

33

WESTERN AUSTRALIA

MARGARET RIVER WINE REGION

DURATION: 3–4 DAYS

DISTANCE: 195KM / 120 MILES

GREAT FOR: WINE & NATURE

BEST TIME TO GO: EARLY SUMMER FOR BEACHES, FORESTS AND AFTERNOONS AT WINERIES AND BREWERIES.

The farmland, forests, rivers and coast of the lush, green southwestern corner of Western Australia contrast vividly with the stark, sunburnt terrain of much of the state. On land, world-class wineries and craft breweries beckon, while offshore, bottlenose dolphins and whales frolic, and devoted surfers search for their perfect break. And, unusually for WA, distances between the many attractions are short, making it a fantastic area to explore for a few days.

LINK YOUR TRIP

32 Western Australia's Southwest Coast
Both trips begin in Bunbury, so joining them up couldn't be easier.

34 Coral Coast to Broome
It's a two-hour, 175km drive north from Bunbury to Perth where this wonderful Perth-to-Broome road trip begins.

01 Bunbury

With long beaches, street art, a great little museum and excellent food options, industrial Bunbury is worth a proper stop. For bottlenose dolphins swimming around your legs, head to Koombana Bay and the Dolphin Discovery Centre (p236). Then pick up a self-guided walking tour of Bunbury's street art from the excellent **Visitor Centre** *(visitbunburygeographe.com.au)*. There's also the **Mangrove Boardwalk**, which you enter off Koombana Dr and which meanders through a 2500-year-old ecosystem, before hitting the beach either on the bayside or for the ocean surf.

THE DRIVE: Take the Bussell Hwy (for Margaret River) that follows the coast south of Bunbury. You'll barely have time to get out of third gear before finding yourself in the small town of Capel. Ignore the town, and head for the winery by taking Mallokup Rd near the centre of the town.

★ BEST FOR:

FOOD

Cullen Wines' biodynamic food and wine package and garden tour experience.

OZIMAGES/ALAMY

Desserts, Cullen Wines restaurant (p243)

02 Capel Vale

Where the Geographe Bay and Indian Ocean coast arcs around to the southwest in a near-perfect moon-curve, **Capel Vale** *(capelvale.com.au)* carpets the green coastal hinterland with vines that produce some of Western Australia's most respected wines; you'll find them in restaurants and bottleshops across the country. It offers free tastings from its cellar door and its well-regarded restaurant overlooks the vines. It has a wonderfully diverse portfolio, from cabernet sauvignon and merlot to riesling and sauv blanc.

THE DRIVE: Ease back onto the main highway at Capel, then cruise on into Busselton, just a few clicks up the road. For a scenic detour take Tuart Drive through the coastal forests.

03 Busselton

Unpretentious and uncomplicated, **Busselton** has a strong community spirit and loads of options for families. Surrounded by calm waters and white-sand beaches, the outlandishly long (1.84km) **Busselton Jetty** *(busseltonjetty.com.au)* is its most famous attraction. A tourist train chugs out to the **Underwater Observatory**, where tours take place 8m below the surface; bookings are essential. There's a great spot to swim by the pier with protected sea baths and an adventure playground onshore. For adults, there's a couple of excellent **bars** with beers on tap. Busselton makes a great stop before heading into the Margaret River region.

THE DRIVE: You're within sight of the shimmering blue of the Indian Ocean almost all the way from Busselton to Dunsborough and Cape Naturaliste, an easy, pretty drive where you may be tempted to park and go for a quick swim. Unless you do, you'll probably be at the cape in less than an hour.

04 Cape Naturaliste

Northwest of Dunsborough, a holiday village with excellent restaurants and plenty of great shopping to distract you, Cape Naturaliste Rd leads out to the cape and some excellent local beaches at

Meelup, **Eagle Bay** and **Bunker Bay**. Whales and hammerhead sharks like to hang out on the edge of Bunker Bay during the winter season, where the continental shelf drops 75m. The cape itself is marked with the **Cape Naturaliste Lighthouse** *(margaretriver.com/things-to-do/attractions/lighthouses/cape-naturaliste-lighthouse)*, built in 1903, which kids will love too if a playground and kangaroos bring them joy. Walk around to the ocean viewpoint with buffeting winds and you'll find it difficult to escape the feeling that you're standing on Australia's final headland, contemplating eternity. If time allows, take the 3.5km boardwalk that runs south from the lighthouse to Sugarloaf Rock. From September to May you may see Australia's most southerly breeding colony of the really rather splendid red-tailed tropicbird *(Phaethon rubricauda)*.

☑ TOP TIP

TASTING TIMES & WINERY TOURS

Most of the wineries offer tastings between 10am and 5pm daily. At busy times (this includes every weekend), consider booking ahead for lunch before you set out.

THE DRIVE: Return to Dunsborough, then take the road that trickles down towards the coast at Yallingup, stopping for a meal or a tasting along the way.

05 Yallingup

You're permitted to let a 'wow' escape when the surf-battered coastline first comes into view around Yallingup – from here the ocean stretches all the way to Africa. Beautiful walking trails follow the coast between here and **Smiths Beach** with its excellent rock pools. Between Dunsborough and Yallingup, the 500,000-year-old **Ngilgi Cave** *(margaretriver.com)* has fabulous formations, which will change your perspective – especially if you are guided by the Aboriginal outfit **Koomal Dreaming** *(koomaldreaming.com.au)*. But magnificent as these attractions are, most people come to surf at Yallingup. It is possible to take a surf lesson with the **Yallingup Surf School** *(yallingupsurfschool.com)* in the morning,

Bootleg Brewery, Margaret River

CAVAN IMAGES/ALAMY

then while away the afternoon at **Caves House** *(caveshousehotel yallingup.com.au)* watching sport on the big screen, or a local live gig, in the extensive beer garden. Romantics may also love the fact that Yallingup means 'place of love' in Wardandi's Noongar language.

THE DRIVE: From Yallingup head back up the hill and turn on to Caves Rd, which winds its way through native bush and almost immediately presents you with spots to stop, stretch your legs, grab a coffee or buy some local art.

06 Canal Rocks

As you head south, Leeuwin-Naturaliste National Park is on your right down to the ocean, with plenty of potential detours to sandy coves and rocky points facing west (great to watch the sun set). The natural formation at **Canal Rocks** *(exploreparks.dbca.wa.gov.au/site/canal-rocks)* is a popular photo opportunity, from a bridge over the water.

THE DRIVE: From Canal Rocks it's around 4km east to Yallingup on Caves Rd, then 11km south to Bootleg Brewery, a 15-minute drive all up.

07 Bootleg Brewery

In a reminder of just how far the Margaret River region has evolved from its exclusively wine-producing roots, **Bootleg Brewery** *(bootlegbrewery.com.au)* is deliberately rustic and an interesting contrast to the excellent, well-heeled **Caves Road Collective**. Good food available and spots to soak up the sun with the occasional live band to watch.

THE DRIVE: Return the 2km to the main north–south road and turn left (south). Keep an eye out for Wilyabrup, a tiny hamlet that is easily missed. A few clicks south of the last house, you'll find Cullen Wines.

08 Cullen Wines

The area around Wilyabrup is where the Margaret River wine story began way back in the 1960s; one of the pioneers, **Cullen Wines** *(cullenwines.com.au)*, is still very much around. Grapes were first planted here in 1966 and Cullen has an ongoing commitment to organic and biodynamic principles in both food and wine. Celebrating a relaxed ambience, Cullen's food is excellent, with many of the fruits and vegetables sourced from its own gardens. But it's the wines it's best known for.

THE DRIVE: Around 2km south of Cullen Wines, look for Vasse Felix on the left.

09 Vasse Felix

Visiting wineries may be pleasurable for its own sake, but some of these fine establishments make sure you don't do it entirely on an empty stomach. One of the best examples of this holistic approach is **Vasse Felix** *(vasse felix.com.au)*, one of the oldest Margaret River vineyards and a good all-round winery with a fabulous art collection: the grounds are peppered with sculptures and the gallery displays works from the Holmes à Court collection. In classic winery style, the big dining room evokes a very flash barn, while the sophisticated flavours are perfectly matched to the right Vasse Felix wines such as its Heytesbury cabernet blend and Heytesbury chardonnay.

THE DRIVE: From Vasse Felix, head south and eventually you'll see the turnoff to Margaret River, affectionately known as Margs. It's inland and on the Busselton Hwy, a much busier road for traffic, including trucks.

10 Margaret River

Although tourists usually outnumber locals, Margaret River (the town) has a relaxed authentic country village vibe. The advantage of basing yourself here is that, once the wineries shut up shop, it's one of the few places with any after-dark activities, from restaurants, bars and pubs to outdoor cinema and markets. Plus it's close to the incredible surf at **Margaret River mouth** and **Southside**, and the swimming beaches at **Prevelly** and **Gracetown**. Margaret River spills over with tourists every weekend and gets very busy at Easter and Christmas. Beyond the town's limits, vineyards producing excellent chardonnays and Bordeaux-style reds segue into rural back roads punctuated with craft breweries, provedores, cheese shops, chocolate shops and art galleries.

TOP TIP

MARGARET RIVER GOURMET ESCAPE

From Nigella Lawson and Rick Stein to *Australian MasterChef*'s George Calombaris, the **Gourmet Escape** *(gourmetescape.com.au)* food and wine festival attracts the big names in cuisine. Look forward to three days of food workshops, tastings, vineyard events and demonstrations here and in the Swan Valley.

PHOTO OPPORTUNITY

LEEUWIN-NATURALISTE NATIONAL PARK

Your footprints on an empty beach in Leeuwin-Naturaliste National Park.

THE DRIVE: Take the Bussel Hwy south of Margaret River, and around 5km south of town turn left onto Gnarawary Rd, then right onto Stevens Rd to reach the next stop.

11 Voyager Estate

At **Voyager Estate** *(voyagerestate.com.au)*, a second-generation family-owned winery, wander the formal gardens and Cape Dutch-style building, and take a tour of the estate, including the kitchen garden that Rick Stein loved. Then indulge in top-notch wines over a seven-course degustation accompanied by fine wines and vine vistas.

THE DRIVE: It's only 3km to the next stop. Continue south along Stevens Rd and take the third left straight to Leeuwin Estate.

12 Leeuwin Estate

One of Margaret River's most celebrated icons, **Leeuwin Estate** *(leeuwinestate.com.au)* revels in the finer things in life – the much-lauded Art Series chardonnay and cabernet merlot, the monthly concerts that occasionally feature the Perth Symphony Orchestra, and an impressive estate with tall trees and lawns gently rolling down to the bush. Different packages are available for behind-the-scenes insights, food and wine tastings. Book ahead.

THE DRIVE: Return to Caves Rd, pop into Mammoth Cave, then drive south through mesmerising karri forest. Another detour to Hamelin Bay for a swim or rock pool investigation is also recommended.

13 Leeuwin-Naturaliste National Park

Stretching from Gracetown all the way south to Cape Leeuwin, **Leeuwin-Naturaliste National Park** is wildly beautiful, known for its forests, sand dunes and a startling variety of endemic wildflowers. The 155-sq-km park explodes with colour in the spring months. The demanding environment of buffeting winds and complicated soil system prevents any one species predominating, leaving instead a gorgeous array of fantastically evolved orchids, sundews, kangaroo paws and the like to flourish in their exclusive niches. Walking in the park in spring (September to November), it's possible to see orchids, banksias, clematis, cowslips, and many other species, including the improbably named prickly moses. When the sun is out, the flowers are in bloom and the deep blues of sea and sky provide a backdrop, you'll wonder if you've stumbled onto one of Australia's prettiest corners.

THE DRIVE: Take any north–south road from anywhere along the eastern fringe of the national park and you'll end up in Augusta, right down at the region's southern end.

14 Augusta

At the mouth of the Blackwood River, and 5km north of end-of-the-earth-like Cape Leeuwin, Augusta can appear to be quite separate from the rest of this region. The vibe here is a little less epicurean, and more languid – epitomised by an afternoon river fishing without a care in the world. Take a couple of close-by excursions and you'll soon see what we mean. Begin with wild and windy **Cape Leeuwin Lighthouse** *(margaretriver.com)*, where the Indian and Southern Oceans meet – it's the most southwesterly point in Australia. The lighthouse (dating from 1896), Western Australia's tallest, offers magnificent views of the coastline. Then, if it's May to October, go whale watching with **Naturaliste Charters** *(naturalistecharters.com.au)*; from January to March, the emphasis switches to beaches, limestone caves and wildlife, including dolphins and New Zealand fur seals. And then there's **Jewel Cave** *(margaretriver.com)*, 8km northwest of Augusta at the south end of Caves Rd. The most spectacular of the region's caves, Jewel Cave has an impressive 5.9m straw stalactite, so far the longest seen in a tourist cave. Fossil remains of a Tasmanian tiger (thylacine), believed to be 3500 years old, were discovered here. It's a mysterious, soulful place to end your journey.

Leeuwin-Naturaliste National Park
AKHDIAN REPPAWALI/SHUTTERSTOCK

STAY AWHILE

MARGARET RIVER

BY ANTHONY HAM

I've always loved Margaret River first and foremost as a destination in its own right, one that's well worth lingering over. Known for its world-class wines and gourmet sensibility, the town and the region it serves always feel like an indulgent celebration of the good things in life.

I like to begin with a primer in ancient culture, curated for me by a guide from the Indigenous Wadandi, the Traditional Custodians of the Margaret River (Wooditchup) region. **Koomal Dreaming** *(koomaldreaming.com.au)* runs soulful tours.

Thus grounded for capturing the essence of the Margaret River experience, it's all about the many wonderful tastes on offer. With so much to choose from, take a deep dive into the region's iconic wineries through **Bushtucker Tours** *(bushtuckertours.com)*. Alternatively, **Waves of Wine** *(wavesofwinetours.com)* is one my gourmand friends rave about, with winery tastings and gourmet lunch.

My visits to Margaret River increasingly complement fine wines with craft beers. It always starts at the **Brewhouse** *(margaretriverbeer.co)* in town itself, but also nearby you can enjoy the seasonal ales and dairy-shed vibe at **Beerfarm** *(beerfarm.com.au)* and the 22-beers-on-tap **CBCo Brewing** *(cbco.beer)*. These are two of the region's OGs, dating back to the days before Margaret River became famous.

And before you return to the open road, plan on having dinner at **de'sendent** *(desendent.com)* – its unique tasting menu is one of the best I've tried.

LINK YOUR TRIP

This town is a great spot to base yourself for 33 **Margaret River Wine Region**.

Left: Wine tasting, Margaret River
Right: Tasting menu, de'sendent

FROM LEFT: GAGLIARDIPHOTOGRAPHY/SHUTTERSTOCK, RYAN MURPHY/WWW.DESENDENT.COM

PLACES TO STAY

There's a wide range of accommodation options through the region. **8 Paddocks** *(8paddocks.com)* are luxury chalets on a secluded Cowaramup property. Enjoy complimentary local beer and fresh farm eggs; there's also a snack box to feed the adorable highland cows with in the joining paddock. Experience an intimate stay at **Southcamp** *(southcamp.com.au)*, with minimalist design and a record player at your leisure at these boutique timber cabins in the heart of Dunsborough. A multi-level lodge and tranquil chalets on a private Margaret River property, **Karriview** *(karriview.com)* is surrounded by 40 acres of bush and karri trees.

34

WESTERN AUSTRALIA

CORAL COAST TO BROOME

DURATION: 10–14 DAYS

DISTANCE: 3150KM / 1957 MILES

GREAT FOR: NATURE

BEST TIME TO GO: APRIL TO OCTOBER. IT'S IMPOSSIBLY HUMID FROM NOVEMBER ONWARDS.

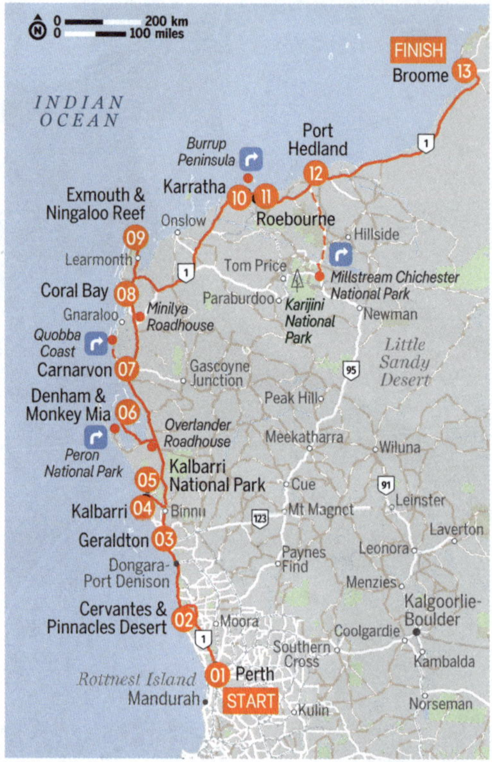

The road from Perth to Broome connects two different worlds, one urban and the other remote, tropical and on the cusp of the outback, with the vast Indian Ocean keeping you company much of the way. There are fabulous places to break up the journey, including many that highlight the intersection of desert and coast that is such a feature of this route, from the Pinnacles Desert to Ningaloo Reef.

LINK YOUR TRIP

03 Across the Nullarbor
Where one epic journey ends (crossing the Nullarbor starts or ends in Perth), another begins.

05 Kimberley Crossing
The drive to Kununurra (1045km) begins where this foray up the Coral Coast ends – joining up the two couldn't be easier.

01 Perth

By some estimates, Perth is one of the most isolated cities on earth, but that's nothing compared to where you're heading. With so many miles ahead of you, soak up the choice of big-city restaurants, the cool breeze of the south and the easy communications of the big smoke. You'll find all of these along the way, but not like here.

THE DRIVE: Head northeast out of Perth as if heading for the Nullarbor, but after 18km swing north, following the signs for Geraldton. At Muchea, take the left highway fork for the Brand Hwy. At 206km out of Perth, at the small settlement of Badgingarra, take the Cervantes turnoff for the final 49km.

02 Cervantes & Pinnacles Desert

The laid-back crayfishing town of Cervantes is a fine place to end your first day's journey. The major attraction here, and it's a big one, is the

INC/SHUTTERSTOCK

★ BEST FOR:

OUTDOORS

Gorges at Karijini National Park.

Hancock Gorge (p255), Karijini National Park

Pinnacles Desert – one of Australia's most photographed landforms. This singularly eye-catching stand of weird-and-wonderful natural sculptures, a vast, alien-like plain studded with thousands of limestone pillars, is 19km south of Cervantes in **Nambung National Park** *(exploreparks.dbca.wa.gov.au/park/nambung-national-park)*. Rising eerily from the desert floor, the pillars are remnants of compacted seashells that once covered the plain and, over millennia, subsequently eroded. A loop road runs through the formations, but it's more fun to wander on foot. In Cervantes itself, walkways wend along the coastline and provide access to some lovely beaches, while Lobster Shack is a great pit stop for a bucket of prawns and cold beer.

THE DRIVE: Instead of returning to the Brand Hwy, head north out of Cervantes along the Indian Ocean Dr. Aside from having far less traffic, panoramic ocean views open up at regular intervals and you'll pull over often to take it all in. At 124km from Cervantes, the road rejoins the Brand Hwy, from where it's 94km into Geraldton.

03 Geraldton

Capital of the midwest and the largest town between Perth and Darwin, sun-drenched 'Gero' is surrounded by excellent beaches. Gero blends big-city sophistication with small-town friendliness, offering a strong arts culture and vibrant foodie scene. Among the best places to bed down is **Mantra Geraldton** *(mantra.com.au)*, and you can treat your taste buds at **Beached Barrel** *(facebook.com/beachedbarrel)*, **Saltdish** *(facebook.com/saltdishcafe)* and **Piper Lane Cafe**. Most activities are water-based: **Midwest Surf School** *(surf2skool.com)* runs surf lessons at Geraldton's back beach, while **KiteWest** *(kitewest.com.au)* does all sorts of things on water and on land, among them kiteboarding courses, surfing lessons and paddle-boarding tuition, as well as fishing, scenic and wildflower day trips. Amid such adventurous pursuits, save time for the **Western Australian Museum – Geraldton** *(museum.wa.gov.au)*, one of the state's best museums, and for a day trip to the **Houtman Abrolhos Islands**.

THE DRIVE: At exactly 100km north of town, take the Kalbarri turnoff – it's 54km into Kalbarri, with a picturesque oceanside stretch.

04 Kalbarri

This laid-back beachside town makes an ideal base for visiting Kalbarri National Park if you want the adventure but wish to return to creature comforts at the end of the day. Companies such as **Kalbarri Wagoe Beach Quadbike Tours** *(kalbarriquad.com)* and **Kalbarri Quadbike Safaris** *(kalbarriquadsafaris.com.au)* take visitors out for exhilarating rides along the sand dunes, while **Kalbarri Abseil** *(kalbarriabseil.com)* runs action-filled trips to the gorges of Kalbarri National Park. Kalbarri can also be used as a jumping-off point for the stupendous Houtman Abrolhos Islands; take a day trip with **Kalbarri Scenic Flights** *(kalbarriscenicflights.com.au)*. Gecko Lodge is one of the standout accommodation options. Treat yourself to a meal at Finlay's Fresh Fish BBQ or **Upstairs Restaurant** *(kalbarrirestaurant.com.au)*.

THE DRIVE: Some 8km south of town, the scenic road passes by the entrance to the cliffside walks of Kalbarri National Park. Heading north, a road runs through scrubland towards the national park's main entrance.

05 Kalbarri National Park

With its magnificent river red gums and Tumblagooda sandstone, the rugged Kalbarri National Park contains almost 2000 sq km of wild bushland, stunning river gorges and savagely eroded coastal cliffs. There's abundant wildlife, including 200 species of birds, and spectacular wildflowers between July and November. A string of lookouts dots the impressive coast south of town and the easy **Bigurda Trail** (8km one way) follows the clifftops between **Natural Bridge** and **Eagle Gorge**; from July to November you may spot migrating whales. The river gorges are east of Kalbarri, 11km down Ajana Kalbarri Rd to the turnoff, and then 20km unsealed to a T-intersection. Turn left for lookouts over the **Loop** and the superb **Nature's Window** (1km return). Turning right at the T leads to **Z-Bend**, with a breathtaking lookout (1.2km return), or you can continue steeply down to the **gorge bottom** (2.6km return).

Abseiling, Kalbarri National Park

HANS WISMEIJER/SHUTTERSTOCK

THE DRIVE: Take the 54km from Kalbarri back to the main highway, where you turn left (north). It's a 158km-long drive through scrubland and red dirt to the turnoff for Shark Bay. Pause at the Overlander Roadhouse for a breather, then turn left; from here it's 128km across some narrow spits of land into Denham.

06 Denham & Monkey Mia

Beautiful, laid-back Denham, Australia's westernmost town, is, with its turquoise sea and palm-fringed beachfront, a terrific base for trips to some fine surrounding national and marine parks. **Shark Bay Scenic Flights** *(sharkbayscenicflights.com.au)* offers a brilliant perspective on the area, while watching the wild dolphins turning up for a feed each morning in the shallow waters of Monkey Mia, 26km beyond Denham, is a highlight of most travellers' trips to the region. The pier makes a good vantage point; the first feed is around 7.45am, although the dolphins arrive earlier. To see more wildlife, take the 2½-hour wildlife cruise with **Wildsights** *(monkeymiawildsights.com.au)* from Monkey Mia. Back on land, learn 'how to let Country talk to you' on the excellent bushwalks run by **Wula Gurda Nyinda Aboriginal Cultural Tours** *(wulagura.com.au)*. Enjoy the wonderful hospitality at On The Deck @ Shark Bay and dine at Denham's Oceans Restaurant or Monkey Mia's **Boughshed** *(facebook.com/boughshed)*.

THE DRIVE: Return to the main highway (128km) from Denham. At the Overlander Roadhouse, head north. It's 193km into Carnarvon – watch for fine Shark Bay views and kangaroos en route.

SHARK BAY

The World Heritage–listed area of Shark Bay, stretching from Kalbarri to Carnarvon, consists of more than 1500km of spectacular coastline, containing turquoise lagoons, barren finger-like peninsulas, hidden bays, white-sand beaches, towering limestone cliffs and numerous islands. It's the westernmost part of the Australian mainland, and one of WA's most biologically rich habitats, with an array of plant and animal life found nowhere else on earth. Lush beds of seagrass and sheltered bays nourish dugongs, sea turtles, humpback whales, dolphins, stingrays, sharks and other aquatic life. On land, Shark Bay's biodiversity has benefited from Project Eden, an ambitious ecosystem-regeneration programme that has sought to eradicate feral animals and reintroduce endemic species. Shark Bay is also home to the amazing stromatolites of Hamelin Pool. The Malgana, Nhanda and Inggarda peoples originally inhabited the area, and visitors can take Aboriginal cultural tours to learn about Country.

DETOUR

Peron National Park

Start: 06 Denham

A magnificent wilderness encompassing the peninsula north of Denham, Francois Peron National Park is all low scrub, salt lagoons and sandy dunes, home to the rare bilby, mallee fowl and woma python. Its rust-red cliffs, white-sand beaches and exquisite blue waters are wonderfully remote and a terrific place to spot all manner of marine life. At **Cape Peron**, local bottlenose dolphins have developed a unique way of fishing, while at **Skipjack Point Lookout** you can spot manta rays, eagle rays and dugongs. Since the park is largely off-limits unless you have a high-clearance 4WD, you'll most likely have to join a tour from Denham with **Shark Bay Coastal Tours** *(sharkbaycoastaltours.com.au)* or **Ocean Park Tours** *(oceanpark.com.au)*.

07 Carnarvon

On Yinggarda country at the mouth of the Gascoyne River, fertile Carnarvon, with its fruit and vegetable plantations and thriving fishing industry, makes a pleasant stopover between Denham and Exmouth. It's a friendly place, though there's little to detain you here besides visiting the luxuriant plantations along North and South River Rds; grab the **Gascoyne Food Trail** *(gascoynefood.com.au)* brochure from the **visitor centre** *(carnarvon.org.au)*. The tree-lined Central Business District exudes a tropical feel and the palm-fringed waterfront is a relaxing place to amble. Check whether the historic **One Mile Jetty** at the Heritage Precinct on Babbage Island, once the city's port, is again open to visitors. If you're travelling with kids, it's worth swinging by the **Carnarvon Space & Technology Museum** *(carnarvonmuseum.org.au)*. Hankering for a memorable meal? **Sails Restaurant** *(carnarvon.wa.hospitalityinns.com.au/sailsrestaurant)* serves Carnarvon's most imaginative fare.

THE DRIVE: It's 140 flat and rather uneventful kilometres from Carnarvon north to the Minilya Roadhouse. There, the North West Coastal Hwy (as it's called north of Carnarvon) veers north-east. Instead, take the Minilya Exmouth Rd towards Exmouth and turn off towards Coral Bay after 85km. The last 13km is narrow.

DETOUR

Quobba Coast

Start: 07 Carnarvon

The coast north of Carnarvon is wild, rugged and desolate, and a favourite haunt of surfers and fisherfolk. Those who make it this far are rewarded by huge swells, relentless winds, amazing marine life, breathtaking scenery and fire-in-the-sky sunsets. Some 24km north of Carnarvon, turn left off the North West Coastal Hwy and drive 49km to the impressive **Blowholes**, where the sea roars upwards through porous rock. Take the unsealed, unpeopled road 75km north to **Gnaraloo Station** *(gnaraloostation.com)*, where you can stay at the homestead. Don't miss the pristine white crescent of Gnaraloo Bay, 7km north. If you're a surfer, you can hit the legendary **Tombstones** wave while camping out at the nearby **3-Mile Camp** *(gnaraloostation.com)*.

08 Coral Bay

This tiny seaside village is one of the easiest locations from which to access the exquisite Ningaloo Marine Park. Consisting of only one street and a sweeping white-sand beach, the town is very walkable. The southern access point for the **Ningaloo Marine Park**, Coral Bay is particularly good for swimming with manta rays year-round; trips are offered by **Ningaloo Marine Interactions** *(mantaraycoralbay.com.au)* and **Ningaloo Reef Dive & Snorkel** *(ningalooreefdive.com)*, among others. You can also swim with whale sharks (April to July) and whales (June to November).

THE DRIVE: Backtrack to the Minilya–Exmouth Rd and drive for 140km to reach Exmouth. Much of the way, you'll see otherworldly termite mounds dotting the scrubland, but the prettiest stretch of road is along the Exmouth Gulf, along the final approach to town.

09 Exmouth & Ningaloo Reef

Once a WWII submarine base, Exmouth is a laid-back seafront town where emus wander footpaths. With great dining options, it makes an excellent base for visiting the World Heritage–listed and exquisite Ningaloo Reef. **Ningaloo Marine Park** is home to a staggering array of marine life – sharks, manta rays, humpback whales, turtles, dugongs, dolphins and more than 500 species of fish. Australia's largest fringing reef is also easily accessible, in places only 100m offshore. Swim with whale sharks (April to July), spot wildlife, dive, snorkel (try the **Bay Snorkel Area**), kayak, surf and fish to your heart's content – the **visitor centre** *(ningaloocentre.com.au)* has the full list of tours available, but our favourites include **Three Islands** *(whalesharkdive.com)* and **Kings Ningaloo Reef Tours** *(kingsningalooreeftours.com.au)*. Outside whale-shark season, marine tours focus on manta rays, while the **DPaW Turtle Interaction Tour** is the best and most ecologically safe way to encounter nesting turtles (November to March).

Whale shark, Ningaloo Reef
LEWIS BURNETT/SHUTTERSTOCK

PHOTO OPPORTUNITY

Underwater creatures at Ningaloo Reef.

THE DRIVE: It's a long road south from Ningaloo Marine Park and you've a long day ahead of you, but we can't imagine it hasn't been worth it. Take the road 86km south of Exmouth, and turn left on the Burkett Rd, from where it's 79km to the main highway. After rejoining the highway, it's 383km to Karratha. Nanutarra Roadhouse is the only petrol stop en route.

10 Karratha

Those who arrive in Karratha just looking to stock up on essentials for the road ahead are pleasantly surprised. Travellers expecting a gritty mining hub instead find a laid-back, friendly town with an excellent dining and coffee scene – **Empire 6714** and **Lo's Cafe Fusion Bistro** *(facebook.com/losbistro)* are standout choices). There is an architecturally striking cultural centre – the **Red Earth Arts Precinct** *(reap.karratha.wa.gov.au)* – and enough natural attractions in the surrounding area to make you linger for a day or two.

THE DRIVE: It's a mere 39km along the North West Coastal Hwy from Karratha to Roebourne.

DETOUR

Burrup Peninsula

Start: 10 Karratha

An absolute must if you're interested in Aboriginal culture is a half-day trip to the Burrup Peninsula. Take Dampier Hwy west past Karratha Airport towards the port town of Dampier, 20km from Karratha, and then take Burrup Rd north after you've driven past the vast salt pans. Several kilometres north, turn right along Hearson Rd towards Hearson's Cove and look out for a sign on your right for **Deep Gorge**. The rocky hills here have the densest concentration of ancient rock art in the world, dating back 30,000 years. As you wander around, you may spot engravings of fish, goannas (lizards), turtles, ospreys, kangaroos and even a Tasmanian tiger. It's particularly rewarding to come here on a half-day tour out of Karratha with **Ngurrangga Tours** *(ngurrangga.com.au)*.

11 Roebourne

The oldest (1866) Pilbara town still functioning, Roebourne is well worth a stop to check out the beautiful old buildings along the town's main street and to gaze out over the parched countryside from the lookout point up **Mt Welcome** (Fisher Dr). The town is also home to a thriving Aboriginal art scene, and the Aboriginal-run **Yinjaa-Barni Gallery** *(yinjaa-barni.com.au)* is the highlight of any art-lover's visit.

THE DRIVE: Take the North West Coastal Hwy east for 203km to Port Hedland. There will be little to keep you company en route besides a few road trains, and no petrol stations between the two.

STAIRCASE TO THE MOON

You might hear them talk in these parts of a strange attraction known as the Staircase to the Moon. No, it's not the WA version of Led Zeppelin's classic, but instead an appealing natural phenomenon whereby, when seen from an easterly facing beach, the light of the full moon rising above the sea (and/or mudflats) resembles a staircase to the moon. Port Hedland, Broome and Dampier are three places where you might see it from March to October.

DETOUR

Millstream Chichester National Park

Start: 11 Roebourne

The spinifex-covered plateaus, tranquil oases and eroded mesas of the Chichester Range make an excellent day trip.

The park is divided into two halves. The Chichester half is a scenic 90km drive southeast of Roebourne along an unsealed road that's fine for 2WDs much of the year, while the Millstream half is around 130km away from Karratha. Highlights include **Python Pool** (Chichester) and **Deep Reach Pool** (Millstream). Millstream has the lion's share of short hiking trails. Millstream Chichester is also reachable from Karratha.

12 Port Hedland

A high-visibility dystopia of railway yards, iron-ore stockpiles, salt mountains, furnaces, a massive deep-water port and striking street art confront visitors to Port Hedland. Yet under that red dust lurks a colourful 130-year history of mining booms and busts, cyclones, pearling and WWII action. Several pleasant hours may be spent exploring Hedland's thriving art and real-coffee scene (try **Hai's Coffee Van** *(facebook.com/haicoffeevan)* for the best caffeine hit), historic Central Business District and scenic foreshore. From the **visitor centre** *(visitporthedland.com)*, popular **BHP Billiton** iron-ore plant tours depart, while the **Courthouse Gallery** *(courthousegallery.com.au)* is the town's leafy arts HQ, with stunning local contemporary and Aboriginal exhibitions. Hungry for more Aboriginal art? Head for the

CHAMELEONSEYE/SHUTTERSTOCK

Historical building, Roebourne

Spinifex Hill Studios *(spinifexhillstudio.com.au)* in South Hedland. And if you're here between November and February, flatback turtles nest on nearby beaches.

THE DRIVE: The Big Empty stretches from Port Hedland to Broome, as the Great Northern Hwy skirts the Great Sandy Desert. It's 609km of scrubland and dust and not much else. There are only two roadhouses – Pardoo (148km) and Sandfire (288km) – so keep the tank full. The coast, wild and unspoilt, is never far away.

DETOUR

Karijini National Park

Start: 12 Port Hedland

Only in the Outback can a 666km round trip be described as a detour, yet Karijini is too spectacular to miss if you've come this far. Comprising 15 breathtaking gorges, spectacular waterfalls and tranquil pools, it's a hiker's playground, with numerous treks to choose from. Whether you opt for an easy stroll along the rim of **Dales Gorge** (4km return), allowing you to admire spectacular views, or test your mettle by wading through an icy stream while traversing the challenging trail through **Hancock Gorge** (800m return), it's an experience you won't forget. Camp under the stars at one of the two campsites or stay in style at the **Karijini Eco Retreat** *(karijiniecoretreat.com.au)*, complete with gourmet restaurant in high season.

13 Broome

Sultry and remote, Broome clings to a narrow strip of red pindan on the Kimberley's far western edge, at the base of the pristine Dampier Peninsula. Surrounded by the aquamarine waters of the Indian Ocean and the creeks, mangroves and mudflats of Roebuck Bay, this Yawuru Country town is a good 2000km from the nearest capital city, and it will feel like paradise after the long drive to reach it. Magnificent Cable Beach, with its luxury resorts, hauls in the tourists during high (dry) season (April to October), with romantic notions of camels and surf. Each evening, the whole town pauses, drinks in mid-air, while the sun slips slowly seawards.

King Island
Yambacoona
King Island
Naracoopa
Currie
Grassy
20 km
10 miles
King Island (35km, see inset)
Stanley Point
Cape Frankland
Sellars Point
Emita
Flinders Island
Whitemark
Lackrana
Strzelecki National Park
Lady Barron
Bass Strait
Truwana/ Cape Barren Island
Clarke Island
Three Hummock Island
Hunter Island
Robbins Island
The Nut
Stanley
Smithton
Marrawah
Rocky Cape National Park
Wynyard
Somerset
Burnie
Arthur River
Savage River National Park
Cape Portland
Mt William National Park
Narawntapu National Park
George Town
Bridport
Gladstone
Port Sorell
Scottsdale
Derby
Larapuna/ Bay of Fires
Ulverstone
Devonport
Beaconsfield
Lilydale
Binalong Bay
St Helens
39
Exeter
38
Launceston
Arthur Pieman Conservation Area
Sheffield
Waratah
Ben Lomond National Park
Deloraine
Westbury
St Marys
Perth
Fingal
Corinna
Cradle Mtn
Mole Creek Karst National Park
Rosebery
Cradle Mountain-Lake St Clair National Park
Walls of Jerusalem National Park
Douglas-Apsley National Park
Zeehan
Campbell Town
Bicheno
Arthurs Lake
Miena
Ross
Queenstown
Derwent Bridge
Lake Sorell
Strahan
Bradys Lake
Swansea
Coles Bay
36
35
Freycinet National Park
Franklin River
Tooms Lake
Macquarie Harbour
Tarraleah
Franklin-Gordon Wild Rivers National Park
Bothwell
Lake Tiberias
Triabunna
Mt Field National Park
Hamilton
Orford
Maria Island
Point Hibbs
Gordon River
Lake Gordon
Maria Island National Park
Bridgewater
Richmond
Southwest Conservation Area
Strathgordon
Maydena
Sorell
New Norfolk
Hobart
37
Lake Pedder
Turrakana/ Tasman Peninsula
Huonville
Hartz Mountains National Park
Storm Bay
Southwest National Park
Geeveston
Turrakana/ Tasman Peninsula National Park
SOUTHERN OCEAN
Cape Pillar
Dover
Alonnah
Port Davey
Bruny Island
Southport
South Bruny National Park
TASMAN SEA
Tasman Head
South West Cape
South Cape
South East Cape
D'Entrecasteaux Channel
100 km
50 miles

KARENFOLEYPHOTOGRAPHY / SHUTTERSTOCK

Port Arthur Historic Site (p274)

TASMANIA

EXPLORE

TASMANIA

Tasmania is something special, and one of Australia's most naturally beautiful states. From the dense and ancient rainforests of the west to the sea cliffs of the southeast, the postcard-perfect bays of the east coast and the wildlife and hiking riches of stunning Cradle Mountain-Lake St Clair National Park, Tasmania has landscapes to stir the soul. Buzzing Hobart, the historic towns of central Tassie and the haunting, tragedy-stained beauty of Port Arthur together ensure that the human story also inspires, and the many wine and gourmet-produce regions bring together the natural and human stories to delicious effect.

Hobart

Arrayed around a natural harbour and in the shadow of Kunanyi / Mt Wellington, Hobart sprawls prettily across the intervening hills. With a world-class art museum, great places to eat and drink, and an atmospheric and historic waterfront area, it's a city brimful of charm and worth a few days of your time. It's also part of most journeys around the state's south and southeast; in these parts, all roads lead to and from Hobart. Even far-flung Tasmanian destinations are rarely more than a half-day's drive from Hobart. The city also has the island's best flight connections to the rest of Australia.

Launceston

Gateway to Tasmania's north, Launceston combines small-town feel with big-city conveniences. There's not a whole lot to see in the town itself, but it's an appealing, relaxed place. It's also easy to reach from anywhere else on the island (making it the perfect starting point for numerous road trips) – Cradle Mountain and the east coast are within a couple of hours' drive, and the Tamar Valley begins right at the city's edge. Launceston has reasonable flight connections to the mainland as well.

WHEN TO GO

Tasmania is at its best, including for hiking around Cradle Mountain, from October to April. For the beach, January and February are the warmest months; remember that Tasmania is cooler (sometimes significantly so) than mainland Australia. There's a greater chance of rain, cold weather, even snow across the interior in winter (June to August)...and sometimes even in summer.

Devonport

Devonport is the Tasmanian port that connects the island to the mainland – the car-and-passenger *Spirit of Tasmania* runs between Geelong and Devonport. The city has some excellent museums and art galleries, as well as some good beaches that lack only a warm climate to be better known. Tasmania's third-largest city also has a good portfolio of cafes, restaurants, craft breweries, distilleries and hotels, not to mention a couple of enjoyable markets, though too many visitors make landfall and head out of town before they have time to enjoy the place.

Strahan

Picturesque little Strahan is a remote town about as far south as you can go along Tasmania's west coast. Apart from its appealing surrounds, Strahan is the starting point for boat trips along the rainforest-clad Gordon River, as well as fascinating former convict sites, a smattering of excellent restaurants and end-of-the-world-style coastal hikes. The accommodation here is some of the best in western Tasmania, consisting mostly of motels and caravan parks, but interspersed with some lovely B&Bs. Book ahead in the summer high season, as it's only a small town and rooms sell out fast, with prices rising for what remains.

TRANSPORT

Hobart and Launceston are the main entry and exit points for the island; both have good flight connections to the mainland, especially Sydney and Melbourne. There's also the Geelong–Devonport car ferry. Roads across the island are usually in excellent condition, but only 4WD tracks reach the southwestern third of the island, and then not much of it. Buses connect major towns.

WHERE TO STAY

Hobart has by far the biggest collection of places to stay, followed by Launceston, Cradle Mountain and the east coast. Perhaps more than any other state, Tasmania is known for its charming B&Bs and historic hotels – central Tasmania, Hobart and the east have the widest selection. Cradle Mountain has some superb places to stay, while camping is typically only possible in summer (usually around October to April). Out in the western rainforest, Corinna offers accommodation in the cottages of an abandoned former mining village. Along the east coast, you'll find the occasional resort.

RESOURCES

Discover Tasmania
Everything you need to know about the beautiful isle. *discovertasmania.com.au*

Spirit of Tasmania
More than just for booking ferries, with articles on foodie itineraries and more. *spiritoftasmania.com.au*

Tasmanian Parks & Wildlife Service
Deep dive into Tasmania's national parks, with plenty of info on campgrounds, wildlife and hiking trails. *parks.tas.gov.au*

WHAT'S ON

MONA FOMA
Offers up wonderfully eclectic performances in Hobart and Launceston. *mona.net.au/mona-foma*

Dark Mofo
Live music, quirky arts, bonfires, red wine and a nightly Winter Feast in Hobart in the half-light of June's winter solstice. *darkmofo.net.au*

Bicheno Food & Wine Festival
Food and wine stalls, cooking classes, live music and home-brew beer competitions take over Bicheno in November. *bichenofestivals.com.au*

35

TASMANIA

EAST COAST TASMANIA

DURATION: 3-5 DAYS

DISTANCE: 226KM / 140 MILES

GREAT FOR: NATURE, FAMILIES & WINE

BEST TIME TO GO: OCTOBER TO APRIL; FROM FEBRUARY, THE SEA IS AT ITS WARMEST.

This journey along the Tasman Hwy's coastal fringe takes in two of Tasmania's most striking natural attractions – perfectly curvaceous Wineglass Bay (arguably Tasmania's most famous image) and wildlife-rich Maria Island. A detour to the vibrant Larapuna / Bay of Fires, blowholes and gulches at Bicheno, and a happy handful of wineries as you approach Swansea all add up to Tasmania at its pretty best.

LINK YOUR TRIP

37 Turrakana / Tasman Peninsula
From where this classic East Coast Tasmania trip ends, at Orford, it's just 55km southwest to Sorell to join the Turrakana / Tasman Peninsula drive.

39 Western Wilds
This drive is 620km from Strahan to Launceston, which is 160km along the Tasman Hwy from St Helens, the East Coast trip's starting point.

01 St Helens

On the broad, protected sweep of Georges Bay, St Helens has always made the best of what it has. it was born as a whaling and sealing settlement in the 1830s, and soon learned to harvest the local black swan population for its downy underfeathers. Today, this town suitably named after a ship is Tasmania's ocean-fishing capital, both for amateur anglers and the state's largest fishing fleet. Charter boats will take you out to where the big game fish play – try **Gone Fishing Charters** *(breamfishing.com.au)*. For nonanglers, the beaches of the Bay of Fires are near at hand, as are the world-class mountain-bike tracks at Derby.

THE DRIVE: The Tasman Hwy leaves St Helens tight against the shores of Georges Bay before briefly turning inland. By the time you hit Scamander (22km from St Helens), however, your wheels will be almost back in the water. South of Scamander,

TOM JASTRAM/SHUTTERSTOCK

★ BEST FOR:

OUTDOORS

Maria Island's curious cliffs and peaks.

Maria Island (p265)

join the A4 and climb over St Marys Pass to St Marys, 17km from Scamander.

DETOUR

Larapuna / Bay of Fires

Start: 01 St Helens

Larapuna / Bay of Fires is a 29km-long sweep of powder-white sand and crystal-clear seas that's been called one of the most beautiful beaches in the world. To refer to Larapuna / Bay of Fires as a single beach, though, is a mistake: it's actually a string of superb beaches, punctuated by lagoons and rocky headlands, all backed by coastal heath and bush.

Curling around a sheltered sandy inlet 11km north of St Helens, gorgeous Binalong Bay (reached along the sealed C850) is the only permanent settlement in the Larapuna / Bay of Fires and the start of the 10km drive to the Gardens area on the C848. This road rolls through the bush, but is stitched with side roads that dart down to various little beaches – Jeanerette Beach, Swimcart Beach, Cosy Corner – and the enticing camp sites behind them. From just past Sloop Reef, it's ocean views all the way to the garden-free Gardens, where there are some phenomenally beautiful beaches and headlands – you could easily spend hours poking about here.

The bay's northern end is reached along the gravel C843, which leads to **Ansons Bay** and then **Mt William National Park** *(parks.tas.gov.au)*. Lighthouse-tipped **Eddystone Point**, just north of Ansons Bay, within Mt William National Park, marks the Larapuna / Bay of Fires' northern extremity. It's about an hour's drive from St Helens.

02 St Marys

Set back from, and 300m above, the coast, St Marys is an unhurried little village encircled by forests and farms. Visit for the small-town vibes and the craggy heights around town, which you can climb for memorable views over the area. The top of **South Sister** (832m), towering over German Town Rd

PHOTO OPPORTUNITY

Wineglass Bay from its lookout atop Mt Amos.

6km north of town, is a 10-minute walk from the car park. To get to **St Lumeragenena Wuggelena / Patricks Head** (683m), turn down Irishtown Rd, just east of town. This steep, 1½-hour (one way) climb, with some cables and a ladder, is a real challenge, but at the top there's a stellar vista along the coast.

THE DRIVE: The A4 searches for the sea for 17km as it turns back east, crossing Elephant Pass (and passing an unexpected pancake cafe). Rejoining the Tasman Hwy at Chain of Lagoons, it's a game of hide and seek with the sea for 27km into Bicheno – when you can see the coast, Bicheno is usually in the frame up ahead.

03 Bicheno

Despite having beaches and ocean colours worthy of framing, Bicheno (bish-uh-no) is very much a functioning fishing port – with a holiday habit. It's madly popular with holidaymakers, with brilliant ocean views and lovely beaches, but it retains an appealing lack of polish. Off the northern end of Redbill Beach, **Diamond Island** is a photogenic granite outcrop, connected to the mainland via a short, semi-submerged, sandy isthmus, which you can wade across at low tide. A foreshore walkway winds along the town's coast, ending beside a rare **blowhole**. To get out on the water, try **Bicheno's Glass Bottom Boat** *(bichenoglassbottomboat.com)*, which will give you the sea's equivalent of an aerial view. Bicheno is one of the top spots in Tasmania to see penguins – take a dusk tour with **Bicheno Penguin Tours** *(bicheno penguintours.com.au)*.

View of Wineglass Bay, Freycinet National Park

TOM JASTRAM/SHUTTERSTOCK

THE DRIVE: The coast is shy here – there's nary a sight of it for the first 12km before you turn onto the C302, which heads south onto Freycinet Peninsula. Look for the waters of Moulting Lagoon to your right – its surface will likely be covered in black swans. When the Hazards mountains bubble up into view ahead, you'll know that Coles Bay is near.

04 Coles Bay

Touching shoulders with Freycinet National Park, Coles Bay township has been a holiday town for generations and yet it remains remarkably low key – a couple of stores, a restaurant, a caravan park, a tavern – for a town that sits on the cusp of arguably Tasmania's most famous natural feature: Wineglass Bay.

♥ WHY I LOVE THIS TRIP

ANDREW BAIN, WRITER

If Tasmania's east coast had the water temperature and weather to match, it'd bankrupt half the tropical paradises on earth. Wineglass Bay is a curvy natural supermodel, Larapuna / Bay of Fires dazzles with colour, and Maria Island brings together World Heritage–listed convict history, extraordinary contrasting cliffs and a meeting with crowds of wombats...and, most likely, a Tasmanian devil or two.

Freycinet Adventures *(freycinet adventures.com.au)* offers three-hour kayaking outings on the sheltered waters of Coles Bay, while **Pennicott Wilderness Journeys** *(pennicottjourneys.com.au)* runs sedate, four-hour cruises from Coles Bay to Wineglass Bay. The boat chugs around the southern end of the peninsula, passing Hazards Beach and Schouten Island en route. You're likely to see dolphins, sea eagles, seals and perhaps even migrating whales in the right season (around May to November).

THE DRIVE: Return 27km back up the road to the A3, then turn left. There are good long-range views of Freycinet as the road climbs past Devil's Corner Winery cellar door; from here the liquid in the view is mostly wine as the highway cuts through a cluster of vineyards around Cranbrook.

DETOUR

Freycinet National Park

Start: 04 Coles Bay

The sublime **Freycinet National Park** *(parks.tas.gov.au)* is the reason everyone is here: a wild domain of sugar-white beaches and gin-clear water. The park's big-ticket sight is the gorgeous goblet of **Wineglass Bay**, and the climb to the **lookout** above the beach (one to 1½ hours return) is deservedly one of Tasmania's most popular walks. If you want to hear the beach squeak beneath your feet, however, you're in for a longer walk. The steep descent from the lookout to the bay takes another 30 minutes, making the out-and-back trip from the car park 2½ to three hours. Alternatively, the 500m wheelchair-friendly boardwalk at **Cape Tourville** affords sweeping coastal panoramas and a less-strenuous glimpse into Wineglass Bay.

05 Swansea

Unhurried Swansea graces the western shore of sheltered Great Oyster Bay, with sweeping views across the water to the peaks of the Freycinet Peninsula. Founded in 1820 as Great Swanport, Swansea also delivers some interesting historic buildings and an engaging little **museum** that covers the plight of the Tasmanian tiger (including a tiger trap from the late 19th century) and features eggs from the now-extinct Tasmanian emu. South of town, the rather amazing **Spiky Bridge**, built by convicts in the early 1840s using thousands of local field stones, is a compulsory stop. Nearby **Kelvedon Beach** and **Cressy Beach** have deep golden sand and rarely a footprint. The **loontitetermairrelehoiner** walk skirts the headland between Waterloo Beach and the Esplanade, passing a muttonbird (short-tailed shearwater) rookery. During breeding season (September to April) the adult birds return at dusk after feeding at sea.

THE DRIVE: The Tasman Hwy's best views live here. Once you pass Spiky Bridge, 7km from Swansea, it's eye-popping coastline as the road skims past Kelvedon Beach (with Tasmania's most photogenic – albeit collapsing – old boat shed) and up and over Rocky Hills, before it retreats again from the coast; Triabunna is 50km from Swansea.

06 Triabunna

Triabunna sits on an inlet of Spring Bay and shelters a small cray- and scallop-fishing fleet. There's a shambling old waterside pub here, but not much else of interest to visitors...other than the fact that it's the jumping-off point for magical Maria Island. **East Coast Cruises** *(eastcoastcruises.com.au)* runs full-day eco-tours to the island, visiting its Painted Cliffs, Fossil Cliffs and the old convict settlement at Darlington before either heading to the Ile des Phoques seal colony or circumnavigating the island. Otherwise, take the **Encounter Maria Island** *(encountermaria.com.au)* ferry.

THE DRIVE: The only driving you need do on this section is to Triabunna's wharf. The passenger ferry will 'drive' the rest of the

Cape Barren Goose, Maria Island

OBSESHNZ/SHUTTERSTOCK

way, across Mercury Passage to Maria Island.

07 Maria Island

Captivating Maria Island (ma-rye-ah), with its jagged peaks and string-thin isthmus, is a carefree, car-free haven, laced with impressive scenery: curious cliffs, fern-draped forests, squeaky sand beaches and azure seas. Forester kangaroos, wombats, Cape Barren geese and wallabies stroll around the World Heritage–listed convict settlement at **Darlington** *(parks.tas.gov.au)*. An insurance population of Tasmanian devils has been released and is thriving – more than 100 devils at last count. The island's unsealed roads are the domain of walkers and cyclists (bring your own bike, or hire one from the ferry operator) and there's also lots to see below the water, with good snorkelling and diving in the clear, shallow marine reserve. It all adds up to one of our favourite places in Tasmania. Just note that the island doesn't have any shops: BYO food and gear.

THE DRIVE: It's a short hop of just 7km from Triabunna to Orford, where the Tasman Hwy bids adieu to the coast. As you roll towards town over Sheas Creek, there are great views of Maria Island rising like a castle from the water.

08 Orford

Orford was once a port for the east-coast whaling fleet and the convict settlement on Maria Island. These days it's a holiday hamlet where Hobartians have their seaside 'shacks' and spend summer holidays on the sand. The Prosser River flows through **Paradise Gorge** as it heads towards the town, and is often mirror-calm with perfect reflections. On the north side of the river is a convict-built road that once ran all the way to Hobart; it's now a riverside walking track. Another coastal track (5km) leads from Raspins Beach, along Shelly Beach, around the Luther Point cliffs and onto photogenic **Spring Beach**, which has improbably clear water and, if the surf gods are smiling, decent waves. The track passes a convict-era quarry that coughed out sandstone for buildings in Hobart and Melbourne.

HYSERB/SHUTTERSTOCK

Devil's Corner vineyard

EAST COAST WINERIES

Along the Tasman Hwy, around Cranbrook and Swansea, you'll encounter a string of terrific wineries where the producers are making the most of sunny east-coast days and cool nights.

Freycinet Vineyard
The Bull family has been growing grapes beneath the east-coast sun since 1980 – it was the first vineyard on the coast. The vibe at the cellar door is agricultural, not flashy – we like it! Super sauvignon blanc. *freycinetvineyard.com.au*

Devil's Corner
Wine with a widescreen view at this cutting-edge cellar door (Eyesore or delight? You decide.) overlooking Moulting Lagoon and the Hazards mountains on Freycinet Peninsula, complete with jaunty lookout tower. *devilscorner.com.au*

Gala Estate Vineyard
Enjoy a red in retroville in this funky pistachio-coloured cellar door – once a post office – right on the main road through Cranbrook. *galaestate.com.au*

Spring Vale Wines
Down a long driveway in Cranbrook, this winery is on land owned by the same family since 1875. The cellar door is housed in a convict-built 1842 stable. Don't miss the pinot gris. *springvalewines.com*

Milton Vineyard
Worth a stop alone for the bizarre twin trees at the entrance – a eucalyptus and macrocarpa seemingly growing out of the same trunk. Tastings are in an elegant, white weatherboard pavilion presiding over the vines. *miltonvineyard.com.au*

36

TASMANIA

HERITAGE TRAIL

DURATION: 3 DAYS

DISTANCE: 257KM / 160 MILES

GREAT FOR: HISTORY

BEST TIME TO GO: GOOD ALL YEAR, BUT AT ITS FINEST FROM OCTOBER TO APRIL.

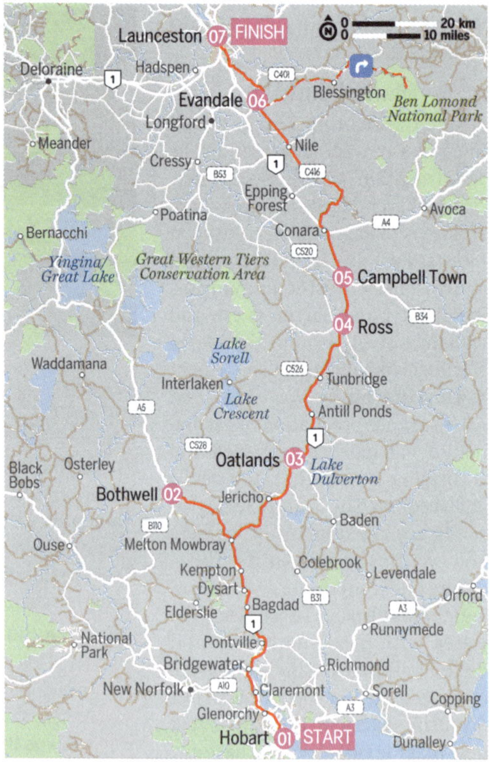

The Hobart-to-Launceston route may lack the epic mountain or coastal drama of many Tasmanian drives, but it more than compensates with its open-air galleries of colonial-era architecture. The town names, building facades and landscapes resemble a jaunt through the rolling farmlands of southern England. The direct route is straight up the Midland Hwy, but meander a little and discover the best of historic Tasmania.

LINK YOUR TRIP

37 Turrakana / Tasman Peninsula
A 125km foray southeast from Hobart towards Port Arthur and the amazing sea cliffs of this hook-shaped peninsula dangling off Tasmania's southeastern edge.

38 Tamar Valley Gourmet Trail
From Launceston, a 186km loop weaves through the wineries, berry farms and wildlife-rich corners of the Tamar Valley.

01 Hobart

Pinched between towering **Kunanyi / Mt Wellington** *(wellingtonpark.org.au)* and the broad Derwent River estuary, Hobart is a city ruled by nature. From the restaurants and bars of North Hobart to the buzz and commerce of sandstone Salamanca Place, with historic Battery Point beyond, the city will rapidly absorb a few days of your visit. The city and docks area are easily navigable on foot, while the world-class **MONA** *(mona.net.au)* museum, burrowed into a peninsula in the northern suburbs (best reached by ferry), is worth a day on its own. The excellent **Cascade Brewery**, **Tasmanian Museum & Art Gallery** (TMAG; *tmag.tas.gov.au*) and **Cascades Female Factory Historic Site** *(femalefactory.org.au)* also vie for your attention.

THE DRIVE: Head north out of Hobart on the Brooker Hwy, following signs for Launceston and passing MONA after about

ANDREW BAIN/ALAMY

★ BEST FOR:

HISTORY

Ratho Farm in Bothwell was Australia's first golf course.

Ratho Farm golf course

10km. Cross the Bridgewater Bridge 21km north of Hobart, passing between crowds of swans, and stay on the Midland Hwy to Melton Mowbray, 35km north of the bridge. Turn left onto the A5 here, crossing a rolling rural landscape to Bothwell (21km).

02 Bothwell

The journey's first echoes of rural England and Scotland come at quiet Bothwell (population 485). Far enough off the main highway to keep visitors to a trickle, Bothwell is becalmed, beguiling, backcountry Tasmania. The town encircles a traditional village green near a slow-roaming stretch of the Clyde River. It has some lovely historic buildings: standouts include the impressive 1891 **St Michael's Church**, and the **Castle Hotel**, first licensed in 1829. Bothwell's Scottish heritage makes itself felt in Australia's oldest golf course at **Ratho Farm** *(rathofarm.com)*. If you've been drawn here by the golf, there's also the **Australasian Golf Museum** *(ausgolfmuseum.com)* beside the village green. In case you missed the wee hints, Bothwell's street signs have a winning tartan motif.

THE DRIVE: Return to Melton Mowbray (21km) and turn left onto the Midland Hwy. The highway tracks northeast, climbing over Spring Hill – at 488m, its the highest point along the highway – and cuts through wide-open farmland to Oatlands, set just off the road, 28km from Melton Mowbray.

03 Oatlands

A small town built on a grand scale, Oatlands contains Australia's largest single collection of Georgian architecture. On the stately main street alone there are 87 historic buildings, and the whole place feels like a cross between a picture-perfect film set and a stately English country town. First conceived in 1821 as one of four military posts on the Hobart–George Town road, the town reflects the grand plans of its early settlers: in 1832 an optimistic town surveyor marked out 80km of streets, on the assumption Oatlands would become the Midlands'

TROOPER
A.E.FITZALLEN
SA

capital. In the 1830s, settlers began erecting solid buildings with the help of former convicts and soldiers who were skilled carpenters and stonemasons, but with the architecture in place, Oatlands settled back into quiet obscurity, and thus it blissfully remains. Don't miss the impressive restored **Callington Mill** *(callingtonmilldistillery.com)*.

THE DRIVE: Follow Oatlands' main street north to rejoin the Midland Hwy, which climbs immediately over heavenly sounding St Peters Pass. From here it's a rather flat, agrarian 28km dash north to the Ross turnoff. At about Tunbridge you cross the unseen beer line – once upon a time, only Cascade beer was drunk south of here, and only Boag's to the north.

ANDREW BAIN/ALAMY

Four Corners of Ross

PHOTO OPPORTUNITY

AUTUMN IN ROSS

Autumn's golden glow along the elm trees on Church St in Ross.

04 Ross

Immaculate Ross is anything but a bridge too far, sitting just 1km off the Midland Hwy. Founded in 1812 to protect Hobart–Launceston travellers from bushrangers, the town quickly became an important coach-staging post at the centre of Tasmania's burgeoning wool industry; the **Tasmanian Wool Centre** *(taswoolcentre.com.au)* offers some fascinating insights. The crossroads in the middle of town, known as the **Four Corners of Ross**, could lead your soul in one of four directions: temptation (the pub), salvation (the church), recreation (the town hall) or damnation (the old jail). Other notable historic edifices include the 1836 **Ross Bridge**, the third-oldest bridge in Australia, and the **Ross Female Factory** *(parks.tas.gov.au)*, once one of Tasmania's five female convict prisons. With a few good eateries sheltering beneath beautiful elms – spectacular in autumn – Ross makes the perfect overnighter.

THE DRIVE: There's barely time to get going once you're back on the main highway – Campbell Town is just 12km north of Ross and the main road trucks right through the centre of town.

Ross in autumn

CANDYAPPLERED IMAGES/ALAMY

05 Campbell Town

With more through-traffic than the other Midlands towns, Campbell Town wears its history a little more lightly. Even so, there's no mistaking its heritage: this was another former garrison and convict settlement and has a slew of mid-19th-century buildings on show. Along High St, rows of red bricks set into the footpath detail the crimes, sentences and arrival dates of convicts transported here for misdeeds as various as stealing potatoes, bigamy and murder. Today Campbell Town is ground zero for Tasmania's cattle-and-sheep-farming industries (the 'Eliza and Ram' statue opposite Zeps celebrates Eliza Furlong, a local farmer who helped pioneer the introduction of Merino sheep into Australia in the 1830s). It is also a burgeoning book centre, with a pair of good secondhand bookstores along the main street. The annual **Campbell Town Show** *(campbelltownshow.com)*, is the oldest country show in Australia (since 1839).

THE DRIVE: Shun the highway sprint by turning off (right) onto the C416, 14km north of Campbell Town. This lightly trafficked road winds through undulating farmland, making a slower and more scenic approach into Evandale. A 7km section of this road is unsealed, but in good condition. Evandale is 60km from Campbell Town.

06 Evandale

The most northerly of Tasmania's historic Midlands towns, Evandale is the prettiest of them all. Stroll along the main street and you'll feel like you've stepped into a period film set (precisely why the entire town is National Trust listed). A few hours spent hanging out in the galleries and cafes here is time well invested. The heritage atmosphere wheels to life each February when Evandale hosts the **National Penny Farthing Championships** *(evandalevillagefair.com)*. There's also an agreeable Sunday morning market, the usual portfolio of historic churches and, south of town via Nile Rd, the neoclassical estate **Clarendon** *(nationaltrust.org.au/places/clarendon-estate)*, which dates to 1838 and looks like it's stepped straight out of *Gone with the Wind*. Clarendon is also (somewhat incongruously) home to the **Australian Fly Fishing Museum** *(affm.net.au)*.

THE DRIVE: Beside Evandale's visitor centre, turn right onto the C412, signposted to White Hills. This road dips into the Relbia valley, where the high hedgerows give the land an English look but the vine-covered slopes give it a French flavour. By Josef Chromy Wines, turn right onto Glenwood Rd and follow this into Launceston.

DETOUR

Ben Lomond

Start: 06 Evandale

As you near Evandale, the drive continues north across the flat, rural Midlands, but it's mountains that begin to dominate the scene, with the Great Western Tiers smudging the western horizon and Ben Lomond rising more abruptly to the east. The tallest point on Ben Lomond is the second-highest mountain peak in Tasmania: Legges Tor (1572m).

From Evandale, quiet roads journey around 40km east to the base of the road-climb to Ben Lomond. Here the unsealed C432 (easily managed in a 2WD outside of winter) begins a spectacular 18km ascent towards the sky, climbing first through tall forest and then finally to the most dramatic bit of road in Tasmania: **Jacobs Ladder**. This 1.5km section of dirt road contorts its way up onto the Ben Lomond plateau through a series of hairpins so tight you half-expect the road to snap. Pull over at the top of the 'ladder' and walk the few steps to **Watchtower Lookout**, which peers down over the road, giving you full perspective on its tortuous design.

The C432 ends at the Ben Lomond ski village. About 1km before the village is a walking trail that leads to Legges Tor. Taking just one hour (return), it's by far the easiest of Tasmania's high peaks to scale.

07 Launceston

Launceston, Tasmania's second-largest city, is a compact, endearing place with a well-preserved cache of colonial architecture and a progressive foodie culture. The centrepiece of the city is not urban at all – **Cataract Gorge** *(launcestoncataractgorge.com.au)* feels a million miles from town even though it's just steps away, with the ice-cold South Esk River pouring between narrow cliffs. Inside the gorge, at **First Basin**, there's a free outdoor swimming pool, the world's longest single-span **chairlift** *(gorgechairlift.com.au)*, huge European trees and sociable peacocks around the now-closed **Gorge Restaurant**. Beer boffins will be equally drawn to a tour of **Boag's Brewery** *(jamesboag.com.au)*, home to the famous range of James Boag's brews. If you're feeling more cerebral, pay a visit to the **Queen Victoria Museum** and **Queen Victoria Art Gallery**, collectively known as **QVMAG** *(qvmag.tas.gov.au)*.

Cataract Gorge, Launceston
TRABANTOS/SHUTTERSTOCK

37

TASMANIA

TURRAKANA / TASMAN PENINSULA

★ BEST FOR:

OUTDOORS

Crescent Bay's impressive sand dunes.

Crescent Bay (p275)

DURATION: 3–4 DAYS

DISTANCE: 125KM / 77 MILES

GREAT FOR: HISTORY & NATURE

BEST TIME TO GO: THERE'S GENERALLY GOOD WEATHER FROM OCTOBER TO APRIL.

The Turrakana / Tasman Peninsula's convoluted coastline corrals plenty of interesting sights into a small area. Port Arthur – a hauntingly beautiful former penal colony – is one of Tasmania's key tourist lures, but there's also the peninsula's legendary 300m-high sea cliffs (the tallest in the southern hemisphere) and other circus acts of coastal rock, all of which will dose you up on natural awe.

LINK YOUR TRIP

35 East Coast Tasmania
Tasmania's classic beach-hopping east-coast road trip (224km) ends at Orford, 55km northeast of Sorell.

36 Heritage Trail
The 257km drive through Tassie's historic heart begins in Hobart and tracks north to Launceston.

01 Hobart

Hobart's days as a provincial backwater in one of the furthest flung corners of earth are long gone. On a perpetual ascendancy since the astonishingly good art museum **MONA** opened in 2011, the city is now a place where the food and culture are as fulfilling as the natural scenes along the Derwent River and **Kunanyi / Mt Wellington**, the two features that shape Hobart. Salamanca Pl and North Hobart anchor the eating scene, and you shouldn't miss a jaunt up 'the mountain', as Kunanyi / Mt Wellington is simply known in Hobart, for the best views in the business (and snow in winter!).

THE DRIVE: From Hobart, cross the Derwent River on the Tasman Bridge and head east, following signs for the airport. As the highway crosses through the low Meehan Range, the Richmond turning is to the left. Turning left again in Cambridge, the road tracks through the

BEC CHIPMAN/SHUTTERSTOCK

Coal River Valley between lines of pinot noir and riesling vines. Richmond is 27km from Hobart.

02 Richmond

A historic town straddling the Coal River, Richmond is the quintessential piece of colonial Tasmania and was once a strategic military post and convict station on the road to Port Arthur. Interesting old buildings abound: check out **St John the Evangelist Church** *(hobart.catholic.org.au)*, Australia's oldest Catholic church (1836); and **Richmond Bridge**, the country's oldest road bridge (1823). Kick up a stink at the **Pooseum** *(pooseum.com.au)*, which is both a scientific and a silly look at poo. More mature tastes should consider a visit to the nearby **Sullivans Cove Distillery** *(sullivanscove.com)* or settle in for lunch with a view at **Frogmore Creek** *(frogmorecreek.com.au)*. If you're in no hurry, consider a 36km round-trip detour to the **Bonorong Wildlife Sanctuary** *(bonorong.com.au)* for a full complement of native critters.

THE DRIVE: Cross the Coal River on Richmond Bridge and drive straight ahead. This road climbs through a low range of hills, descending through more vineyards at Penna. At the road's end, turn right onto the Tasman Hwy and enter Sorell, 15km after leaving Richmond.

03 Sorell

It may initially be hard to fathom, but Sorell is one of Tasmania's oldest towns. Founded in 1808, it once supplied locally processed wheat and flour to the rest of the colony, but the town's historic aura has tarnished over time. These days it's very much a service town, but traces of its origins linger in the presence of a clutch of 19th-century buildings: pick up the *Sorell Heritage Walk* brochure from the visitor centre, or download it from *sorell.tas.gov.au*. If you're here in summer, detour out to the **Sorell Fruit Farm** *(facebook.com/sorellfruitfarm)* and pick yourself a bevy of berries for the drive ahead.

THE DRIVE: At Sorell's traffic lights – yes, there's just the one set in town – continue straight ahead onto the Arthur Hwy, weaving through beautiful green farmland. The area is still scarred by the bushfires of 2013, though the bush is slowly regenerating. About 30km southeast of Sorell, the road curls down to little Dunalley.

04 Dunalley

Strung along one edge of the 895m-long Denison Canal, a boating shortcut that effectively turns the Forestier and Turrakana / Tasman Peninsulas into an island, the small town of Dunalley wears a few historic stars and scars. Abel Tasman made his only landfall in Tasmania in 1642 just near the town, and the first contact between Europeans and Aboriginal people in Tasmania was here, while a horrific 2013 bushfire destroyed a third of Dunalley's homes. The town has well and truly bounced back from the fire, and though there's not a whole lot to see (other than the canal), it's worth stopping for lunch or liquid refreshment at the excellent **Bangor Vineyard Shed** *(bangorshed.com.au)*.

THE DRIVE: Crossing the Denison Canal, the Arthur Hwy skims past Sunset Beach, looking west across the water to Kunanyi / Mt Wellington (and, yes, sunsets). It then climbs across the Forestier Peninsula, the precursor to the Turrakana / Tasman Peninsula. About 17km on, just before Teralina / Eaglehawk Neck, take the turnoff to Pirates Bay Lookout – your utterly splendid first glimpse of the Turrakana / Tasman Peninsula's high cliffs.

05 Teralina / Eaglehawk Neck

Eaglehawk Neck marks the start of the Turrakana / Tasman Peninsula and is less a town than a smattering of holiday homes amid an assortment of natural coastal oddities. The 100m-wide isthmus here (the 'Neck') once had a row of ornery dogs – the infamous Dogline – chained across it to prevent convicts escaping from Port Arthur. A statue of a dog in the middle of the isthmus commemorates the line. For a close-up look at the spectacular coastline around the Neck, stop at the **Tessellated Pavement** as you descend from the Pirates Bay Lookout, and then follow the signs south to the **Blowhole** (*eaglehawkneck.org/attractions*), **Tasman Arch** (a cavern-like natural bridge) and **Devil's Kitchen** (a rugged 60m-deep gulch). At the Blowhole, don't miss the excellent Doo-Lishus caravan for some of Tasmania's best fish and chips.

THE DRIVE: The road from Eaglehawk Neck hugs the shores of narrow Eaglehawk Bay before turning south through Taranna, once the terminus of an infamous railway from Port Arthur – convicts pushed the rail carts by hand – and then through beautifully wooded hills to Port Arthur, 20km away.

06 Port Arthur

The juxtaposition between natural beauty and unsettling human history is nowhere so profound as it is at the **Port Arthur Historic Site** (*portarthur.org.au*). In 1830, Governor Arthur chose this beautiful spot to confine prisoners who had committed further crimes in the colony. Between 1830 and 1877, 12,500 convicts did brutal prison time here, and the fine buildings sustained thriving convict-labour industries, including timber milling, shipbuilding, coal mining, shoemaking and brick and nail production.

Interior of Remarkable Cave

DANIEL KARFIK/SHUTTERSTOCK

Despite its redemption as a major tourist attraction, Port Arthur is a sombre place: there's a sadness here that's undeniable. Add to this the 1996 massacre in which 35 people were killed, and it's a place that will leave you deeply affected – both by its history and its beauty. What surprises many people is that Port Arthur is also a township with a smattering of good accommodation options and a couple of fine restaurants: On the Bay, and the historic site's sleek new **1830** *(portarthur.org.au)*.

THE DRIVE: It's just 12km from Port Arthur to Nubeena and, except in the height of summer, it's a quiet road forsaken by day trippers rushing back to Hobart. From the Port Arthur Historic Site, the road climbs over one final peninsula hill before dipping through pear orchards into Nubeena.

ONLY JAYNE/SHUTTERSTOCK

Tessellated Pavement, Teralina / Eaglehawk Neck

PHOTO OPPORTUNITY

The Tessellated Pavement, a perfect marriage of geometry and geology.

DETOUR

Remarkable Cave & Crescent Bay

Start: 06 Port Arthur

Just 400m past the Port Arthur Historic Site, the C347 turns south off the Arthur Hwy. This road rolls along protected Carnarvon Bay, where, if you have kids in the back seat, a couple of tyre-swings over the beach may tempt you to linger and play. At the road's end, 7km from Port Arthur, a lookout platform beside the car park peers over the water to the jagged tip of Cape Raoul.

A 15-minute return walk from here leads down to **Remarkable Cave**, tunnelled into the sea cliffs by the relentless wave action of the Southern Ocean. Its entrance is shaped a bit like Tasmania itself, but what you can't see from the platform is that the cave has two entrances – the unseen entrance forks away to the left as you peer through the tunnel towards the sea. Hardcore surfers often brave the cave, paddling out through the opening to surf the offshore reefs beyond.

The cave car park also marks the start of one of our favourite Tasmanian day walks, heading south along the coast and past Maingon Blowhole to **Crescent Bay** (9km, three to four hours return). This perfectly curved beach, with its views to Tasman Island and the Blade on Cape Pillar (the coup-de-grâce moment on the Three Capes Track), is backed by some of the highest and most beautiful sand dunes in Tasmania. Local kids (and big kids) often carry in boogie boards or similar on which to slide down the dunes.

07 Nubeena

Nubeena, fanned along the shore of Parsons Bay, is the largest town on the Turrakana / Tasman Peninsula (population 481). It's unapologetically functional, but if all the other accommodation on the peninsula is booked out (trust us, it happens), you might be able to find a bed here. There's also a couple of supermarkets, a tavern and a decent cafe, and Nubeena is surrounded by some of the peninsula's most beautiful and wild coastline. Nearby White Beach is everything the name on the tin suggests, while Roaring Beach gets wicked surf but isn't safe for swimming. Down a side road 3km south of Nubeena is the newly spruced-up hiking trail to Cape Raoul (14km, five hours return), with its side trails to Tunnel Bay and the humbling Shipstern Bluff, one of the world's great big-wave surf spots. Prepare to stand in awe of the Southern Ocean.

38

★ BEST FOR:

FOOD & WINE

The cluster of vineyards at Pipers River forms one of Australia's most underrated wine locales.

TASMANIA

TAMAR VALLEY GOURMET TRAIL

DURATION: 4–5 DAYS

DISTANCE: 186KM / 115 MILES

GREAT FOR: WINE & NATURE

BEST TIME TO GO: OCTOBER TO MAY BRINGS THE BEST WEATHER.

Kangaroos, Narawntapu National Park

You could make this up-and-back journey in a single day, but that would be to miss the point (and many of the drinking opportunities). On this route, you'll meander along a riverbank, go off on a tangent to a winery or two, and plan your day around the comings and goings of wildlife. The valley's western bank is the prettier of the two, but the eastern bank holds some of the bigger-name vineyards.

LINK YOUR TRIP

36 Heritage trail
From Hobart to Launceston (257km) via the historic towns of Tasmania's Midlands.

39 Western Wilds
This 620km journey ends (but could just as easily begin) in Launceston, taking in the great forests, remote rivers, high mountains and beaten coastlines of Tasmania's wild west.

01 Launceston

Laid-back Launceston is a fine starting point for a foodie's exploration of Tasmania's north, with Cataract Gorge providing a dramatic natural counterpoint within walking distance of the city centre.

THE DRIVE: From Launceston take the West Tamar Hwy 13km northwest to Legana. At the bottom of the first dip past Legana, turn right onto the C733 (Rosevears Dr), which runs hard against the Tamar's grassy bank into Rosevears.

02 Rosevears

It can be deceptive to refer to vineyards in the area as being in the 'Tamar Valley', as many sit so far from the river, but this is not the case in Rosevears, where the vines almost tumble into the water. The road runs closer to Kanamaluka / River Tamar than anywhere else along the route, and you can pay a visit to **Tamar Ridge** *(tamarridge.com.au),* a winery best known for

TKPANG.JOSEPH/SHUTTERSTOCK

its quaffable Pirie sparkling wine (named after the brothers who pioneered the Tamar's wine industry) and with a scenic terrace overlooking the river. Back in nearby Legana, **Vélo Wines** *(velowines.com.au)* was christened by its former Tour de France cyclist owner (*vélo* is French for bike) and has the oldest cabernet vines in Tasmania, planted in 1966. The on-site **Timbre Kitchen** *(timbrekitchen.com)* restaurant is Vélo's main attraction.

THE DRIVE: Continue along Rosevears Dr for 4km, turning right onto the A7 and passing through Exeter to Beaconsfield, 23km from Rosevears. Branching away to the east, Batman Bridge crosses the Tamar, but simply make a note of it for now, as you've some essential business to transact on the western shore first.

DETOUR

Narawntapu National Park

Start: 02 Rosevears

Tasmania is one of Australia's most underrated wildlife-watching destinations, and that can be the only reason why **Narawntapu National Park** *(parks.tas.gov.au)* is barely known beyond these shores. So prolific is the wildlife in this coastal reserve that it has been dubbed 'Tasmania's Serengeti'. It used to be called Asbestos Range National Park, but park management thought the name was deterring people from visiting. Go figure...

At dawn and dusk, the Springlawn area – once farmland – around the ranger station becomes a critter convention, filling with wallabies, Forester kangaroos and the star of the show: wombats. Lots of wombats. It's worth **camping** *(parks.tas.gov.au)* the night, if you can, to make the most of the viewing opportunities.

To visit the park's main areas around Springlawn and long Bakers Beach, enter via the main entrance off the B71 near Port Sorell, where there's a ranger station. In Exeter, 17km before Beaconsfield, turn west on the B71, following it for 40km before swinging onto the C740, from where it's about 13km to the ranger station. Rangers run guided walks and activities from here in summer.

03 Beaconsfield & Around

The international spotlight briefly shone on Beaconsfield (population 1298) during a mine collapse in 2006, but these days the gold mine has closed and it's a quiet town in the heart of the Tamar's apple-growing country. Pause long enough to visit the **Beaconsfield Mine & Heritage Centre** *(beaconsfieldheritage.com.au)*, which has hands-on interactive exhibits, including a large display about the mine collapse and rescue. Six kilometres north of Beaconsfield, Beauty Point has two winning attractions. **Platypus House** *(platypushouse.com.au)* is a chance to see the world's only two monotremes – the platypus and the echidna – while **Seahorse World** *(seahorseworld.com.au)* is a working seahorse farm with up to 90,000 seahorses, plus other bizarre sea creatures such as the spotted handfish and Tasmanian giant crab (the world's second-largest crab species by weight).

If you plan on visiting Beaconsfield Mine & Heritage Centre, Platypus House and Seahorse World, the

Tamar Triple Pass can be picked up at the **visitor centre** *(tamarvalley.com.au)* in Exeter.

THE DRIVE: From opposite Beaconsfield Mine & Heritage Centre, turn east on Grubb St (signed to Rowella). From here it's just 6km, crossing a couple of bush-smothered streams, to hilltop Goaty Hill Wines.

04 Goaty Hill Wines

Arguably the most scenic of the Tamar Valley's vineyards, **Goaty Hill Wines** sits on a rise looking over its own vines towards the mouth of Kanamaluka / River Tamar. It's a real gem, with the little corrugated-iron cellar door offering tastings and platters (call ahead to book platters). It's best known for its top-notch riesling, and pinots gris and noir. The tables on the grass, under the tall stringybark trees, are the place to be on a summer's afternoon. Bliss.

THE DRIVE: Turn right out of Goaty Hill, then right again on the C724. Turning left on the B73 takes you over Kanamaluka / River Tamar on the Batman Bridge before heading south along the East Tamar Hwy (A8). Look for Hillwood Jetty Rd on the right after almost 5km and follow the signs another 1km to Hillwood Farmgate.

05 Hillwood Farmgate

Tamar Valley wines may steal all the plaudits, but the valley is also renowned for the fresh fruits that emerge from its numerous orchards. Prime among these is **Hillwood Berries** *(hillwoodberries.com.au)*, which is at its best in summer when the hillsides are almost universally under berry. Pick your own strawberries, raspberries, blackberries, blackcurrants, red currants and blueberries and then make a beeline to the cafe for a berry smoothie, some choc-dipped raspberries or a coffee.

THE DRIVE: Return to the A8, and follow it 22km north above the Tamar's eastern riverbank. Almost as far as you can go in Tasmania without falling into Bass Strait are George Town and Low Head – they are barely divided.

06 George Town & Low Head

Strung along the northernmost banks of Kanamaluka / River Tamar, George Town and Low Head sit shoulder-to-shoulder – you'll barely have time to take a breath as you

Pipers Brook vineyard, Pipers River

WINEPIX/ALAMY

leave one before you hit the other. Low Head is the prettier of the two settlements, but be sure to visit the **Bass & Flinders Maritime Museum** *(bassandflindersmuseum.com.au)* before you just hurry on through George Town – its replica of the *Norfolk*, the sloop in which Bass and Flinders circumnavigated Tasmania in 1798, is a highlight. Low Head looks out over the swirling (and treacherous) waters of the Kanamaluka / River Tamar mouth, with the **Low Head Lighthouse** standing guard. Built in 1888, it's a terrific spot to watch the torrent of the Tamar spilling into Bass Strait. **Low Head Penguin Tours** *(penguintourstasmania.com.au)* leave nightly at dusk from a signposted spot beside Low Head Rd, just south of the lighthouse.

THE DRIVE: From George Town, backtrack 5km on the A8 and turn east on the B82. This road crosses through the low Tippogoree Hills, where the bush is drier and more typically Australian than anything behind you on this trip...but there's an oasis ahead in the clutch of wineries at Pipers River, 23km after leaving George Town.

STEVE TODD/SHUTTERSTOCK

Low Head Lighthouse

PHOTO OPPORTUNITY

Low Head Lighthouse.

07 Pipers River

In the eastern Tamar Valley hinterland, the Pipers River Wine Region is a lovely adjunct to the Tamar's charms. **Pipers Brook** *(kreglingerwineestates.com)* is the region's most famous vineyard, and is accessed from Pipers Brook Rd, about 11km past the Pipers River general store. Around 3km south of the store, **Bay of Fires Wines** *(bayoffireswines.com.au)* is the home of prestigious Arras sparkling and easy-drinking whites and pinots. There's a touch of Cape Cod about the cellar-door design, and the ample lawns and footballs to kick will distract the kids from their parents' wine antics.

THE DRIVE: From the entrance to Pipers Brook and Jansz Wine Room, head south on Pipers Brook Rd. At its end turn right onto the B81, which takes a roller-coasting ride into Lilydale, 24km from Pipers Brook. There are three more wineries en route – Brook Eden, Apogee and Clover Hill – if too much tasting isn't enough.

08 Lilydale

Quiet Lilydale is little more than a main street with a few stores and services, but 3km north of town are the pretty **Lilydale Falls**, seemingly propped up by a fallen log. Energetic types also propel themselves up **Mt Arthur** (1188m; five to seven hours return), which looms – high, cold and austere – above the town. You can swing through the trees with the greatest of ease at **Hollybank Treetops Adventure** *(treetopsadventure.com.au/location/tas-hollybank)*, which has a rope course and zip lines through the canopy of a particularly beautiful section of forest. It's south of town, as you drive towards Launceston.

THE DRIVE: The B81 tracks straight on through Lilydale, heading south. Farmland soon falls behind and bush closes in until you reach Launceston's outer suburbs. Follow the 'City Centre' signs, with the drive ending along the eastern bank of Kanamaluka / River Tamar, 27km from Lilydale.

39

TASMANIA

WESTERN WILDS

DURATION: 14 DAYS

DISTANCE: 620KM / 385 MILES

GREAT FOR: NATURE & HISTORY

BEST TIME TO GO: OCTOBER TO APRIL; AVOID THE DEPTHS OF WINTER (JUNE TO AUGUST).

★ BEST FOR:

OUTDOORS

Cruise to wild Pieman Heads along the Pieman River from Corinna.

Strahan harbour

The west is literally wild in Tasmania, where the Southern Ocean thunders ashore, tall-timbered rainforest scratches at the sky around the Takayna / Tarkine wilderness, and peerless Cradle Mountain stands sculpted by long-gone glaciers. To this, add the historic towns of Stanley and Sheffield, the striking beauty of Boat Harbour Beach and Marrawah's relentless surf, and it becomes clear that just about everything good about Tasmania lines up along this route.

LINK YOUR TRIP

36 Heritage Trail
Drive through history between Hobart and Launceston (257km), passing through some of Tasmania's best-preserved historic towns.

38 Tamar Valley Gourmet Trail
This 186km loop from Launceston is gastronomic heaven thanks to its wineries and berry farms, with some excellent wildlife-watching en route.

01 Strahan

Nestled between Macquarie Harbour (a body of water six times the size of Sydney Harbour) and the rainforest, Strahan presents a mild moment within the wild of Tasmania's west coast. Take a day trip with **Gordon River Cruises** *(gordonrivercruises.com.au)*, exploring Macquarie Harbour, the soulful rainforests and mirror-perfect reflections of the Gordon River, and the haunting penal colony of **Sarah Island**. Also worth a day is the **West Coast Wilderness Railway** *(wcwr.com.au)*, a restored heritage rail service that travels inland through rainforest to the hard-as-nails mining town of Queenstown and back. On one of your Strahan evenings, don't miss the fabulously entertaining theatre performance, **The Ship That Never Was** *(roundearth.com.au)*.

THE DRIVE: It's straight from town to thick bush as the B27 heads out of Strahan, soon skirting the Henry Dunes

OWEN DERRICK/ALAMY

(Tasmania's largest dune field). At Zeehan, 43km north of Strahan, the C249 heads 50km (4km of it unsealed) to the Pieman River, where the Fatman vehicle barge waits to deliver you across the dark waters to Corinna.

02 Corinna

Corinna is the green and gold of Australia made literal – a former gold-mining town inside the deep rainforest of the Takayna / Tarkine wilderness. As a humming mining settlement in the late 1800s, it had two hotels, a post office, shops, a slaughter yard and a population of 2500. These days, it's a tranquil place with only one business – **Corinna Wilderness Experience** *(corinna.com.au)* – providing accommodation in camp sites and cabins, a restaurant, **boat cruises** *(corinna.com.au/river-cruises)* down the Pieman River to one of Australia's wildest beaches, kayak hire and several good walks. There are no TVs, no phone signal and no wi-fi; there's just living.

THE DRIVE: The road north from Corinna, dubbed the Western Explorer (or sometimes the Road to Nowhere), journeys through an all-or-nothing landscape – the thick rainforest of Takayna / Tarkine, or bald buttongrass ridges – to Arthur River. It's unsealed for 70km, but is easily passable in a 2WD.

From Arthur River, the road rolls smoothly on to Marrawah, 117km from Corinna.

03 Marrawah

Untamed and unspoilt, Marrawah is both wild and pure at once. The last stop west in Tasmania before you hit Argentina, 15,000km away over the wild seas, it has vast ocean beaches, abundant signs of Aboriginal Tasmania – especially in the fascinating **Preminghana Indigenous Protected Area** *(tacinc.com.au)* just north of town – and mind-blowing sunsets. A nearby scientific station has decreed that the world's cleanest air blows through here on the relentless Roaring Forties. It's also a place beloved by surfers for its challenging breaks. There's a general store and pub here, but very little else.

THE DRIVE: From Marrawah's southern edge, the Bass Hwy begins its eastern journey, burrowing at first through the northern Takayna / Tarkine and then across some of Australia's most fertile dairy and beef country – the bovine lifeblood of Smithton. Stanley lies 7km north of the Bass Hwy, and this last stretch, with the Nut looming ahead, is the prettiest section. Stanley is 67km from Marrawah.

04 Stanley

At a glance, Stanley could easily just be a line of colourful buildings huddled along the base, the Nut, but there's an undeniable magnetism here. Fishing boats piled high with cray pots bob in the harbour, penguins amble ashore and the blast of the Roaring Forties ensures that the air is exhilaratingly clear. With a couple of top-drawer tourist attractions – **Highfield** *(parks.tas.gov.au/highfield)* homestead and **the Nut** – and an array of good eateries, it's an understandably popular place to while away a day or two.

THE DRIVE: Return to the Bass Hwy and turn left, driving east. You'll still sense the presence of Takayna / Tarkine in the fuzz of forest to the south, but mostly the highway continues across lush farming flats. Around 48km from Stanley, the road to Boat Harbour Beach, located 3km off the highway, squirms down to the coastline.

05 Boat Harbour Beach

This may well be paradise. Picture-perfect Boat Harbour Beach's pristine white sand and sapphire-blue waters make you feel like you've taken a wrong turn off the Bass Hwy and ended up somewhere in the Caribbean. The usually calm seas are patrolled in summer and perfect for kids.

THE DRIVE: Return to the Bass Hwy, following it 24km into Somerset, where the Murchison Hwy (A10) branches away south. It's a contorted drive through Hellyer Gorge before you turn east onto the C132, climbing over the Black Bluff Range for your first view of Cradle Mountain. Shortly afterwards, you descend into the orbit of Tasmania's most famous peak, 130km from Boat Harbour Beach.

PHOTO OPPORTUNITY

CRADLE MOUNTAIN

Rising from the waters of Dove Lake.

06 Cradle Mountain

Cradle Mountain anchors the northern end of **Cradle Mountain-Lake St Clair National Park** *(parks.tas.gov.au)*, part of the World Heritage–listed Tasmanian Wilderness. The 1545m mountain is Tasmania's fifth-highest peak, and by far the most famous and recognisable in the state, if not the country. The most easily achieved views of its bowed figure come from the shores of Dove Lake, while there are also glimpses from Cradle Valley, the settlement that presses up against the national park's northern border. Here you'll find the park

Dove Lake, Cradle Mountain-Lake St Clair National Park

CHAMELEONSEYE/SHUTTERSTOCK

visitor centre *(parks.tas.gov.au)*, **the Devils@Cradle** *(devilsatcradle.com)* wildlife sanctuary and a plethora of free-roaming wildlife – wombats, Bennett's wallabies and pademelons are almost guaranteed along the roadside clearings at dusk.

THE DRIVE: It's a stunning 55km drive from Cradle Mountain to Sheffield, crossing a wide-open subalpine plain and then, at Moina, dipping steeply down to the Forth River. Having ground your way back out of the gorge, the road skirts the flanks of deeply furrowed Mt Roland, a peak as impressive in its own way as Cradle Mountain.

DAY WALKS IN CRADLE MOUNTAIN

With its namesake dangling like a lure at the head of Dove Lake, it's easy to see why the Cradle Mountain region is Tasmania's prime hiking area. It's here that the famed Overland Track begins its 65km journey to Leeawuleena / Lake St Clair, but it's also rich in day-walk possibilities.

- **Marions Lookout** (three hours return) Climb past Lilla Lake and Wombat Pool to an eyeball-to-eyeball view of Cradle Mountain's summit.
- **Dove Lake Circuit** (6km, two hours) Lap the lake, setting out from Dove Lake car park, with near-and-far Cradle Mountain views.
- **Cradle Mountain Summit** (13km, six to eight hours return) A tough but spectacular climb with incredible views in fine weather. Some scrambling acrobatics are required as you near the summit. Begin at either Dove Lake car park or Ronny Creek.

07 Sheffield

Sheffield would be a typical workaday provincial Tasmanian town, were it not for the remarkable profusion of murals that have adorned the town's facades since the 1980s. Based on an idea from Chemainus in Canada, the large murals depict scenes from the district's pioneer days, and Sheffield is now a veritable outdoor art gallery, with more than 80 fantastic large-scale murals – the number grows each year through the town's annual mural-painting festival. For more information on the town, its murals and surrounding walks, visit the **visitor centre** *(sheffieldcradleinfo.com.au)*.

THE DRIVE: Return to Paradise (literally; it's a town) and take the C137 over the Fossey Mountains, descending to Mole Creek, where you might pause to tour Marakoopa or King Solomons Caves. The road passes through Mole Creek township – beware the Tassie tiger on the pub roof! – and the honey town of Chudleigh, before crossing lush farmland to Deloraine, 55km from Sheffield.

08 Deloraine

At the base of the Great Western Tiers, the long wall of mountains that separates the northern coastal hinterland from the rugged central highlands, Deloraine commands wonderful views at almost every turn. Blessed with the photo gene, the town is bisected by the winding Meander River, with Georgian and Victorian buildings scattered around the main street, Emu Bay Rd. It's a crafty town – in the artistic sense – at the doorstep of **Liffey Falls** *(parks.tas.gov.au)*, one of Tasmania's most beautiful waterfalls.

THE DRIVE: Shun the Bass Hwy by heading out of Deloraine on the B54, which runs parallel to the highway but with none of its haste. The road passes through a string of towns – Westbury, Hayley, Carrick – that are like little pieces of rural England transposed onto Tasmania. The drive pops back onto the Bass Hwy just 8km from Launceston.

09 Launceston

Launceston may be Tasmania's second city, but its inhabitants argue that their architecture is more elegant, their parks more beautiful and their food scene more zesty than Hobart's. Art and design are indeed big here, and gorgeous Cataract Gorge remains the sort of natural adornment you rarely find so close to the heart of a city.

STAY AWHILE

STANLEY

BY ANTHONY HAM

Clinging to Tasmania's sometimes-wild northwestern coast, Stanley huddles beneath an ancient 143m-high volcano and is my favourite place in Tasmania's north to rest for a few days. Every time I visit, it's almost a rite of passage for me to climb **the Nut**, either hiking the short, sharp and steep 20-minute **Zig Zag Track** or taking the old-school **chairlift** *(thenutchairlift.com.au)*. This 12-million-year-old volcanic plug is known to local Aboriginal people as Moo-Nut-Re-Ker and was labelled 'Circular Head' by explorer Matthew Flinders. Up here, I can feel nature's raw power, with the strong winds known as the Roaring Forties coming in off Bass Strait and ensuring that the air here is delightfully clear.

Back at ground level, I love watching for penguins from the platform above **Godfreys Beach**, or heading out to look for seals on a 75-minute boat trip with **Stanley Seal Cruises** *(stanleysealcruises.com.au)*.

In town, Stanley has its fair share of heritage buildings, with the highlight among many being **Highfield** *(parks.tas.gov.au)*. Built in 1835, this homestead, 2km north of town, is a supreme example of Tassie's colonial-era architecture. For more, pick up a copy of *Under the Nut – Stanley Heritage Walk* from the tourist office and set out to see 15 historic architectural gems.

Order fish and chips from **Hursey Seafoods** *(hurseyseafoods.com.au)* and head for the foreshore. Enjoy a Devonshire tea from **Nut Rock Cafe** *(nutcafe.com.au)* or a counter meal at the **Stanley Hotel** *(stanleyhoteltasmania.com.au)* – but on no account miss one of the town's legendary scallop pies.

LINK YOUR TRIP

Stop awhile in Stanley in the middle of the trip through 39 **Western Wilds**.

Left: The Nut
Right: Little Penguins, Stanley

FROM LEFT: ADWO/SHUTTERSTOCK, BARRYHATTON33/SHUTTERSTOCK

PLACES TO STAY

It's all style and suaveness at **Ship Inn** *(shipinnstanley.com.au)*, a wonderfully restored historic property – formerly the Bayview Hotel – that exudes a seamlessly curated blend of heritage and modernity. Little penguins come ashore within walking distance of **Old Cable Station** *(cablestationstanley.com.au)*. This treasure, built to carry Tasmania's first telephone link to the mainland, features two beautifully furnished guest units with claw-foot tubs, and serves homemade bread and jams at breakfast. **The Ark** *(thearkstanley.com.au)* has five individually styled rooms, some with sublime water views. Expect polished wooden floors, wrought-iron furnishings, luxury linens, goose-down duvets and espresso machines.

TOOLKIT

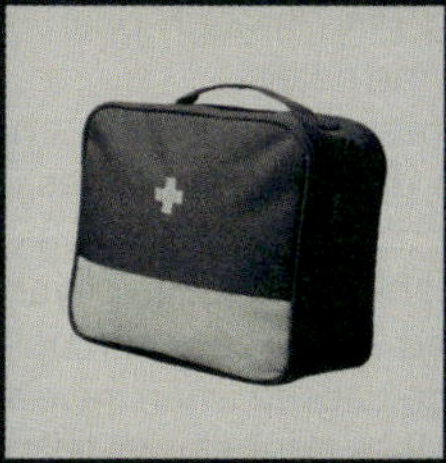

ARRIVING

Most visitors reach Australia by air, typically via the major international airports of Sydney (Warrane), Brisbane (Meanjin) or Melbourne (Narrm). All state and territory capitals have an international airport, as do Cairns (Gimuy) and the Gold Coast. Hobart's only direct international route is to/from Auckland.

AIRPORT CAR RENTALS

Every large and medium-sized Australian airport has car-rental desks inside the arrivals hall; the smaller the airport, the more limited the choice. Shop around on *autoeurope.com.au*. Local car-rental companies (with smaller fleets but often more flexible conditions) don't usually have offices at the airport; they're often easier to find through local visitor information centres and some hotels.

When it comes to 4WDs, check the insurance conditions, especially the excess (the amount you pay in the event of accident, which can be up to $5000). A refundable bond (often payable up front) is also often required. The excess and policies might not cover damage caused when travelling on unsealed roads (which they don't always tell you when you pick up your vehicle). Some also name specific tracks as off limits and you may not be covered by the insurance if you ignore this.

AIRPORT TO CITY CENTRE

	SYDNEY	BRISBANE	MELBOURNE
TRAIN	from 11 mins **from $50**	from 28 mins **$22.30**	N/A
BUS	N/A	N/A	from 30 min **$24.60**
TAXI	from 20 mins **$60**	from 20 mins **from $50**	from 30 mins **from $65**

VISAS

New Zealand passport holders are the only visitors exempt from applying for a visa or visa waiver (ETA) in advance of travelling to Australia. More than 30 nationalities are eligible for an ETA.

WI-FI & SIM CARDS

All of Australia's international airports offer free wi-fi, with SIM cards available for purchase, though SIM-provider options can be limited; Telstra has the widest network coverage.

CUSTOMS

Australia takes biosecurity very seriously – don't forget to declare any food products, and even muddy shoes (which will be cleaned for you, not confiscated, if needed). Above all, be truthful on your passenger arrival card.

BORDER CONTROL

Immigration queues can be long for non-citizens, but you should be through quickly if your documents are in order. If they're not, you probably wouldn't have been let onto the plane.

GETTING AROUND

DRIVING LICENCE & HOOK TURNS

To drive in Australia you'll need to hold a current driving licence issued in English from your home country. If the licence isn't in English, you'll also need to carry an International Driving Permit, issued in your home country.

In inner-city Melbourne, the presence of trams means that you may need to perform what's known as a 'hook turn', which involves waiting for the traffic lights to turn green in the street you're turning into, then turning right from the left-hand lane.

DRIVING INFO

Drive on the left side of the road; all cars are right-hand drive.

Legal driving age varies by state; car rental may require drivers to be 21 or even 25.

.05

Blood alcohol limit is 0.05%.

TRANSPORT CARDS

States and territories have their own transport cards. For example, the Sydney metro area (including Newcastle) uses the Opal card, southeast Queensland uses the Go Card and Melbourne has the myki. Alternatively, tap-and-pay with a debit or credit card (at the time of writing they are trialling tap-and-pay on select lines in Melbourne).

CARBON CONSIDERATIONS

Ensure your vehicle is well serviced and tuned. Drive slowly – many vehicles use 25% more fuel at 110km/h than at 90km/h. Consider ridesharing where possible. Check out the hybrid and electric-car options at major rental companies.

SPEED LIMITS

The general speed limit in built-up and residential areas is 50km/h. Near schools, it's usually 25km/h (sometimes 40km/h) in the morning and afternoon. On highways it's usually 100km/h or 110km/h (110km/h or 130km/h in the NT). Police have speed radar guns and cameras, often used in strategic locations.

PARKING

Inner-city parking (in parking garages and on-street) can be prohibitively expensive, especially in Sydney, Melbourne and other major cities. First Parking (firstparking.com.au) bucks the trend with some excellent flat-rate deals, and not just on weekends or overnight.

TRAVEL COSTS

2WD/4WD rental **$80/180 per day**

Petrol **fluctuates but around $2/litre; up to $3.60/litre in remote areas**

EV charging **$3.80-6.50 for 100km**

Melbourne to Sydney plane/train tickets **from $90/166**

ACCOMMODATION

HOW MUCH FOR A NIGHT IN...

Double room in a B&B or hotel
$180–280

Double room in a basic motel
$130–200

Hostel dorm bed
$50

B&BS

Australian bed-and-breakfast options include restored miners' cottages, converted barns, rambling old houses, upmarket country manors and beachside bungalows. Tariffs are typically in the midrange bracket, but can be higher. In areas that attract week-enders, B&Bs are often booked out for weekend stays.

MOTELS

Drive-up motels offer comfortable basic to midrange accommodation and are found all over Australia, often on the edges of urban centres. They rarely offer a cheaper rate for singles, so are better value for couples or groups of three. You'll get a simple room with a kettle, fridge, TV, air-con and bathroom. The best ones are family-run and have a pool.

TENTED CAMPS & ECO RETREATS

Out in the wilds of some national parks, and in some remote coastal areas, safari-style tented camps are glorious ways to immerse in nature. Based around the same principles as African safari lodges, they inhabit fabulously remote (sometimes fly-in) locations and offer a mix of semi-luxurious four-walled cabins and elevated canvas tents with en suite bathrooms. Rates usually include all meals.

FARM & STATION STAYS

Country farms sometimes offer a bed for a night, while some remote outback stations allow you to stay in homestead rooms or shearers' quarters and try activities such as horse riding. Some let you kick back and watch workers raise a sweat; others rope you in to help with day-to-day chores.

PUBS

Many Australian pubs (from the term 'public house') were built during boom times, so they're often among the most extravagant old buildings in town. Some have been restored, but generally rooms remain small and weathered, with a long walk down the hall to the bathroom. If you're a light sleeper, avoid booking a room above the bar.

CAMPING GROUNDS

Australia has hundreds, perhaps even thousands, of free camping areas, but you can't just camp anywhere – you need to know where it's allowed locally. For national park camp sites, advance bookings are almost always required – reservations can be made through each state's national park website. Popular parks – Victoria's Wilsons Prom, for example – get booked out months in advance over summer. If any sites remain free, they're allocated on a first-in system; payment in such cases may work on an honour system, with an envelope and sealed box for cash payment.

CARS

HOW MUCH TO HIRE A CAR?

2WD
from $80 per day

Campervan
$150–500 per day

EV
$100–350 per day

4WD
$180–220 per day

2WD

Depending on where you want to travel, a regulation 2WD vehicle will usually suffice. They're cheaper to hire and run than 4WDs and are more readily available. Most are fuel-efficient. Downsides: no off-road capability and no room to sleep.

CAMPERVAN

Creature comforts at your fingertips: sink, fridge, cupboards, beds, kitchen and space to relax. Downsides: slow and often not fuel-efficient, not great on dirt roads and too large for nipping around the city. Parking can also be a challenge.

EV

Electric vehicles (EVs) generally cost more to rent than petrol vehicles in Australia, and they're not yet as readily available as you might imagine, but expect that to change. On the East Coast, at least, you needn't suffer range anxiety, as the region is home to the nation's most comprehensive charging network. Chargefox has the widest network, with charging priced at 40–60c/KWh. Download the Chargefox app for network maps and more. In other areas, such as WA and the NT, the combination of vast distances and limited charging stations in remote areas ensures that an EV is not really viable.

MOTORCYCLE

The Australian climate is great for riding, and bikes are handy in city traffic. Downsides: Australia isn't particularly bike-friendly in terms of driver awareness, there's limited luggage capacity, and you are exposed to the elements.

4WD

Renting a 4WD is affordable if a few people get together. For a Toyota LandCruiser you're looking at $180 to $220 a day, which should include unlimited kilometres (but always check, especially in the NT). Vehicles will be more expensive if they include camping equipment such as a rooftop tent.

MACONDO/SHUTTERSTOCK

RESPONSIBLE TRAVEL

CLIMATE CHANGE & TRAVEL

Lonely Planet urges all travellers to engage with their travel carbon footprint, which will mainly come from air travel. While there often isn't an alternative, travellers can look to minimise the number of flights they take and use cleaner ground transport, such as trains.

One proposed solution – purchasing carbon offsets – unfortunately does not cancel out the impact of individual flights. While most destinations will depend on air travel for the foreseeable future, for now, pursuing ground-based travel where possible is the best course of action.

The **UN Carbon Footprint Calculator** shows how flying impacts a household's emissions.

The **ICAO Carbon Emissions Calculator** allows visitors to analyse the CO_2 generated by point-to-point journeys.

Green Travel Guide
greentravelguide.org
Search for eco-certified experiences around the country.

Australian Farmers' Markets Association
Farmersmarkets.org.au
Locate farmers markets around the country.

GoodFish
GoodFish.org.au
Online consumer directory for sustainable seafood.

SUSTAINABLE TOURISM OPERATOR

Ecotourism Australia *(ecotourism.org.au)* certifies tourism operators and destinations for well-managed commitment to sustainable practices. Look for its Advanced Ecotourism Certified and Advanced Sustainable Tourism Certified labels.

FIRST NATIONS-LED TOURS

Australia's First Nations peoples have lived in harmony with the natural world for millennia. Learn about their ancient sustainable living practices on Indigenous-guided tours. Tourism Australia's Discover Aboriginal Experiences *(discoveraboriginalexperiences.com)* is a great resource.

BE A CITIZEN NATURALIST

Photos of your encounters with Australian organisms uploaded to the iNaturalist app *(inaturalist.ala.org.au)* are shared with scientists working to better understand and protect nature.

SAFE TRAVEL

BREAKDOWNS

Under the auspices of the Australian Automobile Association (*aaa.asn.au*), automobile clubs in each state handle insurance, regulations, maps and roadside assistance. Club membership (around $110) can be invaluable if things go wrong mechanically. The major Australian auto clubs generally offer reciprocal rights in other states and territories. If renting, your first call in case of breakdown should be to the car-hire company.

ANIMAL HAZARDS

The risk to drivers from wandering animals is a huge problem in Australia, particularly in the NT, Queensland, NSW, SA and Tasmania. Many Australians in rural areas avoid travelling once the sun drops because of the risks posed by nocturnal animals on the roads. Kangaroos are common on country roads, as are cows and sheep in the unfenced outback.

ROAD TRAINS

These giants of the Australian road (trucks with two or three trailers stretching for as long as 50m) ply outback roads and are an only-in-Australia proposition. Be careful overtaking them; you'll need distance, visibility and plenty of speed. On single-lane tracks, get right off the road when one approaches: stones or debris can clip your car as it passes.

ROAD CONDITIONS

For up-to-date information on road conditions around the country, check the following:

- **Australian Bureau of Meteorology** (*bom.gov.au*) Weather information and road warnings.
- **Department of Planning, Transport & Infrastructure** (*sa.gov.au/topics/driving-and-transport/service*) SA road conditions.
- **Live Traffic NSW** (*livetraffic.com*) NSW road conditions.
- **Main Roads Western Australia** (*mainroads.wa.gov.au*) WA road conditions.
- **Road Report NT** (*roadreport.nt.gov.au*) NT road conditions.
- **QLD Traffic** (*qldtraffic.qld.gov.au*) Queensland road conditions.

TAP WATER

Water is generally drinkable in Australia and is usually signposted if it isn't safe. Never drink from rivers or lakes without first purifying the water.

MOSQUITOES

Mosquito-borne illnesses you may be exposed to in Australia include dengue fever, Ross River fever, viral encephalitis and Bairnsdale (Buruli) ulcer. For protection, wear loose-fitting, long-sleeved clothing and apply DEET-based insect repellent to all exposed skin.

IN CASE OF EMERGENCY

000

Police
Ambulance
Fire Service

106

Text Emergency Relay Service
For those with restricted hearing or speech, the text emergency service number 106 reaches police, fire or ambulance via textphone.

NUTS & BOLTS

GOOD TO KNOW

Time zone
Three mainland zones (GMT+8, GMT+9½, GMT+10)

Country code
+61

Emergency number
000

Population
28 million

ELECTRICITY 230V/50HZ

Type I
230V/50Hz

CURRENCY: AUSTRALIAN DOLLAR ($)

OPENING HOURS

- **Banks:** 9.30am–4pm Monday to Friday
- **Bars:** 4pm–late
- **Cafes:** 6.30am–3pm
- **Nightclubs:** 10pm–4am Thursday to Sunday
- **Post offices:** 9am–5pm Monday to Friday; some also 9am–noon Saturday
- **Pubs:** 11am–midnight
- **Restaurants:** noon–2.30pm and 6–9pm
- **Shops:** 9am–5pm
- **Supermarkets:** 7am–10pm

INTERNET ACCESS

Good in urban areas, unreliable to non-existent (or restricted to a hotel reception area) in regional areas. Free wi-fi at cafes is not as common as you might expect.

TOILETS

Most public toilets are free of charge and reasonably well looked after. See *toiletmap.gov.au* for public toilet locations, including accessible toilets.

CASHLESS PAYMENTS

Contactless payment, where you touch your credit or debit card against the reader rather than typing in your PIN, is now common. Cash is still widely accepted, but the option is decreasing. It's best to keep some cash on you, though, especially if travelling to small towns and remote areas.

ATMS

Australia's 'big four' banks (ANZ, Commonwealth, National Australia Bank and Westpac) and affiliated banks have 24-hour cashpoints (ATMs). You'll even find them in some outback roadhouses.

TAXES & TIPPING

A 10% goods and services tax (GST) is automatically included in almost everything you buy, Australia-wide. Tipping isn't traditionally part of Australian etiquette, but it's increasingly the norm to tip around 10% for good service in restaurants and a few dollars for taxi drivers.

HOW MUCH FOR A...

Major museum entry **usually free**

Concert or theatre show **$100**

Metered parking **up to $10 per hour**

Major Gold Coast theme park entry **$109–139**

INDEX

Drives 000
Map pages **p000**

O

P

Q

R

S

THE WRITERS

This is the 5th edition of Lonely Planet's Best Road Trips Australia guidebook, updated with new material by Sarah Reid, Anthony Ham and Blaze Lopes. Writers on previous editions whose work also appears in this book are included below.

Sarah Reid

Sarah Reid is a freelance travel journalist specialising in adventure and regenerative travel. Between overseas assignments, she can often be found exploring Australia in her Toyota LandCruiser 78 Series Troop Carrier customised for overland adventures. Read her work at *sarahreid.com.au* and follow her adventures *@sarahreidtravels*

Anthony Ham

Anthony has been travelling the Top End and deep into the outback looking for stories for more than two decades. His book *The Last Desert Woman* takes readers into Warlpiri Country in the Tanami and Great Sandy Deserts of central Australia. *anthonyham.com (@AnthonyHamWrite)*

Contributing writers

Brett Atkinson, Andrew Bain, Cristian Bonetto, Samantha Forge, Paul Harding, Trent Holden, Anita Isalska, Anna Kaminski, Tatyana Leonov, Virginia Maxwell, Hugh McNaughtan, Kate Morgan, Charles Rawlings-Way, Andy Symington, Steve Waters

Send us your feedback

We love to hear from travellers – your comments keep us on our toes and help make our books better. Our well-travelled team reads every word on what you loved or loathed about this book. Although we cannot reply individually to your submissions, we always guarantee that your feedback goes straight to the appropriate writers, in time for the next edition.

BEHIND THE SCENES

This book was produced by the following:

Commissioning Editor
Darren O'Connell

Coordinating Editor
Brana Vladisavljevic

Production Editor
Martijn Vos

Image Researcher
Norma Brewer

Cartographer
Dorothy Davidson

Cover Researcher
Daisy Korpics

Thanks to
Will Allen, Aileen Cudmore, Melanie Dankel, Darren O'Connell, Maja Vatrić

Product Development
Sofie Andersen, Melinda Anderson, Marc Backwell, Alison Killilea, Darren O'Connell, James Smart, Saralinda Turner, Robin Yule

Acknowledgments

Digital Model Elevation Data
Contains public sector information licensed under the Open Government Licence v3.0 website nationalarchives.gov.uk/doc/open-government-licence/version/3/

Cover photographs
Front: Great Ocean Road (p100); John W Banagan/Getty Images
Back: Koala, Currumbin Wildlife Sanctuary (p148); rangrezak/Shutterstock

Visit **lonelyplanet.com/contact** to submit your updates and suggestions or to ask for help. Our award-winning website also features inspirational travel stories and news.

Note: We may edit, reproduce and incorporate your comments in Lonely Planet products such as guidebooks, websites and digital products, so let us know if you are happy to have your name acknowledged. For a copy of our privacy policy visit **lonelyplanet.com/legal**

lonely planet

Published by Lonely Planet Global Limited
CRN 554153
Digital Depot, Roe Lane off Thomas Street, Dublin
D08 TCV4, Ireland (EU authorised representative)
5th edition – Sep 2026
ISBN 9781838696726

10 9 8 7 6 5 4 3 2 1
Printed in Malaysia